Advance Praise for Number 788

Number 788 isn't just a book; it's a profound journey into the life of a soldier, masterfully penned by Max Lauker and his co-author, Tony, a former soldier and military historian. This narrative swirls between the harsh realities of war and deep personal inner struggles. As you read Lauker and Tony's words, you're transported into the midst of military actions, grappling with their complexity and moral dilemmas. Their combined perspectives offer a rare look at the development of military tactics post-Cold War, making this book a real revelation. It's an emotionally charged and incredibly valuable reading experience that will deeply resonate with anyone interested in military history and the intricacies of human stories in times of conflict.

Mr Kostiantyn Koshelenko, Deputy Minister for Social Policy and Digital Transformation, Ukrainian Government

The first and most important thought is that it's someone's story with personality, humour, honesty and a genuine reflection of the challenges and struggles he faced in overcoming some extreme conditions. This is a highly enjoyable read… It leaves you wanting more…

Ms Danielle R

A very good and interesting read, certainly different from the technical/tactical level narrative to the Green Beret and SAS-dominated Anglophone publications.

Lt Col (rtd) Eddie Watson (SA Air Force)

Fast paced, hard hitting and providing a unique insight into Swedish Special Operations.

Prof Evert Kleynhans, Stellenbosch University

A book written by a Scandinavian soldier is rare and refreshing amongst the military literary circuit, dominated by the experiences of Americans, Brits, and South Africans – great job.

Lieutenant Colonel Jason McDonald (SANDF)

Hard-hitting. The state of preparedness is incredible.

Brigadier General Peter Sereko (SA Army)

NUMBER 788

My experience in Swedish Special Operations – preparing for NATO and the War on Terror

Max Lauker
with
Antonio Garcia

Helion & Company

In memory of Stonelate.
You went so deep it finally consumed you.
I will always remember the Laurental abyss doctrine.
You never got a star on that wall, but you will never be forgotten.

Helion & Company Limited
Unit 8 Amherst Business Centre
Budbrooke Road
Warwick
CV34 5WE
England
Tel. 01926 499619
Email: info@helion.co.uk
Website: www.helion.co.uk
X (formerly Twitter): @Helionbooks
Facebook: @HelionBooks
Visit our blog at https://helionbooks.wordpress.com/

Published by Helion & Company 2024
Designed and typeset by Mach 3 Solutions (www.mach3solutions.co.uk)
Cover designed by Paul Hewitt, Battlefield Design (www.battlefield-design.co.uk)
Text © Max Lauker and Antonio Garcia 2024
Photographs & illustrations © Max Lauker
Maps drawn by George Anderson © Helion & Company 2024

While all the stories in this book are true, some names and identifying details have been changed, and other parts have been partially fictionalised for reasons of operational security and to protect the privacy of the people involved.

Every reasonable effort has been made to trace copyright holders and to obtain their permission for the use of copyright material. The author and publisher apologise for any errors or omissions in this work, and would be grateful if notified of any corrections that should be incorporated in future reprints or editions of this book.

ISBN 978-1-804514-23-8

British Library Cataloguing-in-Publication Data.
A catalogue record for this book is available from the British Library.

For details of other military history titles published by Helion & Company Limited, contact the above address, or visit our website: http://www.helion.co.uk

We always welcome receiving book proposals from prospective authors.

Contents

Preface

Being good at doing bad things is not always a blessing; you can't be the judge, only the executioner. I never wanted to be a soldier, never planned to be a soldier but I found that I excelled at it. The concept of 'for the greater good' always has a flip side. You are moving and living in the shadows. The ones in control grant you the ultimate power of life but a life lived in the shadows is never your own.

This is my story. I am a soldier and a ranger – a specialist in reconnaissance, intelligence, and covert operations; my development was slow and meticulous, it was born out of necessity and improvised. Now I write about this and what it was like to be pushed past the brink of what I thought was humanly possible. My story may excite some, and bore others, it is not a self-help story for those looking for solutions on paper – my aim is to share my flawed path, lessons learned, relationships forged, revelations of self and the workings of others; and a very small hope of inspiring a few new generation warriors.

I was trained at a unique time, as I joined the forces after the Cold War, in the aftermath of the 9-11 attacks. During my formation, the lack of controls and regulation came with tremendous risks, but also significant opportunities – I seized them. I am the product of brave officers who took action at great personal risk to save a regiment, without permission and by asking for forgiveness later. Officers who believed in the saying, 'Who Dares Wins.' I share my small place as a silent mediator between the light and shadows in the long and imperfect history of Western and Nordic fighters.

Over the years, as is the case with all of us, I started trading time – I exchanged youth, for experience. After 20 years I am out of youth, but I have some experiences saved up. The more adventure I had, the more I felt I had something to say so people didn't have to read between the lines. My story is one of being in the right place at the right time, but the smell of gunpowder is not present on every page – my purpose as an author is to share a glimpse of my reality. I have fired my weapons in anger, I have infiltrated terrorist groups,

I have made and burnt sources, I have served my state; I am not what some would call a good man, but I am not all bad – my calling was the profession of arms.

Let me assure you that I have not written this book because of a selfless interest in contributing to the greater good; it was a need to tell the untold. There are other first-hand military accounts published and being written – between us, there are similarities and differences and perhaps a warrior spirit, framed in our societal cultures.

In meeting Tony, a former soldier, and military historian, I found someone with a unique understanding, with whom I could share my story. With our biased lens, and the mouldable material we call hindsight, I constructed my narrative. We were introduced by an old mutual friend, Jason – also a soldier, and through our connection we found common ground. My experience was different to theirs but at the heart of it was respect for the mechanisms of war. I once heard a Colonel say, that he had more in common with a soldier in Egypt, Nigeria, the US, and China, than with his neighbour who was a banker.

The broader context to this story is that the end of the Cold War, and subsequent peacekeeping missions caught the Swedish military flatfooted when the War on Terror came around. The need for special operations forces was in high demand, but for the most part, Sweden lacked this niche capability. While still in its conceptual form, the International Ranger Platoon, an elite force that became a special purpose unit within the Ranger Battalion, was used to fill the gap. Newly recruited, I was drawn to the challenge and adventure of it all, I took on the tough selection course – the reward was to be part of something new – the special purpose units.

Mentioned in Dispatches

My thanks go out to everyone who has worked with me on this book. Starting as a discussion with an old friend over ten years ago, this book is a mature reflection of my accumulated experiences. I appreciate the efforts of the many reviewers and beta readers, Jason MacDonald, Eddie Watson, Peter Sereko, Jim Thayer, Evert Kleynhans, Danielle R, and Manuel Trucco. Thank you to the reviewers who had to remain anonymous, and a special thanks to Mr Kostia Koshelenko, who while serving in a senior political appointment in Ukraine, during times of war, managed to review this book.

Thanks to Helion and the team for helping it become a reality.

Remember, a book is just a snapshot of one's experiences and thoughts and it will never replace the story behind it. A story not exclusively reserved for authors but for everyone.

Acronyms and Abbreviations

2iC:	Second-in-Command
13e RDP:	13e Régiment de Dragon Parachutistes/13th Parachute Dragoon Regiment
AA:	Anti-Aircraft Artillery
AK:	Carbine mostly referring to the Swedish Automatkarbin
ARF:	Airborne Reaction Force (Usually a helicopter QRF)
ASP:	Armament Systems and Procedures
BC:	Battalion Commander
BND:	Bundesnachrichtendienst/German Federal Intelligence Service (Germany)
CAT:	Counterassault Team
CERTE:	Centro de Re-entrenamiento Táctico Del Ejército/Army Retraining Centre
Comms:	Communications
CPO:	Close Protection Officer
CSAR:	Combat Search and Rescue
CQB:	Close Quarters Battle
DA:	Direct Action
Debus:	Unload or Get Out of a Transport Vehicle
DLB:	Dead Letter Box
Demob:	Demobilisation
DMZ:	Demilitarised Zone
DGSE:	Direction Générale de la Sécurité Extérieure/Directorate General for External Security (France)
E&E:	Escape and Evasion
Embus:	To Board a Transport Vehicle
ERV:	Emergency Rendezvous
FAC:	Forward Air Controller

FARC:	Fuerzas Armadas Revolucionarias de Colombia/ The Revolutionary Armed Forces of Colombia
FOMO:	Fear of Missing Out
FJS IK:	Early Swedish Special Forces reconnaissance unit attached to the Paras
FLIR:	Forward Looking Infrared
FOB:	Forward Operating Base
FOK:	Preparatory Officers' Course
FMV:	Armed Forces Equipment Research and Development Division (Sweden)
FRU:	Force Research Unit (Britain)
Ghillie:	Camouflage Clothing Designed to Blend in with the Surrounding Environment
GIS:	Gruppo di Intervento/Special Intervention Group (Special Caribineri unit that gained Special Forces status in 2004)
HF:	High Frequency (shortwave communications)
HQ:	Headquarters
HVT:	High Value Target
Infil:	Infiltration
ILISA:	Panamanian Private Language Institute
IR:	Infrared
IRP:	International Ranger Platoon
ISR:	Intelligence, Surveillance and Reconnaissance
ISTAR:	Intelligence, Surveillance, Target Acquisition, and Reconnaissance
JTAC:	Joint Terminal Attack Controller
JTF:	Joint Task Force
KBS:	Kompanibefälsskola/Military Junior Leaders School
KFOR:	Kosovo Force
K&R:	Kidnap and Ransom
LMG:	Light Machine Gun. FN Minimi Para version (collapsible stock) Swedish designation KSP90B. Produced by FN Herstal. Also referred to just as Minimi
LRRP:	Long-Range Reconnaissance Patrol
LUP:	Lay up Point
LZ:	Landing Zone
OC:	Oleoresin Capsicum (pepper spray)
OP:	Observation Post

OPSEC:	Operational Security
OR:	Other Ranks
OSINT:	Open-Source-Intelligence
POI:	Person of Interest
PSD:	Personal Security Detail
PX:	Post Exchange (Shop or Store)
MOT:	Military Observation Team
MP:	Military Police
MRE:	Meal Ready to Eat
NATO:	North Atlantic Treaty Organisation
NDA:	Non-Disclosure Agreement
NOE:	Nap-Of-The-Earth. Referring to helicopter flight conducted very close to the ground.
NOS:	Nitrous Oxide System
NI:	Swedish Police National Antiterrorist Unit
NVG:	Night Vision Goggles
PMC:	Private Military Company
PTT:	Push To Talk
QM:	Quartermaster
QRF:	Quick Reaction Force
RedMan suit:	Gear for Reality Based Training
ROE:	Rules of Engagement
RTO:	Radio Telephone Operator
RV:	Rendezvous (in the context of a location during operations)
SAP:	Security Advance Party
SATCOM:	Satellite Communication
SIG:	Särskilda Inhämtnings Gruppen/Special Reconnaissance Group
SIGINT:	Signal Intelligence
SF:	Special Forces
SCOTT:	Special Hybrid Swedish Police and Military Intelligence Unit
SOP:	Standard Operating Procedure
SSG:	Särskilda Skydds Gruppen/Special Protection Group
TLC:	Tender Love and Care
UAV:	Unmanned Aerial Vehicle (Drone)
UV:	Ultraviolet
VHF:	Very High Frequency
WHO:	World Health Organisation

1

The Grind

'It was one of the greatest challenges of my life, with the exception of operations in war.'

I turned 18 in the early spring of 2001, and the only thing between me and my first adventure was my final semester of high school. I wondered if all teenagers have that feeling of being excited, overwhelmed and scared at the same time. For me it was like I had been waiting an eternity to finally start really living. While some friends were going on to university, others were starting new jobs, but somehow, I knew my path would be different. I am not sure if it was intuition. God knows I am not religious, but somewhere in the depths of myself I knew. I can only explain it as that feeling some of us get when we instinctively guess the right answer – I would learn that people in the world of intelligence relied on this instinct.

The white envelope was creased at the edges, I found the middle of the flap, and I opened it. 'Max – you are hereby ordered to attend the Swedish Defence Conscript and Assessment Agency's station, in Stockholm for compulsory military selection and training.' A sharp intake of breath.

Looking at my call up letter, I felt the weight of my father's shadow hanging over me, 'what did it mean to be a real man?' Perhaps all boys have a love hate relationship with their fathers, I don't know. Mine was difficult. He was tall, strong, tough and an asshole.

That white envelope with creased corners, like the suit of a civil servant contained a ticket to a new world. Before this, I had no idea what to do. Further studies were a yawn, and I briefly considered working with my hands. I remember building flat pack furniture once, I am from Sweden after all, IKEA, and all that, but who was I fooling, turning four screws with an Allen key. Building the wardrobes of others was not my future.

Mine was to convince people. I had some talent for speaking and adapting to the 'room', some friends called it playing the game. When someone spoke softly, I lowered my voice, I always listened intently, the clues were in the minor details. What football club, which artist, were they well turned out, unshaven, talkative? I gained their trust and instilled confidence. For a while it made me think that I could be a ladies' man, but I wasn't there just yet. I remember speaking to a brunette, with hair that threatened to touch her shoulders, her smile conspired with her eyes and they were piercing. I listened to her and soon realised that I was the one being played. I wouldn't make that a habit.

No, my skill would serve me well in the practical world, where I had to build relationships and form them to my needs. Somehow, I used rudimentary tradecraft, the skills of espionage and intelligence gathering even before I was trained. I remember a friend, Peter, slim and tall with a polite manner saying Max 'It feels like we have known each other for a decade but I still don't know anything about you.' Being able to make an impression like that, without being memorable, would play an important part in my future work, I just didn't know that yet.

Military service meant that I could postpone my life choices. Yes, we still had conscription for all men, and it was mostly a 'speed bump' that needed to be passed before cracking on with your life for real. It was relaxed back then and since the Swedish Armed Forces had at that stage, been downsizing for about 10 years, you could easily get out of it. Some who had higher education lined up, just postponed it until they became too old, others tried their best to fail on every test and the last resort was to just roll yourself up into a carpet or ball in front of the psychologist. Many Swedes did this during the Peace and Love era.

I always felt an obligation to serve in the military, but in the same breath I wasn't really looking forward to it either, more something that I needed do. I loved my country, but I never imagined a life in uniform as the only way to serve. Did I get goose bumps when listening to the national anthem? Well not always; did I feel pride when I saw the Swedish flag carried by Olympic athletes? I guess so. I was like any other teenager, simple and infinitely complex at the same time. My friends were a mixed bag, and their paths were all clear. Then there was me, not the academic or competitive type, just one of the many who had nothing else lined up. I needed time to think.

I re-read my call up letter. The Swedish Defence Conscript and Assessment Agency's coat of arms in the header gave it a feeling of officialdom. The font was simple, and readable. The letter came with a standard government issued note that allows free travel on buses and trains to get you there. It also said that not showing up could lead to a prison sentence. It put some seriousness to the situation, even though I knew that nobody those days was sent to prison for not showing up. For the first time I felt a sense of ambition, I wanted to show people that I was something more than just average; I needed to show my father that I was a force of nature. I wanted to be the best.

The initial military testing was done at one of the three armed forces testing stations. The assessments take three days and are straightforward, physical, logic-based, and technical tests as well as psychological interviews. My father's service was my benchmark, he did his service as a Coastal Ranger in 1968 and that was of course, according to him, the only true choice for real men.

My father was an accomplished surgeon, but arrogant and egocentric, I couldn't stand him. He was a functioning alcoholic, and I always wondered how he was able to pull that off at work. After a few UN deployments with the army, serving in Lebanon and Saudi Arabia, he somehow stayed in the deployment loop, and later helped to build early Forward Surgical Team (FRT/FST) units in Iraq and Afghanistan. During his drunken ravings on our occasional phone calls, he told me about his experiences in Afghanistan and Iraq. Always quite extreme stories about being attached to secret units. I knew for a fact that he had been there. But there is a slight difference in being an army doctor or being Captain Willard or Colonel Kurtz from 'Apocalypse Now' – a movie he admired and with which he strongly identified. The little he shared about his life was striking, but with drinking comes lies, and liars usually end up taking their truths to the grave.

In my heart I wanted to join the Navy, I wanted to become a sailor and maybe a telegraphist. I loved the idea of a life at sea, but that wasn't a possibility because proving myself to my father and everyone else was more important to me. So, becoming a Ranger or specifically a coastal Ranger felt like my only choice. Testing day came and I was nervous. We filed into the open hall. A sterile setting, fitting for military tests. There were some static bikes on the far end, and another area which had mats, weights and stop watches set out. The walls housed antiquated piping from a different time. The unassuming space was the setting of historic personal battles, one where the dreams of young men were made and broken. My greatest challenge was the cardio test. I knew I would do well in the strength test as I was a gym rat.

The cardio test was done on a static bike. The test applied increasing resistance and was timed using an equation of body mass. Performance was measured on a scale from 1 to 9. A minimum rating of five was required for any unit, and a rating of seven or above was required for specialised units. I had to get into ranger school. So, in short if you are a light guy you will need to cycle for about eight minutes to get a seven, I needed to do 22 minutes to get a seven. So, the doctor that administers the test laughed and said, 'I can give you a five.' That meant that he assessed my physical level based on my strength results and my overall condition. This could be done in cases when the test was going to be very unfair, as it appeared to be in my case. But they were only allowed to assess a five, never higher and I needed a seven.

The whole experience was strange. I found the pedals and started cycling. My first thought was 'this isn't too bad.' After a few minutes I felt the resistance increase. I felt the burn in my thighs and my breathing getting heavier, but I pushed on. After 12 minutes the sweat was dripping off me and I was struggling. I was now in a battle against myself. A part of me just wanted to quit and do my service in a comfortable duty station. My father's words kept popping up in my mind 'Coastal Rangers is the only option for real men.' I refocused, angry at myself for letting his words affect me, determined to succeed. The other boys started low key cheering me on. At 20 minutes my vision narrowed to what was immediately in front of me, and it felt like my whole body was on fire. My eyes were burning from the sweat rolling down my forehead. I squinted, looking up to find the clock on the wall, 21 minutes and 10 seconds... 'come on... come on... I mumbled while exhaling. My heart was beating like a drum, I heard someone shout, '15 seconds more! You can do it!' I made it, 22 minutes, I felt an additional surge of adrenaline propelling me forward and I kept going for another minute. I cycled for a total of 23 minutes; I got my seven and a round of applause.

On the third day, I stood before the placement officer, I was nervous of course; their decision was made in just a few minutes. He asked if I had any wishes, I replied, 'I would like to do my service at the Coastal Ranger Company.'

He instantly replied 'No!'

I froze for a second as I immediately thought my results weren't good enough for ranger training. Then he continued, explaining that the Coastal Ranger Company would not take on any new recruits the following year due to the heavy military downsizing. I had mixed feelings, as my mind was set on becoming a Ranger.

The placement officer continued, 'You have good results, you are suitable for ranger training, are you up for a challenge?'

'Yes.'

He said, 'Very well then *Kompanibefäl*[1] (*KB*), 15 months at K4, you start in January 2002. Now get out! Next.'

I was going to the Arctic Rangers, officially known as Norrland Dragoon Regiment with the designation K4, a cavalry regiment and one of the "true" ranger units. The others were the Paras, the Coastal Rangers and the disbanded Lapland Ranger Regiment with the designation I22, located in the north as well, just a few hours from K4. The Lapland Ranger Regiment lost to the Norrland Dragoon Regiment in what was known as the 'regimental death' and became just a statistic when more than half of all Swedish regiments were closed.

The term Arctic Ranger is the direct translation of the word *Norrlandsjägare*. It was used officially in the older system of naming Arctic Ranger Battalions, *Norrlandsjägarbataljon*, but it cannot be paired with the word regiment as in Arctic Ranger Regiment. Popularly K4 or just Arctic Rangers is used. In 2005, due to cutbacks and reorganisation of the Swedish Armed Forces, K4 seized to exist as a regiment, and became a detachment of *Norrbotten Regiment I 19* in Boden. They were given the new name *Arméns Jägarbataljon (AJB)* – Army Ranger Battalion, still in the same location. In 2022 it regained its status as a regiment, reverting to the old name and designation. I will throughout the book refer to it as the Regiment, even after 2005, as that was the name used by us informally.

All ranger service in Sweden is voluntary, being placed there was just the first step, then one has to pass an extra selection. Most of the guys at school received their placements for military service and went to regular infantry units or decided to "skip". A friend of mine, Martin, short and slim, went to the Navy – I'm sure he did it for the uniform. Another, David was tough but not in a military way, he wanted to do good and opted to serve in the civil service as a firefighter. They became two of my lifelong friends outside of the military circle. Henrik made it into the prestigious and notoriously hard Naval Clearance Divers School. Then we had Peter, an easy-going guy – I liked him. He had the unique combination of being smart and cool, annoying really. It

---

1 *Kompanibefälsvärnpliktiga* or *Kompanibefäl* (*KB*) for short, were conscripted officers who, after completing basic training, were assigned to a wartime unit, with the rank of *Värnpliktig Fänrik*, Conscript 2nd Lieutenant (only wartime rank). *Kompanibefäl* were only trained in the army and the training time could vary between a minimum of 415 and a maximum of 615 days, depending on the type of troop and position. Something equivalent to a conscript junior officer in other countries. This is not to be confused with junior leader/junior officer training. In peacetime they would hold the rank of Sergeant. In practical terms, a *KB* at a ranger unit in peacetime, was a squad leader.

sometimes bothered me that he had dated my old girlfriend before me, but that soon became ancient history. Peter was also selected for ranger training at K4 to start in 2002.

It was 3 January 2002, 16:15 in the afternoon and I was waiting for the train, and I kept looking up to see if the train had arrived, the train that would take me to the far north. I looked up at the information board and saw the overnight train that would take us from Stockholm to Umeå arriving in two minutes. They had several train cars reserved for the military. I swung my backpack over my shoulder and grabbed my small bag as the doors opened and we boarded. Just cattle in the military machine, the air was filled with the kind of testosterone that only 18 year old young men can produce. I felt bad for the few girls on the train who had stops after ours.

Our stop was the infamous train station, Jörn, a deserted platform in the middle of nowhere, like in an American western where you can see the tumble-weeds roll down the street; except that Jörn is just dark, cold and void. It is about a two-hour bus ride from the regiment. A small town that has a famous boot maker, and a story that Lenin once stayed the night there in 1917; that was basically what they had there. Back in the day the small town accommo-dated the workers of the Boliden gold mine, but since then, communications and infrastructure improved and they all moved to the nearby towns of Boden and Luleå. The train stopped at Jörn station at 03:45, it was -30 Celsius and pitch dark. There were two buses standing on the side of the road waiting for us. This stop was only for the new recruits, the serving soldiers got off at the next station. They wanted to keep us separate and not have serving soldiers and recruits returning "home" at the same time. I would eventually come to call it home.

As the buses reached the Regiment and the large steel gates opened, it marked the point of no return. The buses left us on the parade grounds, I was wearing jeans and a leather jacket like a true city kid, I didn't even have a hat. I felt stupid, how could I not bring a warm hat and gloves when going to the Arctic. I was hoping nobody noticed and I tried to look casual. We all stood waiting in the darkness for something to happen or for somebody to say something but there was just silence. It felt odd arriving with no one meeting us. Eventually a few people started walking towards the dimmed lights of the Regiment building. It was empty, just a note saying "Recruits" and an arrow directing us down a corridor.

My first impression was that this was unlike any regiment I had seen before. Regiments are usually housed in beautiful buildings that have hundreds of years of history. K4 was originally located in Umeå and remained there until it moved to Arvidsjaur in 1980; so, this regiment was purpose built and well suited for military activity but had that ugly 70/80s style with little charm. The Regiment was designed and built like a horse, yes, an actual horse. In the "head" of the horse are offices and the mess hall, the body is a 400 metre long corridor that runs from the head to the tail, curiously called "the rubber corridor". The name came from the rubber mat on the floor that dampened the sound.

In the horse's "legs", are Squadrons 1 to 4 and in the "tail" is the infirmary. Each "leg" housed four platoons and in the "hoof" of every leg they had their own storage for equipment, weapons and also rooms for maintenance and laundry. The design left something to be desired, but this was only a passing thought, as I knew I faced a life-changing challenge.

Arriving at the registration desk I would experience what represents 90 percent of all military work… 'hurry up and wait.' A long line formed outside a small door to an office with an older officer, checking the orders and identity cards of all recruits. He handed us our military IDs, dog tags and a plastic bag with hundreds of embroidered name tags with our personal identity number and last name.

If you have never been in the military, the sequence is basically the same everywhere in the world. The process involves getting people registered, clothed, fed, and housed. This might sound like an easy-going period with some mingling, like 1st year university, well it could be, but it isn't, ever. The sweat poured down my face, my heart raced, my spirit was being crushed. Moving massive amounts of equipment in thin plastic bags; they break and tear, no one cares, it is a conveyor belt that doesn't stop. The only option is to catch up. All this and the training hadn't even started yet. We were told to hydrate on command. I realised that this was important as I saw Johan, another recruit, standing next to his bed and without warning he just fell forward like a sack of potatoes. The stress of the first days in the military is well-known and is largely caused by recruits' own expectations and the over-load of a new and unfamiliar environment. Later I came to realise that it is fun to watch from afar, but at that moment it was all very real.

Once we got our gear, all the various uniforms required for the coming 15 months, including winter, summer, sports, and combat, we continued to the vehicle hall next to the equipment depot and formed a big circle around an officer. 'Take off your clothes. In the Army, we will teach you how to get dressed' he said. 'Now put on your battle jacket… now close the strap, now…,' these were the orders shouted out. Every piece was inspected. I made a balls up early when it came to the shirt that is worn with the sleeves rolled up; I just started rolling them up without much thought. I could see the combination of hopelessness and frustration in the squint of the officer's eyes when he came to me, you could hear him clinch his fists while inhaling through his nose. This was Captain H; he would go on to lead our training at *KBS*[2] during the coming months. A short, sturdy man with small eyes and a wide but sharp nose. He did everything with an unmistakable sense of purpose. He had a firm and instantly recognizable step; it was like he was trying to drive his foot through the ground each time his heel hit the floor. My first thought was this is not the appearance you would expect from an officer at an elite unit. I later learned that surviving in the harsh arctic had nothing to do with having a six pack.

Captain H approached me and pulled me out of the circle, placing me in the middle. I only had my underwear on, one sock and my shirt with one sleeve rolled up. He spent seven minutes intensely explaining to everyone how to properly roll up a 2.5 finger's width sleeve. Captain H said, 'This is a piss poor attempt, in fact it hurts me to think that this is how a recruit rolls up a sleeve.' I started to sweat; it felt like I had failed on the first day with the simple task of rolling up my sleeve, 'perhaps I am in the wrong place,' I thought to myself.

Captain H stated, 'there is no scheduled end to the day, in the military, the day ends when you are finished, not sooner or later.' Later that evening we found out what we had to do with all those embroidered nametags. The last order of the night was, 'be sure to sew on a nametag to all of the items you have received, take a look at the list on the wall, and there you will find instructions on how to attach the nametags.' I hardly slept that night, and it was my first experience with needle and thread. Between sewing and doing my own laundry, I think the first lesson was self-reliance. Although the laundry routine differed from other regiments, who had a central laundry, where you exchanged your dirty clothing for fresh ones once a week. Having the soldiers doing their own laundry was an initiative for smaller units aimed at saving time, resources, and the environment, all very Swedish.

I was surprised at the attitude during the first couple of weeks. There was no shouting or screaming, we were not penalised for the sake of it. Everything

---

2   *KBS – Kompanibefälsskola* translates to *Kombanibefäls* school. It is the conscript officers' training course, which runs for 4 to 5 months before the regular soldiers arrive.

was run by professional officers who we respected by virtue of their presence. That is not to say things weren't moving at pace, the tempo was insanely high of course. A few weeks later I stood with 42 other guys that would form KBS 02/03. We had five intense months of training before the specialists (regular soldiers) would join us. Specialists usually did 10 months of basic training.

Training continued over the coming weeks and months, theory was mixed with practical skills and most of the theory lessons were outside, for us to acclimate to field conditions. I learned the basic soldiering skills, shooting, fire and manoeuvre, skiing and just surviving in the arctic. With time I also trained in other specialist areas, including but not limited to radio telephone operator (RTO), light and heavy machine gun, demolitions, intelligence gathering, and field medical training. You don't need to master all the skills, but one has to be proficient to be able to lead a squad. The core of the KBS was leadership. At its heart we were training to lead small teams in difficult conditions.

I remember one day, we were out with Captain H, skiing in the vast forest from early morning to late at night. We took a10-minute break every hour and 60-minute break every four hours. Each time we took a break we followed the standard operating procedure (SOP); we got off the track, took cover from the air, set up a perimeter watch and placed a claymore in our tracks. This is the way to stay alive. You put your coat on, change socks, dry your wet socks, drink some hot water, adjust your skis and Bergen. This is a lot to manage in 10 minutes and in a moment, you had our Bergen on, and you were ready to go.

On that particular day, the sun was up, it was one of those cold and crisp winter days, the sun reflected off the snow, glistening and blinding. Captain H had decided we would stop next to a frozen lake, spirits where high among the men, for a moment it felt like we were on a skiing vacation. He gave the sign for a short break; we went off the track and most people were tired of repeating the drill for the 100th time. We just sat down on our Bergens enjoying the sun and provided cover in their allocated areas.

After two minutes I heard the first scream, I jumped up 'what the hell is happening.' Then I heard the second and the third shrieks. I looked back and saw Captain H on his skis moving up the column and hitting everyone that hadn't put on a coat and followed the drills. His ski pole went up and came down like a soldier in battle striking down the enemy. I have never seen so many scrambling to get their clothes on and socks dried.

He was furious, 'Pulling this kind of shortcut shit will kill you all, four times over before the enemy even has a chance to.' Nobody pulled a stunt like that again. The realisation started to sink in, ranger training had very little to do with blowing things up, fancy tech, cool vehicles, or awesome looking close quarters battle (CQB) raids. It was mostly about surviving and being able to operate under extreme conditions. Captain H's persistence in setting these basic routines right from the start has saved my life countless times. It would do so even later that year, during the second winter of training.

As training progressed, we started to hone our squad and platoon level skills. Even if platoon sized operations are not the main game of a ranger unit it's still necessary to develop these skills. During the spring of 2002 I started to feel more comfortable with military life. Even though the exercises were many, the lack of sleep was tiring, and the rigorous physical regime left me exhausted every day, it felt right. I like this environment, I fit in. And once I got over the initial nervousness, I discovered that I had a natural inclination for tactics and how to run things in the field. It was a work in progress, and I was still a bit tightly wound and not as relaxed as one of my bunkmates Mr S. He was a true natural, maybe not the greatest military fanboy out there, but he was a northerner. Tall and stringy, his body was designed for moving in the snow. He did not have the physique of a weightlifter or a runner; he had lean muscle, toned and electric, an arctic beast. Watching him negotiate the terrain was a sight. He came from a hunting family from one of the remote areas in the far north. So, for him this was nothing new, spending most of his time outside in the subarctic climate was any given Tuesday. That meant that he could focus entirely on the military aspect. He became my rock in the early days. I would often say 'Seriously, this is day one of 30 that we are going to be out in these conditions.' He always smiled and replied, 'well one day less that we have to spend inside in a concrete building.' He was an outdoors man through and through and probably born on a pair of skis.

Mr S was like most northerners, not super talkative; maybe that was why we enjoyed each other's company. During our winter survival training he was tasked with showing and giving instructions, on how to take care of a killed reindeer since he had the right background. He then started to gut and prepare the fallen prey. It looked like he had been doing this his whole life, he was professional but silent. The officer leading the exercise asked him to explain what he was doing and why. Mr S replied, 'I am butchering' and carried on. The officer continued narrating this exercise from that moment onwards. After his military service Mr S studied Russian for a few years and started working for a very different government agency, but that is a story for him to tell. We are still good friends to this day.

With summer approaching we were about to start *baskerprovet*, this was where you earned the green beret with the "ND" insignia.[3] *Baskerprovet* is one of the major accomplishments during ranger training and elevates your status from recruit closer to Ranger. It is usually one of the longest and most demanding tests during ranger school. It tests everything you have learned and has an extreme profile when it comes to sleep deprivation, very limited food intake and extreme physical challenges.

Looking back at this period, it was one of the greatest challenges of my life, with the exception of operations in war. The technical side of it is not very hard and the skill set required is intermediate. Especially if you compare it to special forces units where you have very challenging training, both physically and mentally, and difficult technical challenges to overcome. *Baskerprovet* is a massive grind over a long time and is meant to test if you can break through your limits and keep functioning. The exercise can go on for between 15 to 30 days.

3   Quite a few years ago the beret stopped being the sign of ranger training and became a regimental beret, worn by all military personnel who work in the regiment, ranger or not. At present the sign of having completed ranger training is the ranger tab. Previously the tab was a sign of having completed one of the last major exercises including a long summer survival element with additional physical requirements.

2

Ranger Training

'After 29 days we were at the limits of physical exhaustion.'

The exact start time of the exercise is always a surprise. So, on the first day, 03:15 the lights turned on and we had 20 minutes to report to the parade ground with full kit for Long Range Reconnaissance Patrol (LLRP) duty. Not an extreme record-breaking time to get down there, but you need to hustle. The receiving officer just said, '*Baskerprovet* has started.' He handed the squad leaders one map each, it contained the first destination and then he pointed us to a pile of old army bicycles. We were sure that they had been discontinued 50 years ago, the best kind, heavy, clunky and anything but smooth. The destination was about 100kms away and we took stock of the bikes.

Everyone left the parade ground within the hour. It might sound like an uncomplicated start, but have you ever tried riding a bike with a Bergen[1] that is so heavy that it's hard to stand up? The remote roads were mostly gravel and wet clay. The rains from the night before had turned the ground into a treacherous path leading deep into the wilderness of northern Sweden. Add a weapon that is constantly smacking you in the face with the rise and fall of peddling. The next 100 kilometres would be a nightmare. This was the first gruelling test of a 30-day challenge.

We reached the destination late that night. The activity had required teamwork, as many bikes broke down along the way. Captain H was waiting for us. His face expressionless. We lined up and reported 'First patrol, all present, Second, present…' He managed a nod and said, 'Nice of you all to pop by, but you are late.' He clenched his fists like he always did, his knuckles becoming

---

1   Military backpack normally holding a heavy load.

white, and all we heard was a subtle cracking noise. We formed a wide circle and in the middle was a large pile of paving stones. I didn't like the look of it. I felt like they were going to end up in our Bergens.

Captain H took a paper from his pocket, it was the standard packing order for Bergens: combat kit and uniform. 'Inspection of gear.' He continued, 'Empty your Bergens, combat kit and uniform in front of you, strip off all clothing.' There we were standing naked with all our gear in a big pile in front of us. 'Balls and penis, hold up!' was his next command. He slowly walked around inspecting our crotches for hidden items. It must have been quite a sight. Forty-one men standing in a circle, holding their packages in their right hand. It was funny and a bit grotesque.

I wanted to burst out laughing, but it was not the right time for it. Besides our privates, every piece of equipment was checked for food, tobacco or other gear that could give us an edge. Captain H of course knew where to look and many items were awarded an individually numbered paving stone. Later that night as we were moving out, my Bergen was so heavy that I had to put it on while kneeling and have a friend assist me in getting up.

We moved out. We were now operating purely on training, adrenaline, and determination. The next task was an infiltration exercise where we were required to establish an Observation Post at an airbase. A 12 hour march.

It went on like this, with new missions every day or every other day. Insane amounts of footwork were our staple. The missions included commando-like tasks, reconnaissance, blowing up a railway, raiding and so on. The squad leadership was changed every other mission. We were always made to adapt, and nothing went to plan, funny how that seemed to reflect real operations. We always appeared to make contact with the enemy and our casualties were transported over long distances by foot. Small amounts of food were handed out occasionally which we inhaled. I remember at one point being so hungry and tired that while eating the single piece of hard candy, the size of a small coin, it unfortunately slipped out of my mouth and disappeared on the ground because I was half asleep while standing up. The lack of sleep was unbearable. After a few days I was in a foggy, fuzzy existence, somewhere between being awake and dreaming, where monsters and shadows interplay. Things started to move in slow motion, my thinking and reactions were slow. Even if I wanted to, I didn't have the energy to give up.

After 29 days we were at the limits of physical exhaustion. We headed towards a checkpoint, deep in a valley. We arrived at a small clearing as the morning sun pierced through the foliage, the shades of light and dark came alive with rays of light. The ground was coloured with dashes of green, brown, and white, the grass fought through the overbearing frost. Even Swedish summer battles the winter cold.

I heard a rumbling sound in the distance, the melting mountain ice fed the river and the echoes off the hills were like an untamed horse running across the plains. We saw Captain H standing by two small army trucks, we lined up as usual and reported. He said we should sit and wait on our Bergens, people were too tired to nap, most just stared emptily into the distance.

He came back after a short while, 'leave your gear, just bring your weapon, and follow me.' He started jogging along a narrow forest trail. I sighed, 'Not running, not now.' As the rumbling came closer, the thought of the river gave me a fresh feeling. After a few minutes of jogging, the forest disappeared around us and suddenly we were standing on the rocky slopes. My first thought was that I wanted to shove my head into the water and quench my thirst.

I looked to the side and saw the Battalion Commander and all our instructors lined up. Captain H had to half shout to be heard over the roaring river, 'Two lines, towards me, front and...' it all felt very formal. We quickly came to order and Captain H reported, 'KBS, all accounted for' and then lined up with the other officers. The Battalion Commander stepped forward and addressed us, it was something short about never giving up. To be honest I do not remember his words, but what is permanently etched in my memory is that warm feeling of pride that had worked itself into my chest. I snapped out of my foggy daze and focused on what was going to happen next.

We had been ordered to keep our berets, without insignia, in our left chest pocket since the start of the exercise. They were all wrinkled up and moist. The BC moved through the lines handing out the 'ND' insignia. He shook my hand and gave me his congratulations. I was moved, I imagined that nothing could ever beat this feeling, not even having children.

We tried our best to line up the insignia correctly, so it would sit right over your left eye, on our berets as we pushed the metal pins through the cloth.

He commanded, 'Attention' with a voice that cut straight through the roaring river, then he gave the command that I had been dreaming about 'Hats off, beret on.'

Forming them on our heads, they looked ridiculous but at that point it didn't matter. A collective feeling of relief, and achievement came over the group. I looked around and saw the smiling faces, and I couldn't help but smile.

We arrived back at the Regiment. Captain H led us towards the gates, the sun was at its highest over the parade ground and music started blasting through the speakers. It was Thin Lizzy – *The Boys Are Back In Town*. Captain H shouted, 'Straight backs and heads high boys…you've earned it', you could hear how the marching became firm, synchronized and the timing was spot on. We felt proud, we felt like soldiers.

The whole Regiment was watching, including the newly arrived recruits that had just started their basic training. They would later become our squad members. Another member of our audience was the 42nd man of KBS. Only 41 men earned their beret that day, number 42 had sprained his ankle during a parachute drop just weeks before. He would earn his beret with the specialists later that year. He came down to congratulate us and help with our equipment. I could see he had a hard time holding back his tears. He felt that he was, at least for now, not a part of the brotherhood. He was even though he didn't feel that way. I felt bad for him, but I appreciated his presence.

It was now the middle of summer; the new recruits were still separated from us as they had a few months of basics left to go. For the squad leaders the summer was the last part of KBS, and it was all about honing our specialist skills, digging deeper into demolition, weapon systems, radios et cetera. The heavy lifting was done and to be honest it was a fun summer, relaxed and mostly spent blowing things up. For us it was as close to a vacation as we got because we all knew that when we left KBS for our new squadrons, things would change, and they would change quickly.

In late August it started to get dark and cold again. Some days you could feel the summer still trying to cling on, but winter was winning the fight. Finally, the day arrived when we were assigned to our new squadrons and platoons. In the Swedish Army the designation squadron, called *skvadron* in Swedish, is unique to the Cavalry. It is the equivalent of a company. There are four squadrons each consisting of four platoons. The 1st squadron or company in a regiment is almost always called *Livskvadron/Livkompani,* that is the Life Squadron/Company. Figuratively it means something to the effect of 'the regiment's own.'

Livskvadron this year consisted of only one platoon, a sniper platoon. People that have shown talent for being a sniper are taken aside a few weeks earlier during the summer for extra selection tests, but the results of these tests are kept secret.

The 2nd squadron is the ranger squadron comprised of direct-action units, who are more heavily armed, including weapons such as SAWs, Carl Gustav M/86s, NLAW 44s,etc.. They also have a Forward Air Control unit.

The 3rd squadron is the intelligence squadron with LRRP units. These are called intelligence capable units, which mean that they are authorized to make their own tactical decisions based on intelligence gathered.

The 4th squadron trains the leaders and hosts the KBS.

We were waiting on Squadron assignments to post on the notice board that afternoon. I could feel my shoulder and neck cramping up as I waited to see my future military role. I was hoping to be assigned to the 2nd squadron with heavy weapons and more action. I didn't want to be assigned to the intelligence squadron as it was notoriously hardcore and "boring". They were known for long exercises, being first in and last out. We all agreed that when the post was up, you wouldn't share other people's assignments if they were waiting for their turn to look.

Captain H did the evening roll call, it was quicker than usual. He said that he would post the assignments after we were dismissed. Almost everyone gathered around the notice board immediately after we were released. I went back to my room just across the hall; I wanted some peace and quiet. I could hear the commotion and people shouting out loud, 'YES! I got *Livskvadron.*' Two of my roommates came back in, one of them was Mr S, they were happy as they both managed to get into the only FAC unit, I was happy for them. I didn't want to go to FAC myself so there was no competition.

I was assigned to the 3rd squadron, 34th intelligence platoon. I was slightly disappointed as I wanted something else; not the eternal hard routine – pooping in bags and keeping things on the down low. But little did I know that this platoon assignment would form my future. When you get assigned to your squadron, you spend the evening cleaning out your barracks and common areas and moving to your new accommodation, then reporting to your new platoon commander the next morning.

The next morning the squad leaders of the 34th Intelligence Platoon were lined up for roll call, our specialists had not been assigned to us yet. These were all familiar faces, some you liked more than others but the five months together at KBS had made us close. We were all worried and a bit excited to meet our new platoon commander Captain B He was new to the regiment, and we were his first platoon. The nervousness came from knowing that Captain B had just transferred from the newly disbanded Lapland Ranger Regiment I 22, it was even further north than our unit and they had performed a similar military function. It was rumoured, as it always is in the forces, that the discipline was hardcore. I am not saying we were lacking in anyway, but they were famous for being several levels above everyone else.

He entered the corridor from the left. He was short, his biceps, shoulders, lats, and chest filled out his shirt. His head was newly shaven and had a mirror like finish. He had an almost alien-like appearance.

He was very formal; his movements were firm and solid. I thought if I ever saw combat this is the guy I would want in charge. Little did I know that just a few years later that wish would be granted. Captain B had booked a meeting room, and we sat down. He told us that he wanted to get to know us and for us to get to know him, as trust was everything. His forearms on the desk, his stringy muscles popped up as he brought his hands together and his fingertips made contact. He went on to say, 'In this business you are to be my eyes and ears on the ground. We need to establish trust; this is our foundation.'

He started with his own story, telling us about his family, his life, ups and downs, strengths, and weaknesses. We had never heard an officer speak like this previously. When it was our turn to tell our stories, you could tell he was really listening, asking questions, and paying attention, he didn't do this because he had to, he did it because he wanted to. This is when we understood that he was different.

After our introductions he talked about his expectations of us and what we could expect from him. He said, 'It doesn't matter if you fail, what matters is that you did your absolute best and that you are always professional in your actions, mindset, and heart.'

He pulled out a contract that he had drawn up about professionalism, 'Read it and make notes if you want to propose any changes.' Nobody had any changes. He continued, 'are you ready to sign this contract, not for me but with me, in which we make a vow to professionalism?' The question was rhetorical, and we all signed it without hesitation. He said, 'No one can be released from this contract, and I will destroy anyone who tries, and I count on you to destroy me if I try.' We all left this curious meeting with a good feeling; we liked him. This was not a job for him, this was one of his life missions. And when he said that he would train soldiers to the best of his abilities… he meant it, this was no joke.

We had a week of preparations ahead of us before the specialists were to join us. It was mostly stocking up equipment like radios, heavy weapons, tents, nets, et cetera. Checking inventory and arranging it in order in every squad storage area. Captain B also gave us daily tasks, thinking about tactical and strategic concepts. To our surprise he also participated in PT every morning. He was a real monster when it came to PT, but a humble one, he never thought less of you if you didn't finish first or do as many reps as he did, as long as you gave it your best and tried to work on your weaknesses.

His leadership style felt modern at the time and would probably work at any progressive company even today. The night before the soldiers arrived, he said, 'I expect nothing but 110 percent professionalism tomorrow, these are the men that will be on your left and right side when you are facing death; treat them accordingly.' We looked at each other and everybody nodded, we were all onboard.

Being assigned soldiers is always exciting but being assigned recruits fresh out of basics is something that usually happens only once in your life. An intelligence squad gets the following specialists: a Second-In-Command, medic, RTO, LMG gunner and demolitions operator and an intelligence specialist. As with all elite units, we operated in small well-trained teams, a squad of six in total.

I was unsure about the quality of the recruits, and I remembered Captain B's words, 'You shape these individuals, you do what it takes to make soldiers out of them, there is no such thing as bad soldiers – there are only bad leaders. If they don't "work" I will hold you personally responsible.'

I looked at the five of them lined up in front of me. We had the usual suspects of course: the comedian, the overachiever, the clueless guy, the too relaxed dude and the nervous guy. But I was happy as it seemed like a good bunch. We spent the evening doing some light PT, introductions, and we also explained the contract of professionalism that they would have to sign. It soon became obvious that we were one of the few platoons running it like this, as we heard shouting and the regular initiation rites being performed throughout the night. It felt like we were already working on an elevated level, breathing, and living professionalism. It felt good.

About a month in it was time for Ranger Exercise 1. It's one of the three large exercises of the year and it's the first one where everyone leads their assigned squad. This is also when the soldiers earn their berets, and the commanders earn their ranger tab. As a squad leader I felt confident since I had already completed one of these exercises. I knew I was up to the physical challenge, but I wondered if I would be able to lead my men through it.

The exercise is half as long as my first one had been, roughly 14 days, and it has a different focus. The mission was the focus on this occasion, and it was the first time the squads were doing a complete cycle. The mission cycle entailed operational planning, infiltration, operations, extraction, and debriefing. The key was to work as a unit and to solve operational problems, reaching tactical and strategic goals.

My squad was tasked to do reconnaissance and establish whether there was an enemy presence at a remote airfield. Based on this, if we found enemy forces, we had a number of tasks and objectives. First, we would watch them and provide intelligence up the chain; and then we would construct a battle plan for the direct-action units. We were also required to establish an observation post for target acquisition. The aim of the last task was to be ready to strike against enemy logistical convoys behind the front line thereby slowing their advance.

It was a challenging first task for me and my newly formed six-man squad. But I felt confident, I told the men, 'Trust your training, trust each other, trust me as I trust you, and remember our contract.' I kept it to myself, but I was secretly worried about our radio communications as my RTO was the clueless guy Mr K. 'We are screwed if we have any problems with the shortwave', I thought out loud. Somehow, I had a natural understanding of radios and radio communication. Totally weird as I sucked in math and physics at school. The radio skills came in handy, and I maintained a very close eye on my RTO throughout the exercise.

It was one of those exercises where we spent loads of time by ourselves. We were operating within tight limits and constraints, covering large distances, locating and neutralizing complicated targets. About halfway through, my men started to show signs of fatigue. Naturally a part of the exercise was to test our endurance. Food was low, and we had the standard less than one meal a day. I felt energized by them managing to carry on by watching me push forward. It was leading by example, something to the effect of 'if this man can do it so can we.' I felt proud that I managed to lead, even when things were tough and that they trusted me enough to let me.

In a good squad it's not only the leader's task to be strong and give energy and courage. A good leader also sets the tone and attitude towards the problems encountered. I tried to keep a balance and create an environment where we became a single organism. My squad operated in silence, there wasn't a need for many orders, people knew when to move, when to pick things up. It was an unwritten code, programmed into the senses and muscle memory of my soldiers. This approach requires trust and mastery of skills. It is underpinned by mutual respect, regardless of rank. It is communication, taking note of my team members and them of me, seeing people for who they are and not who they should be.

We managed to reach all our targets and all in all, it went better than I could ever have imagined. The reconnaissance mission was perfect – we observed the enemy, put together the plan of attack and transmitted the messages to our commander. The DA team was flawless, and we successfully stifled enemy supplies. I was proud. I could see that they were proud. In less than two months we were a unit. The beret ceremony was held at our last rendezvous (RV) point, a remote camp deep in the bush. I felt a warm feeling in my chest as I saw my soldiers put on their new but wrinkly berets.

The squad leaders had one challenge left before receiving our tab. A 20km march with boots, combat kit and a 24kg combat backpack. With my helmet on, I could feel a bead of sweat trickle down my forehead. It wasn't warm, and I felt my palms were sweaty, while I held my weapon which of course had no sling. The exercise was to be completed in less than 1 hour and 40 minutes. After being two weeks in the field with limited food and sleep, a demanding test.

I was never a fast runner as my frame was heavy. There are two tactics one could use, find your tempo, slow but consistent or run faster on flat and down-hill parts and then do a quick walk when going uphill. I was tired from the start, but I was driven by the potential humiliation of not making it. I decided to go for the first technique, keeping a slow but decent tempo, no stops. Step, step, step, I kept the rhythm, it complemented my breathing which was heavy but under control. Every time I passed someone that was struggling, I got energized; it was a bittersweet feeling, as we were playing for the same team. You try to get them going but we all knew that this was one of the few challenges that are done one hundred percent individually.

I felt my backpack weighing me down, after a while I entered a state of extreme focus. With my body at full exertion, my eyes always looking up ahead and then down, searching the horizon, then scanning obstacles on the ground. There is no great dash to the ribbon, rather a slow methodical trudge to completion. I was far from the first to reach the finish line, when I approached, my squad cheered me on and shouted, 'You will make it.' I made it with 4 minutes and 10 seconds to spare.

3

Honing Our Skills

'The loud music was deafening. It was the old Swedish Communist song *Arbetarbröder* on an eight second loop. They stripped us down, and I was put on my knees.'

Autumn was approaching, and the coming two months were spent solidifying and developing our LRRP unit and advanced combat skills. Building OPs, photography, SOPs et cetera. Just perfecting the details. Next up on the calendar was Ranger Exercise 2. It's always in late autumn/early winter when the specialists earn their ranger tab. It's a problematic period as it is cold and wet, especially in the south. Up north in Arvidsjaur we already had snow which in my opinion is always preferred over rain. Dry and cold weather is much better for endurance than rain and cold.

The mission was as relevant today as it was then. The Russians had invaded, and regular Swedish forces had managed to secure the Airport in Visby. The Russians got reinforcements through the port in Slite, which they had taken over. Our task was to be airlifted from Arvidsjaur to Gotland by C-130. Then provide the regular forces with a target pack over Slite Harbour and finally assist with creating a diversion and taking out key targets before the main assault.

It was snowing heavily. We had our summer uniforms on since there was no snow on Gotland. It's a few hours flight and we were scheduled to land at 03:00. The airport was only partially secured so it would be touch and go. I knew we had a long night ahead of us as we needed to cover half the way to Slite on foot before daylight then find a good layup position and wait for darkness.

The infiltration proved uneventful but was physically challenging due to the speed of our march and the weight of the gear we needed for the last phase of the operation. The following night, we established our OP and had time to do some footwork before first light checks. We had been handed the northern sector, not uncomplicated since there is a lack of cover in Gotland which makes the terrain very challenging, and even the most inexperienced defenders could calculate one's approach. We put the main OP about 1,000 metres away; it was far enough to safely put up a small antenna.

The first couple of days we managed to get a reasonable picture of the enemy's main activities and started to establish some routines and patterns. We had a few blind spots that we would need to fill in before we could make anything that resembled a target pack. Time was short as we only had a few days before the DA units wanted their first intelligence handover so they could start to prepare for the main assault. I reacted by deploying two forward positions that first night. The first one was through an almost inaccessible route that basically guaranteed surprise; this required the team to traverse steep and rocky beach terrain. This approach got us so close that, when downwind, we could smell what the 'enemy' was cooking; and the second team's forward position was in a field with no cover, we hid in plain sight. It was unexpected but it worked well with the ghillie suits that we modified the day before.

This was not the best of situations for us since the patrol was divided into three parts, and the forward positions were not able to be relieved until they were pulled back which would take around two days, so we all had to dig in and embrace the difficult test for the next 48 hours. The forward positions were pulled back during the cover of darkness two nights later. The intelligence was brilliant, we had more than enough for an extensive target pack, and we could now monitor the show from the main OP. My main concern was finishing the target pack and resting the men, as they hadn't slept properly in 48 hours, and we were on standby for the DA the next night. I left four guys in the main OP, so two could sleep and I took the intelligence specialist with me to the target pack handover meeting.

It was a quick affair, the DA units were positively surprised by the quality and detail of the intelligence; the captain who accompanied the DA unit, who was also an evaluation officer, said, 'You took pretty big risks collecting this intel. Did you consider what would happen if you were exposed?'

'I did', I replied, 'it was either this or nothing, it is always better to ask for forgiveness than permission.'

He replied, smiling, 'Well that only works if you are successful, but here we are. Well done on using the field and the beach, as I wouldn't even remotely consider that someone would try to establish anything there.'

After a few hours of shut eye, it was time to start prepping. Outside of the harbour there was a small pier running along the entire length of the port. It's very narrow and only has one point of entry. It serves as a source of weather protection for the port and in this case, the 'enemy' had deployed an anti-aircraft artillery battery and mortars. We knew that it would be almost impossible to fight our way in from the entry point.

They only had one guard with an LMG. The most likely reason for this was that the 'enemy' believed that the assault on the pier would be initiated through the port rather than from the north. We needed to take the guard out without raising the alarm. It could be done by letting one man crawl through a drainpipe, which ended just behind the guard post. The pipe was long, dark, and cold; not the best task, but it was our only option. My 2iC drew the short straw, as he was the slimmest of us all. We expected it to be a 20 minute crawl. Sitting under cover just 50 metres from the guard post, we waited for the 2iC to make his appearance and make the guard 'disappear.' Our designated marksman provided cover with a .50 from an elevated position 75 metres to the west.

42 minutes had passed since he entered the drainpipe. I was getting worried, 'was he stuck?'

I looked around and started thinking of contingency options. I decided to give it 50 minutes, after which I would send out a search party. On the 46th minute we saw the guard disappear backwards into the ditch while he was sipping on a cup of java. It must have hurt because the guard went down like a sack of potatoes. We dashed towards the gate, without a minute to spare and secured it, the guard was declared "dead" by the wargame umpire. The last part of the mission was a 100-metresprint over open terrain to a pair of rocks just short of the AA and mortar position. 'Mike Sierra, this is Romeo Viking, guard post down, sit rep, over.'

'Romeo Viking, Mike Sierra – all clear, I say again all clear for you to move to cover.' Looking at my crew I said, 'Mike Sierra gave all clear.' We swiftly moved across the open plain taking cover behind the rocks. 'Charlie Sierra, Romeo Viking, we are in position. It's a go.' The designated marksman opened up with a salvo from the .50. This was the signal for the DA teams to commence the attack. After about two minutes we had control of the position, with no casualties. We could hear the main assault on the port had started and we needed to move quickly so we wouldn't be cut off by any enemy forces.

The team prepared the explosives to finish off the AA and mortar positions. We were going to detonate them remotely. Just as we packed up to move out, our heaviest guy, the LMG gunner, fell down screaming in pain. He had been 'shot', I looked at the wargame umpire. He smirked and said, 'You know those stray bullets are a terrible thing.'

Of course, it had to be the heaviest guy who had to be medevaced. Luckily it was less than 500 metres to the pre-determined casualty collection point. We treated the wound and placed him on the portable stretcher. We felt him move to one side and then the other as we struggled to get our balance. We needed to get him to where he could receive better medical treatment.

We got him to the gates where the medic stabilised him and got him transport ready. I was starting up the radio to report in when the umpire switched the radio off. He said, 'Your radio is broken, and you are cut off from your main units, you have one wounded man. Escape and Evasion is in effect.'

'I hate umpires, we are not cut off, you just want to make this final part hell', I managed to hold back these words, but my eyes must have said it all. I called in the marksman and briefed the squad. We were taken from a perfectly planned and executed operation, into the deep and murky waters of life. Our reward was an8-hour march to our emergency RV (ERV) which was outside Visby Airport.

The fighting had stopped in the port, and I assumed all units had met a similar fate. I knew the "enemy" had anti-sabotage units with dogs and we could hear them, it was time to move, now. What followed was a long night; we managed to shake the dogs a few hours in, and we just kept grinding to make the ERV before it closed.

We were the second unit to arrive at the ERV, I was surprised as we had been furthest away. The ERV had been secured by a rear support unit that was halfway to the airport. We were tired but a well-deserved cup of coffee did the trick. We helped them with perimeter defence; by morning all the units came trickling in, each with at least one wounded soldier. Time was tight – we had three hours to prepare an improvised strip for a C-130 to land and take us back.

We all sat heavy in the nets as the C-130 charged down the road, I hate road take-offs and landings as it feels like the aircraft is going to disintegrate. We achieved a lot, but my thoughts slowly started to fade into a dreamy haze as I felt the aircraft leaving the ground and starting its struggle to gain altitude.

Back at the regiment, one of the most intense training periods was about to begin, the winter. This would be the second winter for the squad leaders and the first for the specialists. There is so much ground to cover. Skiing, winter warfare, survival et cetera; and all of this while the squads continue to develop their skills and not sliding backwards. Our winter training period coincided with an interesting event. In January we found out that the first ever delegation of Russian generals and a platoon of "Rangers" from Murmansk was going to participate in a small exercise with us.

It was a tense moment as ties with the Russians had just started defrosting since the end of the Cold War – but of course it was still politically sensitive. Especially for a unit like ours. I know that the Navy in the south of Sweden had already done some friendly visits back and forth to Kaliningrad. But it was all kept from the public eye. Weeks before the Russian delegation arrived, a number of government agencies and departments came to the regiment. Swedish military intelligence, secret service, and what we knew as the state department. All participants were vetted and subjected to interviews and questioning. A soldier from another platoon had participated in a Labour Day march in his youth – he was not allowed to participate. A little harsh perhaps, but we were following orders.

We drilled and rehearsed all potential questions and answers. We were told what to look for and to pay attention to anything and everything and to be prepared to debrief afterwards. They selected my platoon and the FAC group to be the ones interacting with the Russians. First, we would perform a live fire assault, supported by live firing JAS 39 Gripen fighter jets led by the FAC group. They really went all out on this show. Following this we were to conduct a simple joint fire and manoeuvre exercise with the Russian platoon.

The "show" part went as expected, it was a smash hit. They even broke the safety regulations by having the fighter jet firing dangerously close to the front line as we were pulling back. We didn't mind, at 19 years old we were bulletproof. The Russian generals congratulated us afterwards and shook our hands, 'You are welcome to serve in my unit any day,' one said through his interpreter. He winked as a smile crept up on one side of his face. This led to a lot of strained smiles from our officers.

When we met the Russian platoon, we were not allowed much interaction. They looked rough and ready. They had more advanced gear and gave off a sophisticated special forces look. It was their subtle way of showing us that things had apparently changed in Russia. We nodded to each other and carried out the exercise. It was by all accounts a very straightforward fire and manoeuvre drill that was done for the appearance of bonding and diplomacy.

After the Russians left, the Regiment was swamped with military intelligence, and everyone involved was debriefed. They even took the glass model of the newest Sukhoi fighter jet that was given as a gift to the regimental commander. After a bit of nagging, I was allowed to keep my token tin wings badge with a number 'one' engraved on it. I got it from the Russian general for being a 1st class soldier and I still have them today. Of course, I know that this was just a gesture, but us old soldiers often hang on to the mementos.

Winter training ended in February, the coldest month, with Ranger Exercise 3. It's the perfect month to examine our winter skills. Ranger Exercise 3 is just a small part of something much bigger, The Swedish Armed Forces joint winter exercise. So, a lot of moving parts, and all units and headquarters are put to the test. The exercise is prepared a year prior by a special wargame unit at HQ. The briefing pack is extensive and there is a lot of background material to the conflict, movies, news reports, maps, and entire villages are 'created' for the purpose of the training.

My platoon was tasked with surveillance on Vidsel, a remote airbase in the vast wilderness, close to the small town of Jokkmokk. It is used as a live fire-bombing range and test site for new weapons. It was February, the mercury read -42 degrees Celsius. At these temperatures you usually sleep well. Waking up is a different story as the cold usually hits you on a crippling level, but nothing that a cup of ranger coffee can't fix. Ranger coffee is just coffee with pieces of bark and wood that usually find its way into your thermos when melting snow.

During our infiltration towards the airbase, the nights were amazing. They were beautiful as they tend to be in the arctic, and we had plenty of night since there were only a few hours of light every day. While skiing slowly through the forest, the magical northern lights danced above our heads and gave that hard to describe magic shimmer to the frozen snow. The silence is haunting, and the only noises were the dragging of our skis as we made our way through the snow and the thud of exploding trees. They start popping when the temperatures are low and the water in the trees' core freezes, expands and explodes.

After almost a week of static and mobile reconnaissance work, we met up with two mechanised companies from Norrbotten Regiment I19, back behind our own lines. We had an initial dispute with the commanders from the infantry. They always had their briefings inside. We don't; especially during extreme temperatures and we were going back out to the field immediately. There is a good reason for this, as if you go indoors, after being in the extreme cold, your blood vessels dilate, and you get swollen – which makes one puffy, and slow and affects your body and brain. And when going back outside, it takes one about 12 hours to readjust to the extreme cold. Once again during that time we would be slow, low on energy, and tired. Not exactly the way to start the next infiltration.

Being a conscript sergeant standing up to two captains was a tall order, but I tried to come across as polite and calm while I made my case. It was a power play and they resorted to shouting and the usual, 'Who do you think you are?'

By pure coincidence, a Colonel passed by and asked about the ruckus. It was the battalion commander. The captains made their case, adding, 'These rangers think they own the world.'

The Colonel looked at his two captains, 'So, what you are saying is that you will impede this squad's future performance because you two don't want to stand outside for two hours, is that correct?'

'Well not like that,' said the captain, 'It's more convenient inside, better lighting, warm, easier to take notes.'

'Hmm, so you think it was convenient for this ranger patrol to be outside in this freezing ass cold for a week and then ski for eight hours in the dark to hand over their findings to you so you can solve your tasks and then head back out there again to repeat it all?' said the Colonel.

The captains knew they had lost their case, 'Ehm no.'

The Colonel continued 'I will attend this handover myself and I want to see your commanders out here, out of their cosy barracks in five minutes, properly dressed. So, we don't take any more of these gentlemen's time, Go!'

As the captains ran towards the barracks, the colonel looked at us and smiled, 'There are assholes in all walks of life, never give in to them when you know you are right.' As we were preparing to leave, one of the captains approached us and said, 'Hey I am sorry I overreacted, I shouldn't have, good luck on your next mission.'

He probably did it out of shame, we had just delivered him the key to success, including a new and better route for their unit. A path that was not on the map, which would save them a day or two and keep them away from the enemy. It was either that or the reprimand they received from the Colonel.

We had two more missions to complete. The first one was to confirm the location of an artillery radar group, and the second was to conduct disrupting assaults along a logistics route and finally get to our extraction point. The artillery radar group was a cake walk, they were located on a hill, and they were loud. We didn't even have to get close to confirm the number of soldiers and layout of the position.

They found it hard to walk in deep snow, so they always took the same route, in some countries they call it path discipline, but for a reconnaissance team, we were looking at a highway. We could have taken them all out, but it was not our job, we were to confirm their presence, numbers, and any heavy gear. The FAC coordinated an airstrike on the position later that week.

The temperature started to plummet, and we took readings of -48 degrees Celsius. This was dangerous, and severe frostbite was more of a threat than our lumbering 'enemy'; it would hit one like lightning. We relied on our training, keeping dry, changing socks, adjusting our clothing, no short cuts. We also increased buddy checks, where we checked for signs of frostbite. A key part was to help them out before they got too tired and started taking short cuts. Captain H's speech came to mind, 'you will not need the enemy to kill you if you take short cuts!'

One of the perks of operating in the extreme cold is that not that many people are out; so, it provides additional protection. Most anti-sabotage patrols would be cancelled and maybe replaced with a vehicle borne one instead. It keeps the forest quiet the way we liked it.

We were headed towards our last mission; it was roughly two days of skiing from the radar station in the direction of our RV. It was a stretch of road that ran deep behind enemy lines – their main supply route from the west, a heavily trafficked dirt road, which was constantly being reinforced, repaired, and maintained by the engineers.

We had resupplied at the handover with eight anti-tank weapons, our trusted AT4s.[1] This resulted in an added load, so we had to leave some comforts behind to fit them in our sledge. My plan was to strike at two points, one on the main supply route to get a number of vehicles stuck, and the second was an attack on the route planned for reinforcements. This was a classic tactic employed by elite and special forces units, it was a test to see if we were up to the challenge.

We observed the route for about 24 hours. All convoys were following their SOPs, first a small Security Advanced Party, then the main convoy. The first vehicle, oddly enough, was always a heavy truck, so were the last two. The SAP team was always 10minutes ahead, methodical, like clockwork.

My plan was to divide into two teams, with two AT4s each. Timing was central to the operation, with one team striking the front and one hitting the rear of the convoy, to stop them dead in their tracks. As a means of deception, we would move in the direction of the enemy, deeper behind their lines. The 'enemy' would be looking for us on the wrong side while we would strike against their reinforcements. It was a test, and I wanted to see if we would hit the mark.

---

1   A Swedish 84mm single use anti-tank weapon. It is an unguided weapon that can be carried by soldiers in all terrain.

We found a culvert that would allow us to cross the road unseen, we just needed to make sure we covered our tracks. During the night we moved our sledge and Bergens under the road and crept to a layup position about 45 minutes from the road. We planned to hit the early morning convoy. As we came back to our assault position, we made the tracks look like they ran back towards the radar station.

I decided that we were going to use vehicle claymores and flare mines for illumination. We managed to set it up, but I knew we were running short of time. I wasn't happy with how we covered the tracks, but it had to do – I made my peace.

'I hear the SAP team', I whispered. Two armoured sections came speeding by. We could hear the crunch of their vehicles cutting tracks in the snow. They kept higher speed than we expected and had seen previously, but they just swooshed by, we were undetected. 'Was the convoy going too fast, would we miss, had I miscalculated?' I focused, zooming in on the approaching vehicles. I was in the team hitting the front, we would trigger the assault to the rear. I felt my heart beating in my chest.

'Boom' the mines exploded, the illumination was perfect and two seconds later I could hear the thumping when the AT4's were fired. I observed the scene for a split second, the frame froze, we got them. A few seconds of silence, we don't follow up with any small arms fire, there are too many of them and they are too strong. The gunners in the convoy started to lay down fire in our direction, while the armour started to deploy heavier shells. It's a deafening sound, but we keep our cool. To put it into context, they are wounded and stuck and they don't know what they are looking for, it is just speculative fire in all directions.

We got down behind the ridge and followed our own tracks back, we had to get back and hide our tracks that led to the drainpipe. We took our time as the danger was not the convoy – they wouldn't leave the road – I was worried about the enemy's silent patrol. A unit like ours hunting us. On our way through the drainpipe the ground rumbled, the SAP was on their way back.

We could hear the shouting and commands given down the road. 'They had a long day and maybe even night ahead of them', I thought. When we reached our layup point, we heard the helicopters on their way. They were looking in the other direction.

Our second target was a smaller road. We had less time, but luckily it was only 20 minutes of skiing before we saw the road – our estimation checked out, and it was a good enough spot to strike. After a few minutes the ground started to rumble, it was the Quick Reaction Force – two armoured platoons that came roaring by. We waited for the salvage and engineer units who were heading down to support and recover the stuck convoy. Time was limited, and I sent two guys to find potential exit routes and a new layup point for the equipment. Two more team members were tasked with making false tracks in the wrong direction. Twenty minutes later two additional armoured platoons passed us, it was the remainder of the QRF. They had a company size QRF there now, so I knew that it was almost time for us to play our part.

We got the signal from the look out and we used the ploughing sticks on the road as markers – it was at the break of dawn, and we had enough light to fire without illumination. I knew it was all systems go – a part of me just wanted to get it over with, and another enjoyed the moment. Suddenly it was action again. The first two AT4s took out the repair trucks heading up the column. The second group waited, it seemed like forever, then they fired and managed to disable the salvage section. We needed to move quickly now, there was a narrow strip of land for us to use as cover for the first 150 metres; the snow was deep, and the RTO fell into a small ditch. When someone falls into two metres of snow, they just disappear. There is no way one can get out without help.

We managed to get the RTO up, but we lost time; the lookout joined the group, and he told us, 'We have armour on us.' 'Fuck', I said. The last thing I saw before I left my position was a platoon size armour group. They stopped further down the road when we started the attack. With their thermal sights, they could easily cut us down. 'Think fast,' I thought as I looked up.

'Quick, new plan, circle south and then up north to make a wider circle around the enemy, cross the road and backwards again to the lay up.' It was 20 intense minutes where we came close enough to touch them, but we made it over to the other side and back to the layup position.

It had been a close call and perhaps we created too much commotion.

The RV was about a day's ski away, we would be there early. That's unusual but also well deserved. It was to be a helicopter pick up. We had prepared a spot for a night landing, and we waited. No helicopters in sight. The hours went by, and we knew it was a missed pick-up. We had a radio slot an hour later so I decided to move away from the pickup location as it might have become compromised. We found a good spot about 35 minutes away and I left two of my men behind as lookouts. Something was off.

We got the radio up and HQ messaged that the helicopters had been shot down en route. We had to proceed to the ERV where we would probably make contact with the resistance – the plan was to get us out by truck on the back roads. Well, you always know a shabby deal when you see it. I lied about our position and gave them the helicopter landing site; I wanted a head start just in case they were sending 'someone.' I decided not to rest and to get the team to the ERV as fast as I could. We had at least five hours of skiing ahead of us. I knew we would need time to stake it out and I wanted to do it carefully.

The ERV was outside of a small, abandoned village and it was a perfect place for a trap. It was hard to get a good look at it without approaching using the obvious routes. I found a spot for the marksman to provide cover and a LUP for the rest of the team in preparation for our initial meet up with the resistance. It was not too far away because we had to be close enough to get on the truck without much delay. I felt trapped between a rock and a hard place.

I had the marksman in position and three guys in the LUP, ready to go in any direction. I took the intelligence specialist with me for the meeting. An old Volvo pulled up in the clearing. The driver exited the car and walked back and opened the trunk, then sat on the hood and lit up a cigarette. The coal of the cigarette burned bright as he inhaled. That was the signal. We cautiously moved forward and approached him from the front. He was calm and greeted us in broken English, he said, 'Good work on the convoys, they are still busy with that.' I asked him about the truck, to which he responded, 'It's in the barn there', and pointed to a shed 20 metres away.

It was hard to see as there was no ambient light. I said, 'Show us the truck.' We walked down towards the barn, and he opened the wooden doors, I was ready for contact. I had a good angle, and I could easily take out their point man first. The doors hung unevenly and squeaked when he opened them. Inside was an old army truck with a tarp covering the back. I asked, 'Who will drive it?'

He said, 'I will, I'll leave the Volvo here. We need to go now, there will be roadblocks at first light, we need to hurry.'

I hesitated, but what options did I have, I had to play the game. I got the marksman down and the squad out from the forest. We were all on the truck within 10 minutes. The smoking guy hid his Volvo in a nearby garage. He had to try the truck several times before it started, and it jumped to life on the fifth attempt. He slowly rolled out of the barn; the hard, unmaintained suspension would make this a bumpy ride.

It would not take more than 35 minutes to drive us to our drop off point. It was cosy laying in the back with our AKs ready, just watching the forest rush by through the holes in the tarp. Maybe it wasn't a trap after all, maybe it was just a happy ending. Approximately 15 minutes into the ride the truck came to a sudden stop, we heard shouting in Russian, it was a roadblock. 'This is it we need to prepare to fight our way out', I said. One single shot rang out, it appeared to come from the front of the truck, and before we knew what was happening the tarp was pulled away and we had a platoon size number of rifles pointing at us.

They threw us down on the ground, it was a long fall from the back of the truck. Looking up from the ground, I could see that the driver had been executed and was lying in a pool of blood. I knew it wasn't real, but it put fear into you. We were hooded, strapped, and led onto a bus. I could hear our captors speaking Russian. I knew what was coming our way, the next stop was interrogation.

We spent about an hour on the bus. I felt a bit groggy after the fall from the truck and the heat in the bus was turned up high. Our captors walked up and down the aisle poking us with their rifles. I could see through the bottom of my hood that they wore Russian gear and had AK 74s. It felt like there were more prisoners on the bus, but I wasn't sure.

When the bus stopped, we were taken inside. It was sensory overload. The loud music was deafening. It was the old Swedish communist song *Arbetarbröder* (brothers in labour, referring to the working class) on an eight second loop. They stripped us down, and I was put on my knees. I felt the cold hard floor, imagining the fear of being caught in combat. The order rang out, 'Hey, you, back straight.' I felt the butt of a rifle encouraging good posture.

After a few hours it all became blurry, the pain from the stress positions, the repetitive music, the cold, and hard environment. My mind started to drift, and I got numb from the pain. For a moment it felt like I had left my body. My hood was lifted once they had dragged me into the interrogation room. I tried to snap out of it, to have a clear mind, I wanted to know what I was answering. I don't think I said anything. I had no idea how much time had elapsed or what was happening. It was a constant vacuum of pain, a never-ending void. I refused to drink any water that offered from time to time, as I was convinced it was poison.

I was taken outside and put on my knees; they took the hood off. The sense of cold, numbness and fear set in. I could see my comrades kneeling beside me. There was blood in the snow, a firing squad lined up in front of us and masked men with AK74s. 'This is it' I thought. I saw some of my mates welling up and swallowing hard. At this point you have long since lost your grip on reality, this is now real. We faced the idea of a violent end; this was the day we were going to die.

Ten seconds later, with my heart beating like a drum, a lump in my throat, and pain throughout my body, someone from the back said, 'Exercise is finished, cease fire.' It's a formality that must be said out loud when an exercise involving firearms is formally over. The masked men untied us and led us inside, the music was turned off and we were put in chairs. Someone put a blanket over my shoulders and a medic looked me over, as he did with my friends. Someone then came and offered us warm sugar water, and a straw. He said, 'Drink, it's over now you all did well.' I spat it out, since I was still riding on the poison train. He said, 'It's okay, drink it, the interrogation is over. It was 49 hours of torture, one of the longest sessions.'

We still had a bit of winter left, then spring would take over and the demobilization phase would start in the beginning of June. Most of the heavy lifting was done, Ranger exercise 1 through 3, and *baskerprovet* – that was two winters. The next part was a month of specialist courses. Then we would do one more round of summer survival. In the spring, remote weapon systems, counterinsurgency, advanced CQB, advanced platoon level warfare and a few other specialist training sessions. The spring was when candidates applied for officers' school. Each platoon commander recommends whoever they think is suitable to the squadron commander who then considers the candidate and puts his recommendation to the regimental command. Eventually six to fifteen candidates and a few reserves are chosen.

It was an early spring day and I had just come back from advanced demolition training. Captain B called me aside in the corridor, 'Get into my office and close the door.' I thought I was in trouble but before I could even start to consider why, he asked, 'Officers training, Yes or No?' I blurted out a 'yes' without even thinking, He replied, 'Good, I didn't expect anything less from you, this is in your blood.'

Captain B pulled out a bunch of papers and said, 'Let's do the paperwork.' I left his office with a weird feeling, I wasn't planning to stick around in the military, but it didn't feel bad either. I thought let's see where it takes me, I might not even be selected, there are many good candidates. When I came back, my squad said that they had been interviewed about me by Captain B, and the Battalion Commander. 'You bastards didn't say a thing', I said. They smiled and a few comments came flying in. They all smiled, and that was it. Ours was the silent squad, enough was said.

We had one more major event to do before it was over, the final exercise. The hardest part was to keep people in the loop as some had started to check out mentally. They felt the fresh air of freedom and civilian life just around the corner. Of course, you had a few hardliners that felt sad and couldn't see how one could live a civilian life after our experience, but most of us could.

Captain B reminded us about the contract. 'It is valid until the end – keep it professional to the end.' I looked around and knew it wouldn't be a problem with my men, hardly with anyone in my platoon for that matter. One of the guys from the 2nd Squadron was arrested during a drunken night out on the town; he floored a guy that annoyed him. He was a former Serbian Youth Champion in boxing; it didn't end well for any of them. Least of all for the guy who bugged him. I was keen on staying out of trouble since I still had that officer's application grinding in the back of my mind.

The final exercise is one for the joint Swedish Armed Forces. It is more a test of command, structure, and capabilities than hardcore grinding. It started with a long infiltration. We marched through the Abisko National Park, which is a breathtaking mountain range in the Swedish Lapland. We were tasked with monitoring a border crossing, reporting, and analysing units, and potential build ups. It was straight forward but challenging in terms of analysis. Our secondary mission was to blow up a railway line on our way home, a classic sabotage mission that we have all seen in old movies. The recent (2022) Russian invasion of Ukraine showed us again the timeless tactic of destroying infrastructure in the face of an advancing enemy.

I cannot say that this one made any lasting imprints in my mind, but I do remember how it ended. We were on our last leg of the extraction, moving by foot to the regiment, we had a few hours left. And for most of us this would be the last hours in the field during our military service. Spirits were high and we were covering ground quickly. I was moving down the column to check on my guys and I saw that my RTO Mr K looked unusually strained. He was sweating heavily and was obviously struggling. Every squad had a few personalities and Mr K was the clueless guy.

I asked, 'What is wrong?'

He replied, 'It's just so damn heavy today.'

RTOs usually carry one of the heaviest loads but of course he was no stranger to this. I noticed that he didn't have his hip belt on, so I said, 'Ahh you forgot to use the hip belt on your Bergen.'

He replied, 'What?'

I repeated, 'Your hip belt on your backpack it's just hanging there.'

Mr K replied, 'What's a hip belt?'

He had such a sincere look on his face and tone in his voice, I knew he wasn't bluffing. I took his hip belt in my hand and said, 'This one, you wear it over your hips and pull it tight to distribute the load from your back and shoulders.'

'Ahh I never knew what it was for, never used it,' Mr K replied.

I just stood there as the column passed me, I couldn't believe that he had never used his hip belt during 11 months of service. Even though it had been explained several times during basic training. I didn't want to make a fuss about it, so I just jogged back into my place in the column.

The weeks before demobilisation was hectic; gear is inspected, cleaned, and handed in. All this during a time when everyone has checked out mentally. On one occasion a squad in one of the platoons was perhaps over happy, and they played the Soviet anthem while cleaning out their platoon storage – it didn't go down well, but nobody cared, we were almost out.

During the last days before leaving the regiment forever I was called down to the parade ground. Along with 12 other soldiers, we assembled. We had been selected as candidates for officers' school. The commander said, 'Observe the word candidates.' We were to return one week later to complete a series of physical tests, written exams, and detailed interviews.

I told my squad that I made it to the last officers' selection. They were happy of course but also felt sorry for me having to come back in just a week. I didn't care much. I was just looking forward to a week off; it had been a long time since I had a week off. It was a bittersweet feeling; it was emotional and when all the dust had settled from the ceremonies, speeches and handing out of diplomas, it felt empty and a little sad. The thought occurred to me that I would probably never see most of these guys again.

I remember thinking that it felt good that I hadn't closed the military chapter of my life, and I was excited for my next adventure.

4

Number 788

'It was just a train ticket, a location with a time and a date and papers to show the guard.'

I could feel the warmth of the sun on my back, as I sat down on an old bench near the harbour. The wood was worn; the seasons had taken their toll. The plaque on the bench had the name of some person I didn't want to remember… it wouldn't be me – I was after all new and shiny, unvarnished, and robust. Stockholm was beautiful on days like this. I took a moment and watched the boats leave for the archipelago just below the royal castle. Three days had passed since demobilisation. It had been quiet, way too quiet. I had mixed feelings – I felt free in that there was nothing, no one controlling my day. But on the other hand, it also made me feel empty, like when you have had a long-term relationship that you wanted to get out of but once it actually happens it's just a void.

It scared me a bit, I felt institutionalised, but I had this nagging feeling – I needed back in. There was nothing left for me here in Stockholm anymore. I headed off to meet some old friends. I thought that they were clueless about life. Most of them were university students, all cosy and academic, too many soft values. I wanted them to know what I had been through, who I had become. This is one of the first lessons soldiers get when going home – we can no longer relate. 'Are they trying to piss me off?' It was most likely that I had changed. I missed the grind and the violence; it was a strange feeling. But it was true, like many others I was another 18-year-old taught to kill and trained in violence.

I had grown. At least I thought so, what did I know anyway? Maybe I had become weakened by the discipline and indoctrinated by the system. 'Snap out of it.' I had to shake the feeling and put on a game face, so they didn't think that I had become a freak.

My school friends, Mr G, Ms K, and Mr L hugged me, smiling from ear to ear, 'How have you been?'

'Oh my God it's been such a long time. So now you're a soldier, eh? No, a Ranger?' … and so, it went on. I tried to smile and only relaxed after my second lingonberry vodka. Mr G was always joking, 'Loosen up man,' he said. I kept zoning out. My eyes searched the room, black shirt, red dress, and the music was loud.

Mr L was an academic, a syndicalist at heart, always talking about how the working class would lead the charge on world peace and so on. 'Nah, not today mate.'

Mr L looked at me. He took a moment that felt like an hour and slowly said, 'So do you want another drink?' I saw Ms K look at me, the corners of her lips tried to hide a smile, her eyes narrowed, then Mr G came in, 'The tough soldier needs another drink', and he was right.

I arrived at the gates of the regiment. I had a brisk walk from the train station taking off my jacket. Those warm summer nights were lovely. I had to show my papers to the guards at the gate. I was offended, a week ago we owned this place and now I was treated like a stranger. I didn't like the feeling, but I was still happy to be back.

The corridors were silent; I heard the clunk of each step as I made my way down an empty corridor. Only a handful of recruits were around, no doubt going through the process – it felt like yesterday and a lifetime ago. We had been assigned accommodation at Life Squadron. A few of the other candidates had already arrived, I didn't know them well. They asked me if I wanted to tag along to the gym and then go for dinner and beers. This meant either the pizza place or the hot dog stand – they both served beer.

They must have been a little concerned about the assessment as there was lots of talk about tactics to deal with the physical tests. At this point I didn't really care. I remembered Captain B's words, 'This is in your blood,' I was a different guy than the boy who walked these corridors in January 2002.

All the testing for officers' school is very formal, not stiff, but if you compare it to ranger school where there is always an element of surprise and excitement, this was a little different. We received a schedule, and all testing was carried out in an almost methodical and calm manner.

The first day was a doctor's exam. It was straight forward, well except for the regimental doctor.

He had always been a bit weird, a relic from a previous generation, in his 60s; he had come with the regiment when they moved from Umeå in 1980. This man was a piece of work, heavy handed, slap dash and worst of all a hardcore racist -so few people wanted to work in these parts, we were stuck with him. When I had my vaccinations during basics, he said 'Watch that armrest, there was a coloured guy sitting there before you; you don't want to catch anything.' There were many racists in Sweden just like in other places, but this type of blatant statement was not typical. I considered my options. 'This man has no principles', I thought. I always felt I should have said something, but I was too worried about my own success. It disturbs me even to this day.

Day two we tackled the physical tests. Starting the day off with a 10km run and strength tests in the afternoon, it felt like a regular day in the office. I pushed myself through the first five kilometres before hitting my stride. Perhaps a little too bulky to be a natural runner, I got into a decent pace of about 5 minutes 20 seconds per kilometre. I cruised in well under the one hour cut off, drank some water, and headed back. The strength tests were even easier, and I did what was needed without pushing myself too much. With my service still fresh in my mind, I felt a new confidence.

Day three, we were given a written exam, something similar to what people do when they apply for university, just a bit more militarised. Exams had never been my strongest point, and they always made me nervous. I felt that they impaired my thinking. Working through the logic puzzles, analysis, and numeral quizzes I was flustered. Moving from one part to the next made me break into a bit of a stress sweat; it was mostly mind games with me doubting my own abilities. I was flying through it, a few hours passed, and I felt like I ran another 10 kilometres. I finished first with this ten k, but perhaps unlike with the actual run it is not a good sign, at least so I thought.

The evening was dedicated to in-depth interviews with a selection panel of officers from different parts of the regiment. I was more comfortable with this part than with the written assessment. It's nothing hard, one just has to master the skill of sitting alone in a chair and owning the room – all attention is focused on the interviewee – it was my stage to dominate. This is where I realized that soft skills often win the day – talking about your strengths and shortcomings, analysing them. It is tied up with emotional intelligence, some-thing like how we learn to influence each other. I walked out at 21:15; I knew I had made a lasting impression. Everybody was eager to hear my thoughts, and I answered, 'It went okay I think.' We all waited for the next day when the selected candidates were to be announced.

The number of selected candidates was based on how many spots each regi-ment was assigned. The number is preliminary and can change up but mostly down – less is more and they wanted the cream. So, a few reserve candidates were chosen, and the candidates were ranked to avoid any doubt.

I couldn't believe it, but I ranked number 1 – I was very surprised, I had been hoping to make the top five. I look back with pride as my competitors were top notch guys. I felt uncomfortable when I got all the celebratory back pats; I didn't want to be in the limelight, just somewhere in the back or observing from the sides.

The FOK (preparatory officers' course) would start a month later. It's a course run by the regiment, a few months before the officers' school starts in Stockholm in September – the FOK was designed to give candidates a flying start. Only a few units ran preparatory courses at the time, among them were the Paras, Rangers, Costal Rangers… you see the trend, right?

High performing units kept it professional, and I liked the idea of it. A perk was that we got a senior officer as a mentor and started working with our future colleagues straight away.

The last night before we were leaving, Captain B came by the accommodation and asked if he could see me in his office. He offered me coffee and a protein bar, it felt like we were two regular fellows now, not Captain and sergeant. He had a totally different tone in his voice; he was speaking to a future colleague not a conscript sergeant. I struggled with keeping my "Yes captain, No captain" inside of me. He was short staffed on a reconnaissance course, and asked if I would be willing to be an instructor. It started the next day – I was humbled by the offer.

Over the next three weeks we held the course and some of the trainees found it hard – they were after all a crew of officers from an Infantry recon unit, not used to having no protection from the environment. They were accustomed to doing recon from their combat vehicles. We were from different worlds, but there was a mutual respect. I felt a genuine urge to make them as good as I could in the time available. I was a bit to detailed, Captain B said to me, 'you are doing a damn fine job but remember they are only here for a few weeks; stick to the basics, we don't have the time to indulge in the finer details.' I understood, I just wanted to make them better and give them enough knowledge to survive. I realised that being an officer was right up my alley, this is where I felt at home, but the future would be tricky.

The train was nearly empty, and the time approached midnight. My plan was to have a chilled week in Stockholm getting my affairs in order before the preparatory course started. There was no void this time, I knew I was just going to be a visitor, I had found my home.

It was Wednesday, and I was about to go with a few friends to a nearby beach. It was not a beach with sand, just rocks. I liked that about Stockholm and that is how most of the coastline looks in Sweden, rugged.

I was putting my shoes on as I got startled by the mail coming through the letterbox, 'the postman is a damn ghost' I thought; he always moved in silence, probably postal special forces; I had actually never seen him, he would have been an excellent spy, 'death by letter' I thought and smiled. I picked up the envelopes and sorted through some bills and my tax return – I would open them when I got home. As I left them on the kitchen table, I saw a letter from the armed forces. I was expecting the official letter that I had been accepted to officers' school, so I smiled. I had to open it straight away.

After reading it three times I put the letter back on the table and sat down on the kitchen chair. My stomach turned and I felt sick, the feeling of emptiness had returned just like that. The letter was something I couldn't even dream of in my wildest fantasies. 'We regretfully have to inform you that all officers training has been cancelled this year due to funding and the Swedish government have made the decision to cancel all higher military education. You will keep your ranking and have priority for next year's admission.'

I just felt empty as I sat on the chair. My phone rang. It was my friend that was going to pick me up; he said that he was five minutes away. I said, 'Something came up I have to cancel.' 'What came up?', he asked. 'Life', I replied.

I was so invested in this path; I had no idea what to do next. Later that evening I got a follow up call from the regiment. The poor PR officer had the awful task of calling all the candidates to make sure they got the message. He said he had never seen anything like this in his many years of service – you could hear the bitterness in his tone, and he knew that his job could be next. At that point, it was all about survival.

I called my mother later that night; she heard in my voice that it was bad; she couldn't believe it either. She cautiously suggested that it might not be too late to do a late application to the sea captains' programme in Gothenburg, I said, 'Maybe.' I needed to clear my head over the weekend. It was not a bad suggestion, but I had a built-in resistance to going down the academic path.

Friday came and I had managed to muster up some energy to spend the weekend at my friend's parents' summer house in the archipelago. It was a calm place and I wanted him to help me think it though; he was not a military man himself, but a good listener and he usually had reasonable solutions to complex problems. I took the bus from Stockholm city centre to Värmdö, it's a 35 minute ride. The city quickly turned to countryside, and then the coast appeared like a stage from behind a curtain. He was going to pick me up with his boat in the harbour. I felt better, the initial shock had worn off and the change of scenery and its serenity settled me. I knew it would be alright.

I had my phone on vibrate as I had already checked out mentally for the weekend, I could feel it buzzing in my pocket and I looked at the screen "Unknown Caller ID". I chuckled, 'Only government agencies and telemarketers used unknown caller ID', I thought. Well, it is Friday and I had 10 minutes to spare before I reached my destination, even telemarketers need some love from time to time.

'Hello…' 'Hi, its Captain B, do you have a minute?'

This was probably the person I least expected to hear from. I managed to get a, 'Er…yes I do' out.

'Dreadful business with the officer school being cancelled and all, this country is going to shit; but we have to try to keep our heads out of the sewer water, right?' Captain B replied and continued, 'I have a proposal for you; I can't tell you much about it right now, but we are working on something new and unlike the government we don't like to waste valuable resources, I think it would be right up your alley!'

With that cliff-hanger, I asked, 'What is it about and what do I need to do?' and immediately felt stupid.

He just said he couldn't tell me. 'Come to *Livgardet* (1st infantry regiment in Stockholm) Friday a week from now, I can't promise anything, and you are not signing up for something right now, just checking it out. I'll be there, what do you say?'

'I am in', I said. What else could I say?

'Great, I'll have them send out the orders today so you will have them next week, and also expect to be away for some time. See you there,' and before I could say another thing, I heard 'click.'

The second time this week things had pivoted – it was a 360 degree turn around and I felt things were almost back on track; I was curious, excited, and puzzled, why the secrecy? I guess he just wanted it to sound a bit more exciting than it really was.

A few days later an envelope arrived in the mail. No orders, it was just a train ticket, a location with a time and a date and papers to show the guard that I had official business there and the person responsible for me. I recognized the name of the responsible officer, Major M, I didn't know him well. He had been the commanding officer of the KBS School, but we didn't see much of him – afterwards, I think he was attached to the winter research unit. So, I figured it had something to do with my home regiment – things were warming up and I felt confident on my way to Livgardet. I didn't feel any "pre-competition" nervousness, I guess I just assumed that there wouldn't be any competition, I had my mind set on something else.

I presented my orders to the guard. The speaker on my side of the bullet proof glass was broken, he tried to explain where I should go, speaking through the document hatch, gesturing to the right, and speaking animatedly, he looked like a mime. He quickly gave up and came out of the guard building, and pointing across the regiment, said, 'You are going to the old mortar company barracks, they haven't been used for a while. It's down at the end towards the fence in the corner, you can't miss it.'

I had been here a few times when we prepared for guard duty at the royal castle. But I was not very familiar with the layout, also I didn't care that much for the design. Built in the 70s, with ugly concrete blocks decorated with thin lines of the then popular 'puke green'. Walking in, my soul died a bit at the sheer ugliness of the place – I wondered if having design complaints on regiments were common or if it was just me seeing things differently.

I saw a few familiar faces standing outside of the entrance to the building when I arrived. Among them was Mr F, my former intelligence specialist. I was surprised and happy, so weird that we hadn't communicated about this at all. Not even a phone call. But keeping in touch was not my strong suit so I was probably to blame.

The rest were mostly new faces to me, a few officers I had seen before, but mostly older men, relatively of course, they were mid-to-late-twenties. I felt a bit out of place age wise, but it was easy enough to fall in line. The common denominator was that we all had served as Arctic Rangers at different times -some recently, others not so recently – we were around 40 all in all.

An officer came out, he waited for us to pipe down – it was an instinctive and unrehearsed silence. It was the type of thing where former military guys, some half civilian at that stage, didn't really know how to act, but the form and drill quickly took hold. The officer said, 'You are all here out of your free will, if you want to leave, now is the time, otherwise you can follow me.'

I recognised the captain, but I could not remember his name, but I knew I had seen him around the regiment before. We followed him inside to one of the upper floor classrooms. We were told to sit down and in front of us we all had a stack of papers. The captain looked slightly annoyed. He eventually looked up and said, 'Stop fiddling with the papers and listen up. Before you are a non-disclosure agreement and a secrecy act agreement. They are valid for 20 years and the essence is that you cannot speak to anyone about this including your mother, boyfriend, or your army bestie. If you sign this and talk about it, it is punishable by law, so in short keep your mouth shut. 'Anyone that doesn't want to sign? Good. Sign them and pass them to the left when ready.' Military bureaucracy and efficiency.

'I didn't even read it properly, but would it really change anything if I did? Would I walk out because I wasn't happy with a clause in the non-disclosure agreement?' I thought. Nah, they had me at hello.

After that we filled out the next of kin form. The captain informed us that we were insured by the army during this "event", and it was on a volunteer basis. He went on, 'You can quit at any time by stopping during an activity and reporting to the closest instructor.' He then held a short security briefing – it was required by law when people were to be exposed to potentially dangerous elements. At the end of the briefing, we got a plastic box where we wrote our name and personal identification number on a piece of duct tape; it was for personal belongings and valuables like keys, phones, wallets, and watches et cetera. We were told to bring our running shoes and leave the rest behind.

The captain took us down to the equipment storage area and we were handed a very limited and basic selection of equipment – no uniform, only combat boots, and green overalls, the type that was used by mechanics. We received a few additional items, a small backpack and we added a few changes of underwear and some basic equipment like a compass, knife, old mess kit and warm coat. We put our civvies in plastic bags, marked them with tape and left them at the storage unit.

We lined up outside and we were handed a number and four small safety pins, it was printed on half sturdy paper that is decent when dry but that tears easily when wet, I got number 788. 'From now on you are this number, you will attach it to the front of your right thigh, if you lose your number, you will be disqualified.'

An instructor came out from the back, he was dressed in running attire, he just uttered the words, 'Two columns follow me.' Straight off the bat, the tempo was high. 'The bastard had probably even warmed up beforehand', I thought as I felt my lungs warming up. I was first in the column, and I decided to look at the back of his shoes. I would not fall back an inch, as the accordion effect would be horrible for the guys at the back. I immediately felt my stomach turn because I had some weird responsibility to keep it together. He held what I assumed was at least a 45 minute/10 kilometre tempo – so not insanely quick for a normal run, but in boots with equipment it was another story. I recognized the pace even if I was a poor runner, it was ranger competitive pre-selection time.

Just 10 minutes in I was struggling, my boots were not fitted properly, the overall and equipment was weighing me down, I felt this would be a short selection for me, nobody actually mentioned the word "selection" up to that point. They had used the term "event". But I know a selection when I am in one.

The first week was a lot of physical work, running, formal PT tests, obstacle courses, shooting, land navigation, exams and mixed practical test and checkpoints. We were divided into small groups that were constantly changed; leadership was shifted often – we were all given a turn. Sleep and food were limited but not super brutal at this point and we were housed in some old barracks out on the exercise field. Things were run in an ad hoc fashion. There was no schedule, no detailed agendas. It was non-stop endurance and thinking. We got our weapons the first night and we were supplied with extra equipment when needed. I was pretty much fresh out of ranger school, so I was still in it and didn't suffer that much, at least not initially. Some of the slightly older guys, although appearing fit, seemed to be struggling. It was perhaps less about fitness and more about partially losing the military tempo and mindset.

On the fifth night we had been out on an individual night navigation run, the last check point was at an old bunker. We were told to form even lines on each side of the bunker corridor facing each other, two metres apart left and right. It was pitch dark and moist – not ideal, but this was the game. It was one of those long entry corridors, the type that leads towards the blast doors. A small flashlight was put on the floor at each end of the passageway, they hardly gave any light. Two instructors walked down each line and drew the outline of each man's feet with chalk, they said, 'If you step outside the line, you are out.'

'Step outside the line', I thought, 'I can't even wiggle my feet an inch in any direction.' We were given a two-centimetre piece of pencil, with a broken tip. Then they handed out a bunch of papers, it was the previous year's standard university admission test including the essay part – with a four-hour time limit. If we finished early, we were told to just stand and wait until the 4 hours were up and never cross the chalk line. I saw one guy drop his pencil – he watched it roll to the middle of the corridor where he couldn't reach it. He asked one of the instructors who routinely walked up and down the corridor if they could retrieve it. The instructor replied, 'Did you not understand the instructions?.' He looked down at the ground, trapped by the chalk marks around his boots – like the scene of a murder. He knew what it meant.

I had managed to "sharpen" my pencil by chewing off the wood and just using the core; it made it easier to write, and I looked at the guy without a pencil, he was about two metres away, we made eye contact and I signalled to him to form a bowl shape with his papers and press them against his stomach. I chipped off a small piece of lead and signalled that I would throw it by moving my head upwards – like a nod. He realised the bowl was for catching and hopefully his stomach would stop it from falling down to the ground. I was considering an underhand throw, but the piece was too light; I had to throw it like a dart, which meant that if I missed, I would miss by far and it would most likely never be recovered. I aimed at his chest and flicked it in his direction, I saw he was looking at the small piece of lead in his bowl of paper; he needed to move carefully so it didn't roll off to the sides. He managed to retrieve it; he smiled, nodded, and gave me the sincerest thank you with his eyes. It was just a tiny piece, and it wouldn't help him with the essay part but at least he could do the multi choice questions. Taking the university entry exam standing up with my back bent over trying to get some support from my leg in close to complete darkness with a non-existent pen and moist papers took its toll. But I was relaxed as I already knew, language and essays were my strong suit even if it was an exam. I just tried to guess to the best of my ability on the rest of the questions. It was a relief when it was over, and my stiff back was thankful for being on the move for the rest of the night.

On the last day of the first week, we ended up back at the regiment in the early morning. I felt that I was in decent shape, and I was ready for the next challenge. As we stopped outside of the swimming pool, I thought to myself, 'Yes this is my element'; I excelled in swimming, water had been a natural environment for me since I was a kid. We were handed swim trunks and a towel from a black plastic trash bag. They only had extra-large, way too big for me and of course my pair was missing the rope to tie them.

We started out with a standard swimming test; a 500 metre length, using four different styles. This was the standard formal swimming requirement that also included a salvage drill. Then out of the corner of my eye I saw a sturdy guy in a black t-shirt with the text 'clearance diver' written on the front – things were about to heat up. Clearance divers were notorious for running tough water drills.

The tone quickly changed – divers are a "shouty" breed, I don't mind it per se, but it becomes a bit repetitive, and doesn't really add much. It was two hours of up and down in the pool, diving, treading water in close formation and so on. It's heavy work especially for those unfamiliar or who do not like water. We finished it off with a final test, one of my personal favourites – the bucket drill. The bucket drill is fairly straight forward but the fail rate is high.

It worked like this. At the bottom in the middle of the pool was a weight with nine ropes attached to it; evenly spread out in all directions like an octopus. Each rope ended in an upside-down bucket at the surface near the edge of the pool. Painted on the bottom of the bucket were four coloured fields: green, blue, red, and yellow. Each field held a piece of information: a number, a mathematical symbol, a part of a riddle or something like this. The person doing the test started at the 5 metre trampoline. Before they dove in, they were given a starting rope, for example no.1, had the rope positioned at 12 o'clock. People started at different rope positions which added to the test and was another thing for us to keep in mind. We had to complete the tasks in all nine buckets in a clockwise direction. There were two questions on two colours: one colour was a math problem and the other a riddle or story.

We could spend as much time under water as we liked but we only had two seconds to read the instructions when popping our heads up in the bucket. Following the time limit the bucket was pulled up and if our heads were still showing above the surface – we were disqualified. Then with the last bucket we would remain in position while the instructor asked for the combined results of all the questions – and we had to answer on the spot.

I did well, I think, however our results were never disclosed, but I know I had two solid answers. I lost my swimming trunks when I dove in, so I had to complete the bucket challenge naked. I don't know what the fail rate was, but I saw at least four guys being disqualified due to showing their heads or giving up.

When everyone finished, we had seven minutes to shower, get dressed and line up on the outside. I was exhausted, and the worst part was not knowing when it would end. It could be one hour more or a month, we didn't know. It was the uncertainty that was the challenge, as always in the military. We humans aren't built to deal with the unknown and how you handle it is always a big part of military testing. On the outside one of our instructors waited. He said, 'Now the improvised field part of this event starts.'

5

Pushing my limits

'Just like last time you need to sign a secrecy form and a non-disclosure agreement.'

At this point I started noticing that people were missing. I didn't know for sure, maybe they were doing another part of the selection or perhaps they had opted out or been cut. My mind quickly focused on the task ahead and it was going to be a cold night.

We had been divided up into smaller groups, equipment had been added and a task was given. I was going to be in charge for the first couple of nights. We were doing recon on foot and were to confirm enemy activity in a village. I could see that a few of the guys were struggling a bit. They had most definitely been civilians for too long, one of them was a member of the police anti-terrorist task force, so perhaps not a pure civilian, but definitely more blue than green – a nice guy though. He was physically fit – a true PT monster, but the bush had worn him down. We were all doing our best to help everyone through, but a part of me, most likely my ego, felt he was dragging us down. I had to shake those thoughts and I thought of Captain B, professionalism, 'I had to get my shit together, we were a unit now, it was not a one man show.' I hadn't seen Captain B yet. He said that he would see me at the event. Maybe he was watching from the sidelines, or perhaps he was also being tested.

After a night of fruitless recon, we had a contact with a dog patrol that had been tracking us; up until that point I was surprised by how seamless it was to lead a patrol that hadn't previously done any combat drills together and how things just worked. Yes, the distances were tight, the peel off could have been quieter but all in all I was impressed at how well drilled we were, and that muscle memory worked.

But the reconnaissance was less of a success, I guess it was not supposed to be either. We had a super short time frame. By the time we got in range, it was impossible to set up a decent OP, let alone spend time observing our target – they wanted us to take risks. The instructors were tracking us, and the subsequent dog chase was the objective, if you ask me.

The coming days were foggy. One starts to get into a state where your body is working, muscle memory is intact, but your brain goes into slow motion. There was no space for thinking about anything in an analytical manner. They were short missions, of differing complexity, loads of combat drills and lots of technical challenges. The rules changed constantly, and one always had to consider new things, actions, and counter actions. The debriefings were interrogation-like, the instructors wanted to see if we were just clenching our teeth and grinding through it or if we were paying attention.

On the 13th day one of our checkpoints, for the second time, was an old bunker system. Bunkers seemed to be a popular theme even if we as rangers seldom use them. It was dusk and raining. They blindfolded us and walked us, one at a time, into and around the bunker system for about 10 minutes. They took my hood off, and it was pitch dark, I felt the instructor's firm hand on my shoulder. He said in a calm but very clear voice, 'You need to find a briefcase that is located somewhere in this bunker, when you find it, you need to deliver it safely to the old man; not the one with square glasses but to the one with round glasses which has a small crack in the left lens. I will show you a map and light it up with my flashlight for seven seconds. The red dot shows your position, the blue dot shows the briefcase. This is to be completed as quickly as possible. Do you understand your task?'

'Yes', I replied. I wasn't sure – I knew I needed to think smartly when considering how to memorise the map, should I visualise it or count turns and doors? How could I know? It all depended on the map, 'Stop thinking just see what it is when he turns on the light.'

He continued, 'Look down and I will tap your shoulder just before I turn on the light, when the light is off the exercise starts.'

It felt like forever before he tapped my shoulder. When he switched on the light, it was like looking at the sun for the first few seconds. There were three ways out and about ten doors. Only the right-hand path would lead to the briefcase, but all the three paths were connected with side doors. I heard a click, and the light went off, he let go off my shoulder and I stood alone in the dark. I saw that vague shimmering green light that occurs when someone wears night vision goggles in the pitch dark. I grabbed the wall with my right hand – I needed to keep facing in the same direction. 'Orientate yourself,' I thought. I could see the map in my head, but I wasn't one hundred percent sure of my direction – where I was positioned in the real-world versus the map. I was in the middle of the bunker system, and I noticed that I had a door to the left in front of me when the light was on; that meant I needed to turn around and go in the direction we came from.

Time was moving slowly; I knew that it was more important to complete the task than to rush it and fail. 'I had counted two side doors on my right and then I reached the first door across the corridor. My plan was to continue straight ahead, pass the next door across and then take a right. As I fumbled in the dark, I tried not to think too much about the map, I needed to trust my instincts and just follow my plan – thinking would create doubt. I hit my knee hard on something in front of me, I had walked into something immovable. 'This was not on the map.'

I felt around with my hands, tracing the surface. I felt the metallic exterior, bumpy with pieces of rust, and other parts with smoother paint. Eventually my fingers felt the outline of a handle – it was the door across the corridor. I tried to open it, but I couldn't, it was definitely locked. I heard the shuffling sounds of someone's footsteps down the corridor. They had stopped and were no longer walking. They were just standing, and I was sure that they were watching me. 'Control your breathing,' I thought. I need to be rational and not look like this has thrown me off. I oriented myself towards the door trying not to lose my bearings. I tried to visualise the map; I remembered that there were three parallel paths, with the side doors connecting them. So, if I assumed that I was still on the right track. I could follow the wall on the left, retracing my steps back the way I came. Then I could take the first door on my right and step into the next corridor, turn to the right and follow the right wall to the next side door. By doing this I would get to the other side of the locked door. I could then proceed with my initial plan. It sounded like a good plan in my head, 'How long had I been standing here?' Felt like forever, I needed to crack on.

I found the first door after just five metres of backtracking; I counted my steps. I came out in the next corridor and turned right – I stepped on some loose rubble and jolted forward somewhat out of control, my hands instinctively shot out in front of me – I hated losing control, even if only for a fraction of a second. I had to detour around the rubble and while doing that I lost contact with the wall. Still counting my steps, I tried to keep accurate so that I knew when I had passed the locked door. Sweat was pouring down my forehead like a valve had opened. I felt the gravel on my dirty hands as I wiped my face – the small particles smearing across my moist cheek. It was stress sweat. 'I have passed the locked door now,' I thought to myself. I had walked almost double the distance – I got a sinking feeling in my gut, 'Have I missed it?' I couldn't go back now; I had no other plan. As I let my fingers glide along the wall, I felt a sharp sting in my finger – I pulled it back immediately. Using my other hand, I started examining my injury. It was a wooden splinter, I pulled it out. 'Could it be?' I could hardly wait to shoot out my hand again. Feeling for the wall I came across the wooden frame of a door. I breathed a sigh of relief and felt a warm feeling of satisfaction in my chest. Yes, my plan had held up, at least in theory. I stepped into the corridor, turned to the right, and made it back to the locked door – I was on the other side. I found the tunnel a bit further up on the right-hand side exactly as on the map. I started taking larger strides, I felt confident, perhaps dangerously so.

This time I took care and avoided bumping my knee into the dead end. I was expecting it this time. The briefcase was in the door to the left and after that I knew I had to find another door to get to the outside. I cautiously entered the room and saw a small strip of light coming from the door leading to the outside.

The door slammed shut and the lights came on. It was an intense light amplified by the contrast of the dark. My eyes instinctively strained – they pulled closed. 'I should have closed my right eye when entering', I thought, but before I could complete the thought, I felt a sharp pain in my stomach and my ear started zinging. My brain was shaken from a blow to my head from the right. I instinctively brought my hands to my head, 'Keep your guard up and always protect yourself.' A principle and catchline of boxing, and a very real practical tip – I backed up towards the corner. 'Orientate yourself, breathe.' I saw two men in Redman suits.

One man was behind me – he must have been the one who closed the door. He was on my side and the one that gave me a right to the stomach and over-hand left haymaker to the head was in front of me. He charged forward, and while I was still crouched protecting my head. I decided to take the offensive and tackled him, shoving my shoulder into his stomach. He fell over backwards, and I landed on top of him. Both of us breathing heavily now, we were in full survival mode. He pounded my kidneys, but I managed to elbow him to the left side of his head. I knew it landed cleanly, but it only bought me an extra second before the second man grabbed me from behind. I planned to roll over to meet his charge, but in the moment, I couldn't get around fast enough.

He delivercd two blows to my head from the back. Alarm bells started ringing. I managed to roll over and from my back, I launched up with a double kick into his shoulders causing my attacker to stumble backwards. Rolling across the floor and to relative safety and I managed to get to my feet – I clocked the briefcase in the corner. They both charged me at the same time. I tried to sweep the guy approaching me from my right but failed. Perhaps too elaborate a move for a no-holds-barred affair. He rammed into my side, pushing me towards the wall. I regained my balance leaning against him with all my weight. I then pushed away from the wall, giving me a bit of space. Grabbing the initiative, I charged the other guy and tried to take him down. After about two minutes of full on fighting the door opened, the Redmen – the opposing or red forces in a military exercise – retreated to different corners. I started preparing for another assault but then heard an officer on the outside shouting, 'OUT, OUT, OUT!'

On the outside there was a bit of smoke, it smelled like there had just been an explosion. I heard small arms fire, and I crouched down, keeping the briefcase from falling down. Earlier on, I almost forgot the briefcase but remembered it just in time – it had a shoulder sling, and I slung it over my right shoulder. My adrenaline was pumping, 'Breathe just breathe,' I said silently. I saw an AK assault rifle in the grass, half assembled, with its piston and other parts scattered around it, as well as a magazine with live rounds. The officer was shouting, I felt everything slow down, 'listen you need to get out of here now, there is only one way out.' That was the start of the race. The gun sounded.

I knew what had to be done. I was to shoot my way out of the situation and quickly assembled the assault rifle. They were all so similar, and one of the first parts of basic soldier training was stripping and assembling weapons. Just as I was about to put in the magazine, a hand came up, the palm facing me. I instinctively paused and then felt the soft cushions of a pair of ear defenders on my head. He looked me in the eye, I remember the brown constricted pupil surrounded by white and yellow. His hand pointed out the way, 'That direction, go.'

I'm up in a second, and instinctively recognize a classic assault course with remote controlled targets. I rely on the natural alignment of my body when taking aim. No time for fine tuning. The entire course is about 500 metres with a wide variation of targets, all I could do was point and shoot, and they fell. I tried to control my breathing, but the further I went, the more I felt my overalls, and hands drenched in sweat. My rifle jammed. 'No, I think...' I took control, the drills are automatic, 'Two options, option one, cock rifle and remove dud round; option two, safety, remove magazine, check and clear breach, check mechanism is working, reload magazine, cock weapon, safety off.' This happened in a matter of seconds, and option 1 worked; fortunately, the timing was good, and I was able to clear the dud round while moving towards the next target.

At the end the officer commands, 'Cease fire.' He pats me on the back and whispers 'Well done,' I make the weapon safe and hand it back to him.

His mere two words bring a feeling of warmth in my chest. Despite running the assault course, the adrenaline is under control, 'Keep breathing,' I tell myself. It's now a different kind of adrenaline than what I experienced during the fighting. I am proud, but the job is not done.

Another instructor leads me behind a shed and says, 'Hand over the brief-case.' In front of me stand four old men. One with square glasses, the second man with round glasses, third also with round glasses but with a small crack on the left lens and the last one again with round glasses but a small crack in the right lens this time. The instructor says, 'Hand the briefcase over now!' I hesitate, and think back to the instructions, 'You need to find a briefcase that is located somewhere in this bunker, when you find it, you need to bring it safely to the old man not with square glasses but to the one with round glasses which has a small crack in the left lens.' I knew it was between person three or four. Yes, round glasses with a small crack in the left lens. I walked up to the third man, the one with a crack in the left lens. Just before I handed over the briefcase, it struck me that it was the wrong person – I hesitated for a split second, 'my right was his left' – I pulled back the briefcase and handed it to the man that had a crack in 'his left' lens.

The instructor pointed down the road and said, 'There is a truck 500 metres in that direction, you will find your equipment there and your next task. 'I tried to keep the pace up, but I didn't run; I took the opportunity to rest a bit. It felt like I had been in a fight, they didn't hold back, I hoped that I did enough, it felt like I did. But it's like when a close boxing match goes to the scorecards, it could go either way, and each fighter feels they got the victory.

As I approached the truck, I saw three candidates sitting on their Bergens. In the truck I saw the instructor making notes and one of the candidates sitting in the passenger seat. The candidate in the truck had that empty look on his face. He had either been disqualified or given up on his own accord. I felt sad and empowered at the same time – it was a weird feeling. The instructor saw me coming and put his note pad away while getting out of the truck; he had a look on his face that was almost a smile, a smirk, the lines around his eyes creased as the corners of his lips made a move upwards. 'Finally, four of you made it so we can start sending you on your way,' he said in an upbeat tone.

I didn't know how many candidates had cleared the "briefcase bunker" before me. But it sounded like they had been waiting awhile, and I had a feeling that there had been some disqualifications along the way. There were now four of us standing in front of the instructor. He took out a map, it had an overlay, a plastic cover with details marked up, and I heard the creasing crackle as he unfolded it. Taking out his knife, the light reflected on the silver looking steel finish; he pointed with the tip of his knife and said, 'This is your next check point' and then quickly removed his knife. 'I hope you know where you are,' he said in a calm voice. Of course, I did. But naturally a slip of attention and one could have missed it. I double checked and did some mental arithmetic and physical orientation. The waypoint was at least 15 kilometres away. He continued, 'You will make your way to the checkpoint individually.' He tapped the first guy on the shoulder, 'You keep west of the river', the second guy received a tap, 'You keep east of the river.' I felt his hand on my shoulder, 'You keep west of the ridge,' and pointing at the fourth candidate, 'You keep east of the power lines. Now all of you get your gear and GO! These woods fill up with orcs after dark.' We had no maps and had just a glimpse of the one he showed us. I looked around and saw the power lines. I recalled the ridge just to the east of the power lines; although I didn't see the river but thought it was west of the road we were on and running in parallel. The checkpoint was located north of a communications tower where the river met the lake. I could see the tower blinking red in the distance – that would be my guide. Orcs meant tactical movement, 'Expect the unexpected,' I thought. I had a bruise on my shoulder from the fight. The sharp pain alerted me when the heavy Bergen buried its straps in my shoulders.

The third week of selection would be starting at the lake checkpoint. I didn't have any problems on my way there, but I could hear the characteristic hammering of a FN Minimi in the distance, 'I hope they made it.' After making it to the lake checkpoint, we got orders to perform another round of recon missions. The fatigue from almost 48 hours without sleep and continuous activity took its toll. I again entered a foggy state, and the struggle was real. On our next mission and after we reached a checkpoint, I was hoping for some sleep. 'No luck', I thought, after receiving orders that the next mission was going to be performed individually. It was about midnight, and we were to set up individual OPs and observe a part of a small dirt road. It was close, so the infiltration would be short. 'I just needed to find a decent spot and sit down for a while', I thought. It took an hour for me to find a suitable position – a bushy Fir tree with a big rock at its side, the bottom branches were thick and low and hid me well. The road was about 35 metres from my position, I had to remain close to maintain visuals, especially at night with many trees blocking my view – after all I had no binoculars or NVGs.

I had a good view of my designated part of the road, but I had a real problem, I was starting to nod off, and the brain fog was becoming overpowering. I tried my best to stay uncomfortable so I could stay awake. After 15 minutes I heard rustling in the bushes. My adrenaline spiked and I was awake again. Without being able to turn around, I rolled over on my back pointing the AK through my legs, aiming at the entrance. I heard a whispering low voice 'Number 788, are you here… number 788 it's an instructor.' He couldn't find me even if he had followed me pretty closely with NVG. I smiled and internally checked it off as a win. I replied with a short but distinctive hissing sound. It is widely used in the military. I also stuck my boot out through the branches covering the entrance, I hissed again and felt his hand grab my boot. 'I am coming in' he said. It was a really tight spot. 'I see you were prepared for the worst, good, good,' he said.

I recognised him, it was Lieutenant B I hadn't had much to do with him at the regiment. He was a technical officer and had taught some advanced shortwave courses at the ranger school. He kept his voice low, 'So explain to me shortly your thought process of choosing this location.' My mouth was like syrup, I tried my best to keep it short and concise. He nodded as I explained and said, 'Good, good… alright carry on I'll take my leave now if I can find my way out.' I always liked Lieutenant B, he never needed to be stern and project an image of himself, he was very comfortable in his own skin and didn't take things too seriously, he could afford a smile or two, and showed us that he was human – he was also one hundred percent professional but the complete opposite personality of Captain B. I think one needs both personality types to maintain balance in a platoon or group – the common denominator is professionalism.

It had been a few hours, something was happening on the road – I saw lights and movement, I saw it in my head, but it was like a dream, I was starting to nod off. The event passed and I think I captured what happened. 'I need to keep awake.'

Thirty minutes later I heard Lieutenant B on the outside, 'I am coming in!' I was startled. I was not asleep and not awake and had no idea what was happening, or how much time had elapsed.

He said, 'So do you have anything to report to me?'

I said, 'Yes, yes, I do. First a blue Volvo with Swedish military plates arrived, it stopped just short of the bend, a blond girl with a bright red jacket stepped out of the Volvo, she paced around for a moment, then a gnome with a red hat appeared from the left, he handed over something to the girl and then they disappeared.' I didn't reflect on my report at that time, I was just too tired, I reported what I honestly thought I had seen. I hesitated for a moment and asked Lieutenant B, 'Did I get it right?'

He smiled and said, 'We will see.' I felt that I honestly had given it my all, I just hoped it was enough. He said, 'Alright, get your things and make your way as fast as possible to the checkpoint where you started, no tactical implications.'

Just to explain to the reader that might think that what just happened has no place in a military unit, especially not an elite one, I can say the following. This is after two and a half weeks of extreme fatigue, sleep deprivation and stress. It's hard to explain it in just a few pages, but you are operating at the limits of what is humanly possible. In the beginning you have just enough food and sleep; and you have to have your shit together to perform at the top level.

In the end you have been going for more than 50 hours and that is not from a rested starting point. It doesn't really matter if you are a Navy Seal, Delta Force, SAS, or MacGyver – humans are not meant to function at this point. The instructors don't expect perfect results, they want to see if you can solve complicated problems under stress, are trying to cling on and do your best to fight even in extreme conditions. It goes without saying that elite soldiers are not superhumans and have very human needs. They are just taught to push their limits a bit further so they can deal with complex problems, under demanding and sub-optimal conditions. And the way to do that is by knowing your limits; then break through them and get to know how your body reacts. That helps us prepare. Anyone who claims anything else has never tried it themselves. I also acknowledge there are several factors that help, some of which include fitness, mental strength, and ability to evolve, determination to a fault, and controlling one's emotions.

While heading back – taking the shortest way; I saw all the candidates heading back using a similar route. At the checkpoint Lieutenant B and another officer met us. They waited and counted us. I still don't remember how many of us were left. We formed a single line behind Lieutenant B He led us through the forest on a 15 minute brisk walk, my legs were heavy. Years later, I had a chat with a Green Beret, who said something that chimed with my experience, 'When you spent enough time in the military you develop a way of sleeping while you are walking, especially when it's just transport' – in that moment I was transport-sleepwalking.

We arrived at the regiment, and I looked at the small gate in the fence, just below the barracks where everything started on the first day. It was early morning and the sun, and the rays of light warmed us ever so slightly, looking up at the sky, I squinted as I saw the sun pulling up to the middle of the sky. I smiled through my tiredness. Outside of the barracks Lieutenant B said, 'Alright, you will sleep in the corridor', and pointed to the building. 'Half of the group on each side of the corridor, toilets are on the far end to the right; also, there is one sandwich and one juice box each at the end of the hall. Don't leave the corridor and wander off. We will wake you up.'

I felt relieved. I wasn't sure if this was the end. I had been tricked plenty of times before, but I didn't care. I found my spot on the right side of the corridor and set my sleeping bag out. I slung my weapon and headed for the bathroom. On my way there I saw that some had already crashed in their sleeping bags. The steel taps squeaked as I turned them on. I filled up the sink with cold water and watched it whirl round. I dipped as much of my head as I could in the sink. It was a fresh feeling, the cold energising my skin. I breathed deeply and filled my lungs. Exhaling I felt strong, proud, and battered. I knew I had some chores to do before I could go to sleep.

I was not planning to take any more shortcuts now, not at this critical time. On my way back, I grabbed a sandwich and sat down on my sleeping bag. I did a quick cleaning of my rifle, checked my feet, and hung out some gear to dry. I would be ready when it was go-time. As a few rays of sun greeted us through the open barracks doors I felt calm. The gnome and the girl in the red jacket were probably mistakes. 'It was okay', I thought as I started to drift off.

Five hours later we were woken up. My eyes felt like they were filled with gravel, and it felt like a hammer was pounding away in the back of my head, like a massive hangover. My body was sore, and stiff as a plank – of course no one stretched before hitting the sack. Instructor X woke us up and continued with a loud and clear voice, 'Time is now 09:30, breakfast is available outside of the barracks. At 10:00 I want you to be lined up outside, with your gear, not looking like bums. Any questions? Good carry on.'

I quickly assembled my gear and cleaned up, wanting to enjoy breakfast in the sun and hoping for coffee, I needed coffee. While enjoying two cups of coffee and a porridge breakfast I counted 25 people and saw Mr F standing on the side. I headed over and put out my fist, which Mr F met with his. 'Rough night?'

He smiled and replied, 'No shit.' We didn't talk much about what we had been through.

Mr F asked, 'Do you think it's over?'

I replied 'I don't know, it feels like it, but I don't care, I am too invested now, I need to see this to the end.'

He nodded in agreement.

Instructor X led us to the storage building. 'Hand in all your equipment, weapons go next door, keep your overalls on and keep the receipts!' We had to sign for any equipment taken out, as in all militaries, so they know who to hang when something goes missing. At this point we knew that the worst part was over. The military is too lazy to set a sophisticated trap for after you hand in your equipment – too much paperwork.

Instructor X took us back to the barracks. Captain B stood there calmly and casually looking at us. This was the first time I had seen him since the selection started, I remember him saying, 'I'll see you there.' He must have had faith in me. We made eye contact, I nodded discreetly, but he didn't reply. He was way too professional, no fraternising. That had been the line all this time, except for maybe Lieutenant B, it was a selection after all.

Major M, who signed our orders to get here was receiving us. His message was short 'You will all wait under the trees over there. You will be called individually by Instructor X; he will assign you a room. The rooms are marked with numbers on the door. When you are finished wait by the bench', he pointed to an old concrete bench on the left. It must have been a remnant from the seventies, it looked so hard and uncomfortable, 'Who even makes a bench in concrete', I thought to myself. He finished, 'No talking amongst each other.'

In the first round, four people were called by Instructor X, and I was one of them. It made sense as there were four rooms; I was assigned to room number three. I knocked on the door and I was called in, it was Lieutenant B He smiled and said, 'Welcome, have a seat.' It was a deep interview, I was glad I had been assigned Lieutenant B, as his mood always lightened things up a bit. But he was a consummate professional, no shortcuts were allowed. It made sense since he was the one who monitored me during the last part in the field and maybe for the entire duration of this so called 'event.'

It was a fast-paced interview, with a lot of questions and my description of the last two and a half weeks in detail including places, events, people's clothing et cetera. They wanted to see if we had been paying attention to detail. Then a lot of questions about other team members' performances, my own performance and so on. What would my value and contribution be to a military unit? The interview was precisely an hour. On my way to the door, I turned around and asked him, 'How about that gnome?'

He smiled and said, 'We will see.'

Instructor X waited in the corridor and directed all who had finished their first interview to the end of the corridor, he said, 'Form a line outside that door, you will be called in individually.' I was first to be called in. 'Sit down,' someone said. I sat on the chair in the middle of the room. In front of me were Major M, Major T (later Colonel T), and Captain K (later Major K). All these guys had leading roles up at the regiment, commanding the winter unit, and various squadrons. At that point Major T was on his way to becoming a battalion commander.

It was a short interview. Mostly regarding how I see my future. They wanted to find out if I was willing to invest time, a considerable length of time to this career, or perhaps more accurately to this way of life. My answer was 'Yes to everything.'

Major M finished off the meeting, 'I remind you about the secrecy and NDA you signed on the first day. You can't speak of this to anyone, not even to the people you have met during this event.' They still insisted it was an event. Why couldn't they just say it was a selection, we all knew the truth anyway. He continued, 'You might hear from us, or you might not. Did you drive here?'

'No, I took the train.'

'Good you can report to Lieutenant B outside, thank you for your participation.'

I knew it was over when they asked whether I drove. It's a formal requirement; people are not allowed to drive after exercises that cause a lack of sleep, or anything that might affect your ability to drive safely. Lieutenant B was waiting at the concrete bench. 'First out I see', he said. 'Alright, I need your equipment receipt and weapon receipt then find your bag of civvies and you can shower and change in the next barracks to the left. Leave the overalls in one of the black bags in the corridor. When you are done come back out to sign for and pick up your valuables.'

After being in the field for a while, a shower is one of the best things. It is a weird feeling because it leaves you almost slightly sore, like the water and the soap are foreign agents on your skin, but it's fresh. I felt reborn. I dropped my overalls in the black bag on the floor. As I headed to the exit I stopped. I turned back and picked up my overalls again, I wanted my number. It was still hanging on to two of the safety pins. One could hardly see the number through the dried mud. I carefully removed it and brushed off the loose mud, folded it and put it in my back pocket. I wanted a souvenir. I was number 788.

It had almost been four weeks since the selection, I hadn't heard anything – it was unbearable. I had just waited and worked out, not applying for any schools, not looking for jobs, just waiting. I was fully invested in this. A few times it struck me, 'What if this wasn't a selection for a job or a unit, what if it was an experiment or something?'

It was Thursday, I had a gym date with my training buddy, and it was arm day. He commented, 'You have to stop doing this Army shit, you look flat.' He was not wrong; these kinds of selections eat away at your muscles like they were a buffet. 'You still have some lifting in you', he said laughingly as we had our protein shakes out in the sun.

When I got back from the gym, there was mail on the floor. I didn't count on any mail that day since it was after lunchtime. The mailman usually delivered letters in the morning. 'Maybe they were late', I thought. There was only one letter. It was upside down. As I picked it up, I felt it contained more papers than usual, 'probably some advertising', I thought. Turning it over, I read 'Swedish Armed Forces, Norrland Dragoon Regiment', on the letterhead, my address was handwritten with blue ink by someone who didn't pay attention to cursive writing in school.

I had a good feeling about it, but I tried not to get too excited. As I opened the letter, I immediately saw the very recognisable travel order. The tickets were for the following Wednesday, leaving Stockholm Arlanda for Arvidsjaur. Up until then, I had never flown up – it had always been by train. This felt important. The tickets were signed by Mrs S, the regiment's head of HR. I guessed that her signature was needed for air travel. I hadn't seen it before.

I looked at the attached letter, it was a short and formal, call up order, signed by Major M. It didn't give you any clues about the purpose. Under his signature it said, 'Note, if you are not planning to attend, please inform us, by telephone.' 'Pffft who in their right mind would not attend?' I thought. Also, I felt annoyed that they only gave five days' notice before our travel. 'Who do they think they are? But who was I kidding? I had cancelled everything and just waited for a month. This was it – they called the shots, and I was cool with that.'

I recognised a few of them at the airport. One was Mr F, I smiled. 'So we made it.' he said.

'Yeah, it looks like they accept anyone' I replied with a smirk. We were just happy to be a part of it. Mr F was overflowing with ideas and theories about what it could be. I mostly listened but I felt the same. I kept my excitement on the down low, maintaining my cool composure. But in reality, I just wanted to run around and ask everyone what this was about.

I sat with Mr F on the plane, it was a bumpy ride, lots of turbulence – I am not a big fan of small propeller planes. When they were finally able to serve dinner Mr F ordered a beer, I looked at him. He said 'Lighten up, we are already in whatever this is. Do you seriously think they will start with some hard charging shit tonight? And if they do, I'd rather be one or two beers in.' He had a point, I had that "stick up my ass" thinking and needed to chill out. I guess at times I was a mix of Captain B and Lieutenant B. I ordered a beer, and looked around me, as if I had taken it from the cookie jar. Mr F held up his beer, 'Cheers to the next level.' I wanted to believe him, and I guess I started to.

The guard told us we were supposed to head to the 4th Squadron. We were familiar with it, and 15 people had already arrived. A note on the notice board in the corridor read that all 'Event Candidates' should be in the upper corridor meeting room at 19:30, late dinner was available in the mess hall up until 19:00. 'Was this going to be the moment of truth? We just had to know, we earned it,' I thought as we were waiting in the conference room. We were sitting down; conscripts and recruits never sit down before the NCO or officer arrives. We were not conscripts anymore.

Major M came through the door, instinctively everyone got to their feet to the screeching of 20 chairs being pulled back at the same time. 'No, no, sit, sit,' he said, 'Everyone here?' he asked, and did a quick headcount, 'Twenty, ah perfect.'

I had never experienced this informal tone before, not from a senior officer. It felt collegial, I liked it, but it felt weird. As I looked around, I saw beards and long hair. This was definitely an odd bunch.

'We are just going to have some formalities dusted off first.' He picked up a bunch of papers. 'Just like last time you need to sign a secrecy form and an NDA. Send them to the end of the table when you are done.' He leaned back against the desk and waited for us with his arms crossed. It was a quick process, no one read it, I guess. We could have sold our soul for all we knew, and maybe we had. 'Anyone that didn't sign', he asked – it was silent.

'Welcome to all of you. Each and every one of you has earned your spot to be here. Welcome to the International Ranger Platoon,' I looked at Mr F and smiled. He was right, we had made it.

6

Colonel X

'If you don't deliver after that you are on your own.'

Twenty of us had successfully been selected and approved for training – we were to form the International Ranger Platoon. This was the first independent special operations forces unit with reconnaissance, Joint Terminal Attack Controller, and Arctic capabilities. Sweden now offers similar capabilities to NATO – and this was an early iteration.

We were independently commanded from the HQ and were the first unit made up of former conscripts and officers – we were the first ever 'formally' recognised contract soldiers in Sweden.

Let me give you a brief run down:

Ranger units were traditionally and often cavalry units, but this was not a prerequisite. Ranger Units were formed around the ownership of a specific skill set and linked to the key capability of endurance. The Swedish military command stated that a ranger unit should be able to conduct reconnaissance and sabotage missions behind enemy lines, independently and without external support for up to 30 days. This was similar to the British historical long-range units and patrols. We had Arctic Rangers and the Paratroopers, commonly known internationally as Paras; while the Coastal Rangers, although technically not rangers in the sense that they were a direct-action and maritime assault unit with limited endurance – however, their diving platoon was their reconnaissance unit, which was why they held the ranger designation.

At this time there were no formal or rather standardised special forces units, and all special forces operations units were comprised of officers and some old conscripts from the elite units – we did not have any contract soldiers, only contract officers. One of the earlier units was the *FJS IK* – a special purpose unit[1] inside *Fallskärmsjägarna* – the paratroopers, made up of paratroop officers. Their focus was mostly reconnaissance, of course. At this interesting and evolving time, it was like the tectonic military plates were shifting; slowly but irreversibly, we were reforming.

We had the embryo of what would become the Special Protection Group (*SSG*). It was made up of a range of officers from around Sweden, all qualified in different areas, experimental yet operational – a design in progress. With the advantage of hindsight, and official histories being what they are, they smoothed over the edges of a hesitant and cautious organisation. If you read the Swedish Armed Forces' official history, it claims that the first Swedish SF units were formed in 1994. This is not incorrect but, in this case, they refer to the *FJS IK* and the *SSG* embryo units. Two loosely formed groups with a handful of good men. There certainly was nothing wrong with their capabilities but they were organised and run in an ad hoc way – it was an exercise in improvisation – which, as in many historical cases, was not necessarily a bad thing. This was fine for the time being but was light-years away from modern SF units. Some administrative elements were also lacking, such as formal designations, definitions, and organisational structure, but those were mostly formalities. Although important aspects, especially in formal bureaucracies, operational effectiveness was the key.

There are some similarities, when referring to international special forces operations, including a sharp edge and a supporting element. SF can traditionally be made up of any unit that has a specialist skill and that meets the requirements for working under the broader special forces operations umbrella or command. At this early time, we did not have formalised requirements and definitions, and perhaps I could say that the doctrine, concepts, and organisational structure part of the military was catching up to what was happening on the ground.

Special forces operations units are generally kept closer to the top of the command chain. In Sweden and also broadly, SF serve directly under the military command HQ or an SF umbrella within the broader hierarchy. The key consideration is that SF have, within reason, freedom of initiative, and action, to achieve political objectives through unconventional means.

In practice the command line does and doesn't have an impact – it could for example impact logistical supply and funding, and perhaps other elements, but in the same breath a team of committed fighters could, through improvisation,

1   Special operations unit.

achieve much. Our units existed in the grey area. It came to bear, when we were covertly put into action overseas – that having someone looking out for you, whether a military HQ, or an active operational unit, was very important, perhaps even critical. But the reality was a little less well planned, and our success was less a result of formalised forethought, but rather improvisation and professionalism. The Swedish military played the hand it was dealt and that provided the lessons for the future Swedish Special Forces.

Military HQ saw the need for a more conventional SF unit in 2000 and decided to formalise the SSG. This group was formed under great secrecy and was staffed by handpicked officers from the Paratroop and Ranger Regiments. They set up camp in Karlsborg, which was the home of our Paratroops. They now had a formal base and application procedure.

SSG was a very small unit at this time and their main focus was DA and close protection tasks. This was one of the first attempts to create a NATO compliant *JTAC*. The first effort that I can recall was when two Arctic Ranger officers were sent to the *JTAC* course in the US. On their return, we got our first Viking call sign. In 2011 *SSG* merged with other units to form the SOG (Special Operations Group).

In doing a gap analysis, the *SSG* had a strong tactical and action component in the modern strike and anti-terrorist style, however it lacked an intelligence capability. To remedy the gap, HQ recognised the *FJS IK*, originally under the Paras, as an official unit – Special Reconnaissance Group (*SIG*).

SIG became a standalone special purpose unit, an elite force, but it was set outside of the special forces umbrella due to technical issues of definition. The reason that *SIG* fell out of the special force's definition, was that it did not meet all of the requirements: direct assault, specialised reconnaissance, and or other expert capability. The HQ based their SF draft blueprint on what the *SSG* could deliver. That was something that needed revision. Now well-established, they have a formal base and serve under the military HQ command.

To start with we had in effect two special forces units with separate desig-nations – two formalised standalone units. They had separate budgets and reporting lines; even though *SIG* was the reconnaissance component of *SSG*. So, on a theoretical, command and control as well as financial level it mattered, making it difficult to deploy, especially as a rapid response unit. Despite the higher-level administrative matters, the day-to-day operations were run as one organisation and used mostly the same resources.

In the early 2000s Swedish Armed Forces was under extreme pressure. In practice this meant that we were perpetually downsizing. We lived in a contradictory time – despite attempts at reducing our military strength, we were adding new capabilities to the inventory that could later be included in a future SF umbrella. This essentially made the Swedish Armed Forces' blade shorter but sharper. At least this is what they tried to do, and what we understood at the time.

They were rough times and basically every regiment was fighting for survival. Having a special purpose unit in your regiment would guarantee survival. But a pre-requisite was that you had something to offer that was needed in the special forces operations department. That disqualified most regular regiments; many commanders and soldiers started getting creative. Some regiments proposed their units become part of the special forces fraternity and other units were asked to set it up. The Amphibious corps, mostly involved in costal offensive operations and also the home of the Coastal Rangers, were creative and found their approach in creating a boarding unit with handpicked personnel from the Coastal Rangers and the Amphibious corps – *l 1 Livgardet*, a regular infantry regiment, that housed the military police, and their close protection unit, who regularly provided their services to dignitaries in high-risk environments. This capability, although to a limited extent covered by SSG, provided a deeper specialist skill set.

The Life Hussars – *K3*, a light mechanised "ranger" regiment, located in Karlsborg, was an air mobile unit with limited endurance – they had the ability to operate in relative isolation for approximately three to four days. The Life Hussars were jumping on the reconnaissance train – for survival they tried to form a 'sub support unit' to *SIG*, an SF support unit. We regarded these as grey units, who filled the gap between SF and conventional forces.

And then there were the Arctic Rangers. They had already been trying to solidify their unique position in winter warfare and had been asked to set up a unit that could operate in a broader range of extreme climates like Afghanistan. Also evaluating the possibility to become ISTAR compliant and to dig into the HUMINT scene, provided the regiment with plenty of opportunities to find a niche.

At this time all ranger regiments as mentioned above battled for survival – it was a race, but more it was hope that the hypothesis was correct – being able to become special forces or support special forces operations, would lead to more but no promises were made. The only fixed players in the game at this point were the *SSG* and *SIG*. Everyone else was just tasked to research the possibilities by HQ – this was the start of the competition.

A major area of interest for the HQ at this time was increasing the quality of surveillance and intelligence capabilities, like photography, transmitting live video; and HUMINT in general. These areas had typically been reserved for military intelligence and secret service units in the government – so there was a steep learning curve and the experience, SOPs, and equipment varied widely and there was not a grain of standardisation. The *SIG* used civilian photo gear and SOPs developed by themselves; the Paras did the same but slightly differently. The Arctic Rangers weren't really up to speed at all since there had been very few developments outside of the more classic recon style which they had mastered. As Sweden made moves to engage personnel in more advanced roles in increasingly complex arena, the War on Terror was starting, and we had to make adjustments and fast.

Our main competitor was the Life Hussars – *K3*; they had less experience with intelligence and reconnaissance work, but they were technologically highly sophisticated. A big bonus for them was that they were located at the same regiment as *SSG/SIG* and had close ties to them – they could offer a seamless integration with those units without being a threat to them. The Arctic Rangers on the other hand had very solid experience in traditional surveillance and reconnaissance work, but they lacked the technical component. They had an ace up their sleeve though, arctic capability – a critical consideration for warfare in the Nordic region. With the current war in Ukraine and the Russian threat – this is a very important aspect.

HQ viewed the arctic capability with great interest as research and experience showed that soldiers who are trained in one extreme environment usually perform well in other extreme climates. The reason for this was that they had a trained, learned and often built-in respect for the climate and an understanding that you had to work with it and how to do so.

The Norrland Dragoon Regiment had another unique selling point – their winter unit. The winter unit served the whole Swedish Armed Forces with research and training in winter warfare; they also served foreign SF units coming to train with them every year. But there were talks of moving the winter unit to the "nearby" Norrbotten Regiment I 19 in Boden.[2] The reasons for this were that they were not on the list of units to be disbanded and they were the only mechanised regiment left in the North.

---

2 Boden is located a couple of hours drive east from Arvidsjaur, close to the City of Luleå.

The search and marketing of unique skills and positioning created a weird competitive environment, something not very common in modern militaries. A degree of competitiveness is always good to keep people on their toes, but it went beyond that – it got to a point where units didn't share anything with each other – many tried to downplay their units' abilities to keep others in the dark. This actually obstructed progress. If war had broken out at this time, we would have had units with totally different tactics, techniques, and procedures – it would most likely have been a catastrophe. But those were the times and we had to adapt to that.

The Norrland Dragoon Regiment understood early on, in the mid-90s, the need to be active in building unique capabilities, the traditional arctic capability would not be enough on its own. They had been trying to make a road map of how to get there, but funds were almost non-existent. They sent quite a few officers to both Swedish and foreign Intelligence services through more informal connections; and acquired advanced HUMINT training, ISTAR Tier 1 and JTAC certifications, which was important to align our skills and training with that of NATO. US, UK, Israeli and German connections were the main unofficial allies with parts of the regiment.

So, after that brief historical review, I will try to retell the story of how the IRP developed, from an instinct to survive, out of necessity, as it has been told to me over the years.

In 2002, Major M got a call from a senior general at HQ. We can call him General G; he was a former Arctic Ranger, so he knew exactly what they could do, and he had been in the loop for a long time – he gave his silent okay for the unofficial training. The sandbox had just started to heat up and they were on the hunt for more specialised intelligence and reconnaissance resources, the SIG was not enough.

General G said, 'I can convince the HQ to grant you the funds and the freedom to form a special purpose (special operations) unit within the arctic regiment. I can only guarantee the funding for the training period of the operators. If you don't deliver after that you are on your own, they might also change their minds after the training period, but that's more unlikely as they don't want to lose their investment. The catch is you need to sell it to them now; you need to act like you already know what you are doing.'

So, he wanted Major M to sell something he didn't have yet – 'fake it until we make it' – it was a daunting thought. It also needed to be kept secret, and to make matters more challenging, he stood without the necessary funding for the 'show and tell' that was needed to win them over. It was not optimal, but it was the break he had been looking for – he knew that if we handled things properly, we would be upskilled, and it could save the regiment.

A small group was formed at the regiment, and they started to sketch up the training programme. They needed to come up with a new and unique set of skills – as the arctic capability was already known; it had to be something new that didn't require any money. They had to show that we could provide Tier 1 operators or as close as we could get. The first obstacle, or opportunity, was approaching quickly – a group from HQ were going to visit in a few weeks to listen to what the group at the regiment proposed as a concept, and decide if it would be a go for the creation of a special purpose unit at the regiment.

The concept of the "International Ranger Platoon" was created. It was quickly understood that to be a competitor we needed more and better technical capabilities. The rest was already in place, in the form of ISTAR, HUMINT and JTAC instructors, not officially recognized yet but they had the skills. Lastly, they were up against an organizational and human resource challenge – how to source soldiers and then critically how to employ them.

There were already ideas of how to work with contract soldiers in the armed forces, but most of them relied on the premise that a soldier, once accepted to a special unit, needed to complete an officers' course before they could start the operators training. It was time consuming and excluded potential operators with valuable competence from 'civvie street.'

It was kept simple, and a friend of mine, a young officer at the regiment Lieutenant A, who I knew from Stockholm, was a part of the group. He was an avid amateur photographer and a programmer – they needed him to contribute to the photography department, as this was crucial. Lieutenant B who was also already attached to the group played a pivotal role with his technical skills. Together they were going to be a part of creating a modern special purpose unit, even if it was going to be far from a smooth ride.

Lieutenant A got his task, the order was, 'We need to be able to take an ID photo at a distance of 1km. You need to put together a kit that would work for that; the parts need to be available on the civilian market.' Lieutenant B got a similar order, 'Find a solution on how to transfer a picture from the field to a computer somewhere else, instantly, with no delay and minimal losses. Also, the parts should be available on the civilian market.'

This skill set was not unique and already existed in the armed forces, but this needed to be something better, smoother, and quicker – a slick solution, one that would be light, mobile, and efficient – something that could compete with international militaries.

They were told to make minimal noise about this and had a two-week deadline. Meanwhile the group was working on a concept for the unit structure; they had already formed the baseline. It should be a platoon like formation, not in size but in structure. Four patrols of three soldiers each, led by an officer, to increase the decision-making capabilities in the field. One support group with seven soldiers, led by a technical officer, with the soldiers, ranger qualified, with additional civilian competences like a mechanic, engineer or in the IT field. On the human resources end, the proposed model offered soldiers direct contract employment as operators with pensions and all the mandatory benefits, while serving officers would be assigned to the unit as a regular transfer. The special IRP selection was to be organised by the regiment itself who would also set the requirements. As setting a SF standard was a work in progress, it would also include different physical requirements for highly skilled civilian personnel with a ranger background, to enable the direct onboarding of specialists. The candidates would be selected from the recent ranger conscript pool, so there would be a predictable flow of potential operators – the best conscripts got a shot at selection. The operator training would be around 400 days. The minimum age limit was set to 23 years, to ensure maturity; Mr F and I were special cases here, and we were lucky to be part of the initial batch.

The International Ranger Platoon would be under the direct command and control of a select and more shadowy part of HQ, the IRP commanders had to use their own extensive international network to acquire and secure competences that were needed without HQ involvement. It was a solid and half-revolutionary concept in many ways, periods of innovation are of course exciting, but it came with a set of problems. Like with short-term contracted soldiers, Swedish labour law dictated the regulations of work time. This provided an added layer of security for employees, ensuring that employers didn't abuse their workers' rights and provided a healthy and safe work environment. This worked well for most businesses and even the officers were regulated in a similar way. It gave clear directions on the number of hours to work every day, week, and month and compensation for irregular hours, night work et cetera.

Well, you see how this could be very complicated to sort out if they were going to train operators for 400 days with no days off – in short it wouldn't work. Also, the cost of running soldiers in the field under the financial conditions of the time would break the bank immediately. So, at the time, when setting up a unit like this, it was important to look at it, end to end. It was not only about training operators, but it was also about figuring out the full circle from contract to organisation and funding.

Perhaps it was the training talking, as it was also assumed that all functions would be led by a military officer. This was perhaps an early lesson on the importance of finding the right person for the job, not necessarily within the ranks of the Army. During this period, "the most unlikely of persons" came up with the make it or break it solution. But of course, with hindsight why wouldn't she have known – she was after all a professional, who had worked in this area her whole life. A middle-aged woman, unassuming yet assertive – with tied back brown hair, and eyes that smiled when she gave advice, a kind person, and to the group forming the IRP a breath of fresh air and a lifesaver.

The head of HR, Mrs S, overheard a discussion while visiting the regiment on routine business, and said, 'You could use the unregulated Labour Act for specialised government work.' They all looked at her, with an expression of surprise. Major M said, 'Go on.' 'Well, there is an Act that is not used often that allows highly specialised government employees to work on a contract where they sign a waiver stating that they agree to have unregulated working conditions, including time and financial benefits, for a fixed monthly salary. That means you can have them work basically unlimited hours, but they have to agree to it themselves and the salary must reflect it by being higher than that of a regular employee in the same category. We used it sometimes in the state department where I worked before; I think this unit would qualify.' State department, she probably meant intelligence, which would be even better, since special operations and supporting clandestine missions was on the IRPs humble radar for the future.

Everyone looked stunned, 'Could this be exactly what they had been looking for?'

Major M said, 'How much time do you have on your hands?'

Mrs S replied, 'Well we are not that busy at this time of year, so I have some time to spare.'

Major M couldn't hide a small smile which betrayed his excitement, 'Could you perhaps research the matter for us? We are keen to find out if this will hold up and sorry to add to this ask, but if this is a goer, would you be willing to draw up a contract for us to review?'

'Yes', was her simple and clear answer.

Major M now made no attempt to conceal his smile, 'Keep it secret, make it happen. Welcome to the international ranger platoon.'

Mrs S smiled, reflecting the Major's smile. She made her way out clearly beaming; she couldn't believe that she was needed for something this exciting. That is how life unfolds sometimes – being at the right place at the right time, with the right toolbox, then suddenly interesting projects or opportunities will appear. She was methodical, she would leave no stone unturned, this was her chance to get out of the HR office and the mundane routine work and contribute to something bigger.

Two weeks had passed; it was now time for the group to reassemble. Mrs S, Lieutenants A and B were going to present their results for the group, it was late on a Friday evening, and the regiment was empty. They had picked the time wisely as they didn't want any accidental disturbances.

Lieutenant A went first – his presentation was about the photography question. It hadn't been easy, he said that he had been in contact with a friend of his who was a nature photographer who specialised in documenting a rare variant of the Mountain Ripa, which has to be photographed over long distances. The idea, as with the principle of conservation, is not to cause the animals stress as the parents could leave the nest if pressured or intimidated by an outsider. He explained that they had been out together the previous weekend and Lieutenant A got to know the equipment.

He started his PowerPoint; he suggested a competent Canon camera with two high performance lenses, a remote trigger, a Manfrotto tripod that could be adjusted for a low profile, which was also compact and lightweight. All of these fit in Pelicases, with additional soft cases for when deployed in the field. The group looked satisfied. Lieutenant A continued, 'then it's just about the price and availability. The camera and accessories are not a problem, the lenses are. They are usually made to order in Japan. The nature photographer could assist in securing two that were available right now, but then we need to act quickly. The lenses are $10k a piece and with the rest of the equipment it would land somewhere around $25k in total.'

Major M and Major T looked at each other, 'There is nowhere in the regimental budget I could shake out this kind of money,' Major T said.

Major M replied, 'Agreed I can't even start to see where we would find it.' There was a short silence and then he said, 'Let's go on with the next presentation.'

It was Lieutenant B's turn. 'Well, using what we have at the regiment today, the shortwave ALS modem will not get us far, we can divide a picture into a large number of parts, compress it to the max and hope it shows up okay on the other side, then use a programme to assemble it as we would usually do. But that is not what we are looking for here. We need speed and simplicity. I took a trip down to the Signal Regiment, located in Enköping, to test the waters and asked about their SATCOM units. But got a hard no on using them as we would need full circle encryption, HQ approval et cetera. So, with the assumption that this kit doesn't have to be used in wartime but merely functions to show off our capabilities at our future meeting with HQ – I went full civvy on this. I went to see a friend who works with maritime SATCOM solutions, and he has what we need in stock right now.'

'It would be a BGAN compact, as for the satellite terminal, it has a built-in antenna and a low profile, I would use one of the high-performance Sony Vaio compact laptops, it's not rugged but it has the capacity for photo editing and connectivity. We can make a power bank with an MC battery and package all of this nicely in a Pelicase. The satellite subscription is expensive, but we can sort that with a prepaid card. All in all, around $6k US, directly available with no questions asked.'

Major T nodded, 'Good, good, nice work.'

'Well, my presentation is not that long,' Mrs S said from her chair, 'And I don't have a PowerPoint. But I have a draft contract ready that will work if military HQ signs off on it. The Labour Department just needs approval from HQ that this is necessary for them to be able to perform their duties.'

She handed Majors T and M a copy of each, they read it quickly and nodded. 'This is good,' 'This… is good,' Majors T and M said one after the other. 'Is this a salary level you made up or is it viable and a reasonable reflection?' asked Major T.

'No, it's real,' said Mrs S. I discussed it with the Labour Department, not the details of course, but they said it was acceptable.' The number was $2,800 per soldier per month.

Major M said, 'Very, very good work, could you draft the agreement that HQ needs to sign with the Labour Department as well?'

Mrs S replied, 'Yes I have a good contact there, I can do it discreetly.'

Major M looked up and nodded, 'Good, we need to lead HQ to the water on this one, otherwise they might back out, it needs to be all ready to go.'

Mrs S quietly said, 'Do you need me any longer? I need to pick up my son from football practice.'

'No, no you go, thank you.' said Major T and he continued, 'But one last thing, how long would the HQ draft take if you had to guess?'

Mrs S leaned in through the doorway, 'I could probably get it done next week.'

'Good, good, make it happen, go now so you are not late,' Major M said as he waved her off.

Once Mrs S left, they looked at each other, 'Where do we get $30k next week?' No one said a word. Major T broke the silence, 'I could mortgage my house.'

Major M looked up and said, 'Are you joking! Are you going to fund the army with your own money! And by the way you would never get it back.'

Major T paused and replied – it became personal as he used Major M's first name, 'Mike this is my job, my livelihood and my kid's future, not the army, but me providing for my family, I am ready to take risks.' Major M sat quietly. No one could argue with his reasoning. Major T continued, 'I can't get it all, but I could maybe get a loan for 10k.'

Lieutenant B entered the conversation, 'I have 5k in my savings account.'

Captain K said, 'I also have about 5k.'

Lieutenant A joined in, 'I have 2.5k, not much, but it's something.'

Major M looked around the room, searching the eyes of these soldiers, he knew this was a pivotal moment, and said, 'Fuck, we are really doing this aren't we?' Another moment of silence, then, clearly doing mental arithmetic added, 'Okay I can get the remaining 7.5K if I mortgage my house, but we can't go in blind. Let me call General G.'

Major M left the room and Lieutenant B said ironically, 'You know the armed forces are in a bad shape when you need to fund it yourself, what's next buying our own bullets?' No one laughed. Everyone just looked down, nodded, and continued to wait, in the way that soldiers often do. They all knew the truth – the joke was not that far from it. In current times it may be hard to believe, but at that moment it was the reality.

Major M returned after 5 minutes, 'I spoke with the General. He has given us his word that we would be reimbursed, but only if the platoon got the go ahead, otherwise we would be on our own. Also, if this gets out, he knows nothing about it, and will personally fire us.' He looked round the room, 'This is some *Lord of the Rings* shit, that is about to go down. Are you all ready for this? No shame in backing out.' No one flinched. 'Alright, let's get this show on the road.'

It was the night before D-Day. Lieutenant B was helping Lieutenant A prepare the camera kit in the basement, it needed to be ready for the field. Lieutenant A was about to put the first layer of green camouflage paint on the lenses. Lieutenant B said, 'Are you sure you can paint those?'

'Yeah, the nature photographers do it all the time, you just have to mask the sensitive parts, just like we do with the AKs.'

'So have you done this before on something less robust than an AK?'

'No.'

'How do you know what's sensitive or not?'

'I have asked professionals...'

'You mean the weapon mechanic?'

'Maybe, do it yourself then!'

'Hell no, I am not going to be the one ruining 20k of equipment that we will never get back?'

'Thanks for the help, really encouraging,' said Lieutenant A with a grin starting to appear, which broke the tension.

'By the way,' said Lieutenant B, 'What if they want to see a written SOP?'

Lieutenant A stopped painting and said, 'I have written one and have a 28 slide PowerPoint to explain the process, haven't you?'

Lieutenant B yawned, 'Eh… no, it is all in my head you see.'

Lieutenant A countered, 'So if they want to see an SOP for the SATCOM system?'

'They won't,' Lieutenant B replied, looking confident, 'I'll bore them to death with technical details before that happens.'

They both knew that everything depended on the next day, their jobs, the future, a part of a 30k investment and perhaps most importantly, pride. They all felt the same – if they couldn't convince the HQ group, it would be a personal failure.

'Does it look okay?' asked Lieutenant A.

Lieutenant B took a few steps back from the camera opening in the OP, 'Yeah it looks really good to me, come and check yourself!'

Lieutenant A joined him. 'Damn it looks tight; we really got the colour on the mesh right.' It was Friday morning and Lieutenant A was proud of the mesh in front of the camera lens, camouflaging and blending with its surroundings. They had used a very fine mesh that was made even thinner by using a fork or a serrated knife. It was not a new concept, but taking photos at such a distance required a finer type of mesh – it made it possible to establish the focus – it had to be super crisp.

The group from HQ was scheduled to arrive at 11:30. They only expected a briefing and a theoretical run through. It was decided that something practical was needed so we had something to show – after all, the proof would be in the delivery. The group at the regiment had prepared to start with a standard, lecture type presentation, but with a twist. Without a camera in sight, they planned to photograph the meeting from a considerable distance – this was one element that the HQ was looking for, the pictures were then going to be emailed to Major M, the lead presenter. The plan was to simulate a reconnaissance operation, showing pictures of the participants in the meeting room, as well as photographs of their arrival at the regiment including their cars and number plates. This was the twist, not only talking about future capabilities but showing the senior officers how it was done, an intelligence gathering operation unfolding before their eyes. Then to end the day with an OP and equipment demo.

A few dry runs had been performed during the week and the concept worked, but when it came down to business, much like real operations, there was only one opportunity to get it right. There was also a technical issue. What may now seem very minor, was taken very seriously back then – there was a delay in receiving and processing emails to a military inbox due to the filters and scans. In practice, that boiled down to having Major M use a regular Hotmail address. A small thing, but the generals would be frustrated if they saw Hotmail when pulling up the pictures. A detail, but one that needed to be solved.

Captain K went to the airport, to pick up the HQ group. Only a 15 minute drive from the regiment, he got there in no time, and parked the minibus right outside the arrivals gate. One of the advantages of a 1,000 person town was that not many people arrived by air. They flew in with a Swedish Armed Forces Gulfstream 5, or G-5 as it is popularly known. Captain K saw the Gulfstream complete its landing and later commented, 'Typical top brass riding in style.' He did a last-minute check to make sure the van was presentable and adjusted his beret in the mirror. He knew he had to represent now – a high standard of discipline, without giving the feeling that he was kissing ass.

The entourage were quick to come out of the terminal; Captain K counted five people; it was only supposed to be four. He recognized General G, as he was a regular visitor to the regiment and at this point overseeing *SSG/SIG* and international operations, General H the commander of operations at HQ, Colonel C from the HQ financial department also known as the "money man", and a Major that was an aide to General H He didn't recognize the 5th officer, an extra guy, he was a Colonel and wore a plain name tag and generic HQ insignia. Let's call him Colonel X.

They nodded and said a short hello to Captain K and got into the back of the van, continuing their discussion about the upcoming weekend plans. General H joked that he wouldn't mind if they burned a bit more fuel on their way home as he had a dinner date with his wife in central Stockholm that night. They were after all just regular men with lives, their world was different, they had perhaps lived their glory days.

In a practical sense it was late morning, and they were leaving back to Stockholm at 16:30 so time was limited. Captain K didn't like the relaxed attitude; he later said that he feared that it was just a show for the gallery and that they wouldn't pay attention. He didn't have too much time to think as he was quickly approaching the regiment. Lieutenant A was manning the camera and Lieutenant B was handling the communications. They had brought two soldiers that were on guard duty that weekend and kitted them up with ghillies and a PSG 90,[3] these were just place holders for the show, but they had to sign an NDA. The two young men didn't seem to mind that much as they also got an extra day of leave for their trouble.

As Captain K approached the gates, he later recalled feeling a slight nervousness. He wondered, 'Were we ready, what about the plan, the OP, was he driving too fast or to slow?' It didn't matter as the ball was already in motion – no plan survives the first contact – Clausewitz's friction in military operations and all that.

'Shit!' Lieutenant A called out; the tripod must have moved since the test shots. The camera had rocked slightly when the shutter closed. Lieutenant B saw that there was a small gap under the left tripod leg as a small piece of rock had rolled away. He threw himself forward and in one swift move drew and pushed his knife in between the tripod and the ground, 'Go, go, go,' he shouted.

It was Major M that held the presentation, technically it should have been Major T, but since he was on his way to becoming Battalion Commander, he had taken a few steps back. His support and approval were of course crucial, and he needed the initiative to be approved, otherwise he would not have a regiment to command.

Major M had started with the basics, the organisation, selection, capabilities, and this went on for about an hour. The military brass nodded, occasionally asked a question and sometimes their eyes drifted as they watched the scenery – to be frank the group looked borderline disinterested. It looked like they were on the route to checking out, except for the insider General G, who was making an effort to activate the others by asking the right questions.

Captain K said that he was sitting in the back and thinking, about their behaviour, wondering why they weren't more interested 'they were the ones that had asked for this, or maybe General G had half forced them up here?' When it was time for a 15 minute coffee break, the HQ group headed to the officers' mess, and Captain K asked Major M, 'Who is the 5th guy.'

---

3   A PSG 90 is a Swedish sniper rifle, a development from the British L96A1 Accuracy International PM. The Swedish version is called Accuracy International Arctic Warfare, due to the cold weather specs required by the Swedish Armed Forces.

Major M answered, 'Military Intelligence.'

'Military Intelligence! What are they doing here? Is it good or bad?'

'I have no idea', said Major M, 'I trust that General G has it under control. Have you heard anything from the OP?'

'Nope, not a word.'

'Send them a text that we are having coffee, and they better not screw this up.'

Major M had just explained the contract. It was novel, and an ace up his sleeve. He had saved it until after the coffee break, as he needed his aces for the finale so their last impressions would be good. The contract was something new and unique, everyone was now wide awake. The document was straightforward, concise, and ingenious. General G, clearly impressed, said, 'Let me start gentlemen. This is ground-breaking but before I get ahead of myself, I have a few questions about the contract layout.' Major M's expression changed – a flash of panic overcame his normally calm face. He knew nothing more than what he had already explained.

Almost as if it was planned, Major T intervened and calmly added, while walking to the door 'We have brought our HR specialist that drafted the contract to answer all of your questions.' In walked Mrs S, and Major M managed a small smile and a nod to Major T.

Mrs S did a brilliant job, and the HQ group thanked her as she left the room. Major M took the floor, and the money man couldn't contain himself, saying, 'This is really well thought through, I am not sure about the capabilities and if we need them as that is not my job, but you did a great job on the contract, I will remember this for the future.' "Ping" an email arrived in Major M's inbox.

'Oh, sorry I just got an email.' He fiddled with the browser and downloaded the attachments, it felt like forever, and the group from HQ were clearly baffled. The last bit was just showmanship. The Major continued, 'This is you gentlemen one minute ago, he said as he presented and flipped through five pictures that showed all members of the group – clearly identifiable. 'This is when you arrived, and your number plate is proof that is was your vehicle. And this is me talking to you a few moments ago.'

Major M now definitely had their full attention. Colonel X was leaning forward observing, thinking, and analysing. Major M continued, 'This is just a crumb of what we are offering gentlemen, real time, ID quality intelligence, from the field to anywhere. You don't *just* get a top-notch ranger platoon here with all the traditional capabilities. We can work in the whole ISTAR spectrum and beyond. We will provide Tier 1 operators. It sounded like a sales pitch for a high powered multi-national company.

'Where is this taken from,' asked Colonel X. Major M took up the last slide of his PowerPoint, it showed a map where he had marked the OP and their position.

The Major added, 'It's 1,056 metres away, if you are interested, we can go up to the OP before you leave for the airport.'

General G said, 'Although the capability is not unique, I have never seen it in the hands of a ranger platoon, and it is definitely an interesting added value.' Colonel X asked, 'Can you do this in a civilian environment?'

The Major replied confidently, 'Yes, mobile and foxtrot.[4] All patrols in the platoon will also be Tier 1 HUMINT capable.' He knew that human intelligence was the Colonel's forte and played for the crowd. The Major basically just said that the International Ranger Platoon was going to be able to develop and run their own sources, he knew it was a gamble. Major M added some credibility, 'And as additional support two ranger officers recently qualified for the HUMINT level 3 instructors' course.'

Colonel X leaned back in his chair, 'I like it. This is exactly the type of multirole, special purpose unit that we can branch in under the SF umbrella and a damn good set of unique capabilities.' General G nodded and smiled at Major M, it meant he had attracted the right kind of attention here. Major M would later learn that Colonel X was the key player as his role was to assess the capabilities and make a recommendation.

Colonel X lingered in the meeting room as the group headed out to look at the OP. He looked around and then asked Major M in a lowered voice, 'Are you still in bed with the US and the Israelis.' He was asking about the unofficial network that had been developed through informal means over the years.

Major M thought carefully, knowing full well that it could be a trap. But he had to go all in now, if he had the same plans in mind as Colonel X, then his non-HQ managed contacts would be very valuable assets on many levels. Major M replied, 'Yes, we are also tight with the British Force Research Unit and the Germans too.'

Colonel X turned to Major M before catching up with the others, 'Keep them close and out of the circuit no matter what,' the circuit here being HQ and the government.

---

4   Foxtrot in this context means on foot.

Inspecting the OP was a mere formality, and they were impressed by the setup, the attention to detail, and laughed when they learned that the two main players in the OP were officers, but they understood, this was for a tight circle only. As they were about to leave the OP, Colonel X looked at Major T and Major M, 'Can you really make this happen and have the operators ready in a year and a half?'

Major T said without hesitation, 'Yes, I can personally guarantee it.'

Colonel X held his stare at Major T for a few seconds before he turned to General G, 'And you?'

General G nodded, he turned to the money man who without being prompted, said, 'Yeah it's not a problem from our side if you give the go ahead, I have some grey wallets in mind that we can use.' Colonel X looked in the distance for a few seconds. 'Alright, alright, you got your platoon, *don't* disappoint me on this, if you can pull it off you will be running a one of a kind unit here.' He looked at General G and said, 'You make sure it's set up from our side ASAP. Keep the amateurs on a need-to-know basis, I want a very tight circle!'

General G nodded, 'Will do.'

Swedish society is very flat and fluid when it comes to its hierarchy, the military wasn't any different, between senior officers and general officers, there is often an open and frank understanding, which is why Colonel X could ask General G straightforward questions, and what may come across as sharp, was just regular conversation. In this case it was accepted that Colonel X held the power and was the decision maker regardless of rank.

As Captain K drove the group to the airport it was a strange vibe in the van, mostly silence, broken by short questions and answers regarding the set up. He felt pride for being a part of something new and bigger, possibly saving the regiment. And on a personal note, he didn't lose his investment. As Captain K parked the car in the garage he got a text from Major M, 'We are in the officers' mess.'

The regiment was always dead quiet on Fridays except for the guard platoon. Lieutenant B pulled out a beer for everyone, and Major T raised his glass 'We did it. We fucking did it! We made history today.' They stayed up late and chatted until 2am. It was mostly about life and general stuff. They already knew what they had accomplished, and it was time to let off some steam.

Major M told me years later that before he closed his eyes that night, he spared a thought for the task at hand. He was about to start training Tier 1 operators shortly and knew his international connections played a significant part in making this happen. He had promised Colonel X access to his contacts, and wondered if it would have any consequences, but he left that problem for another day.

Back in Stockholm Colonel X, General H and the Money Man needed to start constructing something that would look like a regular unit, so they had coverage for the money influx without attracting attention. They had found the front they needed for the money, *"registerförband"* a new type of high readiness unit that fell under the EU directive for defence contributions. A more well-known example of a *registerförband* was the Nordic Battle Group. The unit type was very new and at that stage they were mostly infantry type mechanised units. It was the perfect front as they were registered outside of the official capacity, each unit had a separate budget path so there was little centralisation. This kind of unit was generally assigned a reserve force designation and there was no real follow up on what really happened daily, as it was a paper product. The tricky part was to keep the unit from being recorded in the EU high readiness unit register, because that would mean they had to obey EU command and that was not the way this was going – these were the first steps in forming an elite unit that lived somewhere between conventional, irregular, and covert operations.

So, the way forward was to use the ambiguity of flying under the radar and explain away the extra money. To keep things above board it was crucial that the money was not taken from the EU dedicated budget. The funds eventually came straight from Colonel X – the root of this cash is still a mystery, but most likely an anonymous government account.

If you do a quick Google search nowadays on the platoon you will only find a few lines on Wikipedia stating that it was a high readiness unit for a few years. That's how you hide a Tier 1 unit properly, in plain sight. That's the narrative being put forward, but the next chapters will give a bit more detail about these special operations units, and our escapades.

7

Fast cars and fast ropes: infiltrating an extremist group

'...she has hate and protecting her children is her motivation. I think she will work hard.'

Our five-man patrol had taken up positions in a natural depression on a small ridge. The evergreen trees that surrounded our position moved slightly with the north-easterly wind. It provided us with two key military elements, protection, and a good vantage point.

Lieutenant W told me, 'Get a hold of HQ on the radio.' I was the RTO and instinctively reached for my combat pack to get the radio ready. I had the antenna fitted – it was standard procedure to have it fitted but collapsed and held together by a rubber band.

Ten minutes earlier we'd had heavy contact and I slid down a mud slope. As I unclipped the lid of the backpack and saw the base of the antenna I thought, 'Shit', it was cracked. The drill was to switch to the flexible march antenna that is carried as a reserve. I fiddled around in the backpack, each passing second I felt my heart rate increasing. I hit the bottom and felt around – I then frantically unpacked all its contents. No antenna in sight, the whole patrol was waiting – I had forgotten the spare antenna. There are no words that could express what I was feeling.

I tapped Lieutenant W on the arm, 'We don't have an antenna.' He looked at me and said, 'Just use the flex!'

I said again 'We have no antenna; I forgot the spare one.'

Lieutenant W looked at me 'You are telling me that we don't have a radio?'

I needed to face the uncomfortable situation head on. 'Yes.' He managed to make an ironic snuffled 'ha' sound. 'So, you are my new RTO, how will this end?' he said rolling his eyes.

'Alright boys, on me, let's head back to base.'

This was also the night when I got my nickname 'boner', we might get back to that in another book… or not. It's a story that is better told with dimmed lights and over a few beers. It had been one week since we were all welcomed by Major M. Since then, we had met Mrs S and signed the contract that basically handed over our lives to the army. The contract said permanent employment, so I guess it was a long-term lease of our bodies. No one minded though since the pay was significantly higher than it usually was – to be honest we would have done it for the standard pay. Major M had a powerful but gentle presence, which garnered him much respect from everyone. He said to us, 'The operator training will run until we are done, no days off.'

The tempo was high from the start, the requirements were substantial, the tasks more advanced and 110 per cent professionalism was expected. But the tone was different, more collegiate but sharper when needed, like brothers.

We were housed in the 4th Squadron, earlier used for the KBS school. This was possible due to the robust downsizing of the armed forces which had more than halved the number of conscripts at the regiment. The doors leading into the squadron had been fitted with code locks, and the windows with mesh to keep prying eyes out. Each housing unit had been remodelled and fitted with a custom-built rack system; all the old metal lockers had been thrown out. A large portion of the space had also been converted into a planning and mission preparation area with projectors, map boards and other bits and pieces. The housing units were originally built for eight but with only four people living there, the additional space was well used.

When it came to equipment, they had vacuumed the armed forces of anything and everything that was new or highly specialised. Except for the standard ranger gear, it was a lot of odd equipment picked up from different units, foreign kit, civilian and even privately bought pieces, if it passed inspection.

Cold weather gear was from Arc'teryx, Mossad issued rigs for plain clothing operations, American plate carriers, the amphibious corps combat uniform adjusted to our needs by a seamstress hired locally, the air force's Nomex gear, FLIR thermal imaging cameras and Gen 4 night vision goggles (NVG) as a gift from our friends in the West.

A lot of experimental equipment had been sent our way for field-testing by FMV (Armed Forces Equipment Research and Development Division). We were lucky to receive the new untested winter and summer Gore-Tex uniforms; these may seem like small things today but back then it was significant – top tier radio equipment, flowing in from Harris and the SATCOM store was like walking into a Starbucks or a 7-Eleven.

When it came to weapons there was also no disappointment. Right off the bat we were equipped with the experimental AK5 CF[1] – it was the prototype for what is today the standard rifle for the Swedish Armed Forces AK5 C. I still remember it today. It was a majestic weapon. All black instead of green, bolt catch, picatinny rails, Aimpoint red dot sights with NVG mount and a laser pointer. Before that I had only seen this kind of stuff while visiting foreign units. But it didn't stop there – the prototype version AK5 D[2] was also issued and was a fresh mint julep. On top of that we had the Glock 17C with tritium sights and picatinny rail. Perhaps the pistol and rifles seem ordinary, but the context is important. The Swedish armed forces had been on a hard-core diet for 10 years, some units were issued around 20 live rounds per year. Only the MPs and guard commanders had pistols at this time. It was scarce to see them. I felt that they had gone all in on this, and we wouldn't be wanting for anything. We were more likely to be almost force fed at this point.

Having been assigned to one of four patrols, I was placed in the second. Each patrol was led by an officer. Second was led by Lieutenant W. He was unknown to me but seemed to be a good guy, with a competitive attitude; he had been trying to get into the embryo of SSG and FJS IK for years – Lieutenant W was always on, always focused.

Our 2iC was a Mr K, a 27 year old. His age meant that he was quite far away from his initial ranger training, but he had worked up until now as a member of the Police National Anti-Terrorist Unit, so he appeared rock solid.

I was assigned to be the RTO; I had been personally recommended for the position by Lieutenant B since I had shown an "unnatural" ability in mastering and understanding radio communications on a "deep level". Our intelligence and photo guy was Mr N who had done his service two years before me. Tall, lean, and multi-skilled, he had been trained with the High Alpine rescue services in his civilian career. Our medic, Mr P, was a Stockholm native like me, he had worked as a trauma paramedic for a few years in the busy Stockholm district. He always walked around with blood stains on his crocs like a doctor – not that I knew any doctors with blood-stained crocks.

1 AK5 CF was then an experimental assault rifle – the C stands for the model and F stands for *Försök*, 'test/experimental.' Today the rifle is in common use in the Swedish military.
2 The AK5 D was a shortened version of the AK5 assault rifle designed for plain clothed operations and drivers.

Finally, we had Mr A, the 'Beast' – this really was his nickname, and he was a true beast. We were in basic training during the same year, but he was in 2nd Squadron as an LMG/demolition specialist – and slotted in nicely as our new machine gunner and demolitions guy. He was ripped and super fit, a former elite cross-country skier; but how he kept in peak shape was a mystery to all of us since he ate anything and everything. He had what we jokingly called borderline personality between being humble and a grunt. But he was primarily a grunt. As long as he was fed and occasionally got laid, he didn't have any questions, except for when it was time for food and sleep. He didn't care about the overall picture, he just wanted to blow things up. And he didn't mind being 'forgotten about' for 12 hours at a time. He would just crack on, keeping watch while the others were building observation posts or stuff like that – he just did his thing until the next task came along. He was the backbone guy all patrols/squads/teams need – and everyone needs a beast on their team.

3rd patrol was led by Captain B. I had secretly been hoping to be assigned to his patrol. But it was good to have him close by for now. Mr F, my former intelligence specialist wasn't happy with his position, so far, he was not overtly complaining, he was happy to be in, like all of us. He was assigned to the 8 man strong support squad as a driver/LMG gunner and demolitions specialist. It was a cool group, many sporting long hair, a bit of a rolling stone section but with epic skills. They all had ranger training, passed selection, and had acquired additional abilities in their civilian roles.

Lieutenant B led the support squad; in addition to Mr F, they had a radio engineer from the armed forces R&D agency, a computer programmer that had done some time in the slammer after hacking government databases, a carpenter, and a truck mechanic. They valued people with added skill sets that joined both military and civilian parts of our brain and body. A person who had seen nothing else in his life than military work left the civilian side empty. While a person that has experience from both worlds – maintained balance and wouldn't stick out like a sore thumb, especially when wearing civilian clothing – we needed to learn how to blend in and many colleagues actually knew how to be civilians.

As for the quartermaster we had been handed a bona fide regimental, and Swedish military legend. Many people thought he was a myth. Captain L was his name, and while his last name looked Swedish, it sounded French when you pronounced it. He had done 19 winters at the regiment. As a young 2nd Lieutenant, he left Sweden and joined the French Foreign Legion, which was highly controversial back then. But even more controversial was that he was allowed to get back into the Swedish armed forces as an officer after serving 5 years in the Legion. Nobody really understood how that happened. He never talked about it, but we found out that he had served with the 2nd *REP* Paratroopers in Corsica and done several tours including many combat jumps over Chad.

Captain L was hardcore, and like many seasoned veterans he balanced a hardnosed approach with good doses of humour. He wore his hair slightly longer than other officers and some of it would sometimes show from the line of his beret. Most of all he took his position as Quartermaster very seriously as only the best was good enough for his boys. He had deep-rooted connections with the French SF and was our private direct channel to them, which helped us over the years in various operational theatres, as well as many unforgettable training opportunities on the Riviera. More on this later.

He had a lot of pull with the top brass and was not afraid to call them out when needed. His main area of expertise was not being a Quartermaster though – this was a convenient front. He had for decades built up and developed the Swedish sniper capability – he was one of the front figures and founders of modern Swedish sniper training. For many years he had overseen the sniper platoon while serving in the *Livskvadron*. He was responsible for making Swedish snipers among the best in the world – evidence of this was how the Swedes often finished in the top 3 in the sniper world cup. He also developed and set the standards when it came to shooting from mobile and moving platforms like boats and helicopters.

With the team set up we spent a lot of time establishing new personal skill sets and routines such as dynamic shooting, mission purposed cross fit training, advanced krav maga, free climbing et cetera. A regular office day was from 06:00 until 22:00 or midnight as we needed to amass a large amount of repetitive training to set muscle memory.

Some instructors were in-house, but most came from the civilian world, other government agencies or military units. All of them were managed through personal connections as we had to find the best in each category (and they were usually not found in the army); most importantly it needed to be done in secret.

This was especially true when it came to pistol training, we couldn't rely on the army's poor standard, we needed someone that could make the pistol an extension or our arm and quickly – Captain T was the answer.

Captain T was a peculiar individual, he worked at the regiment, but I had never really seen him. The rumour was that he was Northern Europe's most evil captain. He had once put two ranger conscripts in a car during an exercise, blocked the doors and lit the car on fire with napalm. They got out by kicking out the windshield, which was the purpose of the exercise, 'Training for reality,' he said. He was a light version of Jack Nicholson in *A Few Good Men*. I cannot say that I would use similar methods, but he emphasised that reality seldom has safety regulations.

He was about 175cm tall with a well-groomed moustache that had that eighties porn star look. At around 45 years old, he was still in good shape, but his male pattern baldness gave the look of a middle manager; unlike most of us he didn't shave his head, so he had somewhat of a monk look. When you saw him, you could imagine him pushing papers all day in a headquarters somewhere.

His unique skill was that he was able to teach anyone how to master the pistol. Besides running the local pistol club, he was one of the best IPSC competitors in Sweden, winning Swedish, European and many other international competitions. He was also brought in to train intelligence operators, secret service agents, the police, royal close protection details, and cloak and dagger agencies.

It was day 1 of 21 of pistol training. The day started at 06:00 at the range, which was after our morning workout routine. Captain T received us and said, 'Some of you know me. Most of you don't. I am the most evil captain in northern Europe, maybe even in the northern hemisphere.' He looked too serious to be joking but some nervous laughter emerged from the crowd. He went on, 'I am here because they pay me, and you are here to do what I tell you and if you follow my instructions there will be no problems.'

We started with an hour or so to adjusting our stance, grip and aim. He walked around with a slim branch, whipping people not doing it correctly. 'Pain reinforces the learning process,' he said. I am not sure about the method, but I stopped trying to aim with one eye closed after I felt the sharp crack of his improvised whip on my neck.

The trick to being good at pistol shooting is to get your position right from the beginning. The basics are very much like with the rifle; you look at your target over your rifle with both eyes open, hence aiming with your body. After enough training, one ends up hitting the target through natural alignment and looking ahead. There is nothing different with the pistol except the barrel length. But to be fair, it is a massive difference. In brief a shorter barrel means that one needs to have a consistent and stable stance, grip, and arm position. Again, this can only be achieved by repetition to create muscle memory.

After the short dry instruction, we started to put lead down range. I felt that this weapon system would have a sharp uphill learning curve for me. Everyone wanted to be a natural of course, something I was not. It may sound cool to some, perhaps I may have even tried to make it sound cool in retelling the story, but it was a lot of work firing a pistol from early morning to late night. Fatigue creeps in and I would feel my arms getting heavy with the limited weight of the pistol. My eyelids would betray me at times – I needed to focus. The first week was just Captain T teaching us the basics. Trying to get us in line, drawing our weapons, practicing a double tap in the chest and one in the head, holstering, using both hands, learning about our strong and weak hand. This was all about getting a solid foundation, a critical first step to be able to do the advanced training, including but not limited to stoppage drills, and extreme positions.

On the seventh day most people were ready to move to the next level except two – myself and an LMG gunner from 4th patrol. At 22:00 everyone except the two of us were dismissed. Captain T said, 'There are always a few handicapped people in every group, and I congratulate you for being a part of that special team. Unfortunately, we don't have time to wait for you two to get your shit together. So, we will stay here until we get this sorted.' I felt the pressure. 'What was wrong with me, why couldn't I get a grip on this like everyone else', I thought.

It came down to being able to produce consistent results. He was never interested in favourites, groupings or first place, he said, 'You are in the killing business not in the competition business, competitions are for divas.'

He monitored us closely to see what we were doing wrong. I was trying so hard to maintain a 60/40 push pull grip. Captain T said, 'You are trying too hard, relax your grip, you need to let the pistol move in your hand. Having a solid grip has nothing to do with trying to hold the gun one hundred percent still when firing.

I tried hard but I didn't really get it, 'How could I grip and still relax?'

It was almost midnight, and it was down to just me. The LMG gunner had shaped up and passed the test. Captain T walked up to the targets about 15m away. He positioned himself between two figures and said to me, 'Kill the target on my right.' I probably looked like a question mark. He repeated, 'Do you have a hearing problem? Kill the target on my right.'

'I don't understand captain,' I replied.

He pulled his gun from his pancake holster, pointed it at me and said with a loud voice, 'Draw your weapon, hold it with a loose grip and fire two bullets in the chest and one in the head in the target on my right or I will kill you.' He started to count, 'One…' I drew my pistol, I felt my sweaty hands tightly holding the pistol grip, and I slowly eased my hold. Exhaling, I hesitated for a second and then I squeezed the trigger. 'Two,' I heard the count. Bam, bam, bam. 'Three, good I thought I had to kill you for a second there,' he said. 'Again,' he shouted. I drew and fired. 'Again.' And I repeated the exercise. In less than a minute, I had emptied both my 17 round magazines. 'Let's see how you did,' he said.

As I reached the targets, I could see that all chest shots were grouped in a 5cm circle bang in the middle, and the circle in the head was on point. 'Ahh so you were only acting handicapped I see. Well next time don't waste my time like this,' he said with a pat on the back. I had finally figured it out, I just had to use a loose hold, look ahead, and squeeze the trigger, that was it. But it apparently just needed to be scared out of me. Captain T knew what he was doing.

The following two weeks and nights was drills, drills, and drills, close protection situations, shooting from moving cars, inside of cars, under cars, kill houses, obstacle courses, low visibility scenarios including being blinded by pepper spray (although we called it OC Spray). I had become one with my Glock.

After 21 days and more than 50,000 9mm rounds fired I had gone from the worst to one of the best. We would see Captain T a few more times during the year to check how we were doing and to keep us on our toes. A running theme through the operator's course was personal competence training. Several times a week we had time to prefect and hone our skills with our personal weapons and Krav Maga. The amount of live fire exercises was unmatched to anything I had ever heard of in the Swedish army. A five man patrol could without blinking spend an annual platoon size amount of AK rounds in one day. The exercises were short, diverse, and almost always live fire.

With daily training and no days off, we quickly became good – we started to believe in ourselves 'we were becoming professionals.' Now only training with foreign special forces would help us gauge our progress and develop further and we did not have to wait for long. Next up was training in France, more precisely with, the *Direction Générale de la Sécurité Extérieure* and the *13e Régiment de Dragon Parachutistes*.

Four, three, two, one – *feu, feu, feu* (fire), the helicopter was oddly still when the shots rang out. 'Become one with the frame', Captain L said to his sniper protégé over the intercom. 'Easier said than done,' I thought. I felt lucky that I wasn't a sniper, it wasn't for me, but they did impressive things. I could relate as it's the same principles that apply when working the camera from a helicopter. It's not the general movement but the vibrations, about 16,000 per second, you can't see them, but they can potentially change the course of a bullet and blur a picture beyond recognition. This is particularly the case if the shutter is open for too long. It's all about isolation from the airframe or rather being one with it.

Captain L was like a fish that returned to the lake after years on land. His French was perfect, and it was like he had never left. He was our liaison with the *13e RDP*, an elite French SF unit, and this was not the first or the last time they would collaborate. *13e RDP* has an exceptional skill set and commanded international respect regarding their HUMINT capability; because of the personal connections developed they were our primary training partner for human intelligence. They are a regular supplier of operators to the DGSE, France's equivalent of MI6 or the CIA.

We were invited to participate in a full-scale French Intel-SF exercise. It was always a double-edged sword for me, I felt honoured of course but at the same time I wondered what we were doing there. I often had a feeling of 'are we good enough' when we were training with or being trained by foreign SF units. At times it felt almost embarrassing, who were we to claim to be a part of this world? We had no pedigree, no famous embassy raids to show – although we had skills, I was battling imposter syndrome. Later on, I discovered that many soldiers and leaders have some amount of this strange invisible ailment.

Captain L always said, 'If you are a household name you are doing it wrong.' I guess he was right, and all units started somewhere I just hoped that we could deliver when it came to game day. As we had been working closely with the French in a bi-lateral "training deal" they had been up at the regiment many times as well. We gave them sub-arctic and winter warfare training in exchange for HUMINT and NATO compliant JTAC training. The French SF is a very "unfrench" organisation, if we consider stereotypes – they are incredibly friendly, ultra-professional and humble operators. Their personal skill level was through the roof, and the only thing they weren't that good at was operating in the cold. Something happened to them in the cold, they froze, becoming more like a National Guard unit from Texas having a weekend warrior showdown.

I remember a winter in Norway, during the Cold Response Exercise, which had SF units from around the world. We were tasked with tracking down "enemy" SF units operating in the area. We caught five SF patrols that night: two Italian, one French, one Spanish and one American. Our night's work started when we saw a light on a ridge. We thought they were civilians or a home guard unit; but it was a six man French SF patrol sitting in a circle around a gas stove on full blast warming themselves. We couldn't believe our eyes. We caught the other four units in similar ways. The Americans were playing with light sabres. It was a cold exercise I will give them that, at around minus 40 degrees Celsius – it would test anyone.

Let's get back to France…

We had a few days together before splitting up into smaller teams. 1st and 3rd Patrol were going to do direct action and a few of us, me included, were going to join the more "bum like" looking people of the deep intelligence section. These are people you could easily see living in a half rough neighbourhood in Pakistan for a few years working as an NGO, fully immersed in the local setting.

We arrived at the 'swimming pool'. I had been there once before. It is one of those places that gives you the feeling of a boring office building. Everyone seemed to look so perfect, almost too perfect. We never did any training there and we wouldn't this time either. This was a headquarter location. We always came here to wait outside an office on wooden benches for a few hours with people pacing up and down the corridors like doctors in a hospital – looking at the same time busy but also not that busy.

We were told, 'You are getting your picture taken and getting a photo ID with an identification number on it as well as a telephone number. The card also specifies that you are authorised to carry a weapon and where the police can call to confirm if you are arrested for real.' It's always a bit complicated when doing operational exercises in plain clothing and carrying a gun with live ammunition, especially in a foreign country. Well, if you do your job well no one will ever know, but if you don't there can be problems and the last thing you want to do is to have the police mistake you for someone dangerous because I guess that will be the end of that.

I am not sure if the ID would help to protect you from poor performance, but if you find yourself in a sticky situation during training like this, you are instructed to give up immediately, 'with ease' so to say. In Sweden the armed forces are obliged to coordinate with the local police when conducting plain clothes exercises with concealed weapons and live ammunition and get clearance from the National Police Command. This is not necessarily the case in France or many other European countries as the intelligence services often live in their own bubbles and don't care much about the concerns of the local police. To be fair, their argument is that it would take the realism out of the exercise. Well, I can't deny that – no point in playing poker without money on the table.

There were five of us and we waited to get picked up by the van that was supposed to take us south, to the area of the exercise. The side of the van showed the bends and bangs of a vehicle that had been through an urban war, forget screws, the license plates were duct taped on. Two Frenchmen were in the front seat and one in the back. The man in the passenger seat nodded hello and tilted his head in a 'get in' motion. The guy in the back slid the side door open. As we got in and loaded our small bags in the middle row, I noticed that the frog in the back had a G36 sticking out of an open duffle bag on the seat next to him. He nodded as we got in. The driver was speaking on his mobile. The sharp sounds of a language I didn't properly know kept me in the dark, but I knew irritation when I heard it.

As he hung up, he turned to us and said, 'Welcome', with a bit of a forced smile, 'I am sorry to say we are a bit short on time, so I hope you don't need to stop, I have a briefing pack for you, read through it and we talk after, okay?' He handed me a brown government-circular envelope that was sealed with one of those old-school cotton string closures.

As the van was approaching the on-ramp for the highway the five of us leaned in over the briefing. The first page was an extract from the French police register:

Ahmed al Khaleed, 46 years old. Arrested a few times for petty crimes; he has been under surveillance for collaborating with Islamic State training wings in Somalia and Afghanistan. He has also been suspected of being a recruiter and a money man.

I looked at the guy in the passenger seat, 'This looks pretty authentic man,' I said.

'It is,' he replied, in a dry and frank way, his eyes looked up for only a moment. He went on, 'The contact just called us and said that the meeting is going to start soon.'

The five of us looked equally surprised. We knew that the French usually mixed exercises with low level operations, but this was not a low-level target.

'Were we being thrown into a live operation?' The answer was clear – the guy in the back was filling up magazines with live rounds as we went through the briefing. Four men were going to be at the meeting. "Jacque", the man in the passenger seat, would attend and we were his support. They were buying

Makarovs and French passports. The target of the operation was to identify the other three who were believed to be 'operatives' being smuggled into France to carry out terrorist actions.

Ahmed was suspected of helping ISIS members into France but up to that point, he had been very careful, and the authorities had not been able to gather much evidence on him during their investigation. An undercover operation was the only option. He had let his guard down after a few previous deals with Jacque, including small arms and a passport for Ahmed himself. The passport had a silent flag which meant it was a real French passport, but his border movements would be recorded, and the appropriate authorities notified if he travelled; but no action was to be taken – it was purely surveillance and monitoring. As Jacque proved his ability to deliver real government documents, he gained Ahmed's trust; Jacque said he had good connections with 'silent' supporters of the cause, strategically placed in important government offices. Ahmed had been using his passport, travelling freely for over a year without problems. The goal of this operation was to identify Ahmed's operatives, put a tail on them and let them lead us to their respective homes and hopefully expose more people in their circle. The end goal was a DA against all involved.

Jacque had some trouble getting Ahmed to bring the suspected operatives to the meeting. Of course, Ahmed was a seasoned smuggler, and looked for every way possible to keep his clients out of it. But Jacque insisted that he needed to collect their biometric information and photos in person as it was a requirement for the passports. Looking fully legitimate, he had a government fingerprint reader. As a consolation, and hook, Jacque offered Ahmed fake passports, but Ahmed needed the real deal – French Government issued ones.

So, this would be a one-shot kind of deal, with no margin for error. Our job was to man a mobile OP. One man in the van taking photos, and two foxtrot guys to keep track of the operatives during the first 500-1,000 metres from the meeting spot. The handover gap was kept short to not raise any alarms. And the last two team members were to do counter surveillance and be able to act as a counterassault team (CAT) under the lead of the 'backseat guy' – he never even told us his alias. Mr N, our best photo guy was manning the mobile OP. They had a Canon camera with a 350mm lens that he hadn't used before. I watched him drum his fingers over the camera – his ring, middle and index fingers were like drumsticks. 'You've got this,' I said. He was going to cover one of the possible six exits, so a big chance that he would have marks coming his way.

Mr K and Mr P were doing counter surveillance and CAT, myself, and Mr A were tasked with foxtrot duty, which is a delicate business. We had solid training, but now it was the real deal. I didn't want to mess up like I had during my first training exercise. I had been surprised by the mark walking around the corner in a coffee shop and I just downed my coffee in front of him and walked out as smooth as I could after that 007 move.

We only had a few hours to set up before the meeting and we were going in hot as we expected their people were already watching the scene. I was dropped off about a half an hour away from the meeting spot and Mr A about 10 minutes closer than me. My cover was that I was going to a meeting at a language school on the same street, so it would be natural that I didn't speak French and I didn't look very French either. DGSE had booked my meeting, but I had to keep track of the timing myself – I would have a two-minute heads' up or so before I needed to walk out after I got my cue, if I got it.

As I was getting the rundown of the language starter package by the very kind and fully invested French lady selling the language course, all I could think about was, 'Are they pulling our leg here? This shit can't be real, we are not being dropped into a major French operation, that they had been running for a few years. Why risk it by bringing in a few Swedes?' I decided that this was a well-planned and realistic training exercise, nothing else. I smiled and the language lady smiled back and said, 'That is the feeling we want to give here.'

I replied, 'You have so much positive energy so it's hard not to smile.' Right then I got my cue.

My phone buzzed again, I opened the text, it said, 'Your package is ready for pick up.' Which meant that Ahmed Al Khaleed was coming my way. I had less than two minutes. I looked up and interrupted the French lady and said, 'I am so sorry, my wife finished early, and I need to get going.' 'Damn,' I thought that sounded odd, 'Did I mention a wife before, or did I just make it weird?'

She smiled, 'Of course,' turning around and grabbing a folder that had a little plastic compartment at the front for a business card. She started looking for a business card on her desk.

'I don't have time for this I should have wrapped this up earlier' I thought to myself. I got up from my chair as she was going through her desk drawer.

'Ahh here they are,' she said with her metropolitan French accent. 'I am sorry, I just got new ones the other day and I forgot where I put them. Please give me a call when you are ready, I really think we can be a good start for your French language journey.'

I took the folder and probably seemed weirdly rushed as I turned around and left. While thinking to myself, 'Next time, you need to play it cool all the way, things like that are what can give you away.' Perhaps I got away with it that time as I was just the weird foreigner, but I was probably weird enough to make an impression; and that was the stuff that could make it or break it if she was working for the other side. The good part was that I knew what Ahmed looked like. This made my task easier. The language school had decent windows so I would see him walk past and I could naturally get up behind him.

I saw his profile pass the window as I stepped out of the building, the street was crowded, and people were walking forcefully as they were either getting to or from work. He was engaged in a conversation on his phone and was walking with someone else. I could see Mr A on the other side of the street so I figured it was the second mark. I kept a comfortable distance, Mr A fell back a bit more just in case they stopped for some reason, and I was forced to carry on walking past them.

We had about 500 metres left to the subway station intersection where we had three operatives waiting to take over. If the mark or marks went down the subway, they would fall in behind us and keep their distance. We would ride one station staying on the mark and then get off, so they had enough time to roll into position. If they were not going into the subway, we would do a flying hand over and still go down the subway and make our way back to the RV.

I needed to decrease my gap as we were approaching the chokepoint, and the subway entrance was crowded. It seemed like they were heading into the subway together. Mr A fell back in behind me and let me take the lead. I could just spot the handovers as we walked into the subway station. I was responsible for both of them now and it was very unlikely that they were taking the same train. The station had four platforms, two on each level. As I approached the ticket barrier, I had two people between me and the mark. Mr A manoeuvred himself farther to the right to be in a better strike position if they went to the second level. I reached for my subway pass in my front pocket, empty. The other pocket, empty. I was building up a sweat, 'What did I do with the ticket?' As I patted myself down, I checked my chest pocket, 'Found it, thank God.' It felt like several minutes had passed but the person in front of me had just passed the barrier. Mr A was already in, but my handover had to close the gap if they were to make it. Mr A disappeared downstairs towards platform four following the second mark and his handover was close behind him. I was on Ahmed's tail up towards platform two. The train was arriving at the platform, and I needed to put one foot in front of the other to keep up.

The train was packed, and I barely managed to squeeze in. My side was pressed against Ahmed's – danger close. But it was hard not to be in contact with anyone as it was Tokyo full. As the doors closed, I saw the handover standing on the outside, 'Great, he missed it…' it was up to me now.

I hoped he would stay on the train long enough so they could intercept us further ahead and get on, but either way I needed to keep my cool. We passed two stations and people squeezed in and out at every stop. I tried to shift a bit to the side and position myself further from the exit, so he could make the first move when it was time to exit, and I could follow more naturally. He was busy texting on his phone and looked up at the station map from time to time.

As we approached the third stop, he made his way through the crowd towards the door. As the doors opened, quite a few people got off, which made for a natural exit. He walked toward the northern exit. Looking up and down, trying to keep my eye on the mark I fiddled with my phone and managed to send, 'Anvers, N. exit.'

I got four street names in return. The French weren't too thrilled about just being given a station and a direction. It felt like forever and as we exited the station, we came out to a massive four street intersection; I had briefly studied the map, so I had a clue about where I was, but felt slightly lost as I tried to orientate myself. I then changed my approach and focused on finding street names instead. I got a text with a '?' They obviously thought I took too long.

I tried to get a better look at the street signs as we crossed the large intersection, as we came to the other side, I saw a half match, it was similar to one that they sent. I texted the street name and got 'ok' back. It was like a large boulevard with a few intersecting streets on our side. The phone vibrated, 'At intersection.' At about a 3 minute walk ahead I could see another largish intersection. As we approached, I saw it was a red light at the pedestrian crossing and 76 seconds before green. Ahmed stopped and fiddled with his phone. I had increased the gap so I could see my handover take position and I could make the turn. I didn't know who the handover was yet, and it was getting crunchy time wise – my phone vibrated. 'Blue jacket, green pants.' I tried to look around carefully but didn't see anyone. I continued walking along while looking for my exchange. I was now at the crossing, close to Ahmed. I was committed and couldn't turn. As we got the green light and started our crossing I saw the blue jacket, green pants man approaching from my right. Ahmed was in front of me at 11 o'clock. As we approached the other side of the street. I fell back slightly to give them space. Ahmed seemed to be heading straight ahead but stopped for a second and headed for the crosswalk on the right. I had plenty of room still as the blue jacket and green pants headed to the right crosswalk. Ahmed looked around like he was orientating himself and suddenly continued straight ahead, the other agent couldn't change direction for fear of looking suspicious. I wasn't committed yet to a particular course – I continued after him. At this point I started to worry, I had been tailing him for a long time and I think I had gone unnoticed but if I hadn't it would be suspicious by now. I saw blue jacket, green pants crossing the other road as I continued ahead. My phone buzzed, 'red backpack, khaki cap overtaking.'

I fell back discreetly and I saw the red backpack, khaki cap from the corner of my eye on the right. I felt relief but also, I felt like I wanted to see it through, the only catch was I didn't know the playbook – I only knew my role. At the next corner I turned left as Ahmed and the red backpack continued straight ahead. I was about 5 minutes from the subway station. I felt good, like I did my part, 'I hope I did at least, we will see soon enough.'

Back at the RV I got a pat on the back as I jumped in the van. The operational commander was there, 'Well done' he said in broken English before he continued to communicate on the handheld radio.

Mr A whispered, 'That was a detour,' with a smile. After a 30 minute drive, we arrived at a small garage in the suburbs that allowed us to covertly move into our compound. The compound appeared to be an extended suburban house with a yard. We did a short tour and then ended up in a modified living room that was actually an operations room. A large map of Paris and photos of the ongoing operation decorated the walls. Mr N's photos were there, and he did a good job getting two of the bad guys' faces – the snaps were crisp.

It was bustling with activity, and I saw officials from the Gendarmerie and DGSE kitting up for a raid. Jacque said, 'They are hitting the marks tonight; we will keep Ahmed on a tight leash just to see what he does and who he calls and most of all who informs him of their arrest; also, who is he reporting to.' At that point I was sure we were not in an exercise.

We spent the next three weeks honing our skills and tapping deeper into managing and running sources, agents, helpers, informants, assets …. they have many names, but the rules are the same. Running sources are at the top of the HUMINT pyramid and is a practice usually reserved for the real cloak and dagger agencies. Luckily, the IRP founders had good and longstanding relationships with the cloak and dagger units, so the sharing of tradecraft was made possible – as a military diplomatic gesture, we had been trading with them providing a lot of training and resources.

There is no black magic to these covert operations – it just requires a lot of training and it's not for everyone. It's like being a fighter pilot or a submarine officer, it demands that special type of person, who has certain traits, and can be trained and groomed to reach the right standards. Covert operations have a couple of differences to conventional missions. Firstly, they require a higher level of operational security. Running sources gives you a lot of personal exposure to unfriendly elements and the risk is elevated even when you decide to leave – it is more than a job. The second is that it usually involves techniques and methods that could break national and or international law, and most countries will not openly endorse these types of operations. It's like a necessary evil for most governments out there – espionage, and intelligence driven covert operations are a country's first line of defence short of armed conflict.

So how do you hone your skills in the HUMINT field? With theory and with exercises? Well, you don't. The theoretical training and exercises are mostly to enhance what one already possesses: communication skills, people reading skills and a strong social game that allows you to adapt to any room, any group and any individual to reach a pre-determined goal. This can be tricky and requires you to have a natural sense of manipulation and the social skill set to fit in; but at the same time gaining trust which means you must have a broad knowledge of your mark, and their context, as well as the inclination of how to adapt it in a natural way. Nothing sticks out like someone who has read up on something well but who can't apply it themselves. Those who cannot do, teach, and those who cannot teach, do, and so on.

Equipped with a basic set of tools, a lot of the training takes place in the real world with real people and real reactions. This is the only way to get exposed to the real thing. It all starts off with low level and low risk interactions. It has some similarities to the movie *Spy Game*, like gaining access to someone's house in a short period of time just by talking or being thrown into a wedding with unknown people; or being told that you have a slot for speaking on the groom's side in an hour. It's a pretty intense experience, but when you are standing there, relying on social pressures – that many people are too afraid to not remember you. And then seeing them "actually remembering" you and laughing at your jokes, that's something special and definitely empowering, you just walked in, and convinced a bunch of strangers on the biggest day of their life that you are a part of their lives. The crowning jewel is when the groom hugs you afterwards and says, 'I missed you buddy'. The alcohol helped me in that particular situation. As I said it's not for everyone and one needs to become the person you are projecting, to be able to play the game all the way.

In the third week we had our last live exercise: 'The Aid Worker', and it took us outside the borders of France this time. It's a common concept, unfortunate for the humanitarians doing good work in conflict areas, and failed states, but for us, it's a very good environment to test one's skills in front of a real live audience. The aid worker role is often exploited by intelligence services as it provides a natural way to keep foreigners in a given country and gives them reasonable freedom of movement and access to one of the main intelligence resources, refugees. Veteran refugees are usually hardened to foreign intelligence grooming and are known to provide information in exchange for favours, money, or benefits – information that might or might not be accurate. That's not the route you want to take, the preferred route is to establish a personal relationship, keep them open for recruitment but don't attempt to recruit them in the initial meetings. One has to wait until they reach their destination country; make sure to play a role in their 'release' from the camp and then, when trust is established, you recruit them in the destination country. Firstly on a humanitarian basis, and secondly because their cosy existence in their new country is 110 per cent dependent on you. Of course, on a human level there is a duty of care, but in the practical world of intelligence, it is self-interest first – Machiavellian. The balance is tricky.

But one can't push too hard, it needs to be balanced, so they aren't too prone to deliver information. By growing the relationship slowly but surely, you will have direct access to the inside of the refugee community and that's where all the action happens; most bad shit that is about to go down is in one way or another filtered through this route.

The background to this exercise was that we were introduced to a group of refugees who were being granted asylum in France within two weeks of meeting them. The catch was that they didn't know that they were being granted asylum. So, we had a week to find the right person, establish a connection, and become the 'helper.' Another week to reinforce the connection and to fast track them through the system – then wait and reconnect.

My cover was a World Health Organisation researcher who was transferred to the French desk four months earlier, which explained my lack of French language. It was a good cover as being a health researcher gives you access to female refugees in a better way. In my opinion the women are the key in at least 50 per cent of the cases as they are silent observers who move around seamlessly. In many cultures the men don't care or respect women, but they have ears and often a lot of hatred built up, plus they often care more for their kids' welfare which is easier to exploit then egocentric men. This work is not for the faint-hearted, and the manipulation of refugees is terrible to some. We keep that in mind, but our aim is to prevent even greater evils. Ultimately Islamist terrorism and the situation in France was complex and nuanced. Some may say that diplomacy, trust, and development is central to successful integration of refugees – they are right, and this works for the majority. While keeping this in mind we face the harsh and frightening reality that a small number of extremists remain active and must be neutralised. We only hope that this work does not inspire more fighters but promotes the integration of the majority of refugees looking for a safe place to live, work, and care for their families.

A refugee woman was sitting outside her tarp; they should have had a tent, but she had spent the last two and a half years under this tarp with her four children and her cousin who had been training as a foreign fighter with Al Qaeda in Pakistan and Afghanistan. A few years after meeting them he would become a lieutenant in Al Shabab, but I didn't know that then – he had been flying under the radar. I knew they were extremists, not so much her but she was almost certainly a silent supporter and along for the ride. Perhaps she didn't have a choice and neither did her children. But they were not hiding their views that well. After all hatred grows well in camps like these – similar to criminals in jail.

I had observed 'the cousin' visiting the Imam a few times. They seemed tight and he was a known and flagged recruiter usually living in the *15e Arrondisment* of Paris, when not recruiting refugees abroad- he had been doing it for years. He would not be my way in, he would just make me more credible, the way in was through a football.

I had seen them for a few days and her kids were kicking around rolled-up plastic bags as a football. They probably had dreams of becoming Ronaldo or Zlatan. I saw the boys' eyes open wide when they saw the football and I rolled it to them from afar. They looked at the ball and then looked at me, I smiled and pointed at the ball, *'Hadia, hadia'*, Arabic for gift, the boys hesitated for a moment then they all threw themselves at the ball. I walked away and saw their mother smile and nod at me.

As I was walking back a few hours later after doing a few interviews, they were still playing, I shouted, *'Daena nadhhab,'* which translates to 'go' or 'let's go.' It was the only word I knew that would be appropriate. The boys got it and passed me the ball, I charged forward and tried to score through their improvised goal posts, but the goalkeeper managed a save holding on tight. I gave him a pat on the back and said, *'Jamil'* which means 'beautiful, pretty' or 'good', he smiled and looked proud.

I then joined my interpreter, a British woman in her late thirties dressed way to fancy for being in a refugee camp. I think she only did that job so she could put humanitarian work on her CV. 'You shouldn't interact with them, and definitely not touch them,' she said with a frown. Perhaps it was more than a frown as she looked as if she had just eaten rotten eggs. 'They are children, they need some smiles,' I said.

'Yeah, but protocol...' she countered.

I interrupted her, 'Fuck protocol, its theory and these kids are the reality. Are you sure you are here for the right reasons?'

She smirked and rolled her eyes, 'We can't save everyone you know.' She was a perfect companion for this as she didn't care at all, and she just wanted to get out of there. I was also not there for the right reasons, but I cared.

Back at base that night, I was preparing my file on the mum of the four kids. I did this while sipping my French beer – it is not really beer it's more like water – like a pilsner but very, very light. I wasn't sure she was going to be a good source, but she was the only reasonable option I had. She seemed to have a good head on her shoulders, and she looked like she wanted out or at least the possibility of a better life for her kids. What was worse, her cousin regularly beat her and she had fresh wounds every morning.

I didn't put her down as a possible informer in my file. I thought she would be a better fit as a community asset, someone who we could interview from time to time to get insight into what was going on, no specifics just like a temperature gauge. That was my plan for her. We hadn't talked yet, but she was up for the pre-selection interview the next day, and if she was selected, she would spend two days with me and the interpreter. She could decline though, but nobody ever did, as they got some perks with more food and other benefits.

We showed up at her spot just after eight, but she was not to be seen. Her cousin looked out from the tarp, 'We don't want anything, we don't want anything,' he said through the interpreter.

I said, 'We are from the WHO, and we are doing health interviews, you will be helping us help you and you will get some extra food for your family.' He looked suspiciously at me, I smiled back and said, 'I know the Imam is a very busy man these days, I know him a bit, maybe I could ask him to free up some time for you?'

I could see that he was thinking hard. 'Okay, but I don't have the time for the interview.'

'It's okay, are you approving that we talk to your cousin and her kids? No personal information will be collected, and all answers will be anonymised.'

'Yes, yes you have my permission,' he said as he walked away.

'Do you know the Imam?' the interpreter asked. 'We are doing research, and we need access to help these people. Sometimes you have to bend the truth a bit for the greater good, but we are seeing him on the way out, okay?'

'I guess we are,' she replied.

I peeked in under the tarp. I could barely see her in the dark, she was covering her face. I waved the interpreter in to give her the speech. She shook her head. 'We spoke to your cousin, and he approved, but it's up to you of course,' I said and smiled. I continued, 'My name is Matt; we have some extra food packages, and we won't take much of your time.' I reached in through the opening with two food packages.

She hesitated, grabbed them and replied, 'I am Aaden.'

I tried not to look at her wounds, but it was hard. He must have beaten her with a blunt object or something. I asked her if she needed medical attention, and she said no. I knew that was the end of that discussion. The first day of interviews followed the regular protocol. I took my time with the questions. Her answers were short in the beginning, but she warmed up quickly. Refugees usually do. It's often the case that it's hard to get them started but once they do, they want to tell their full story, like to get it off their chest. The stories are always the same and you need to keep being an active listener which is a bit tricky as the interpreter often dehumanises the content a bit. Also with the delay, you need to choose your points, themes, and narrative, as well as which battles to fight to keep the conversation flowing.

As we were wrapping up for the day, it was as if she didn't want to stop talking. I reassured her that we would be back tomorrow. She knew that it meant a night of some relative peace. I handed out some candy bars to the kids' great joy. As we left the interpreter said, 'I think I know where we can find the Imam.'

'What?' I replied.

She pointed to the food tent; he was having tea. The Imam was a scared and suspicious man, he did not like NGOs, but he needed to be friends with them as his existence hinged on their collaboration. He greeted us in an overly friendly way, like people who have a lot to hide often do. I assumed he didn't know that I knew all his secrets, well maybe I did not know all of them, but enough to have him extradited to the US.

I got straight to the point, 'Do you know Aaden? 50 metres down on the left with four kids and a cousin.'

'Yes, yes, I do, very nice couple,' and he smiled.

It creeped me out, his statement about the couple thing. I said, 'We are doing the last day of health interviews tomorrow and the cousin asked to spend some time with you?' He knew it was a game, that we were trying to protect her from being beaten, and he also knew he had to play along. I supposed that he didn't know that my real intentions were more complicated than that. But the NGO "compassion card" was working well. After all he was used to that, and it was a common reaction of Westerners.

'Yes, I have been trying to make time to see him, I am free tomorrow,' he said with a very forced smile. I had to hide my 'no shit' reaction and thanked him with a handshake.

As we were leaving the camp, the interpreter said, 'Why are you doing all of this? You know it doesn't help right?'

'If we can help just one person for one minute it's all worth it.' I didn't believe that myself, but I sounded like a real humanitarian, I was just about to hook and exploit this woman for 'the greater good.'

Back at the base we had a run in with Jacque and presented our cases. Jacque didn't look impressed, 'You are putting all your eggs in one basket with Aaden. She hasn't given you anything and does she even have any value?'

'I have a good feeling about her, she has a lot of hatred on the inside, and protecting her children her driving force. I think she will work hard with the right motivation.'

Jacque smirked, 'Well it's your call, I think it's a waste of time, but we will see.'

Mr A was trying his luck with a lone young adult, he was playing the 'sympathy for the cause' card. I never liked that approach as it is a double-edged sword and hard to make believable. I mean honestly, 'How many Westerners will just randomly sympathise with their cause and not even being Muslim?' Anyway, he chose the approach, and he would learn from it.

It was the last day of interviews and Aaden talked like she never wanted it to end. I was tired of filling out forms with a life story that probably would end up in the trash, maybe Jacque was right, and she was a waste of time. I still needed to make my move, I felt more like I had been the listener and that we were lacking the connection one needs. I had won the kids over though, but that was the easier part as kids can be bribed with smiles, attention, and small gifts.

I said, 'We are doing a long-term research programme about refugees' health when granted asylum and reunited with parts of their family in their destination country.'

The interpreter looked at me before translating 'Is this a new programme?'

'Yes, it's a new focus group that will be run over 5 to 10 years to see the effects of assimilation in a new country with or without family members that are already assimilated.'

'Ahh yes, I have heard about that.'

'You haven't,' I thought, 'Because I just made it up.' I continued, 'And my records says that you have family members in France, right?' This was the make it or break it moment; if she accepted this, she was onboard. She looked at me and looked at the interpreter, I needed to help her on her way. As I said, 'Our records have it that you have family in France and that you will qualify for the programme if you want to participate? It would mean that you would have expedited asylum, but you must agree to six follow up interviews a year, all confidential of course.'

Aaden looked at me while the interpreter was speaking. She didn't really listen, she was assessing my lie and considering whether to take the offer, and if I had good intentions?

She hesitated for what seemed like an eternity, I kept my casual and charming smile up front. Aaden finally nodded and said, 'Yes, we have family in France, and we would like to be in the programme.' Her eyes were focused, and she stared right through me.

I replied, 'Great, I will set up the paperwork and clear it with your cousin and the Imam. We will get back to you next week, okay?' She only nodded her reply. I had her, she put herself at risk for something unknown. She knew that something would be asked of her at some point, but she would rather take that risk than stay there. It was cruel of us as she didn't know that she would have been given asylum anyway, but that was my secret, and my burden.

That weekend I prepared her case file. I would see her one last time to hand over the papers then she would be handled by the DGSE. She was on board; the Imam was excited to get the cousin out and she would be around to listen in on those two and take the temperature on the situation. At least that is what I hoped would happen. There was always the risk that a source could become useless, a dud.

Jacque passed my desk and after reading my draft report, said, 'Maybe I was wrong, she could be useful' and patted me on the back again. I was counting, because there was a lot of back patting here, it felt confusing, but I knew it was a sign of approval.

I saw Aaden one last time when I handed over her asylum papers, she smiled and her boys were excited, even the cousin gave me the nod of approval. 'I will hand you over to my colleagues who run the programme and they will help you get sorted, and take care of yourself from now on okay? Do you have any more questions for me right now?' Aaden hesitated and then took my hand and said, 'Thank you,' as she smiled from the heart. I knew then that she was in, no matter the cost. She was recruited. From there we parted ways and I returned to France; I never saw her again – this was the intelligence game. I heard a few years later that she had been playing her part in exposing Al Shabab warriors training as foreign fighters for Al Qaeda and taking down a few recruiters.

We were leaving France; it had been an intense but very rewarding time. The team and I gained immense experience, and we also made some mistakes. Overall, it was a success, and we came out stronger and more confident. We were starting to become a force to be reckoned with, but it came with a high price tag.

8

The Force Research Unit

'Lessons Learned is about attitude and not so much about making technical changes… It's about understanding the problem, the enemy and the objective and then being able to pivot and respond to achieve a better result.'

'You idiots would all be dead by now!'

It was Alan, our liaison in the Force Research Unit. We had just arrived, and we were puzzled. He carried on, 'Not looking and behaving like a grunt is not an on or off kind of thing, it's a lifestyle, you all look like operators trying really hard not to look like operators. It will get you killed!'

I looked around and I honestly thought we pulled it off, the hair, the beards, the civilian outfits. As if he heard my thoughts, Alan went on, 'It's not the look, it's the attitude, you exert an energy like you don't belong here, you look like damned US Secret Service being all vigilant like that. You need to be receptive without being Hawkeyes, just absorb the environment and become immersed in it. You may miss out on some details, but it will keep you alive.'

He knew what he was talking about, as he had commanded several intelligence units in Northern Ireland during 'The Troubles.' They had gained considerable experience and found creative tactical solutions to almost impossible challenges – everything aside from the political, but let's leave that for someone else. Much of his unit's success had come with a heavy price. We were told about a time when two FRU operatives took a wrong turn and ended up in a catholic funeral procession. They didn't live to tell the story. We were there, learning from an experienced operative, to stand a better chance of not ending up like that.

We were in for a roller coaster ride with the FRU. Most of us had of course heard of them in connection with their operations in Northern Ireland and their role as an intelligence provider. What we didn't know was the training

116

that we were in for. We were fresh out from advanced HUMINT training with DGSE, but this would add another layer.

The training requested by our commanders was with a specific mission in mind, one where the Brits were second to none. The British training style was more hands-on, or some would say that robust would be a more accurate description. In contrast to the cultural stereotype that Brits are polite and skirt around an issue, their military culture is different.

To be fair, with this level of training everything was direct, and a lot of the nonsense was cut out – for those who experienced training with the Brits, especially those from another nation – they will understand. It's like they take the fancy out of it. When you enter the upper tiers of military or intelligence training it sometimes has that aura of being better than other units, don't get me wrong most SF units are very humble. It's just those subtle moments of rubbing each other's backs that bother me from time to time. The British, like the Swedes, cut a lot of that out, with the difference that the Brits have even more experience to back up their humility.

We were housed in barracks in Bulford, it looked like an operational base – a base within the base all fenced up and covered in mesh to avoid curious eyes. After a short introduction we were told to get ready. They didn't mess around with time here – that was made clear. As we assembled in the briefing room in our civvies the instructor checked each and every one of us from top to bottom. 'You all look like regular geezers with no money, good, good.' I thought finally some approval for our civilian gear. 'The problem though,' he continued is that bums don't wear £350 Sterling tactical shoes…. you are all dead. Take your bloody shoes off!'

He walked around and collected all of our shoes and threw a box of used trainers on the floor. 'Staying alive and being comfortable are two different things entirely, remember you are not on a forward operation base now lads, combat is not your main job, keeping a low profile is, innit.'

He was right; and that kind of shows what HUMINT is all about… details. If it wasn't for the details, anyone could do it. When we had our new-old trainers on, we got a short briefing. We were going out on a navigation and reporting exercise. Aside from the left-hand side driving it felt simple enough. We were divided into pairs and got assigned a civilian car and handed a map and a radio. We were told that the cars were ready to go.

I walked out with Mr A, who was going to drive while I navigated and handled the radio. I said, 'it feels like a familiarisation exercise, I don't trust these fuckers.'

Mr A said, 'They definitely have something in store for us.'

It started smoothly, and we had no problems for the first hour, then the map started to deviate from the beaten path. It was not uncommon so there were no red flags. However, it was a reminder that we had to start paying attention, especially as we were passing through a scruffy neighbourhood. All of a sudden, the car started jerking but we managed to keep driving. I looked at Mr A and he shrugged his shoulders. Two minutes later it happened again and then again until the engine died. As Mr A pulled to the side I check the gas gauge, and it was almost full. We tried to restart it a few times and Mr A said, 'No fuel is getting to the engine.'

'Damn,' I thought, this was embarrassing. I told him to open the bonnet. Everything looked okay at a quick glance. I closed the bonnet and crawled under the car. I tapped the bottom of the fuel tank; it was as dry as the desert. The gauge wasn't working, we were out of fuel.

A car had stopped in front of us and a pretty mean looking crew stepped out, 'Problems lads? We haven't seen you here before,' the taller guy said as he walked towards us.

I remembered a larger town indicated on the map about 20 minutes north from our position. 'Yeah, we were on our way back to Northbrook, we were out test driving as my friend here isn't really familiar with the left-hand side of things, and I think our fuel gauge is broken.'

Mr A got out of the car and closed his door, it was clear they were up to no good. I stood behind my door, used my foot to move the radio and map under the seat. I then swept my hand past my Glock, tucked into the back of my trousers, to make sure my shirt wasn't stuck on it. I moved back to keep them in front of me, they discreetly peeked in the car like they were looking for something.

'Where did you say you lads were from?' the tall guy asked.

'We didn't,' I replied, 'But we are from Norway; we are here for the music festival. Do you think you can give us a hand getting back to Northbrook?' I tried to break the tension. I smiled and looked to Mr A, 'Pop the hood, these guys are probably better with cars than you and I.' I was ready to draw my Glock and cover Mr A as he went in to pop the bonnet.

Mr A took the lead knowing I would cover him and started talking about what we had checked and not, he looked at the tall guy as he leaned in over the engine. 'What do you think?'

'It sounds like you are out of fuel' he replied quickly. He nodded to the man who had driven their car, 'Check the trunk I think we got a can.' He came back with a red petrol can, 'Found it!' he said upbeat. Their driver refuelled our car. The tall guy said, 'Give it a go.'

Mr A glanced at me before he got in, he made sure I had these guys covered in case things got ugly, I was ready.

When he turned the key in the ignition the engine coughed a few times before starting. I reached for my wallet and grabbed two £10 notes handing it to the tall guy. Money in the left and a handshake ready with my right, I smiled and said, 'Thank you for helping out, this could have been embarrassing for us.'

He hesitated, then took the note and shook my hand. 'No worries lads, we weren't in a hurry to get anywhere. Have fun at the Indie music festival' he said in the weirdest of ways. He certainly didn't look like an indie music festival guy, more like a football hooligan.

Before I got in the car again, I made sure Mr A was ready, he had squeezed his 9mm under his right thigh, he was ready. As I got in, I waved and said again, 'Thank you, we couldn't have done it without you.'

He replied, 'Safe travels.' They started walking back to their car.

I said, 'Let's go in the most civilian way possible.' I waved as we drove off. Something must have felt off to those guys, as they stared us down while we left. I said, 'Go straight ahead and take the freeway on ramp and let's find a gas station.'

I took out my notebook and made some quick notes about the encounter, 'Did you get the license plate?'

Mr A nodded, 'I had it almost except for the last number.' As I reported in, we were ordered to return to base.

When we got back, we had a debriefing. Alan pointed at the different teams, 'You are dead. You are dead. You are almost dead. You made it. Almost dead. You made it.' Me and Mr A were in the last team, and I was happy we had made it. 'Alright lads, all in all it was not bad, some of you clowns need to get your cover story straight but the main thing here is don't trust anyone. You trusted me and that's what got you into trouble, you know this at this stage, and you trusted me automatically because I am your instructor. Always check for yourself even if things were prepared by "friends", friends can forget and friends are not always friends, remember that.'

'Who were the team going to the music festival?' I put my hand up. 'You were paying attention, very good, but you don't look like Indie/Folk music people, but what do I know, people are strange these days' he said as he cracked up.

'Lads it will be a busy couple of weeks', Alan continued with giving us the run down on the coming weeks and it was a mix of ISTAR, HUMINT, lessons learned and more honing of our skills. It was all geared towards the British way of working – their style of intelligence led operations. We recognised most of it, but they were more detail oriented than the French and definitely more than the Swedes. Their experiences in Northern Ireland were unique but the impressive part was how they learned from those experiences and developed a new modus operandi and SOPs. Of course, the British had a long history of counter insurgency operations, from their Colonial Empire to twentieth century operations including, the Anglo-Boer War, SAS support in Greece from 1945–1950, and the Malaya counter insurgency campaign to name a few. But this was all ancient history as far as we were concerned. Intelligence, human intelligence operations were a practical matter, and something we didn't do well in Sweden.

Maybe it was our lack of bulk experiences or maybe it was just our attitude. I think it was mostly our attitude – meaning the format was always good according to Military Command, it was always operator error or 'unforeseen events' in their opinion. We knew this would be a weak spot if we did not start to learn new skills and embed them into our military and agencies. Captain K and Captain B always took debriefing seriously and really tried to implement lessons learned. But the problem was always with practical implementation. This would change over these 400 days of training. As the patrols got more detailed and professional, we all developed our own SOPs, but at its core we implemented lessons learned – it was about attitude and not so much about making technical changes, even if that may be the first move, and ultimately the end result. It's about understanding the problem, the enemy and the objective and then being able to pivot and respond to achieve a better result. On a deeper level, lessons learned are about being able to look at an issue from more angles than just your own and your opponent's. It's immersing yourself completely.

Over the weeks we had quality training come our way. Meet ups, drop offs, running established agents, urban and rural operations in a civilian setting, driving... It was intense and all scenarios were built on real events, so we had the added perspective to see how it turned out in reality. We analysed what they did right and what they needed to improve and compared it to our performance – we ultimately learned lessons and plugged them into our training.

Having the privilege to receive training from different countries gives you the opportunity to get different perspectives, from many varied environments and learn about their tactics and approaches. The basics are the same, but the details and quirks are always different. It's a privilege and honour to tap into that as they have all paid in blood to perfect those skills, their detail and approach – it keeps one humble, especially since we paid nothing for it… up to that point anyway.

British training is even more heavy-handed than that of many other countries. They will let you know about it when things go wrong. At the end of our training cycle, we did a civvie-green drop off. It's basically an operation where one hides uniformed military personnel in a civilian environment. It is commonly used when transporting operators to and from operations in a rural setting. For example, a civilian van with plain clothed operators driving it, with uniformed soldiers in the back. It's a sensitive game, since hiding military personnel is never popular anywhere.

We had about a 45 minute drive to the drop off, and it was supposed to end with a green to civvie transition. This means that you carry plain clothing with you so you could start working on the ground in civilian clothing, while uniform would be required at a later stage or vice versa. It could be that after manning an anchor OP during a direct action one would need to put on civvies – sometimes to watch over your own units, or perhaps a concealed withdrawal, but most of the time the reason was to see what happened after. That's usually when local key players emerge out of the woodwork for assessment and damage control.

We had been driving for 15 minutes through an industrial complex. I couldn't see where we were at the time, as I was seated in the back, in the dark, but I knew where we were from the checkpoint reports and by doing my homework – a time and map analysis. The van slowed down and the drivers said, 'It might be trouble ahead, it's a crowd, maybe a demonstration or something.'

A minute later the van was rocking, the vehicle commander gave the order to abandon the vehicle. 'Contact, contact, contact, wait out,' was the driver's final report to HQ as we did a hard reset on the radios in the back. The banging on the van was loud, it felt like they were going to tip it over. We needed to get out and now! I did a quick sweep; the team was ready. Mr A opened the side door and as soon as it was halfway open a heavy wooden chair and four bricks were thrown in. 'Hell! These guys aren't messing around' I thought. I applied some pressure on Mr A's back to help him out. It was a roaring crowd, easily 100 people, shit was flying in from everywhere, and our first objective was to help the drivers as they had less means to defend themselves.

I saw Mr A was bleeding from just above his eye, 'Didn't fancy a helmet on the exit? Are you okay?' I asked.

'I will live,' he groaned as he hit a man in the head with the butt of his rifle.

As we were making our way around the front of the van, under a constant barrage of bricks and garbage, the windshield got smashed; the van and us were getting dented and marked up. I saw the driver being pulled into the crowd. I hesitated for a second, brought my AK up and shot the man dragging our driver. He dropped down in pain when the FX ceramic bullet hit him, and the driver was freed. The remainder of the crowd pulled back and scattered a bit.

We had only a few moments, and I knew we had to use that window – now that we had introduced weapons there was no turning back, and it would almost certainly boomerang. We picked up the driver – he was a bit groggy from being punched in the head. 'Alleyway to the left, GO!' I knew the alley would take us to what was probably a fence at the outer perimeter of the industrial complex, then railroad tracks, and the forest. That was our only option.

As we entered the alley, the crowd started reassembling, we had to move tactically but fast – key to this was to prevent being enveloped from the side at the end of the alley way. We reached the fence and luckily the rusted poles were almost flat on the ground. We put some weight on it and rolled over the minor obstacle. The crowd was charging down the alley and I felt my heart rate accelerate. 'We need to disappear,' I whispered. The railroad tracks gave us a bit of cover and we had about two minutes to disappear into the woods. We made a dash for it and pushed a few metres into the dense forest before taking up defensive positions. I saw a few folks on the railroad tracks, one with a pistol and another with an iron pipe. They scanned the horizon, looking ahead at the bushes and trees, their anger was palpable. 'It was just a matter of time before they would search the forest' I thought. They looked around, some with binoculars. The man who seemed to command the crowd turned to the left and chose not to head directly into the forest. We needed to move quickly and silently – we had good cover and headed in the opposite direction away from our attackers, we needed to go over a mountain to reach one of our ERVs on the other side. We loaded up the driver's backpack on top of one of our own and Mr A took point.

As we reached the top of the mountain, I took my binoculars out and scanned the forest beneath us. I saw the flashlights beaming through the dense vegetation, and they had a few 4x4 pick-up trucks join the search; they drove up and down the forest's dirt roads. I did a quick inventory. 'I hope that nobody lost any kit on the way up,' I thought.

We took a 5 minute break. Before continuing we activated ERV2. We estimated it would take an hour to get there but we had to pass through some obstacles along the way, so we added some additional time. The extraction was planned to be a rolling pick up on a dirt road. We were early and the amount of traffic on the back road worried me. It was at a natural point to slow down, just before a light curve, which gave us about a 5 minute warning.

We were ready and it would be quick and dirty. 'Four…Three…Two…One', I counted as our extraction party rolled up. The side door slid open, and we loaded the heavy guys first as the van slowed to a crawl – Mr A was the last man and he lost momentum as he struggled to grip his feet in the loose soil. Scrambling, he took a few quick steps, regaining some distance and jumping in. 'Unbelievable, not a good showing', he said, when we were all loaded up.

As the side door closed, the driver said 'Lights.' We had a vehicle behind us, he couldn't have seen us loading up; and the van was almost at normal speed by then, so I hoped that they would keep their distance.

'Without rocking the van, one at a time change into civvies,' I said. I made the call as they were obviously looking for military men. The hardest part was always getting the face paint off. It leaves one looking like a hooker. We had one man left in military attire as we approached an intersection. The pick-up behind us was bumper to bumper. We needed to come to a full stop.

'Be still' the vehicle commander said with a low voice. We were not blocked from the front, but we had to wait for a gap in the traffic, to join the next road. From there our next objective was the highway.

As we turned right the pickup was still close behind us. 'Quietly get that last man in civvies,' the vehicle commander said. We all pitched in to get him dressed, and some of the boys maybe enjoyed it a bit too much.

We were just two minutes away from the on ramp to the highway and relative safety when the driver called out 'flares ahead, might be an accident or a checkpoint, stash everything but be ready.' I did a final sweep and inspected the weary faces – we looked decent. 'Guns. Checkpoint,' the commander called out.

We came to a full stop. I was leaning against my bag and had my 9mm tucked in under my thigh.

The driver rolled down his window, the man on the outside said, 'Where are you headed?'

'We are returning to Bulford; we have been working up north. What happened here?' the driver said.

'We had some problems with insurgents earlier today, we are looking for military men, do you have anything in the back?'

'Yeah, I have six workers in the back and some equipment', the driver said.

The guard said, 'I need you to turn off your engine and open up the back.'

We were ready, I counted to at least eight people – we could do it.

The side door slid open, the guard and his colleague both had AK74s. He popped his head in and looked around. We had some farming equipment in the middle of the back area and Mr A and Mr P were "sleeping" with their hats covering their faces.

'It smells terrible in here, let them pass', he shouted, closing the door. I relaxed my grip on my 9mm, as the driver started the van and said, 'Have a good night and hope you catch those insurgents.' I felt maybe we had just made it.

As we came up on the highway I thought, 'Who is cut out for this? Are we? Is anyone?'

Don't get me wrong, I liked it, but I wondered if this was a reasonable line of work for anyone? And this was just an exercise. Immediately I thought about what my life would look like if I did this full time. I needed to stop thinking, get onboard and just roll with the punches. No one ever spoke about the things I was thinking about. I guess the rest were just happy to be here, I should settle for that.

Alan held the debriefing, 'You need to read the situation, you are already in an impossible situation when you need to exit your vehicle.' The man we saw at our 'running out of gas mission' took the floor. He gave it to us straight, 'You did well but you should have made the kill earlier. There is no chance your situation will improve; you need to get space and move. To get space you drop someone. You do it early on, you almost lost your driver there, but you saved it. Pick up was good, you handled the checkpoint well. So, all in all good work, but never assess these situations as a regular riot, get the kill and move.'

We left Bulford with a lot of new experiences; we were tired, bashed up and glad to be on our way. We needed a bit of rest, but we knew that there was no respite, not yet.

9

Evading capture

'We had to explain how four worn out soldiers with frostbite and with their position compromised could manage not only to escape but to create a two-hour gap.'

We had just arrived at Muskö, one of the Navy's main bases on the Swedish east coast, covering the southern part of the Baltic Sea. It's located outside Stockholm close to Nynäshamn. The base has always been one of the more secretive ones in the Swedish armed forces. The main reason for this was that it houses the bulk of the submarine fleet in a bunker port constructed in the mountain. This allows the submarines to pass in and out without ever surfacing. The security is intense, and all personnel are heavily screened. It's the only Swedish military base that has scent dogs on guard to detect divers. They are positioned alone so their sense of smell is not distorted by their handler's scent. On a system of small piers, the lone hounds stand guard, and are equipped with microphones so barks can be detected by the command centre.

We had landed with a C-130 at the closest airport, Skavsta, just south of Stockholm. It's a sleepy airport with a low volume of commercial air traffic – this meant we avoided any unnecessary attention. We loaded our equipment on military trucks parked close by. At that point we hadn't been briefed on the mission, just that we were going to use Muskö as a forward operating base. It was October and we came from the snowy and relatively cold weather in Arvidsjaur, to more cold and rain – the worst combination with soaking wet days and freezing nights.

As we approached the Muskö base we passed the main entrance, passing through a side gate that led directly to the harbour. Two guards removed the heavy chains around the gates and pushed them open. We rolled straight in to one of the most secretive bases in Sweden, no questions asked.

Down at the docks we stopped outside a shabby looking "schoolhouse". It was a wooden building with traces of aged charm. It appeared to be unused, and a bit run down. It was used up until the 1970s to train navy telegraphists. It had a big hall in the middle like an indoor sports court that was previously used to practice setting up different types of antennas.

This was our FOB. As we offloaded our equipment, we felt the cold wet wind from the sea. We knew whatever they had in store for us was sure as hell going to be cold. Each of the four patrols claimed one corner of the hall and the support squad installed themselves upstairs as they set up a communications centre.

Mr F grunted and looked disappointed as he carried the radio equipment upstairs. He said, 'What the fuck, I signed up for cool stuff not for radio shit.'

'So, you would rather man the checkout at the local supermarket instead?' I replied with a smile.

'No, but still,' he whined as he worked his way up the stairs.

As an RTO one of my duties over the full mission cycle was to handle equipment. Having extremely detailed inventory lists of every single item we had with us and on us, and bringing a copy with me in the field was essential to keep control of and facilitate our handovers. Every item that every member of the patrol carried, I had on a list, even the tiniest piece of candy. This was because after the mission and during the debriefing one of the RTO duties was to inspect that every piece was accounted for. The key principle here was that we leave no trace, which included empty candy wrappers.

So, before a mission it was always hectic. I needed to prepare, not only the communications, but all the squad equipment needed for the task; and then inspect everyone else's equipment. Like a mini-QM, and it comes with waking up first and going to bed last. In our mission planning area, in this case our corner, every piece of personal and squad equipment was organised in a special pattern, so it was easier for me to get an overview and check it off the list. I was also present when the patrol leader received the initial order so I could start arranging any special equipment needed.

All the commanders and RTOs were present at the briefing. Terrorists had taken over the small military island of Utö, about 40 minutes by boat from our FOB at Muskö. I looked at Lieutenant C, who had replaced Lieutenant W while rolling my eyes, 'Loads of terrorists hanging around Sweden these days apparently', Lieutenant C said with a smirk.

Captain K presented the target pack, 'The enemy is a platoon size SF-like unit, with dogs and access to helicopters and they are supported by a regular army recon platoon. The island only has a few roads, but they have access to military vehicles. They have taken over an old navy base. It is littered with tunnels and bunkers.'

'Wow that's a shit ton of people on that tiny island,' I thought. I knew this would require 'Hard Routine',[1] not optimal with this weather.

All patrols were going to be inserted at the same time on the most eastern point of the island, supposedly unprotected due to the very rocky beach. From there the teams would split up. The CB90, combat boat, commander and his skipper were called forward. They were both assigned to us from the Amphibious Corps. The commander pulled out a sea chart and showed us the route, breakaway points, and the point of no return. They pointed at a photo of the landing spot, it was just a pile of rocks, and it looked impossible to land there. The skipper explained, 'This is the only part that is deep enough for us, and you have to do a ballerina exit, quick and smooth as we will only be able to push and hold the boat against the rocks for 60 to 90 seconds and it will be wobbly.'

'Great,' I thought. Wet rocks, heavy backpacks, and a wobbly boat, sprinkled with little time would guarantee an epic start to this mission. I could visualise half of us in the water before it was done. The boat would leave at 03:00 the next morning, which meant that we had roughly 12 hours.

After the briefing, Lieutenant C and I lingered, looking at the charts and talking with the boat crew. 'How wobbly is wobbly,' asked Lieutenant C.

'Well, the forecast looks shitty, half storm and raining, and it's an exposed position. We will take most of it from the side. If we can't hold her for long, we will need to go back out and reload for every group, but we will see when we get there. I am glad I am not you at least', said the skipper with a firm look.

We looked at the map, and the infiltration would be simple if all went according to plan. Two patrols were to follow the northern route and two would pursue the western approach. We would take the western route, the island had little cover and there were very few routes into the forested area. The key to the plan was that we needed to move quickly and find a layup point before the graveyard shift ended. The plan was to layup during the day and do careful mobile work during the night. There was no other good way to do

---

1   Hard routine is usually executed by special operation forces, infiltrating, and remaining concealed close to the enemy – without cooking, external heat sources, smoking and with one cold meal a day. Also, extra clothing is kept to a minimum and sleeping bags are shared.

it – at least that was our initial thought. Maybe we could manage to find an observation post for the day. There was no water on the island, so we needed to carry a 14 day water supply with us. Lieutenant C looked at me, 'It will be a heavy infiltration. Cut everything unnecessary, we need to go super Hard Routine on this one. Can we ditch any comms equipment?'

'Yeah, we can ditch the HF and just bring a handheld VHF for the boat and then the laptop and SATCOM plus the car battery of course; always the car battery.'

The weakly framed skipper showed up on the ramp of the combat boat in his woolly hat. He looked bothered by having to leave the cosy warmth of the boat. 'Let me help you with that' he said as he lifted one of the Bergens from the ground. He dropped it before it got to the boat. 'I can't even move that! You have to load it yourself.' We were going in really heavy, mostly because of the water requirement. The Bergens were steel framed but when we go heavy, I always bring some truck cargo straps to use, if the textile part can't bear the load and rips away from the frame. If that happens one must be on the ball and force the sack back onto the frame and think about the repairs later.

As we left the harbour, we could feel the wind taking a hold of the boat. At 22 m/s, we thought it was rough, but the skipper assured us, 'It could be worse.' Our equipment was tightly secured in the middle under the deck of the CB90, and we sat along the sides on what reminded me of racing car bucket seats. When we left the harbour area the skipper turned off all internal and external lighting except for a tiny red light for reading the charts and a small red light down below where we were sitting. The skipper popped down and did a round to make sure everyone was securely fastened, he said, 'We are going dark and tactical now so hold on to your pants. If you need to puke, everyone has a plastic bag in between their seats on their right-hand side, I will give you a 10 minute warning when we are approaching… good luck gentlemen.'

'Good luck is never a good sign,' I thought.

Tactical in the Navy world has another meaning and includes darkness, high speeds, and sharp turns. We were doing 40 knots in the pitch dark, on an October night in a storm in a notoriously hard to navigate archipelago. You could hear the roaring sound of the water jets and the mechanical sounding commands from the commander, who was navigating, to the skipper. It was clear that they had done this before or at least I hoped so. The turns were razor sharp and precise and they were navigating by watch, similar to submariners. It was not as bumpy as I imagined, more like a roller coaster ride with many swift direction changes. Nobody was prone to sea sickness, but I could feel that we were not far away from someone throwing up. The skipper showed his clinched fist and shouted, '10 minutes.' I looked around and most looked happy that we were getting off soon. At 5 minutes the commander came down and started to make preparations for a quick exit. The boat was still rushing through the water, although at this point, with fewer turns. The commander called out, '2 minutes.'

The boat was not slowing down and just then it felt like the crazy amphibious folks were planning to ram the island. Just then the commander called out, 'Brace, brace, brace.' I clinched my seat with both hands, as the boat shot up, and made a manoeuvre similar to a nosedive. I felt extreme pressure on my arms and legs, as I tried with everything I had to hold on. I never did a crash stop before. The boat slowed down and it was like feeling the reverse thrust of a jet plane when landing, and then gently bumped against the rocks. We heard the engines revving to keep the boat firmly pushed against the rocks. We all got up and tried to get our backpacks on as best we could. I felt the weight on my knees. I hoped the rocks were going to be better than they looked in the picture. 'Ramp', the skipper said, and the commander lowered the ramp. 'Clear exit, clear exit. Go, go, go.' They wanted us off the boat as quickly as possible, they were exposed here and didn't want to make another approach.

I was surprised how well the ramp covered the worst part of the rocks; it was not that bad. The air was fresh and cold. No rain in sight, maybe our luck had turned. We formed a firing line to cover the boat while it departed. Then it was all quiet, and all we could hear was the wind coming from the west. I looked through my night vision goggles and saw no movement.

All Bergens were taken off. One doesn't kneel with a 60 kilogram Bergen on a rocky surface. We covered the two patrols that were taking the northern route. When we saw that they had taken up defensive positions in the tree line it was our turn. I wiggled up my Bergen to get one arm into the shoulder strap. While halfway standing I heard a snapping sound, and I could no longer feel the weight of my Bergen; it had detached from the frame. To make matters worse, the rest of the patrol had already reached the tree line. I tried to lift it from the ground, but I couldn't carry it in my hands. I needed to get out of this exposed position and to cover. Mr K spotted me having problems and quickly returned to help without his Bergen. When he arrived, I had already managed to lash the sack to the frame with the truck straps. He helped me to get it on my back. We needed to hustle.

At the tree line Lieutenant C whispered, 'It's that damn car battery, we need reinforced gear, can you fix it in 5 minutes?'

'Yes,' I had the whole group's supply of zip ties as well and managed to strap it back into its original position, I just hoped it was going to hold. The upside was that the extraction would be much easier. As we headed off west, I could feel the zip ties flexing a bit, but they were holding up. The moon was up, and the sky was clear. We had an hour ahead of us before we reached our layup area. Even if we had a rocky start, I had a solid feeling, I think it was mostly that there was no rain, but that was about to change. We reached our layup at 05:00 in the morning. The rain had started to pour down. We had our new Gore-Tex jackets which were still performing well in the rain. The only catch was that they were loud, like rustling loud – it was something to do with the material.

We were late to our layup as we detected a few static guard posts along the way. They were "loud", so we heard them far ahead and easily avoided them. In evading the guards, we needed to pass across a road and that was time consuming. We quickly realised that the days were very much going to be about laying low. The layup was far from optimal – it was in a valley formation of rock ridges, with dense vegetation and no protection from the rain. We just had a few hours before first light checks. I could hear a helicopter in the distance, although it quickly became clear that the helicopter was not looking for us and we saw it landing in the direction of the main "enemy base".

We managed to surprise ourselves with a very minimalistic patrol base. The reason for this was that when I performed the first light checks I couldn't see, or even begin to fathom that people were inside that part of the bushy tree. The type of terrain made it impossible, but this was not our first rodeo. We had managed to crawl under a very small tree that was hiding a large hole underneath its branches. Our set up was two standing at all times and two laying in a circle formation at the bottom. The only worries now were the dogs. We deployed solid counter measures on the way in but if they walked straight over the patrol base it would be very difficult to hide. But it would have been a gruesome task for a K9 unit to make their way down to our position.

It had been seven days; it was just after midnight, and I was about to move out to do another wide goose egg around the base.[2] 'Hopefully get some pictures too,' I thought. I was going with the 2iC. We looked at each other, as it was really not a good night. For seven days straight it had been raining and for seven nights it had been freezing. Around minus 20 degrees Celsius, which

2   A goose egg is a defined area on a map that might or might not have good places for an OP or temporary reconnaissance mission.

is extreme for the season and location, but the worst part was the combination of rain during the day and low temperatures at night which don't make for an optimal mix. The Gore-Tex uniforms were not good in that type of weather and the hard routine wore us down.

When doing hard routine in a small place like that, there are no extras, hardly any clothes, just one change of socks and one shirt, one or two sleeping bags total for the patrol, no stoves and one cold meal per person per day. We always kept a few very sugary energy bars for combat or extraction though. The poop bags and the filled piss bottles transferred a weird smell to your Bergen, even when they are properly sealed. And then sitting 30cm from a guy trying to fill a piss bottle in the dark without washing for seven days and maybe helping him wipe his ass or hold the poop bag doesn't help. These are also valid points for you to think about if you are ever considering joining an intelligence or reconnaissance unit. There is nothing more hardcore when it comes to sacrifice. No blazing guns, no parades, just first in, last out – never to be seen or noticed. Most units that are in the same mission often don't know that you were there, and even the medals are handed out separately... we do our duty though and for many it keeps them alive. I know you all want to hear more about the comforts of manning a small OP and I will tell you all about that in Appendix A.

We needed good pictures that night. We had some decent snaps from the previous week, but they were limited. Most of our intelligence were either written or sketches, since we had a hard time getting good angles to identify any of the players on the ground. At that stage we could tell that the enemy had a range of equipment including two helicopters with thermal capacity, two combat boats, and an assortment of vehicles ranging from jeeps, quads and 6x6s. As for personnel they had a National Guard Recon platoon, forty-five operators from the police National Anti-Terrorist Unit (NI), and five K9 units. They were clearly tasked with tracking us down as they used their assets day and night to look for us. We had a few close calls but being on a windy island, the drafts often kept our scent out of the sniffers' noses.

With the sheer number of people moving around and looking for us, every-thing had to be done in slow motion. It drained our energy, and the situation was made worse by the freezing temperatures and our one meal a day. That night, we were lucky, and we managed to get good pictures of the helicop-ters and their equipment as they were grounded, probably due to the weather. Our way back up the hill to our observation post was much slower, especially because the recon platoon was firing illumination flares all night. They weren't close, but they obviously knew that we would be doing our recon work at night, and probably just wanted to try and put some pressure on us, hoping we would slip up.

As we approached the end of the second week, we were all in rough shape with first-degree frost bite on our fingers and toes I am ashamed to say. Despite being arctic rangers and familiar with handling cold and wet conditions, we weren't immune to the extremes. We got trench-like frostbite. We managed to recover quickly but I can still to this day feel the nerve damage when it gets nippy outside. We were too competitive or stupid to let that hinder us and we continued to deliver the best results towards the end of the second week. We all felt pretty good that we had survived and remained undetected for two weeks despite the enemy's pressure and resources. The time had come for our extraction, and it was about a two and a half hour operation that would take us to a remote point on the western shores of the island where we would be picked up by boat.

We were in high spirits and ready to leave this God forsaken island. Before we moved out from our patrol base and headed for the extraction route we reported in our position. We later learned that our HQ passed this on to the 'enemy.' As they had been unable to find us, they needed to get their victory. We had just passed a small clearing as the last man in the patrol signalled dogs, they were on our trail, but we were undetected so far.

Our point man took up position and prepared to engage the 'enemy' patrol from the front while the rest of us were lined up on the left side of our trail. We almost had the first of the two patrols moving past us. The point man engaged with a full magazine from the front, and we immediately started a peel off heading in their direction. We moved quickly and as we were used to fighting with the NVGs, we soon passed the second patrol, with coordinated fire and movement, laying down massive amounts of lead in their direction. I could see how surprised they were, and they failed to grasp that we were moving towards them. Shortly after we passed the second patrol, we broke contact. As after violence comes silence. We moved quickly as we were lighter at that point than on our way in with most of the water already used. We managed to create a small gap, but our time was limited as every asset on that island was surely active and out to get us. We did some false trailing on our way. We could only pray that it would work as we needed that gap to grow significantly for us to survive this. The pressure was on, and we saw vehicles roving the roads and the helicopters were getting airborne.

We had more than two hours until our pickup; and had to do something drastic. We regrouped in a ditch, trying to figure out our next moves. In the distance we could hear the dogs barking. Lieutenant C looked at me and whispered a one-word question, 'Road?' I nodded. Road was our only option now. We had a small road leading out to the point where the pickup was going to be, we needed to find a gap between the vehicle borne patrols so we could use the road for speed. The hard surface also helps with the dogs as it's easier to break the chain of your scent. We sent one-man false trailing in the direction of what the 'enemy' might have considered a more probable pick-up point. It was a big risk, but we had no other option. After 30 minutes we passed the small causeway that led to the extraction point. It was just rock, no vegetation but at least the rocks could provide good cover. There was a small fishing shed close by and we left a man behind it, and set up two, four minute timed smoke grenades. His job was to pull the pins when he saw the enemy approaching and it would give us a good opportunity to hold the point for a while. It all hinged on the size of the gap between us and the 'enemy'.

As our former elite cross-country skier Mr A joined us after false trailing up and down a number of hills and back again, we still had about two hours before our pickup. As the RTO I took up a position furthest out on the point close to the water and got all the Bergens and gear ready to go. I had good cover, and my role was to prepare the VHF and to lead the boat in with infrared Cyalume sticks. Everyone was on a hundred and ten percent alert as the time ticked on. We expected contact at any second. One hour and 55 minutes later the VHF crackled, 'Bravo 2 Bravo 2, this is Seagull. Inbound 5 minutes. Standby, Out.' I managed to crack out a smile as I signalled to the others "5 minutes". I couldn't believe it. I reached for my pocket to take out the IR Cyalume light sticks as I heard the hissing sound of smoke. I looked towards the shed; I saw Lieutenant C pulling back under the cover of smoke. 'Two patrols down the road,' he said as he slid into cover. The smoke was perfect and covered the road entirely. No shots were fired at that point, and it soon became evident that the trailing patrols were waiting out the smoke. They surely thought they had the upper hand for the breach. If they knew the boat was less than two minutes out, perhaps they would have made a different calculation. We pulled the rest of the patrol down to my location with the LMG gunner holding the top eagerly waiting for the smoke to clear.

I saw the dark boat speeding towards our position through my NVG. We did an ID exchange with IR Cyalumes, and it checked out. I gave the PTT on the VHF a tap, 'Hostile inbound 12 clock shed.' I didn't have any more time, as I got ready to fight. I took one of my IRs and put it on the LMG gunner's rig near his neck as he held the highest position; in the hopes that the boat gunner could use it as reference.

The smoke had outperformed any expectations by far but eventually started to fade out. The boat was probably 30 seconds away, when we saw shadows moving behind the smoke, the LMG gunner opened up with a few solid bursts. I reported on the VHF, 'Contact, contact, contact, 12 o'clock IR friendly.' I got a PTT tap back as confirmation. While the Minimi hammered away the combat boat did a crash stop just 20 metres from the edge of the point we were at, and as the ramp hit the rocks, we heard the .50 on the boat starting to pound down the road. A deafening wall of sound. The commander stood on the ramp waving us in, and I was the first in with the task of receiving gear. In less than 20 seconds the LMG gunner was with us on the boat, and we started back out in the dark waters to the sound of the hammering .50.

We helped the commander secure the gear. He shouted, 'Get strapped in.' He did a quick round to see that we were properly strapped in. 'Hang on we are taking *låset*,' (*låset* is Swedish for a lock or a padlock). We didn't know what the *låset* route was, but we soon learned that it is a very dangerous passage – even during daytime, due to the rocky shallow waters. It required precision even under optimal conditions. Nighttime, dark, and high speed was probably less than ideal. We needed to keep our speed up while exiting the area. The helicopters were a threat, but our biggest worry was the other combat boats. We couldn't allow them to even see a shadow of our trail.

The ride in was a breeze compared to the way out. One could pick up the focus in the communication and the intense relationship between the skipper and the commander. When we moored at our home base there were a few back pats between us and the boat crew. They were true professionals. And we got away intact, almost. The smell in that hall has been described to me as the 'most horrible ever.' Of course, the members of the support squad who hadn't been out in the field for two weeks, had an entirely different experience. A patrol in bad shape rolling in smelling like ammonia and dead dog, was a small price to pay for a victory. Fortunately, one cannot smell it yourself.

I managed to get the patrol through a complete inventory before the debriefing; the showers had to wait as the debriefing took priority. We were still amped from the ride home and we had coffee and fruit waiting for us during the debriefing so we wouldn't dip. We were the last patrol to be pulled off the island. 'Typical,' I thought, 'Always the last out.' We all felt good though. The debriefing went well, and we displayed solid intelligence, good visual material, and sketches. Hitting the showers and getting a dry pair of underwear was even better than the hot meal. I had a hard time sleeping that night – riding the wave of adrenaline, it felt like something good had happened. The morning after as we were packing up and preparing to leave for the airport, Lieutenant C came to our corner, 'Are we ready to go?' 'Yes, but we aren't leaving until lunch, right?' I replied. He said, 'There have been a few changes. Load the gear on the bus and bring everything, meet me outside in 5 minutes.'

We looked at each other, 'What now! We've had enough fun for a while,' I thought. There was a blue military minibus waiting for us outside. The QM was driving, and he said laughingly, 'So you get to meet the big boys, not too shabby.'

We were briefed in the bus that we were heading to the NI Police HQ. They had requested a personal debriefing from our patrol, to explain how four worn out soldiers with frostbite, and a compromised position could manage not only to escape but also to create a two-hour gap from six of the best K9 units in Sweden, two helicopters and about 100 soldiers and specialised police officers looking for them – all on a few square kilometres. I can't share the details of that particular meeting as the NDA is still in effect, but I can say that it worried them a lot as this was Sweden's finest hunting us. They were after all the people who were doing this day in and day out. We had a solid exchange of experiences, and we also got a letter of appreciation from the head of the NI.

Appendix A

On the subject of the comforts of manning a small OP, it would be negligent of me not to tell you about the queen of all OPs. So, what kinds of OPs do we have? Or rather what is an OP in general terms? An OP is an Observation Post that is either static or temporary. It doesn't have to be hidden; it can be a watchtower, a bunker, on a roof or that guy standing guard under a pine tree watching the perimeter of an Infantry base. But in the case of recon and intelligence units they are always temporary. Even if they sometimes last a long time – like years, they are always hidden, even if that is in plain sight (hidden purpose) and there is never a trace left that could indicate what happened there. Most of the time the physical protection lies in camouflage, not in sandbags or *hescos*.

So, with that in mind OPs are usually roughly divided into rural and urban which is self-explanatory. There are some specialty variants of rural OPs but it's basically just different designations of the same thing. In the urban environment we have a few more options, we have the basic constructed or non-constructed OP. The non-constructed one might be a roof top that has a good hole in the wall and doesn't require any materials to be added as you can just pull out your binoculars or camera and lay flat on the ground. The constructed one, often an apartment that needs modification and you may have to bring your building materials in with you. Then we have mobile OPs in vehicles, on foot or just a person having a coffee at a very convenient location.

So how does one build an OP? There are as many ways as you wish, and it is only limited by one's imagination – but we have a few basic techniques. In a rural setting it always depends on the season, where you are and the tactical situation. You often use camouflage nets of various sizes and panels made of canvas and steel nets that are easy to paint – these assist in getting the right colour and texture. An option is to bring along aluminium or wooden poles that are flexible which allows one to make shapes. A lot of this is done in the prep work, by analysing photos from the area, and familiarising oneself with the type of forest or surroundings. It's natural to want to keep the OP as small as possible as it's harder to make a big area look natural. OPs can look very different for example at the rocky coastline you might add a few metres on a rock formation, here texture and colour match are extremely important. You should be able to walk straight past an OP without knowing it is there, sometimes even stand on top of it. So, it's not just throwing up a net like hiding a navy boat or a tank, it's an art form. Everything you need must be carried in

– you shouldn't within reason disturb the local environment, and everything must be carried out.

To build an urban OP is far more complicated and they are a bitch to work in, that's why they are the queens of all OPs, I'll explain why.

First of all, you have to man it and in order to do that you and your team have to look the part, you can't waltz in looking like typical military guys in their Arc'teryx clothing and Suunto watches, you will be blown in a millisecond. Think about it, how would you get to an OP with four Swedish looking military guys in downtown Kabul, suburban Belgrade, a Damascus apartment complex or in the poor parts of Brooklyn, New York? It's hard; people are usually vigilant and know who belongs and who doesn't. You need a reason to move around there. And how do you even acquire a location? In the forest it's easy. But in the urban environment you need to rely heavily on other people. In some cases, the government agency owns or operates the building that you are working from; it could also come complete with a running business as a front often with a convenient place to unload gear and people, like a garage or a car repair shop. But most of the time you rely on the assets you are running, helpers, traitors, people under duress, where your government holds their family hostage – they open their homes for you. There are several motivations: gold diggers do it for money, others for ideological reasons and so on. There are many options, but they all rely on one trusting your asset that might or might not be onboard, it usually depends on how afraid they are. But in general, they are understandably very unreliable people. They might be handled by your team, by another team or even a different or foreign agency. Are you starting to see the many moving parts yet? Good because there is more beauty to it.

When you have trusted the un-trustable, made your way through urban enemy territory and are entering your lovely apartment it is "all cookies and milk right?" Sleeping in soft beds, running the AC in the summer, using the toilet... No nothing like that because no one can know that you are there. Usually in an apartment OP you have a window that you are going to look out from. To hide yourself one often constructs the OP on the wall opposite to the window or if it's a large apartment, on the side wall, so you can look out of the window sideways. To hide, you need to create an illusion; you must move the wall forward. That is done by putting up a canvas mesh from floor to ceiling that is the same colour as the wall or alternatively a dark colour. The new improvised wall should be about one shoulder width away from the real wall. It is done with collapsible wood poles or telescopic metal ones. Any furniture or paintings need to be moved in front of the fake wall, so one of the first things you do when you enter the apartment is to sketch up where everything is, measure where everything is, take pictures and mark everything you move with non-residue tape. And behind the new shoulder wide wall is where you operate, sleep, eat, poop and all of those things. You can't run the water, you can't use the heating, crack a window open, you need to move around like a ninja in your soft slippers. You can just imagine the smell on a hot summer day after a week or two like that. Like manning any OP your body hurts by being in weird positions all the time and with an urban OP it is even more accentuated, because there is no space to really stretch out to one's full length. And despite this, within the limited space one must do stretching exercises every day to prevent becoming as stiff as a plank. For these reasons urban Ops, in my humble opinion, are far more exhausting to man than rural ones.

You also have the vehicle OPs, usually made in a blacked out back portion of a van with reinforced suspension so it remains stiff. It can be very uncomfortable, but they are usually very temporary, you park them, the driver runs some errands; and upon their return they drive away. They require a lot of focus with your movement – and vehicles for obvious reasons, without having the engine running or climate control, can become excruciatingly hot when operating in sunny parts of the world.

10

Eastern Promises

'I need to know, is your team ready to handle a possible attempt on my life, organised and executed by the GRU or FSB?'

The International Ranger Platoon had just completed 400+ days of training and was for the first time "operational", which meant that we were not listed as an official asset other than as a part of a reserve unit; but for the people involved in planning more dark matters, we were the new kids on the block – we had entered the world of covert intelligence operations.

At this time MUST, Swedish military intelligence, an autonomous agency, were the main players in the field of HUMINT, SIGINT and the broader cloak and dagger business. MUST was never an endangered agency, like the more conventional military units who were threatened by budget cuts. MUST, perhaps equivalent to the CIA, or MI5/MI6 were the only one of its kind and had been operating since the end of World War 2. We were never in competition with MUST but rather seen as a future ground operative complement to them.

So, it meant that we had to keep a low profile – we maintained the appearance, pretending to be a reserve unit. We needed to achieve some operational successes – we had to become something so valuable that they couldn't take us out of business. We were on the radar of a few people at the top, but they kept their cool. They wanted to be on the right side of history when judgement day came, and since the right side had not been established yet, they just hovered.

We had to disguise our unconventional profile and training needs. Most of our "maintenance" training from that point onwards, like language, HUMINT, close protection and other forms of training, could have been covered within the armed forces, but it was not. To give it some context: in 2005 the army was still dissolving units and firing officers like it was nothing;

funds were slim for most units, except IRP and a few others that struck gold, but these units were still a well-kept secret even within the Regiment.

The armed forces were restructuring what they had left and with very limited funds. These were definitely the poorest years for the armed forces in modern times – we didn't see any of that deprivation in our unit, but it was hard watching from the sidelines; we just stood there in a bubble with almost unlimited resources while a lot of people worried about their jobs.

At the same time contractors were recruiting at an all-time high for private military companies (PMCs) serving in Iraq and Afghanistan. Officers from elite units were in high demand and were offered large sums of money up front for short-term lucrative contracts. Many officers, a lot from the Arctic Ranger Battalion, joined the ranks of Blackwater, DynCorp, Aegis, Triple Canopy, and other PMCs. I think many of the Ranger Regiments lost dozens of officers just like that and the army as a whole, a lot more.

The recruiters were even invited to regiments by the Commanders to give their men a chance to get a job should their unit be closed down. A handful of Ranger officers were also handpicked by IKEA, to run their new stores in Russia (it required firm leadership they said). So, contacts with commanders and representatives from the PMC world were common and of course personal relationships were forged.

The commanders of the IRP were no strangers to making personal connections, they already knew how valuable the PMC world was as a bridge between units, governments, and nations. They provided a grey area where nations could meet, train and work in an almost unregulated environment. It was the perfect storm for the intelligence services, hiding professionals with rednecks, mercenaries, extremists, and gold diggers.

It was a spring Tuesday and I had just got back from the range with a few guys from 3rd patrol. Captain B popped his head into the weapon maintenance room, 'The Major wants to see you in his office at 15:00.'

'What about?' I replied.

Captain B just shrugged and said, 'Get ready man you don't have much time.'

With three minutes to spare I knocked on the Major's door. I felt late. Five minutes early was the practice. 'Relax,' I said to myself, 'You're not a conscript anymore.' Some parts of our training die hard.

Casually the Major said, 'Come in.' I saw he had assembled operators from several patrols and Lieutenant C – we were five in total. 'I hope your shooting was better than your time keeping,' he laughed. He knew I was anal about time keeping. 'I need you guys to go to the UK as a training opportunity has presented itself.' We had recently been in the UK, but I didn't mind going back – one quickly got tired of the regiment walls. With a mixture of pleasure and pain, I remembered the bashing we got with the FRU.

The Major continued, 'You will be doing close protection and executive protection with a private company in London, MC Consulting, run by an old friend of mine Mr D. And you all know we have to keep a low profile so it will be a different approach this time. I have booked you all flights to Stockholm tonight for some much needed R&R. You will book the course using your cover identities. So, you are doing this as private citizens. Ex-military people looking to join the security circuit, you have all the details here.' He handed us each a sealed brown circular envelope. 'And this is to cover your expenses.' The bulge in the brown envelope was striking, especially for young soldiers, around £10k in cash. 'And you need a dark suit, not a cheap one, make sure you pick one up in Stockholm before you leave, and you are going for R&R don't forget that.'

As we left the meeting I wondered, 'Why the secrecy?' Usually, we were open when it came to training. It was late when I came home but my mother was still waiting up, this was the second time we had seen each other in 1.5 years. She was no stranger to me being away as I left for boarding school at 16 and never returned after that, but it was a happy reunion and I had missed her. She was in true motherly spirit and had prepared my favourite dinner and the fridge was stocked with my favourite snacks and drinks, I felt like a kid again.

'How long are you staying? You look tired. Are they giving you a hard time up there?' she asked.

'No, it's a been a lot of fun – it's just been a long day, I am going for a two-week vacation to London with a couple of friends who are also off. From there I would like to go down to the coast, but we will see.'

'It's good to have you home,' she said and smiled.

I woke up at 10:00 the following morning, it was a bit on the late side, my local bank closed at 14:00 and I needed to book the course, receive confirmation, pay and send the proof of payment back. I opened the brown envelope; it contained a course flyer with a Chinese restaurant budget look, booking instructions and a receipt for a sale of farming equipment for about 5k, the same amount that the course would cost, as a proof of where I got the money from.

I went downstairs to make a cup of coffee and my mother was sitting out on the terrace. 'Can I borrow your car for a few hours?' I said.

'Of course, you can, it's not work, is it?' she asked.

'No, I just need to go up to the travel agency and sort out some papers,' I said.

'Sure, can we have dinner tonight or are you meeting friends?' she said.

'I will be having dinner in the city with some friends on Friday so we can have dinner today and tomorrow.'

She nodded, and a small smile lit up her face.

As I came back upstairs, I had a new email waiting for me, it had only been 10 minutes. It was my course confirmation and payment instructions. I now needed to go to a bank where I was not a customer, since I was paying as someone else, and I wasn't looking forward to it. Cash has always been wonky in Sweden; we were not as cashless as we are today in 2024 but we were halfway there. Always the questions and suspicion. And farming equipment on the receipt was shady, well it was a snowmobile for forest farming purposes, so I guess it half checked out.

A young woman helped me when I got there. I sat down and opened my folder. Without much prompting I started explaining, 'I worked in the army before, and well you know the state of the military these days, right? I was so lucky to get a last-minute acceptance on this security manager course in the UK and now I need help to pay for the course that starts on Monday.

Her smile was replaced by a concerned nod, 'I know, it's horrible what is happening in the armed forces right now, what are the politicians thinking?' She leaned over and lowered her voice, 'I had a family last week, where both parents got sacked from a regiment and they needed to sell their house as they could no longer afford it. I felt so bad for them, good you found something to do.' She was on board.

The cash flipped through the counting machine as she was typing in the account numbers I had written down. She looked up, 'This is strange, wait a second I need to get my manager.'

An older gentleman showed up behind her and smiled at me before he looked at her computer. 'No, that flag means you have to check his identity...' I held my breath, he continued, 'And you have done that, so you just check this box, "Government issued ID."'

'There you go,' she smiled. 'Sorry, I have only been working here a few months and this was my first real international transfer.' The printer squeaked as it was pushing out the receipts of the payment. She stamped and signed at the bottom and said upbeat, 'All done and good luck with your course.'

The travel agency was close to the bank. 'I can help you,' a bubbly large woman boomed, like a bus coming to a stop she pointed at me, her long finger-nails were like a mural. 'Are we planning your next vacation?'

I wondered how many times she had to say that line. 'Not really, more study to be honest, I need tickets to London.'

With those two things off the list, it wasn't long before I was fitting a suit – but this was a special fitting, as I needed to consider the measurement of concealed weapons in my outfit. 'It's a bit tight over the waist', the store clerk walked around me. 'You pull it off, any larger, it will look like a bad fit.' I needed room for a piece so I couldn't go with a slim fit, no matter how good it looked. 'We have this model, it's more of a classic fit' and the clerk held up a dark blue suit. It was perfect or that was my estimate at least, but I needed my suit altered – it needed to be made combat ready. I was a Velcro man and I needed to make some modifications.

The tailor was an older gentleman, and his white beard framed a leathery face; he had a slight hunch. 'I know you close in an hour, but I need some small modifications if you have the time' I said.

'I can try, let's see what you got.'

'I need to make the belt loops 0.5 centimetres bigger.' This was to fit my reinforced civilian gun belt, but I left that part out.

'That we can do in 10 minutes,' he said.

I added, 'Then on the jacket I need some Velcro under the buttons for more relaxed access.'

'Put your jacket on,' he said. 'Are you going to have it buttoned up all the time or is going to be both opened and closed.'

'Both,' I replied.

'Well, what I would recommend then is to keep the top buttons as they are, fix the bottom button on the front and put Velcro under that, it would look good and natural in both positions.' He clearly knew what he was doing, so I did not ask any questions and neither did he, my type of tailor. 'It will be ready in 30 minutes,' he said.

While waiting for the tailor, I will give you my two cents on gun belts in Appendix B at the end of this chapter.

Before I knew it, we were at dinner and ready for action. 'Any problems?' asked Lieutenant C as he looked around the table. 'Everyone suited up?' We nodded. 'Well don't look so grim, it's not a funeral, let's get some beer in our systems.'

It was almost 01:30 when Lieutenant C and I arrived, we had a later flight than the others, and our flight had been slightly delayed as well, we missed the train and had to take the night bus. Mr R had already checked us in and waited for us in the reception, 'You guys took your time,' he said.

It was a shabby hotel on the outskirts of London, the wallpaper was falling down, and the carpet was heavily stained. But it was quiet, and the reception was unmanned after 17:00. The company that ran the course had booked it – 'included in the course,' they said – all on the cheap.

We had a short assembly in Mr R's room. 'All activated and all numbers are copied in each of them,' he said as he handed out cheap Motorola burner phones. He also had maps for all of us and gave us a quick rundown of our surroundings and where the course would be held the following day. He had done excellent prep work as always.

I woke up to a loud banging on my door, I sat straight up in my bed, 'Fuck I overslept' was my initial reaction. I looked at my watch, it was 05:15. My alarm was set for 06:00. I opened the door. Lieutenant C was standing outside smiling, 'Good morning sunshine, breakfast just opened, and I didn't want to eat alone, so you got the honours.

'Fuck you,' I thought to myself, 'Your honour couldn't have waited until 06:00?'

'Come now it's a glorious day.'

We all looked like used car salesmen in that shabby environment and with our new suits. Mr R sighed, 'No...,' as he had just got bacon grease on his shirt.

'Ever heard of a napkin' Lieutenant C said. It was a dangerous game eating in shirts, it could have happened to any one of us.

We stood outside a warehouse in the London suburbs; it was enclosed with a rusty fence and looked pretty rundown from the outside. A discreet sign said MC Consulting. I rang the bell and the intercom crackled, 'Are you here for the course?'

'Yes', I replied. The door buzzed open, I got the feeling that I was entering a decaying jail – no one was visiting, and the prisoners were lifers.

Inside it was a different story – a remodelled garage with an open office landscape, rustic but modern, completely opposite from the outside. A girl greeted us when we came in, 'Welcome, you can take a seat in the conference room down the hall to the left. Mr D will be with you in a minute, can I get you anything to drink?' As true Swedes we all wanted coffee. She laughed and said, 'I'll bring it right in.'

As we sat down in the meeting room three other suited men came in. They introduced themselves and asked, 'Are you also here for the course?' as they extended their hands. They were an ex-Royal Marine and two former police officers. We were in good company. It all felt very civilian in a way. Just after we got our coffee, a tall, impeccably sharp, and handsome man stepped in. He was probably in his late forties with a perfect smile and a well-fitted suit. He looked around the room and smiled, 'Welcome to MC Consulting, my name is Mr D.'

Mr D was a legend in the security world. We didn't know that then, but we learned that he was a former Mossad operative, a permanent member on the security industry council board in the UK. He lectured often and wrote a lot of articles on global security. He was an established player, not very clandestine, he seemed to know everyone and everything – he was so overt, that he may have been covert.

As he laid out the course plan, I was struck by how basic it seemed. I didn't know what to expect but this was an entry level course that led up to the UK SIA license that is required to work as a close protection operative. 'Well let's see where this takes us,' I thought. Before finishing his introduction, he presented his assistant instructor Mr T, A short man with a slim build, grey hair, and a good smile, he looked like he had been around, but also a typical Brit and perhaps an extra on a Bon Jovi set, with his worn jeans and a nineties leather jacket with spandex in the waist. We discovered that he was a former 21 SAS operator who had spent the last 20 years in the private security industry in the UK, Latin America, Africa and most recently Iraq. He definitely had a story more fitting for our purposes. He may have been a stone-cold killer but the tune of *It's my Life, It's Now or Never*, burned a hole in my ear.

The first week of training was child's play – we were run through a standard syllabus of an entry level close protection course. The five of us went out for beer at the end of the first week.

'Wtf is this,' Mr R said, 'I was all excited on day one, with Mossad and shit and now this? Was the Major drunk when he thought this was a good idea, this is like backwards training.' Mr R chugged half his pint in anger.

Lieutenant C said, 'I know this is not what any of us expected. I don't think the Major fucked up, or maybe he did. But let's do the best of it, we don't know who is watching and we will see this through as professionals to the end.'

The second week was a "final exercise", two days of planning and two days of mission. We left most of the work to the three civilians in the group. One of the former police officers said, 'You guys have done this before haven't you?'

'We touched on close protection duties during our army days,' I replied.

He smiled, and half rolled his eyes 'Must have been an extensive touch.'

I gave him the 'you know better than to go down this avenue' look.

He got it.

The course ended with dinner and a diploma ceremony. It was held at the 21 SAS Artists Rifles Club house just outside town. They brought in quite a few interesting people to entertain us, and we got a lecture on the 21 SAS and its history – that might have been the most rewarding part of the course. As we were mingling after dinner, Mr D approached me, 'So what did you think of the course?'

'It was… rewarding, lots of good stuff in there, you and Mr T are really good instructors.'

Mr D smiled and put his hand on my shoulder, 'I appreciate the feedback, but you need to work on your lying,' he said as he walked away.

'Wtf should I have told him?' I thought. He knew we were overqualified, why did he even ask.

I had just managed to score four pints, from the closed kitchen back at the hotel. We sat down in the lobby and just took a moment. Lieutenant C walked in, grabbed my pint, took a sip, and said, 'I am sorry to interrupt the party, in my room now. Alright, I don't have much information, but I do know that we need to sleep.' It was just after midnight, 'Not the best timing,' I thought. Lieutenant C continued, 'We need to be at MC Consulting at 06:00 tomorrow. I have ordered an early breakfast at 04:00 as we need to leave at 04:45. Don't wear your suits but bring them.'

I was lying in bed thinking, 'Maybe they had just been vetting us or maybe this was the real start of the course?' I felt the excitement of the unknown. That's the problem with operators; they get easily bored and need constant entertainment, like dogs. You start to crave action like an adrenaline junkie. It makes you risk prone but it's also necessary to function in that type of environment, you must want it. 'I shouldn't get my hopes up, maybe they just wanted to say something to our group in private,' I thought before I closed my eyes.

'Welcome gentlemen, the Major sends his regards and best wishes,' Mr D said as he entered the meeting room. We assumed he said that to reassure us that the Major was aware and approved of what was going to happen. 'We are a bit short on time, so I'll try to keep it snappy.' Mr D shook the mouse on the desk and the projector came alive. 'This is Boris Berezovsky, Russian businessman although oligarch is probably a better word for him. He is coming back to London from Rome today, wheels down at Heathrow at 15:35.'

Now we are talking. I felt an eruption of energy – this was my element. We were his security detail for the weekend.

Known to change his mind quickly, we had to adapt to Boris's evolving itinerary – we just planned for the main events, a musical, dinner, business meetings, et cetera. So in-between those we just had to be flexible, dynamic, smooth.

Boris's codename was White Fox. Years back he had gotten into some trouble in Russia and fled prosecution in the late nineties. He held deep connections to the Russian sub economy – a middleman for Russian money flowing out through Gazprom. The Russians tried to control him but with political in-fighting, he soon fell out of favour with Putin. As with many others they tried to silence him, however, all attempts have been unsuccessful. With opponents like the GRU and FSB we knew that if they came for him, it would be full on. Poisoning and armed attacks were a big concern. Boris only ate food that was prepared by his own chef and only drank bottled water. He also had a weak spot for prostitutes and cocaine. This visit to London wouldn't be any different. Cocaine and hookers – a complicating factor for a close protection unit.

'I assume you are familiar with these?' Mr D asked as he handed out Browning Hi-Power pistols and M4s. We all nodded – this was our bread and butter. 'Use it if it will save his life but avoid it at all costs. You have no licensing whatsoever for this and you will be taking the hit as civilians. If you save his life, you will stand a better chance in court.'

It's always like this, enormous personal risks, low pay, and no insurance… we just loved it. I don't know if it was youthful naivety or just the required madness that you had to have to be there in the first place. I am guessing the latter – but maybe a bit of both.

We had been chosen as Mr D couldn't use his regular PSD team. Luckily for us we could use his drivers. Always tricky driving in a big city without having sufficient knowledge of the roads. 'You and you,' Mr D pointed at me and Mr R, 'You will be rotating as his close protection officers, the rest of you will be security advance party and counter assault team.' (SAP/CAT) The SAP was the vanguard – our scouts and they had to make sure any intelligence was fed back to us. 'It will be a slim and tight operation. It's meant to be low profile, so I am counting on a good dynamic from you all. I want to see initiative as the scene changes.'

Me and Mr R were chosen largely due to our stature, we also had a similar look and interestingly, in this game, the look and feel of a team was important. The White Fox was short, he walked with his head slightly low, as if he was always concerned; his dark eyes were penetrating, and they never revealed if he was happy or sad. He was smart, he had made his calculations – quick changes in itinerary and no expense were spared. In practice it was simple, get the best, and for physical protection he wanted big guys marking him.

The drivers were preparing the vehicles, extra shirts, water, food, guns, and ammunition as well as, IV bags, adrenaline, tourniquets and most surprisingly even small bags of cocaine, which had been sealed after being analysed by a lab to confirm it was pure. I was impressed at the attention to detail. I assumed they didn't go to their local pharmacy to check the quality of the coke. We had an intense morning ahead of us, scouting hospitals, talking to doctors, driving routes, trying restaurants, and looking at clubs. It's not difficult work but the key is to pay attention to detail. We had to provide a seamless experience for the principal, which was usually not the case when protecting army top brass.

The armoured car was spotless in the sunshine at the tarmac – it reflected the image that we wanted to portray – professionalism, and safety. The sound was deafening as Gulfstream V rolled in. The flight attendant had barely opened the door before Boris was on the tarmac and heading to the car. A man who was used to getting his way, he looked like he was in a rush. As I closed the door, he said, 'I want to go straight to the hotel, I need to relax and change before the dinner.' He looked at me, 'Are you my guy?'

'Yes sir, me and Mr R in the front seat will serve as your CPOs this weekend.'

'You can cut the sir crap right now; I don't care for it.'

I swallowed hard and thought, 'Did I just offend him?' I analysed it for a few seconds, 'I didn't, he was just not a "sir" kind of dude – and a straightforward person – I could appreciate that.' As we drove off, I felt a bit uncomfortable "bugging him", but he didn't have his seatbelt on. I leaned in, 'I just need to get your seatbelt on as we will be driving at high speeds.'

He looked at me as I clicked his belt in, 'Army? Intelligence?'

'A bit of both', I replied.

Mr R gave the orders to the SAP team, as we now had some practical use for them. Boris fiddled with his phone. 'I got the heads up that my arrival has been causing a bit of "chatter" in the Russian channels, it might just be smoke and mirrors or it might be something, are you ready for heavy action?'

I didn't hesitate, 'Yes, we are ready for any and every eventuality that might arise.' I left the sir out this time. He brushed his hand over his face.

'Okay let's try this again, without the CPO voice. I need to know, is your team ready to handle a possible attempt on my life, organised and executed by the GRU or FSB?'

I looked at him, 'This is not our first rodeo and it's not going to be amateurs' night; you can count on us putting in our maximum effort to keep you out of harm's way, if it goes down, then we will do our best to keep you alive, as we also want to live. We will utilise every tool at our disposal to protect you and ourselves.' Did I just quote the movie *Ronin*? I thought. I felt that this was the kind of answer he was looking for and it came from the heart. Mental note for next time, I should package it better.

He gave me a stern look, 'Good, good that gives me more confidence than the sir stuff.' He answered his phone and started speaking Russian.

At the hotel the SAP team got out of his room just as we got to the door, Boris turned to me, '19:30, I will leave for the restaurant,' and he closed the door behind him. Mr R took first watch on the chair outside of his room. I was going to be the CPO during dinner and would take the last watch. Mr A was manning the lobby. The rest of us had the room next to him and we assembled the remaining operatives and the drivers. Lieutenant C and the drivers held a short presentation regarding the dinner event. We were leaving the armed car and going for a lower profile Mercedes. It would be a better fit outside the city centre. We cased the place – a local Russian restaurant, with two exits, one in the back and one in the front. The car would be parked near the back exit in the alley. We had been scouting the restaurant beforehand, so the staff knew we were coming. However, the owners were personal friends of Boris, and no doubt expecting him. We then did a reconnaissance of a number of the local clubs – we needed to come up with options. The drivers knew of a few suitable clubs in the vicinity, and they went with Lieutenant C to make their choices; en route they also dropped off his chef at the restaurant. Interestingly Boris's chef had a bunch of cooler boxes with padlocks- nothing was bought locally, and everything was brought in.

Boris was more relaxed in the car en route to dinner; he had had a few drinks in his room. He was not drunk, just a bit more friendly. 'I want you to sit on my right, if I cut a piece of food and slide it to the right of my plate, I want you to try it. If you have any doubts on the taste, you spit it out and we are off, look for chemical flavours and excessive garlic or almond taste.'

I didn't know if he was joking, I couldn't help but think, 'When did I sign up to be a poison checker.' I felt a bit uncomfortable as I knew the Russian agencies were partial to poison, this felt like going in kamikaze style. There was no protection against it, just me protecting him. Maybe this was the Major's gift to him – the harsh end of signing up for covert intelligence operations. I remained unsure whether it was his dark Russian humour, or if he was serious – his eyes gave nothing away.

We were eight at the table, and it felt like a movie. Serious looking Russians – most of them exiled Soviets who made their fortunes in the post-Cold War privatisation and gangster boom. With Putin's rise to power, the Russian leader and judoka made it clear that no one was above the power of the state. As a result, many of them had to leave the country. London was a convenient location, and soon Russian money had bought up half of the real estate.

Dinner went smoothly except for the feeling of being the third wheel – only I wasn't. I was treated like I didn't exist, but most importantly I didn't get any food to taste. A few of the other dinner guests had their own security details, and we shared nothing more than the focus on our purpose.

Towards the end of the dinner, we and the other security personnel were told to move to a separate table. Most weren't that talkative, and neither should we have been, but I started to learn that one of my almost natural skills was to draw out information from others. One CPO was a former marine infantry Spetsnaz from Kaliningrad. The other two claimed to have 'mixed' backgrounds. I left it there as they looked tired. Boris shouted, 'we are leaving in 10 minutes.' I looked at my watch – at ten past midnight it was a good time to leave. It had been a long day. Boris, in a gruff voice half yelled to the driver, 'Hey, I need to stop on the way home.'

'Not clubbing, not clubbing' I prayed.

'I need cigarettes' he said. As we breathed a sigh of relief.

I had to plan for the following day's business meeting. We had already scouted the venue, it was a high-profile location, and he was invited in a semi-official capacity. This limited our tactical options in regard to embus and debus locations. The lunch meeting venue was busy; it was on the top floor of an office building in the city centre.

The SAP was already in. Outside a small climate protest filled the street – it was aimed at the oil company working in the building. The driver said they were regulars so probably nothing to worry about, but we changed the debus location to the garage just to be sure.

The office building was loaded with Middle Eastern and Russian oil representatives – it looked like a mini-OPEC meeting. The meeting took place in a small part of the top floor, it had a magnificent view, which I couldn't fully appreciate. His chef had been there a few hours earlier to prepare lunch. It was a hot day, and they served a traditional Russian summer dish, I don't remember its name, but it was a salad with cold Kvass poured over it – the meal had a peculiar taste, not almonds and garlic of course, but I could see the charm.

Mr A was holding his position outside. The radio crackled, 'We got some tension down here, it's not us, just in general, but getting out of the garage will be a stretch.'

'Let's use exit two and just slide out, prep the second driver and take the BMW.'

'Wilco.'

The radio crackled again, 'There's been a small car accident out front, a taxi and a private car had a fender-bender.'

'Alright, standby, prepare for departure.'

I walked over to Boris, and half whispered, 'If you are ready, I think this would be a good time to leave.'

He looked at me, his gaze hid a mixture of concern, mild irritation, and practicality. I took a step back, and he said, 'Thank you all, I need to move on.' The other parties stood up, 'Of course, we have been taking too much of your time, thank you for your hospitality.'

'Standby we are on the move,' I snapped over the radio.

Exit two was the main exit on the backside – it was a bit rowdy when we got out, but nothing like the protests in the front. We remained alert, kept it tight but at the same time tried not to look too business-like. The police were monitoring, however I focused on the hands of those around us. It was the perfect environment for an assassination attempt with a .22.

Boris refused any body armour. During the elevated threat level that we were experiencing, I would at least have liked to see him in a stab vest. The crowd was booing, it was not at us, it was at one of the oil executives leaving the building. We reached the car and our commander Lieutenant C.

'Good you guys cut that meeting short, I was tired of all the pleasantries,' Boris said. I couldn't imagine how different people could be – Boris was like a regular businessman when he met others, he had a sense of humour, and at times he was humble. When alone he was cruder, but I guess it took a toll being him – the pressure, the performance, the trust and knowing that everyone wanted something- perhaps similar to the toll of running sources and then burning them.

As we made our way through the dense London traffic, Boris told the driver, 'Take me to Harrods, I need to buy a gift for my niece.' He had family coming to his country house on Sunday and our last task was to take him there and hand him over to another team. It was crowded, and Lieutenant C and I were with him, the SAP was stuck in traffic as they had gone back and recovered our other vehicle from the garage.

Boris appeared a bit tired, but he smiled and greeted the staff – they seemed to know him. I can't say he made a lot of personal choices as he mostly took the staff's recommendations. The necklace on the desk had an £8,000 price tag and the girl showing it had a Hollywood smile. He looked at me, 'What do you think, is this enough for a 14 year-old?'

I bit my tongue and for a moment thought about saying, 'Maybe if she's spoilt,' but I didn't of course. 'I would say so, what type of person is she?'

'She's a teenager, notoriously hard to buy presents for,' he said.

I tried to be polite, 'Is it for a special occasion?'

'No, just meeting the family,' he said.

'Then it will do fine,' I replied. I knew my input had zero value, but I couldn't really react in any other way.

He picked up a few more things before we left. He was happy and so was I as we managed to time things well and coordinate our exit with the arrival of our car. 'I will leave at 20:00 for dinner and then we will see,' he said before going back to his room.

'Pretty smooth day,' Lieutenant C said.

I nodded. 'But after doing this for two days I miss shady alleyways, combat boots and canvas bags with guns and ammo' I said.

'And a 30k salary' Lieutenant C said smiling.

'Well, this is for free, so I guess so, but point taken.'

The music was pumping, and the stroboscope was intense. A picture-perfect girl was licking her lips while undressing me with her eyes. The tones of Warp Brothers blasted through the speakers. I looked at my watch – '02:07', the night was getting old. We were in a cellar Gentleman's club with Boris and his Russian dinner friend. We fitted right in though. I think it was Russian owned and Boris seemed to know the owner.

Mr R and I held the inside and Lieutenant C managed the outside. The bar was crowded, and the vodka had been flowing for a few hours now. I could see Boris getting irritated on the growing rowdiness of some of the visitors. A man that lost his jacket approached us from the bar with a drink in his hand. He had rolled up his sleeves and was noticeably drunk. 'Do you know this man?' I asked Boris.

He shook his head. I got up and took a few steps forward towards the man. 'Oh, aren't we aggressive tonight...' he blurted out as he stopped short of me.

'Your presence is not wanted here, go back to your friends', I told him with my nicest voice. The man stared at me and as he tried to pass me, I grabbed his arm and lightly pushed him backwards.

Mr R was already on his feet, and I heard him say to our company, 'We are leaving now.'

The man I pushed backwards, stumbled, and spilled his drink. 'You fucking spilled my drink!' he shouted and threw his glass on the floor.

'All out! Knife at the bar.' It was Mr A who had come in after loading Boris and his friend. I saw the knife had been pulled by one in the drunken man's party. This was the third time in my life I had been in a situation where someone drew a knife at me. They were all far away and the situation was frozen, we were not there to engage.

When I closed the door to the second car, waiting outside, the driver commented, 'Damn quick, less than 30 seconds all in all,' and sped off, it felt longer.

The principal and his friend were already well on their way with Mr R and Lieutenant C, 'We will catch up with them on the highway,' the driver said.

Boris had already been escorted to his room and we sat down in our room. 'That was a poor excuse for action', I said.

'Well, as we are not in the business of action but rather of avoiding it – it went pretty well', Lieutenant C said with his officer's voice.

'It was still more like a doorman's job', I said rolling my eyes.

'It was our job,' Lieutenant C replied and killed the rest of the whining. I had thought there would be hookers and drug dealers, but he seemed to have been on his best behaviour that weekend. It was all good though, we all needed sleep, so the night chat was not long lived.

Sunday 11 o'clock, the sun was intense as we rolled in at the country house. I opened his car door; he stopped and looked at me, then grabbed his leather cardholder from his inner jacket pocket. He wiggled out a business card and handed it to me, 'If you ever get tired of working for your current employer.' Boris turned and headed away, I stared at him leaving for a second before getting into the car.

'I think he offered me a job?' I said to Lieutenant C as we drove away.

'Could you bring a friend?' Lieutenant C said laughingly and added, 'I am not really joking.'

We all knew we did okay, it was not the world's most complicated, dangerous, or hectic mission – it was different, and if nothing else, it gave us one unique contact for life. Mr D thanked us for the help, and we handed in our equipment. 'The White Fox was happy; he is a hard man to please,' Mr D said and looked at me. I nodded, I don't know why he liked me, but it was a team effort so I couldn't really take the credit.

The last flight and the final leg of our return journey up to the regiment was empty as always. 'What was the purpose of all this?' I asked Lieutenant C.

He shrugged his shoulders and half asleep with his eyes closed said, 'Fuck knows, I have stopped thinking about these things. I guess it will be clear sooner or later… or not.'

Appendix B

If you have ever carried a gun, you quickly realise that the belt holds the holster; and needless to say, the gun fits in the holster and needs to be sturdy. The belt is critical, and it is important that it doesn't flex or bend when you draw your gun. More than that, the belt keeps the holster reasonably close to the body. If you are doing uniformed work, you usually have an equipment belt for that purpose when carrying a gun at your hip. You might also have your gun on your chest, fitted to your rig, this is especially well suited for vehicle work or perhaps you could have a classic drop leg holster.

These are all good options when you don't need to conceal your weapon, which is usually the case when working in plain clothing. You could use a shoulder holster, but they are not super common and usually one has some type of slim pancake holster that is moulded for your gun or just a generic pocket which will squeeze the gun. In any case the gun belt is, in my opinion, one of the most important pieces of equipment that is often overlooked. A bad belt might tilt your gun outwards and give it a profile under your shirt or jacket, it may also jam the gun in the holster when drawing because of the belt flex causing an angle.

So, what are we looking for in a good gun belt for use with plain clothing? Sturdy on the height axis for drawing and keeping a true position, normal thickness to keep a tight holster profile, and slightly wider to not leave too much gap at the holster and last but not least the look. It might sound crazy, but most gun belts look like cowboy belts. South-western handmade stuff with pearls and stones and shit or they are *uber* tactical. None of these are acceptable for low key work, it needs to look like a normal belt that fits what you are wearing and doesn't give you away. You would never believe how hard it is to find good-looking gun belts – they are so scarce – and I mean 'hen's teeth scarce'. Key is that they must be comfortable and should not need to be pulled super tight to work. I had one of those steel reinforced ones that just cuts into your skin like a knife, when sitting down. Now I have three gun belts, all custom made by an old school leather man. One is dress black; another is dress brown and the third one has a more sporty, casual feel. The sporty, casual one has textile as the outer layer and looks like a belt that could be picked up at any sports shop. The common denominator is that they all have a brilliant construction; the inner layer is made up of small, thin pieces of leather overlapping each other, keeping it sturdy, flexible, and thin. And the belt buckles allow for endless adjustment and have a piece of flex hidden just at the buckle, so it keeps the snug fit with room for movement, they are also the perfect level of fancy, so they go with most types of clothing.

The tailor finished far before I finished my gun belt rant.

11

Extraordinary Rendition in Latin America

'The risks of putting a drugged man in a box for over seven hours was high…
I think he will come of his own accord.'

The sweat poured down my face as I made a dash towards security. I had less than 55 minutes to catch my next flight after landing at Charles de Gaulle. It was just enough but I had to hustle. Since 9/11 the security had been beefed up significantly and in 2005 Europe had seen quite a few domestic terrorist attacks, so needless to say, airport security was tight. An additional layer of heat was always added by the fact that we were using cover passports.

The border control officer looked at my passport and gave it back to me with a nod. I was more worried about the opening and closing of the passport. At this time there was a manufacturing issue that made the Swedish passports weak. The actual plastic ID page had a problem at the seam – I think it had something to do with them cheaping out on materials.

As I left the gate behind me, I looked at my ticket stub again, I was headed to Panama the second leg and closer to the final destination of this journey.

The platoon was still spread-out doing specialist training, most of the drivers in our unit were down at the Navy base learning how to skip boats. I was jealous of them. Other colleagues still at the regiment were doing helicopter drills: long line, fast rope, rappelling, and night operations. I was jealous of them too, not that I have not had my fill of heliops, that I truly enjoyed, but most importantly I also had a fear of missing out (FOMO). Very common in the army, probably quite a few guys were feeling the same about what I got up to – a never ending circle really.

The Major had only done a very quick debrief of our UK mission, so we never got to know more about its purpose or our performance.

On the second day Captain B called me into the Major's office. 'Did you enjoy travelling?'

'I liked it, it was different,' I replied.

'Good, good, what would you say about going again?'

I looked at the Major, 'I am good with that, no problem at all.'

The Major replied with a smile, 'Good because it was not a question.'

Captain B continued, 'I will be organising a small project in a month or two in Colombia. All the details are not worked out yet, but it will be a six man team and I need someone reliable on the ground before the main team get there.'

It felt good to be Captain B's trusted man, he was after all the one who recruited me to the IRP, but this felt like something bigger. 'So, I am going to Colombia? What is the mission?'

'You will all be briefed when we reassemble and no you are not going to Colombia.' I looked at Captain B for an explanation.

The Major took the opportunity to shed some light, 'We want you to set up a presence in Panama, well not really a presence, just go there, feel the temperature and poke around a bit, try to get a good grip on Colombia and the activities in the Darien region, South of the DMZ and FARC.'

I had questions, 'Okay so...'

The Major interrupted me 'So the order is: Go to Panama, start taking intensive Spanish lessons, learn the ropes, be prepared to either receive the rest of the team in Panama or join them in Colombia.'

'Got it.'

The Major slid two envelopes across the table, they were thicker than the UK ones. 'There is a fresh PGP mail in there and if we ever tell you to pick up a package, call Johan at the Swedish embassy, his number is in there. You don't have to live like a rat, but it can be 1 to 2 months so take that into account. Any questions?'

I had a million but no relevant ones, 'No, no questions'

'Good, good, use the same identity as in the UK.'

'Will do.'

As I was heading for the door the major said, 'Oh one last thing, if anyone asks, even within our own ranks, you are going to the signal regiment in Enköping for a SATCOM course.'

I looked at them both with a smirk, 'Right, SATCOM course.' There was a lot of money in envelopes, 'Were we army or intelligence?' I thought. The pieces were falling into place, I started to see the big picture – the details were not clear, but I had a sense that 'this was some 007 shit.'

I had a duffle size bag and a small backpack, with all the gear I needed from the regiment. I did not stop by my mother's this time, for all she knew we were on a longer exercise in the North. When I landed in Stockholm, I headed for the airport train as I needed to get to the central train station in the city. I was not taking a connecting flight from Stockholm Arlanda airport as that would be a bit too much overseas activity for one person in such a short time, and I didn't want to attract any attention – I had time. I took the night train from Stockholm to Malmö and then the fast train to Copenhagen, there were rarely ID checks on the trains between Sweden and Denmark. My plan was to fly out from Copenhagen as I knew they didn't automatically crosscheck their registers with Swedish authorities and vice versa.

I bought the tickets with cash in Copenhagen, not at the airport but at a travel agency. The reason for this was that the airport sales were often vetted by the police – it tended to look a bit shady. My itinerary was Copenhagen-JFK-Panama. I hadn't booked a hotel for the first night as I wanted to check out the place first – it was visa on arrival, so I was confident that the authorities would not check for a hotel reservation.

I flew out on a Boeing 757ER; they were getting old – a single-aisle plane with little legroom – it gave the distinct feeling of cattle transport. The flight attendant had dreams about working for the top airlines and was not short of enthusiasm; it was certain that she was happy to be off the regional flights. She made her best attempt to welcome us to the US, by showing us the Statue of Liberty on our approach, like a tour guide, she stopped short of 'Give me your tired, your poor, your huddled…' I interrupted myself my ass hurt too much to care at that point, I just wanted to get up and off that damned plane.

The DHS officer that checked my passport during my transit asked, 'What is your business in Panama?'

'As if that is any of your business,' I thought to myself. 'I am going for a language course,' I said. The officer started speaking to me in Spanish. I should have guessed it from his surname 'Garcia.' 'Hopefully I get it on my way back,' I replied.

'Have a nice stay in Panama,' he said and smiled.

It was later than I thought when I arrived, around 22:00. My eyelids were heavy, and my clothes started to stick to my body due to the humidity – it was a real tropical night.

On the airport bus to the city centre, I watched the world go by – the mix of Spanish colonial architecture, modern buildings, and Latin flair. I was in a new world. The practicalities took over and I decided to go with one of the larger central hostels, I didn't care to look around on my first night and they had a 24 hour reception. It was a tired hippie backpacker with dreadlocks that manned the reception desk, 'Hola! *Buenas noches*, a room for the night?' He gave off a very chill vibe – just what I needed on my first day in a new country.

'Yes, one night and some baggage storage for tomorrow.'

'We have a few beds available, no private rooms, but I have a bed available in a four bed dorm that has only two guests in it.'

'That will do,' I said.

'Cash or Card?'

'Cash,' I said while I reached for my wallet.

We were on the second floor and the hippie walked me through a larger living room area with a balcony. A girl who looked stoned was watching MTV with bad reception. 'The bathrooms and showers are down the hall.' The hippie pointed down a hallway with flickering lights, which illuminated and darkened the bottle green walls accordingly. 'This is your room' he said pointing to the bottom bunk closest to the door to the right. I sat down and was struck by the two Italian guys already in the room snoring like lumberjacks. The bed looked disgusting, and the wall of noise didn't help. I locked my bags to my bunk with the bike wire lock provided by the hostel. I had my money and documents in my covert waist bag inside of my jeans.

I headed out to the common area and passed the MTV girl; she didn't even notice me. I walked to the hippie in the reception and asked, 'You got cold beer?'

'Sure', he said and turned around and opened a rusty white fridge behind him.

'I'll take three,' I said. I took my beers, walked out onto the balcony, and sat down on a soft couch; the street was bustling down below, a typical touristy street with bars and nightclubs. A pleasant breeze took the edge off the humidity.

'Are you okay?' a girl asked, as she tapped my shoulder and smiled at me. She was pretty with typical Latin features. I felt dehydrated as fuck and had a slight headache. The sun was on the way up, I looked at my watch 06:10.

'Great,' I thought, I had fallen asleep on the couch on the balcony. 'I am all good, my roommates snored,' I replied, with a small smile.

She chuckled, 'Well the balcony would be my spot if I had to sleep here,' she said as she walked away.

I needed a shower, coffee, and more coffee.

On my way out I looked at the overfull bulletin board in the reception, 'Looking for something special?' the receptionist asked.

Not sure what she meant with 'special', but I decided not to dig deeper into the specifics of that. 'Do you know someone nice that rents out, not too far from the centre, I am sticking around for a while, taking a language course.'

'Actually, I do,' she said. 'There is a nice older couple that rents out a small house on their property, they don't like backpackers, but you look a bit more regular.' She scribbled down an address on a piece of paper and handed it to me. 'Just take the number 5 bus outside on the right-hand side, after about 10 minutes you will reach a big intersection with a shopping mall, you can't miss it. Get off there and walk two blocks up hill, it's the steepest road and when you get to the top you will be there, it's super easy to find.'

I had two cups of coffee and a bagel at the bakery and assessed my options. I needed to look around town before I decided, so I made the decision to go by bus on the ring line that went in a loop; and I also picked up a map on the way.

She was right; one couldn't miss the intersection and the steep hill as I got off the bus. 'It's rare that people give accurate descriptions,' I thought and felt like my hope in mankind was restored, if only for a moment. I had been making my way around town for a few hours and I had a good feel for the main areas and a first impression of the housing situation. It was pricey, and most rentals were aimed at tourists or businesspeople. I wasn't lacking in funds, but I needed something a bit more low key. And the location of the couple the reception girl recommended was good, right outside the city centre – a quiet residential area with all the stores and amenities nearby, including a gym, I really needed a gym after all of that travelling.

I found the house, a charming white wall enclosed the property, and a lush garden was hiding behind it as well as old iron gates, it was very Spanish. I looked for the doorbell as the smallest guard dog noticed my presence. A lady opened the door to shush the dog; she saw me standing behind the gate. I smiled and waved, '*Hola*, do you speak English? I got the address from the girl at the city hostel.'

'Ahh come in,' the lady said and smiled. She invited me in and offered me something to drink; her husband came out from the living room and introduced himself. They were both professors at the University and rented out their cottage to students and businesspeople. 'So, you are looking to rent?' she asked.

'Yes, I just got into town yesterday and I am planning to take Spanish lessons, so I am basically looking for something from today and for one to two months.'

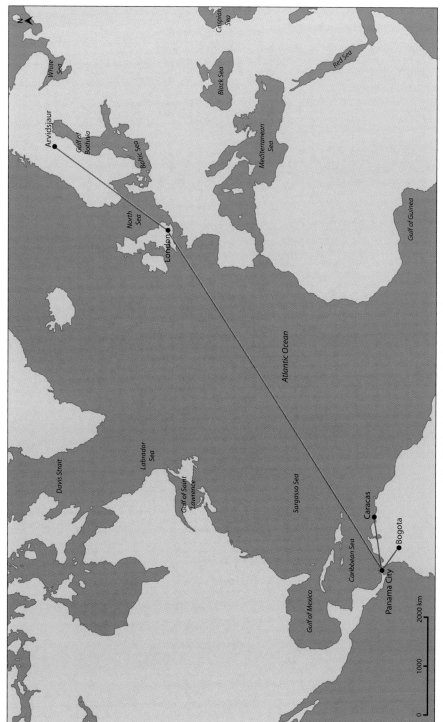

Map 3 Travels during the first part of my career.

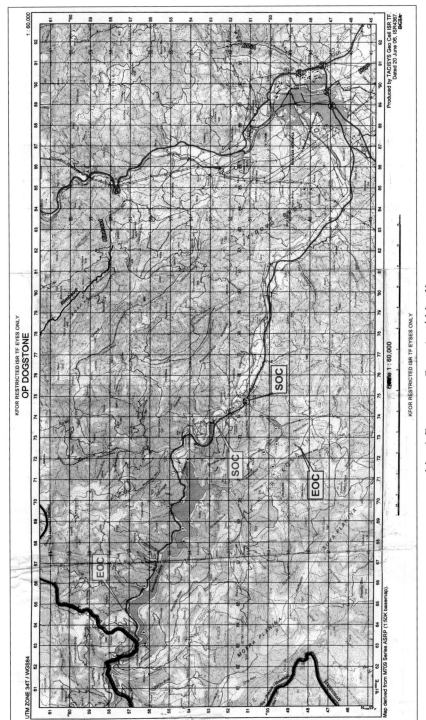

Map 4 Dogstone – Operational Map Kosovo.

Max, Mr F and Mr AN with hard earned headgear, *Baskerprovet* done and dusted.

The Regiment seen from Prästberget. Can you tell it looks like a horse?

The Arctic at its finest.

Walking into the endless white nights of the Arctic.

Pre-operation planning in the early days.

Winter is coming. Gearing up for a stormy night on the mountain.

Where it all started.

Romeo 13 honing their skills with Mr N in the rear with the gear.

Beating them at their own game. Winter hide-and-seek with the anti-terrorist police on Utö.

Unloading a CB90 in icy waters.

Another day at the office, just missing the watercooler.

Ranger taxi during a deep Arctic insertion.

Home is where your tent is. Platoon digging in for the night.

Mr Q enjoying the comforts of an urban OP.

Bored soldiers are a dangerous thing. Still don't know who brought LEGOs with them on a live operation.

Max at the map and pre-action prep in Colombia.

Mr R warming up in Colombia.

The troika, from left – Mr N, Max and Lieutenant B.

Reflexes die hard, unloading at Prizren AB.

Mr A sleeping it off during the Mansion gig with Mr N on the camera. All under the watchful eye of Max.

Blending in. OP Eastern Border Kosovo.

Romeo 12 and Romeo 13 enjoying the German hospitality in Prizren. Lieutenant B embracing the summer vibe with Hawaii shorts.

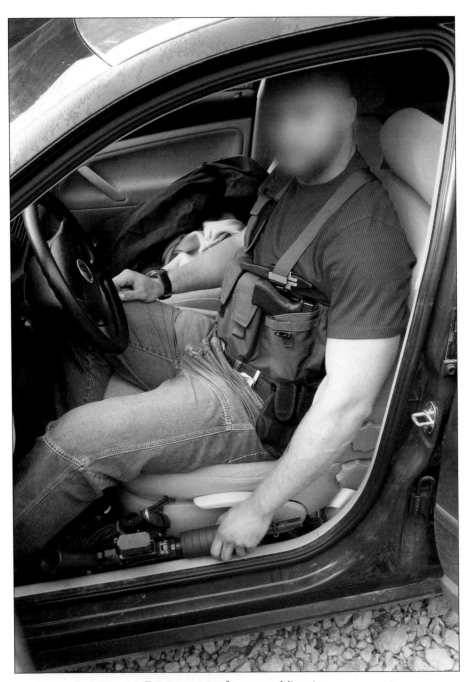

Driver preparing for a run to Mitrovica.

Fashion was different in the early 2000s. Max preparing for urban ops in Kosovo.

Parts of Romeo 12 ready to roll out on mobile surveillance.

The money shot with Cossack and Benchwarmer.

Fast rope insertion of Romeo 12 and 13 courtesy of the French.

ASSOCIATED TO U25

CHERRY	VW GOLF	236 KS 639
BLACK	MERCEDES 190E	153KS287
BLACK	BMW 5 SERIES	DK 24927
RED	OPEL VECTRA	163 KS 041
WHITE	NISSAN PATROL	SWISS VRN 34441.

ASSOCIATED TO COMPOUND ONLY

BLUE	OPEL VECTRA	492 KS 151
BLUE	VW GOLF ESTATE	501 KS 969
RED	VW GOLF	435 KS 204

Low tech gets the job done.

'Oh, I am so sorry,' she said. 'That would have been perfect for us, but two days from now we are getting a language student from the ILISA institute. He is doing a full immersive language course and is staying for four weeks.'

'It's okay,' I said, 'I just came on the off chance, and she didn't make any promises.'

Her husband said something to her in Spanish. She continued, 'I don't know what your budget is and if you would consider something more central, but our daughter, who also works at the university, has just moved in with her husband and they are renting out her apartment. It's very central, three rooms, a good kitchen and AC, fully furnished.'

It sounded expensive, 'How much are they asking?' I was just being polite without any real expectation.

'Well...' she looked down at the table and appeared uncomfortable '$300 a month, but it is including everything she stressed.

'Is she kidding? That's a damned bargain,' I thought. 'I can take a look,' I said.

She picked up her phone and called her daughter right away, after a short conversation she took the phone from her ear and said, 'Are you able to meet them now? They are there now cleaning the place.'

'Sure, I can do that, how far is it and what is the best way of getting there?'

'No no we can take you there, we will drive you.' They seemed too sincere to have any hidden agendas, and I accepted her offer.

Her husband was driving, and she was riding shotgun. She kind of gave me a tour as we went down one of the main boulevards. 'Which language school are you going to?'

'I haven't decided yet, I was going to look around when I got settled.'

She took up her notebook and started to scribble down. '*Toma*' she said and handed me a note. It read, 'Herman' and was accompanied by a phone number and address. 'We often take on students from them who are doing full immersion courses, they have a good reputation, and the owner Herman is a Dutch expat, and a really nice man. Reasonably priced as well.'

I took the note and said, 'I will look into them.'

She said, 'They are located at the old army base near the Miraflores locks, its just 15 minutes by bus, from the apartment and then a two-minute walk.'

It sounded like she already sold me the whole package, I needed to be careful not to settle too early.

I sat on the bench waiting for the number 7 bus. I flipped the keys to my new apartment in my hand and I couldn't believe my luck. The apartment was stunning, and her daughter and husband were lovely – a super sweet couple. She worked at the university and her husband was a lawyer. She had just moved out of her apartment and into his flat. They were planning to put her apartment up for rent for a few months before selling it. They had barely finished cleaning it when we got there. It had three rooms and a flat screen TV, modern kitchen, and a great balcony, as well as being on a quiet street bang in the city centre. Even a parking spot was included, it was a find.

Her husband went down to a print shop and came back with the rental contract and a bottle of wine. He said, 'Sorry we were not able to do more to get the place ready.'

'Don't mention it, your place is perfect,' I said and signed and paid for two months with the option to extend. Even if I only stay for one month it would be cheap. The whole renting process was over in 45 minutes. I took down the husband's number just in case I had any questions or if there were problems with the apartment.

I found a phone shop just a block away that provided me with a burner phone and a prepaid sim card. I decided to call Herman right away and he suggested I pop by. Either I was lucky, or I had fallen straight into a counter-intelligence operation. I sat at the bus stop, which was just a one minute walk from my door. I was waiting for the bus that left every 15 minutes and would take me straight to the language school. This school had to be really expensive or bad for me to not take it, it was way too convenient.

The language school was located in the outer part of the old army base. It was a green and lush area just by the canal. A part of the extended university campus was situated close by, including a large track and field arena. A good reuse of an old military structure.

Herman's assistant Anna greeted me at the door, 'Welcome, I'll give you a quick tour and then we will meet Herman.' It was a small but modern school, with lots of classrooms and a nice lounge area.

She introduced me to two American businessmen, in Hawaiian shirts, who were taking private lessons; they waved enthusiastically, and said, 'Hello.'

Herman was a middle aged, tall, slim and very Dutch looking man. His octagon shaped steel framed glasses made him look like a nerdy James Bond villain. He told me the story about how he and his wife moved to Panama and how he started the language school. 'Soo what are you looking for?' he asked, in a direct yet kind tone. I told him a bit about the state of the Swedish Army and that I had recently left due to the state of things – I was trying a different path. 'Are you looking for group classes, or an individual one, and for how long?'

'I am planning to do at least one month of classes and maybe extend to two depending on how things work out. I would like the intensive course, and preferably private, but it depends on the cost of course.'

He gave me a rundown of the options, it was the low season, so most courses were discounted. The last option was a private and super intensive course, one to one, five days a week, five hours a day with one excursion to the old town. Fully adjustable to your individual needs. 'It's usually $1,700 a month but we could do $1,400 per month and if you choose to extend, we could do the second month for $1,200.'

I thought, 'Rather expensive at $2,900 for 2 months and 5 hours a day. Although weekends were free. It was not the cheapest, but for the price I got a shitload of training, and I had more money than I could count left. 'When can I start?'

Herman flipped through his book 'Tomorrow, we could set you up with Jorge, he gets results fast.'

'Can I pay cash?'

Herman smiled, 'Of course.'

I settled in quickly and I felt at home in my apartment. I found a gym and a place to run. It didn't feel like work, it felt like I had just moved and started a new life, and I had to remind myself who was paying the bills.

I used my first week to explore the city, do some touristy things to get a feel for the place. I didn't put that much into Spanish practice after the actual lessons. The classes were enough, and I made progress every day. I found the Spanish language to be very forgiving and at 5 hours a day without a single word of English one gets results. Spanish speakers are also generally forgiving, and as long as you try to speak to them in their language – they would try to help you.

Not far from my apartment I found a bar, *El Pavo Real*. It was an expat bar run by a Brit. One level above a spit and sawdust bar, it was a good place to take the temperature, get information, hear gossip, and just make connections. I was always comfortable with the social game, it had always worked in my favour, so I had minimal problems establishing myself there, I didn't keep a low profile, but I didn't stick out either.

At *El Pavo Real* I met Anna, she worked there and after a few days we hit it off. She had flowing dark hair, and cute dimples – a beautiful mix of Spanish and Latin. She would laugh at me for using Spanish sayings in the wrong context and I bought her dinner. She lived in a very poor neighbourhood and had two children with an American soldier who had left her. It was clear that she was looking for the security that a decent looking foreigner could provide, she worked hard on that. The first time that I left her apartment I thought, 'This is a 9mm kind of place.' It felt unsafe and as a *Gringo* I stuck out like a pirate on Halloween. Most people thought that I was an American and that made it worse. I knew the relationship would be short lived. I knew she would be hurt, but I couldn't resist it, it was a pure dick move that I am not proud off – but we all play the game.

The second week Herman took me and the two American business guys at the school out for lunch at the causeway, a beautiful place that symbolizes the division between the rich and the poor – Herman was definitely in the first category. The purpose of the lunch was purely business from Herman's side, he thought he hid it well, but he didn't. The Americans probably bought it as they enjoyed the 'asslicking'. He invested in us believing we could bring more business; it was very unlikely that I would though, but I played along as I had other interests, he was knee deep into the expat community and I wanted to tap into that.

Herman said, 'We have a guy in our expat group that meets every month, he was in the military I think.' Herman had no idea as the military didn't interest him at all but tried to give me added value because of my service.

I took the number of the soldier and thought, 'I wouldn't mind hanging out with some military guys, just for fun or maybe they could provide me with insight.' I just needed to be careful depending on if the person was a grunt or something else; often military types are easy to play but if they are observant speaking out of turn can be one's downfall. But I didn't worry too much as it was my backyard.

His name was John, and I gave him a call on my second weekend, it was around lunchtime on Saturday. He answered the phone in Spanish, and I managed to convey that I got his number from Herman, in Spanish, he quickly turned to English, with a thick southern accent. Sounding happy he said that Herman had texted him and said I was going to call. 'You were looking for possibilities, right?' he said.

A strange way to put it, I was sure he meant "opportunities" – I hesitated for a second, but my mouth didn't. 'Yeah, that's correct, I am doing a language course at ILISA,' and I explained about my previous experience in the army and what happened with the forces in Sweden. As a military man, he was saddened by the fact that this could happen in this day and age.

'Do you have any plans today?'

'No, I don't,' I said.

'Pop over to my office if you want. I'll be here until 17:00.'

As I jumped on the bus I reflected on the conversation, I knew I had mentioned to Herman that I was looking for opportunities, but I hadn't really thought about it. 'How much was I willing to invest in this and how deep in should I go?'

It was a middle-class business area mixed with some residential blocks – a lot of concrete. His office was on the second floor in a two-storey building that looked like a residential complex, only the ground floor was a hardware store combined with a garage. John's office had double reinforced steel gates protecting his door, and video surveillance. I rang the doorbell.

The security locks made that distinct metallic clunky sound of constraint as the door cracked open. John was a man in his late fifties or early sixties, wearing shorts, he was a little heavy but strong, and his calf muscles showed a man who had done some miles. He broke out in a genuine smile and greeted me, waiving me in like I was an old friend. 'Was it hard to find?'

'No, I have familiarised myself with the area over the last few weeks, so I knew where I was headed.'

He smiled, 'You can leave the service, but the service never leaves you,' and chuckled.

We walked through the converted flat. It was messy – he looked like a bit of a hoarder or maybe he was just lazy. Halfway down the corridor, lined with piles of magazines and books, he pointed to an open door, 'That's Magdalena, my trusty secretary.' I popped my head into her office, and she gave me a smile and a wave and continued talking on the phone. 'You want coffee, juice, beer?'

'I'll take a beer.'

John signalled to his secretary with the "beer opening" hand gesture and she nodded and responded with the hand signal for "just after this call".

His office was of the chesterfield type, a leather seat that was creased like its owner's face, oak desk, large oak bookshelves along the walls – the room was framed with books, and pictures of him, diplomas, and a USMC pendant. A file cabinet and a gun safe were located in the corner. The safe door was halfway open, and I saw a rack of Sig Sauers and two shotguns – 'interesting business,' I thought.

'Tell me a bit about yourself and how you ended up here?' he said as I just sat down in a blood red worn out chair across from him. The desk between us gave the meeting some formality – it wasn't putting me a football field away, but it felt like an interview. I gave him the run down, the disgruntled ex-army guy who wanted to tap into the private sector but thought that Latin America was the future and not the Middle East – I wanted to level up from being a glorified guard in the sandbox. I gave him a cleaned-up version that indicated that I had done more than just regular duties. He looked pensive, a look that managers and university professors seem to have mastered. 'So, you are telling me you don't want to make $30k a month as a PSD team leader in Iraq? Most guys from here are going that route, I can arrange that!'

'It's not primarily about money and I want dynamic work that challenges me and hones my skills rather than dull them, soldiering is not the future. The playing field in Latin America will always be complicated, so establishing myself here would be a long term win I think.' It was bullshit, but even I was convinced.

John smirked, 'Wise choices, you don't sound like an army man, maybe the Swedish turmoil was your blessing?' He told me his story. He was an ex-spook, he had been there since the Noriega days, a former station chief back then and he never left. He came across like an analyst – he could definitely pull off being station chief, but he was not an operator. Maybe briefly in a previous life, but he didn't have that typeset, maybe that is what made him the perfect operator.

Magdalena interrupted with bringing in two cold Heinekens, her smile said, 'Sorry it took so long.'

John continued giving me a rundown of his business – it was a security/investigation company. His main focus was surveillance, due diligence, kidnap, and ransom negotiations and from time-to-time manhunts.

'I like you! Would you be up for managing a surveillance team, I need fresh eyes on the ground. I have about 20 taxi drivers that I have trained – they work for me in this capacity.'

It made sense, taxi drivers can be anywhere and everywhere, just sitting in their cars in weird places waiting to drive, that was what taxi drivers did mostly in Panama, so it was perfect.

He continued, 'I have a guy, Raul that runs the show, but we would need to split the teams and have better control on the ground.'

'I would be up for that,' I replied.

'Well you need to meet Raul first, I will let him make the call. If he is onboard, then it's a go. I know you are still in school, but most work happens over weekends, evenings, and nights anyways.'

Before I could reply he picked up his phone and made a call. He spoke fast and I could only pick up a few words. He covered the microphone, 'Could you meet Raul tomorrow?' I nodded. He scribbled a name and an address down on a 'post-it note'. 'Tomorrow at 19:00, the place is called *El Pavo Real*, its located...'

Before he could finish, I said, 'I know the place.' John smiled, 'Of course you do.'

I called Anna to cancel our evening plans, she was happy that I got a job offer – she was worried though. Jobs meant meeting people, meeting people meant that I might find someone else, my experience with Latina women, and perhaps others will agree – is that many have serious issues with jealousy. If she just knew what I had in store for her.

Raul was a tall gent in his late forties, his skin was tanned with salt and pepper hair, and his eyes were hawk-like and serious. He spoke surprisingly bad English, but my Spanish worked above all expectation. He took a liking to me at the meeting, and he spent most of that Sunday evening driving around explaining their local grid. The firm had developed a grid net over the city with waypoints, static positions, holding areas et cetera. It was all coded and made a lot of sense.

Raul handed me an envelope, 'It's for the first two weeks. If you do well, there will be more.'

It was $1,000, I mean it was not bad by Panama standards, not too far away from army pay but crappy for this kind of work. I was thinking 'maybe I was jumping into the deep end of the pool.' It wasn't a maybe, it was risky, but I loved it.

I was starting the following day, it was a Monday evening, and I took five guys to monitor a senior customs official who was thought to let drugs and weapons enter the country under the radar. We were to establish his routines and complete the basic groundwork. It would probably be an operation longer than what I had time for. They had to build a case against him, and that took time. I was surprised that he let me start this operation, but perhaps they needed skilled people.

After my lessons I was hyped to start the operation. I had an hour to get to the "taxi garage" owned by the firm, and used as a FOB and ops centre. It was a chilly reception from the five drivers, they were sizing me up like they would with the new kid on the block, but I knew this game and machismo wasn't going to put me off.

'I have been told that you are experienced photographers. Take a camera and follow me', I went upstairs and to the window that overlooked the busy street. I grabbed the man closest to me, 'You have 30 seconds, I want a number plate from a moving car.' He looked surprised, '25 seconds… 20 seconds… If you are good enough to wait it out, I don't mind.' He moved to the window and fiddled with the ISO settings and managed to snap a few shots. He looked like he was ready to kill me. 'Next.' I lined the butt hurt men up in front of me and showed them their pictures, 'Shutter time… exposure… white balance… stability… shutter time.' None of the pictures were good enough, the second one was the best, but still unacceptable. They all looked pissed.

The first man said, 'You can't do it better!'

'Give me your camera.' He handed his camera to me, and I walked up to the window, took a deep breath, and fired. I was damn lucky, I managed to get the plate and the driver on my first car and first shot. I showed them, 'This is what we need, I don't work with amateurs. You are not amateurs are you?' They were silent and looked down, I had proved myself, at least I was off to a reasonable start.

The unofficial leader of the taxi drivers said, 'We thought about taking him when he gets home from work?' I paused for a second before replying, 'I want to grab him at work, can we do that without attracting attention?'

One of the younger drivers replied, 'Well they park outside the freight terminal, and there is no good place to park a taxi around there. But taxis park on the grass divider at the onramp. By waiting there, we will be on his route, and once he passes us, we will be able to start a tail.'

I replied, 'Good, I like that. I then want a rotating tail with short turns.' They had done this before, and we quickly put together a plan. I was going to be in the car, as part of the first tail, ready with my camera, we had a good opportunity to make a fresh ID and tie our mark to a given car. It also helped that all the cabs were blacked out in the back, it was standard in Panama.

We parked on the grass next to the on-ramp. It was perfect; taxis were coming and leaving all the time. We had positioned ourselves at the first spot, which gave us less of a heads up, but we were sure no one would park behind us.

Bailando played on the radio. I looked at my watch and tapped my fingers to the rhythm of the song. At that point he should have left work 15 minutes ago. There were no other exits for him to take. Earlier that day we had verified his car at the parking lot with a drive-by. It was an easy car to detect, a white Cadillac, 'Not at all suspicious for a government employee' I thought.

I was fiddling with the camera, when suddenly the driver said, 'Up!'

I immediately looked up; the white Cadillac took the onramp. It was excellent mirror spotting by the driver. I put the camera up, the headlights were blinding, I had to wait for him to get closer so the lights would spread out, 'Come on come on,' I thought, I started snapping – click, click, click – and I fired 15 shots. The Caddie passed us, and the driver let one more car in ahead of us before pulling out. I flipped through the pictures. The first five were just crap, the one after was better, but one couldn't see the plate or the driver... fuck...12 crap...13...YES I got you. Both pictures 13 and 14 were perfect, they were slightly overexposed but that didn't matter. I was relieved. Nothing would have happened if I had failed, but I had something to prove.

I ran the crew for the entire night, and they dropped me off at the language institute 20 minutes before my class started. It had been a long night, and it was going to be a long day. But it was worth it.

After my lessons I needed to be there to get the operation started off properly before I could get some shuteye. On my way to the taxi garage, I stopped by the firm, John was about to leave. 'Do you have a minute?'

'Sure, sure come in, everything going okay with your crew?'

'Absolutely, I just wanted to drop off my initial target pack that we compiled last night.'

'A first target pack already?' He flipped through the bio, report, and pictures. 'You did all of this yesterday?'

'Of course, we are not sitting around wasting time,' I said and smiled.

'It's always a pleasure to have people onboard that know what they are doing.'

'It's just basic stuff,' I replied. It was true, I get that he didn't know what to expect, but what we did in one night wasn't anything spectacular, it was just basic information gathering. Maybe I should have been humbler about it, but this is when my true work persona kicked in.

Four weeks had passed, and my Spanish was evolving. After my third week I started communicating with my five man crew mostly in Spanish. At least I was making progress with the language and working towards one of my operational objectives. Most weeks I had a few emails from HQ but nothing more than a few short reports, but then things changed! 'Four weeks from now your team will be arriving in Bogota, you will be there one week early to set things up and make contact.' The email also provided a mobile phone number. I was excited but also a bit sad, I thought, 'I have a good thing going here, but I knew this day would come.'

John almost seemed to expect it, 'Quality people always get better opportunities quickly' he said. 'You have set up this operation on a better level than I could ever have expected and the guys like working with you – you brought in a lot of knowledge.'

I guess I did; before I came these drivers were static in their cars. I had developed a mobile approach and I had them doing solid foxtrot work now. In following a mark, this new skill gave them crucial reach beyond their cars.

Maybe I did change the way they worked. They were certainly more than just drivers. I had also honed their photography skills, and they had improved way beyond their initial crude 'private detective' pictures.

'If you are okay with it, I would like you to still run the operation this week and prepare a hand over to Raul on the weekend.'

'I could still run it for two more weeks' I replied. I wasn't ready to let go earlier than needed.

'I will ask something else of you' he said, 'I will brief you after your handover to Raul. Is Saturday good for you?'

I would miss working with these guys a bit, they were fun to be around and most of all not very military. My mind focused on the practical as I still had to make my travel arrangements to Bogota, settle the apartment, and write up my final report and update my target pack on the ongoing operation. What we had discovered was that he was dirty, with eleven dodgy connections and a whole police station on his payroll. Given the size of the operation, I guessed that John would have to up the resource allocation, running double crews. Then my thoughts turned to Anna. 'What to do what to do?' I thought and I decided not to tell her. I had to think about it.

Saturday finally came and I was busy compiling the last reports and all the handover material. I had made a board in the office, and we had over 3 hours of video and 500+ images, which all needed to be indexed and labelled. Of course, I was not working for free. After the first week John bumped me up to $850 a week so I was making decent pocket money, the tab still ran on the army though, but I would never tell. John joined the handover meeting with Raul, and both seemed to be impressed with the work. Maybe I overdid it a bit on the analysis, and I am sure it reinforced their feeling that I was more than my resume.

As Raul left for the Taxi garage we stepped into John's office. He slid a paper across his desk, 'I am sure you have seen one of these forms before!' It was a DoD secrecy and waiver form, 'It's that kind of work. Next weekend, or more like a long weekend of Thursday to Monday. Are you up for that?'

'I believe I am' I replied.

'Do you have a clean passport?'

'It's clean enough.'

'Good, I need you to be here at 08:00 tomorrow morning. Bring your passport.'

Anna said that I was quiet at dinner that night. I wasn't quiet for those reasons she thought. I was thinking about the next day. I had a feeling something big was going down.

I arrived 10 minutes early as John greeted me at the door, 'Take a seat outside my office for a few minutes.' Six guys were already waiting outside the office. 'We will be ready in a minute, don't talk!' John said before he stepped into his office. These guys were definitely ex-military, a mix of a few locals, some Europeans, maybe Eastern Europeans and perhaps a Yank or Brit.

'You were all here early, did I miss something?'

The Eastern European looking gentleman gave me a stern stare, 'No talking.'

The third man chuckled lightly, he seemed to get it. It appeared to be a mixed bag of grunts.

After 15 minutes of silence, we were called into John's office. John was accompanied by an accountant looking type, his round glasses, shirt, and braces gave the impression of a man who had spent his life around paper.

John handed out the DoD forms, 'Fill this in and hand me your passports.' The official looking accountant type took the passports and opened up his briefcase. He took out a sheet of Venezuelan visas, and put one in each passport, then meticulously like a well-trained civil servant, lined them up, adjusted his sights, and signed and stamped them. He shook John's hand and left, they seemed to have done this before.

I looked at the DoD form and smiled. It was a waiver, stating that we didn't work for any US government agency and that they could not be held responsible for any sub-contractors or other parties that might or might not claim to represent the DoD. It was also an NDA, that basically said we couldn't talk about the waiver – this was going to be fun.

'Alright gentlemen let's get this show on the road,' he said, 'The mark is Elon Vazquez.'

John's firm had been hired by a foreign government, not officially, to recover an individual that they wanted extradited. But the catch was that they didn't have a strong enough case against him.[1] Secondly, he was moving in jurisdictions where said government has no reach and lastly, they would never want it to go public that they were involved because it would be controversial or even illegal. Typical CIA stuff.

So, our task was to find Mr Vazquez, track him, take him, and covertly transport him to a jurisdiction where he would be extradited and of course he would just 'magically' appear there. It was a snatch and grab or possibly a kidnapping I was not sure, but in the world of diplomacy they use the

---

1   Usually, the case when the information this person has is important and he might not have even committed a crime.

euphemism extraordinary rendition – either way it was too late for me to back out.

I thought to myself, 'This is sanctioned by the DoD and Panamanian authorities, it will never be recognised by them if we fail, and if we succeed, we will get a pat on the back. We are basically doing this as civilians, with their government's unofficial blessing, so don't fuck it up.'

The plan was for us to fly into Caracas under the cover of being businessmen in the used farming equipment trade, funnily enough that was the second time of late that I had been involved in the agricultural industry. Of the two local looking men, one was Panamanian and the other Peruvian with the Panamanian most likely working for intelligence or another state agency. The two Latin Americans were leaving the next day, Monday, to set up a safe house and get a vehicle. The rest of us would arrive on Thursday, prepping and spending the night in the safe house. Friday, after his arrival in Caracas, we would follow Vazquez to the outskirts of the city, where he was believed to be staying. The intelligence was that he was arriving alone, with no external security arrangements. Despite his high profile, and dangerous line of work, he had apparently been operating without close protection for the past 10 years and felt safe in Venezuela. His itinerary was to have a business meeting in Caracas on Saturday around lunch time and then again on Sunday morning. After that he would move further into the interior of the country to visit friends and family. We did our calculations and decided that the best time to grab him was after the Saturday meeting which gave us until Sunday when he most likely would be missed. The extraction was planned from Churuguara Airport using a cargo flight to Colon Panama. It was a small airport about 7 to 8 hours west of Caracas and the play required us to enter the airport between 22:00 and 05:00.

My take is that with all the super precise intelligence, knowledge of his movements, having the airport staff on the payroll et cetera. It all pointed in one direction, big government agencies were supplying intelligence in the background. 'Why didn't they do it themselves?' I wondered. It went without saying that they had resources for this kind of thing. But on the other hand, contractors provide deniability. John was definitely well entrenched in the system, 'Did he really leave the agency?' He probably did but still ran errands for them.

Just thinking about it left me with a sour taste in my mouth, but I liked sour candy, so it wasn't all bad – I was curious and wanted to know more. We were leaving at 04:00 on Thursday and weapons were to be supplied locally. It was going to be an intense week. One of my final days before the mission was spent on a mini cruise with Anna. She knew something was afoot. I suppose I was "being distant". Women sometimes think that the absence of being present is about other women. Maybe some of the time but if she really knew – I was excited and on the edge about the mission. But I had put myself in this situation and emotional entanglement during an operation – nothing new I suppose. In retrospect it was not worth it, not by a long shot. But I certainly was not the first or last person to be making that claim. Now I just had to play the hand I dealt myself, she was more a liability than an asset. On the plus side, and in cold hard intelligence terms, she added 'normal' to my picture but that was so minimal it was not worth the effort. I needed to shape up and be a bit less distant with her, just for the time being and then I would be out of her hair.

On Wednesday I told the language school that I was going away for a long weekend, and I wouldn't be back until Tuesday, but they shouldn't be alarmed if I was a few days later. Herman liked the idea but was also clear that I would not be reimbursed for cancelled days with short notice. 'Cheapskate,' I thought but I didn't really care at this point.

After my lessons I decided to send a short communication to HQ. I don't know why but it was like I wanted to flag that something was going down. I was looking for their blessing even if I couldn't have it. 'I am going for an excursion this weekend, I am hoping for good weather and will be back next week, so checking out early,' it was at least something if this project went south. I imagined the news articles 'Swedish Mercenary arrested for attempted kidnapping in Venezuela.' My mother wouldn't be proud, and I would probably do a couple of years in a Venezuelan prison before I could be transferred. If I survived that is. People often went missing in the remote regions in South America.

At 04:15 we left the firm, escorted by drivers from my old crew. The driver looked in the mirror and said, 'May God be with you.' I am not sure if it was a common expression, but as a non-religious man it gave me an ominous feeling.

There were not many people checking in on this early flight and they had that extra visa/passport control; this is often the case when the destination country provides their own border control at check in. He flipped through my passport, closely inspecting my previous stamps. He reached the newly acquired visa on the sixth page, looked at me and said, 'What's your business in Venezuela?'

'We are a team that is going to the agricultural expo.'

He looked at me and closed my passport with a snap, handing it back silently as he reached for the next man in line. I am glad he didn't want to see our business documentation; we had some folders, business cards et cetera, but it was shaky at best. While going through security, I thought that if they had suspicions, they would surely have just flagged us and then grabbed us in Venezuela. We pulled off the tired businessman look with slightly wrinkly shirts, rolled up sleeves and sweaty armpits. The problem was that I was still a bit young to have sold being an established businessman – I was maybe a junior associate at best.

The aircraft did a dead cat bounce before finally getting airborne, it was a Venezuelan airline which rattled so much I could feel the vibrations through my arm rests, and if that wasn't enough the engine sounded like a Stuka dive bomber. I was not afraid of flying and had been in a lot of different and wonky aircraft, but this one just reeked of a lack of maintenance, most likely due to embargoes, sanctions, and a general decay in professionalism.

As we completed our descent, our landing was a repeat of the take off, and we bounced down two thirds of the runway. Luckily it was a small turboprop aircraft and when we finally had wheels down, we had some space to break. The humidity and heat hit you like a hot wet rag in the face.

We only had hand luggage, so we were quick to the border control line. I was a bit tense as I moved up to the officer in the booth. He took my passport and shouted to a colleague, he left the booth and his colleague just stood there weirdly and looked on. He hadn't even looked at my passport yet. I asked, 'Is there a problem?' the colleague just put his hand up in a 'stay and wait' motion.

It took what seemed like forever and the border guard returned, looking upbeat and thanked his colleague with a tap on the shoulder. He sat down in his chair, quickly took up my passport, glanced at it and just like that I heard the double tap of' two stamps on the visa. 'Sorry for your wait, I had to use the restroom,' he said as he chuckled to himself, 'Enjoy your stay.'

I could barely get a 'thank you' out of my mouth, and hurriedly continued on my way.

I thought to myself, I had such a bad feeling and it ended up with a man going to the bathroom? I hope he washed his hands. Even if it seemed like an honest thing, the suspicion lingered in me. It is the curse of working in intelligence, you end up trusting no one and analysing everything, and by analysing everything, one starts going nuts, and at times one sticks out like a sore thumb. I remembered Alan from the FRU and his words 'You will miss things, but you will look the part,' he was right about that, you have to dial your senses up and down accordingly because being on high alert all the time makes you conspicuous.

The arrival hall was fiesta loud and crowded as always in Latin America. Perhaps a myth, but apparently during the Spanish Civil War the Germans said that they had never seen such a well organised chaos as in the Spanish military lines – and this certainly rubbed off on their airport culture. We spotted the SAP crew, and they waved and cheered hello, we greeted each other like old friends. The best way to be camouflaged in a cheery, bubbly culture, is to act the same.

They had an extended Dodge van from the late eighties. It looked the part and was the type of vehicle parents told their kids to avoid. But surprisingly when I looked around in the parking lot it was a fairly common vehicle. In practical terms it made sense, as we needed the space in the back. When we rolled out of the parking lot one of the SAP guys swept the bags and made sure we weren't tagged or bugged. It felt like I was missing out on information – this was a well-planned mission and I wondered about my role in this. Were there underlying purposes? Or were they just one man short?

The SAP crew were pros and navigated the busy streets of Caracas like locals, they were used to the no regrets driving style. Our safe house was about 60 minutes outside the central parts of Caracas. They hooked us up with a kind of town house with the living room on the second floor and a workshop/garage on the ground floor. The neighbourhood was one step up from a *favela*, but it gave privacy. And the police tended to stay away from those types of areas.

The garage doors closed behind us, and only the crack in the door and a single light bulb illuminated the room. A ray of light from the door marked a line across the floor and up the wall crossing a sheet of black plastic that hid where the window was. A ladder gave us access to the upper floor. 'The ladder is wobbly so climb carefully,' one of the SAP guys said. The upper floor was run down with a stained couch and plastic chairs, the type that were found almost everywhere in Latin America. They had been sleeping on camping mats as they wisely didn't want to try the bed. They had been preparing well, sleeping bags and mats for everyone, radios, MREs, bottled water, an assortment of pistols (Makarovs, Chinese licensed Stars, no name ones) AK47s and a shotgun. The American took the floor and it became clear that he had a leading role in this operation.

'Okay listen up, it's not a four-star hotel but the neighbourhood is off the government radar, and they will be quiet as we are in good standing here, we also have quick access to the highway. We have a lot of ground to cover so we need to get moving.'

Vasquez was landing at 09:35. We knew where he departed from and what he looked like, but we didn't know where he was staying or whether he had beefed up security – we had to prepare for any outcome.

The SAP had arranged two sedans that they parked behind the garage. We needed to be glued to our mark from the airport. The plan was to keep a rotating team at his accommodation, trying to establish habits and movements and then grab him in a suitable location after the lunch meeting Saturday. We had a seven plus hour drive to the airport and our guard window was 22:00–05:00 so we had to leave Caracas at the earliest by 15:00 and absolutely no later than 19:00. Also, we didn't want to be too early as we didn't want to wait around with Vasquez in the car.

'How do we transport him?' said the Eastern European who I later learned was from Ukraine, or at least born there.

'Well, we were thinking of building a box in the back of the van. We have the parts of a cultivator here and export documents for it. That is what's officially going back on the return flight. James here is a paramedic, and we have intramuscular haloperidol and promethazine.' These guys were obviously not fucking around, as haloperidol and promethazine were often used in psychiatric emergency wards to tranquilize violent patients. It usually puts people to sleep or in a drowsy state within 10–15minutes and can also cause respiratory depression in patients with underlying health conditions. It didn't feel like the right approach, and I had to say something.

'You are overcomplicating things,' I said, 'The risks of putting a drugged man in a box for seven plus hours is high, he will come by his own will.'

'What?'

'I said he will come by his own will.'

'I heard you the first time,' said James with a grin. He was in his early thirties, of average height, and he had a badly healed scar on his right cheek which made him look seasoned. He asked, 'What makes you think that he will.'

I stood up and paced. 'Firstly, he is a survivor; he has been a money man, not a fighter. Secondly, he has stayed under the radar for a long time, and we can assume that he would have had to have made several compromises to stay out of trouble for such a long time. Thirdly, he has a family, and he will try to protect them. Fourthly he knows his information is valuable and he can make a deal with whoever is on the other end. Lastly, he will be more afraid of us than we are of him. And if that doesn't work, we always have the option of violence, but if we go down that route, just keep him in the back, splash some vodka on him and he will pass for a drunk.'

'I agree, keep it simple,' said the man to the right. The Ukrainian nodded, and the leader looked around. 'Okay, I am down with that.' He looked at me, 'Will you convince him to go?' I nodded. I just hoped my approach was the right one.

The night before, we did some final preparations and tested the equipment. The two locals were going in the first car – they were the primary tail as they were better suited to the frenzied Latin traffic. The Ukrainian and I would run the position of back up tail; our other duties included taking over as the first static shift when the mark reached his destination; and taking over again when he went to his business meeting. We would also be a part of the snatch later that night. The van would hold the rest of the crew and carried the real stopping power if needed.

The clutch had to be maxed out to the floor, for the gears to engage. 'The clutch cable probably needed to be replaced. Always the lack of maintenance on the cars and planes' I thought, as the car jumped a few times as I backed out of the driveway.

I looked at the Ukrainian with a 'sorry' look. He shrugged his shoulders, 'They got shitty cars, what can you do.'

It was 06:00 in the morning, and we had a 45 minute drive. We needed the buffer time; traffic was a nightmare. The airport had a lot of good spots for parking and a circular route in and out which made it easy to follow our mark without raising any red flags. The lead car found a good position. I parked closer to the exit with sufficient distance from the lead car; our primary task was to mark the target when he exited so that the first tail didn't miss him.

We sat down and had breakfast in the airport restaurant and took the opportunity to take one last look at his most recent picture. It was 3 years old, and he wore a Panama hat, it looked expensive. It wasn't the best picture, but it was taken from the side, so one got a good look at his nose and profile. He had strong features, a well worn moustache, and droopy eyes.

The airport started to fill up as the morning inbound flights started to arrive. The arrivals exit quickly became crowded. The sea of people made it easier to blend in with the crowd, except for us gringos that is. Vazquez's flight was on the tarmac 15 minutes early, and five flights arrived just before his. I took up position on one side of the exit and the Ukrainian on the other.

I thought to myself, 'It always feels like forever waiting for people coming out from the baggage claim,' but this felt like that on steroids. After 25 minutes the automatic doors slid open. I noticed, two kids and a woman coming through the doors waving, they waved at what I assumed was their husband and father who stood in the crowd. Then a single man exited. He was around

175 centimetres, a bit chubby, with a tired look, and a wrinkly linen suit. He had no hat, to cover his long, messy hair, and bald spot – it was him.

He stopped 15 metres from the exit and pulled out a rolled-up hat from his bag. It was the same Panama hat and he looked like he did in the picture, just a bit heavier perhaps. He looked relaxed, strolling along, he certainly did not have Captain H's determined stride.

He moved towards the terminal exit, I maintained a comfortable distance, and picked up my pace. As he exited the terminal, he walked towards the taxi line. There were plenty of taxis. It served us well as the taxi line was on the way to our parking spot.

He got into a taxi in the middle of the line. I stopped short to mark the cab, and the Ukrainian tapped my shoulder and greeted me with half a hug, and I returned the greeting by patting him on the back. We started talking as we walked towards our car. As the taxi left, we saw that our crew had sights on the mark and were positioned a few cars behind Vaquez's cab.

As they passed the corner we hung back as we wanted to see if there were any other security agents tracking his movements. It didn't seem like it, for now the coast was clear. We knew we would be a good five to ten minutes behind the mark, but the traffic leaving the airport was moving at a steady pace so we would catch up.

We had about a seven-minute gap to the lead. I drove as fast as I could, as the lead tail and the mark were also moving at pace. The lead did a good job guiding us although we had a pretty dense waypoint system mapped out.

The taxi stopped, the lead gave us the address; it was a shitty neighbourhood. The hotel looked like an American motel, where the rooms have their doors on the outside. The layout was a bottom floor and a top floor with a balcony like structure in an L-shape. The reception was rudimentary, a hut on the bottom floor.

The mark had moved into the reception area at the same time as we arrived. The lead group asked if we had this so that they could roll away. We took over but only one snag, we had no good place to park. For the time being, we parked at the gas station like many others who popped out to get cigarettes. The key was to find out which room was his before we regrouped and planned our next steps. Vasquez came out with the receptionist. They both looked sweaty, but to be fair it was as hot as hell. The receptionist pointed to the far right at what looked like the upper floor.

The mark went to the staircase that was located on the right part of the L shaped floor and walked up. He proceeded to take a right and entered the second to last room. The front of the hotel faced the main road. The staircase was on the ground floor in the corner of the L at the intersection between the main road and the alleyway. Conveniently Vasquez's room was located in the leg that overlooked the alley way. We found a good spot down the alley way, the problem with that was that we needed to be on his ass when he moved as we only covered his door and not the front.

Our shift ended at 22:00, and it had been an extremely long day. He had only gone outside twice, once to go to the gas station to pick up some snacks and the other time to the courtyard of the hotel. It was a green area in the back where they had some tables and chairs and he sat there for a couple of hours working and flipping papers and drinking coffee. His lights went out at 21:30. We were relieved by the lead car team, and I briefed them a block away while the Ukrainian covered the room.

We were all concerned with his static behaviour, but we assumed that he was just tired. Static wasn't necessarily bad, but it gave us nothing to go on. On the other hand if he was on the move that would have been harder. My shift was going to start at 09:00 the next morning, and I needed sleep.

Back at the safe house we coordinated some of the remaining details. I had snapped a few photos with my pocket camera, and we gave the crew a detailed map briefing.

The van needed to be in place when we got back from the midday business meeting and from there on it was all improv in terms of how we would pick him up. Unfortunately, we had to come back to the safe house with Vazquez in the van and leave our cars behind; not optimal but we had no alternative. For a while we considered it, but we couldn't burn the cars. The van crew had orders to pack up and clean the place – it would be a rolling drop off.

I slept lightly that night. Up until that point we had been unarmed but with D-Day's tasks at hand we took a piece from the bag before leaving. I went for the Makarov as the Star was so rattly, I was not sure it was going to fire if it came to that. The van crew brought the heavy fire power, so we had to rely on them if shit went down.

The Ukrainian and I talked it over on the way to the hotel. Vaquez was not the threat. Maybe he would return with someone after the meeting or maybe there was counter surveillance we hadn't detected, but the real danger was if someone got wind of the snatch and alerted his family or the authorities. I wondered what kind of family he had. He looked like a stiff zombie and on the surface his life looked damn boring.

The lead car team looked tired, and the driver was half asleep. 'He had breakfast and went to buy the morning paper, that's it. Not really an active guy.'

'Alright, we got it from here, go get some sleep. Next time we meet it will be with Vazquez in the back of the van.'

'Let's hope so, let's hope so.'

At 11:15 a cab arrived and 5 minutes later Vazquez was on his way. They were heading towards central Caracas, and it was hard keeping up with the busy morning traffic. He stopped outside Mar Plaza, a big shopping centre. The Ukrainian dropped me off, time was against us. 'Hey,' he said as he tapped my shoulder on the way out, 'I will find a spot after the taxi line', and he pointed 50m down the street.

'Okay' I had no comms, only a pocket camera and a Makarov – could be worse I guess.

He hit a brisk stride this time. It was 11:57, and we guessed his meeting would start at 12:00. He looked stressed but determined. Vasquez headed towards the food court. As he approached the Lebanese restaurant a man got up from a table and greeted him. I passed by them both as they sat down at a table close to the aisle. I grabbed a table at a coffee shop next to the restaurant. They were fiddling with their briefcases; I swept my hand over my right hip, to check if anything was caught on the Makarov. It was a bit bulkier than the Glock that I was used to, and I was afraid it would snag on my shirt. I always check my piece when leaving my vehicle, but sometimes I need reassurance.

I didn't need to get that close, but it was just old habits. As they ordered food, I got my pocket camera out and concealed it in my hand. I zoomed in and snapped twice, repositioned my hand and snapped a few more. I couldn't properly check the pictures, I just glanced at the screen, and it looked like I had something. I shouldn't take this risk with the camera. 'Keep it simple,' I thought, 'The mission was to deliver him, that's all.'

After their lunch they signed a few papers and shook hands. It was all over in 45 minutes. Vazquez got up and left first. His meeting partner lingered. I didn't want to be stuck between them, but he didn't move. I took the escalators down to the ground floor, as I knew he had to come out the same way. I could still see Vazquez walking on the second-floor balcony. I lost him from time to time as he was window shopping before he reached the escalators leading down to the exit. His meeting partner caught up with him, they shook hands again and exchanged a few words. The partner then came down the escalators and went straight out and to the left. Vazquez finally came down the escalator; he made one last stop in a liquor store just before the exit to the street.

He exited the mall and got a cab that just dropped off a customer, shit I had to move 100 metres down the taxi line as they speed away, I walked quickly but tried not to draw attention to myself. As I reached our car, I said, 'The blue taxi.'

The Ukrainian looked at me before pulling out, 'Are you joking, half of the cabs are blue?'

'It was less than a minute ago, it had a green light on top, and the left part of the light was broken. He had just vanished, traffic was heavy, and we had to go with the flow. He could easily have disappeared down any of the many off ramps.

We drove for 15 minutes without a sign. 'Fuck me we lost him', I said.

'Don't worry', said the Ukrainian, 'He will get back to the hotel at some point and our mission is not to see what he is up to but rather to grab him.'

He was right, but it felt like a missed opportunity. 'How the fuck could we be so unprepared? It felt a bit like amateur hour', I thought.

'I am heading back to the hotel,' he said, and I nodded.

I reported in on the radio, and no one seemed to react to the fact that we had lost him. It was 14:05 when we got back to the hotel, and he hadn't appeared yet, I didn't like losing him or control of the situation.

The van that held the rest of the crew was positioned in an adjacent alley. I could just imagine how hot it was in the back. 'Take a break and get some refreshments', I said.

It was silent for a minute, then the response came, 'Yeah we will take a spin and get back shortly.' We had found a good spot in an alley on the opposite street, from where we could see his room, the reception area, and the staircase.

At 15:00 you could feel the tension rise a bit as we knew we were entering our window of opportunity which ended at 19:00. Still no sign of Vazquez.

At 16:40 he arrived in a cab; he carried shopping bags. As I reported it in, now it was my show. I wanted to wait until darkness, but still grab him before dinnertime so we didn't make it more complicated than necessary. We had an hour or two of wiggle room, but I didn't want to use that at this point.

At 17:45 he left his room for the ice machine. I knew I needed to move but catching him outside was a gamble. I waited. At 18:35, I said, 'Move the van to the alleyway stairs when I move. We will leave the car and the Ukrainian will take it back afterwards.' I received a PTT double tap back. I looked at the Ukrainian, 'It's time. Bring the duffle bag. If he resists, we drag him down and leave. If not, you clear the room and leave in our car.'

He nodded.

The adrenaline was starting to build. I walked across the street vigilantly. It had just become dark, which gave us additional cover – it was the calm before the storm.

I tightened the black Nomex flight gloves that I wore to prevent fingerprints being left at the scene. I had a baseball cap to cover my face, and we already checked for cameras. The van rolled up quietly as we moved up the stairs. It was calm. 'Had I thought this through, should I knock? Would he create a scene, was he armed?' Many questions, and there was no time for answers. I knocked softly twice, and I heard movement, like he was getting up from his bed. As the handle turned and the door cracked open, I pushed my foot in, firmly but not aggressively.

He had dress pants on and a shirt that was half unbuttoned, with no shoes. He had probably been resting in bed. 'Hi,' I said with a big smile as I watched his hands. 'Are you Elon Vazquez?'

'Ye... yes I am, who are you?' he stuttered.

'Come with us; take the easy way and you will survive this.' He looked like he had seen a ghost, I pushed further into the room, 'Shoes.' I grabbed his neck, and repeated, 'Shoes.' He pushed his feet into the untied dress shoes, the heel bulged a bit as he pushed in his foot. I took a sturdy grip of his arm and peaked outside, 'Go,' and I half pushed him in front of me, squeezing his arm. I held him up a bit as we went down the stairs so that he wouldn't trip on his laces. The street was still calm, with no one to be seen. I had to make an effort, so it wasn't obvious that I was forcing him. When we were two metres away, the van door slid open, and I let him step in by himself.

I looked around and saw a person walking into the gas station. Everything seemed normal. I slid into the seat next to Vaquez as the door closed. I heard a fast movement and then I saw was one of the Spanish-speaking guys getting up behind him and putting him into a chokehold. His hands grabbed the forearm of the agent who had locked in a rear naked choke, and he kicked frantically. I could see his eyes tear up. This is often a physiological reaction to being choked as part of the fight or flight response. But there was something more, I saw in his eyes that he thought this was his final moment. As the van drove away, I asked him, 'Will this be a calm and easy ride?' He was still struggling; I gave the look to the agent, and he eased his grip. 'Will this be a calm and easy ride,' I repeated in a calm voice. He nodded as he gasped for air with tears running down his cheek. I zip tied his hands in the front and patted him down; he only had a packet of cigarettes and a lighter on him. I put them in a bag that I had prepared. I hooded him with a canvas bag and tied his shoelaces before we moved him to the back. I felt bad for the chokehold as he had come with us without a fuss, since violence was not his game.

I looked around and saw only serious faces and a few nods of approval. We took a detour to give the team in the second car time to prepare the safe house. As we approached the safe house it was pitch dark. The Ukrainian and the driver came out of the garage with three bags. They got in silently, and we rolled – it was all systems go. I looked back and Vazquez had also been fitted with ear defenders. I tapped the Ukrainian's shoulder and gave him the bag with the lighter and cigarettes and pointed to the grab bag. He nodded and put it in with the other items he recovered from Vazquez's room before sealing the zippers with zip ties.

I needed to wind down a bit. I whispered to the Ukrainian, 'Any Reaction after we left?'

He shook his head, 'Nothing at all.'

I looked at my watch, it was 22:00. We had left the safe house at around 20:00 and we had approximately five hours. There was not too much traffic and not too little to single you out on the road. The van crew had prepared pee bottles, there was no stopping here... Unfortunately, I had to use one right away. It was a standard 1.5 litre coca cola bottle. They were trickier as you had to aim. I probably spilled a drop or two in the darkness. I took some hand sanitizer on a cloth and wiped the floor.

The Ukrainian smiled, 'We haven't robbed a bank you know,' he whispered.

Well, I was not about to leave my DNA in this van. Strange that somehow the extraordinary rendition was a lesser thing to robbing a bank.

We took turns sitting with Vazquez, he didn't move other than when the car rocked a bit. I offered him water but with no success and wondered what he did, or what information he had to warrant this, it better be good for someone. It was an uneventful ride and we made good time. It was 02:50 when we stopped 5 minutes short of the airport. There were almost no vehicles on the road except for the occasional truck and car.

One of the Spanish speaking team members went outside, lit a cigarette, and made a call. He said with a low voice, 'We wait here for 15 minutes.' I took the opportunity to stretch my legs. It was a humid night, and I couldn't wait to change shirts, but that was for later. We drove past the airport and turned onto a track that ran along the fence. These were normally reserved for security and emergency vehicles.

I saw lights ahead; it was from an airport runway friction testing vehicle.[2] He had opened a gate in the fence that was locked with a heavy chain. We drove in and stopped close by. Then the unknown man locked the gate, came up to the driver's window and said something like, 'Just follow me,' it was clear that they knew each other. We followed him to the furthest away part of the cargo ramp where we found a small airplane. It was lit up, and the pilot was walking around the plane doing his checks.

He had an American accent, 'You can load the cargo, the heavy items in the back and the precious cargo in the cabin.' The locals and the Yank boarded the plane with Vasquez. Me and the Ukrainian loaded the very awkward shaped cultivator part and a few of the bags.

'Did you get his phone?'

'Yes, I put it in the lead lined bag, I checked everything else twice. Most of his possessions were just regular things, and the presents were actually presents. Do you think anyone would mind if I took his whisky?' I just looked at the Ukrainian.

'I know I know it's still a waste,' he said.

Before I boarded the plane, I did a sweep of the van. I walked up the ladder to the plane with the weapons duffle bag slung over my shoulder. The pilot commented, 'You are responsible for that bag, no cowboy business okay.'

'I'll try,' I replied.

Vazquez was placed in the back. He was still hooded and had his feet tied. I sat down in the front with the Ukrainian and the Yank. The man who opened the gate, came onboard, he collected everyone's 'entry slip', a piece of paper you get when you enter the country and that is matched and collected when you leave. 'Was he going to sign us out of Venezuela?' I thought. The Yank said, 'He will bring them to Caracas, so it looks like we have left from there.'

'That will hold up until they check the flight records,' I said.

'Let's hope they don't then,' he replied and smiled. I never liked the Yank, he was weird, always in the background playing second fiddle, like he was observing.

'Read the folder if you want to know what to do in an emergency, but for now sit in your chairs and keep your seatbelts on because we are leaving, they are lighting up in 5 minutes.'

'Lighting up?' I asked.

---

2   A vehicle that is used at medium to large sized commercial airports to test runway friction. They are also referred to as skid vehicles, or runway testers.

The Yank answered, 'The airport is not manned this early. It's lit up remotely from Caracas.'

He knew odd details, 'Definitely not his first rodeo,' I thought.

The gate opener pulled out our blocks and waved us off as we taxied down the runway which lit up like a string of pearls. The engines were loud and the whole aircraft shook as we sped down the runway. I trusted this pilot more than the one who took us here and nodded off against the window after takeoff.

The Ukrainian bumped my knee, 'We are almost there.' I looked out and the sun was rising, I saw the glittering ocean beneath us. The touchdown was smooth as silk, even if it was one of those scary ones when you think you are landing in the water because the runway was so close to the shore. We had landed in Colon, Panama.

I could see a black van and a black sedan waiting just off the runway. As soon as the door opened four men came in, and walked straight back to Vasquez, two of them dragged him out and put him in the black van. The Yank stood up and shook the hand of one of the men, 'His gear is in the back', and they both walked out. I saw them unloading his duffle bags from the cargo hold.

The black van drove off and that was that. I took the weapons bag and stepped out on the tarmac, 'This is me,' said the Yank, as he shook my and the Ukrainian's hands and said, 'Pleasure working with you.' He walked to the sedan that was waiting for him, turned around and walked back to me. He took a moment while he looked for something in his wallet. Eventually he took out a wrinkled business card and gave it to me. It was nearly blank having only an email address on it. 'If you or any of yours ever need some help or want to collab, give me a holler. Take care now,' and he shook my hand.

As he walked back the Ukrainian asked, 'What's a holler?'

The Panamanian and I both started laughing.

'What? I don't watch MTV.'

We laughed as we unloaded the rest of the equipment.

It would take a few years before I saw the Yank again, it was in the Sandbox, and he was still working for the same agency for which he apparently always did.

I did my last week in Panama, and I had taken a few extra days off language school. I needed to sleep and just wind down. I had a bit of trouble accepting what had gone down. It was quick and intense and then over just like that. I just needed to let it sink in, I guess.

I headed over to see John at the firm one last time, he had invited me for a farewell lunch as he called it. We hadn't seen each other since the briefing before Venezuela. He greeted me with a hug, 'I'll miss you Swedy.'

'Sure you will,' I said ironically.

'I will, it's been an odd pleasure,' he said.

I felt the same. It had been a pleasure, and it was an odd one. Not the working together part but rather how our paths crossed and where we ended up. Entangled with forever secrets, from starting out as strangers to this. 'I got something for you, this is for the last gig.' He threw an envelope across his desk. 'Are you not going to open it?'

I took the envelope and weighed it in my hand, 'I trust you and I'll keep it as a memory.'

He laughed, 'Just don't forget it in a drawer somewhere, I put my contacts in there, I'll be glad to hear from you, in good times or in bad, never forget that.'

I felt a bit sad as I left, I had been living and working in this bubble for some time. But it was just a fantasy world of sorts created by my other persona. I knew I had to get back to what I was supposed to be doing, I had to stay sharp. I looked up at the apartment from the street, 'You served me well,' I thought. I was heading out to the airport. My flight to Bogota was leaving at 14:00.

As I walked towards the terminal, my phone rang, it was Anna. I picked up. 'I'll have dinner ready at 18:00, is chicken and rice, okay?' she said.

'It will be perfect, see you then, love you.'

As I walked into the terminal, I removed the sim card and dumped the burner in the first trash can and the cracked sim card in the next. I looked back at the exit. 'Goodbye for now.'

12

Fighting the FARC in Colombia

'Joint Taskforce Omega – White Raven, it was a unit exclusively manned by foreign soldiers – a strike team.'

Arriving in Bogota, I was surprised how clean it was, especially when compared to other Latin American cities. It was organised and in order, not German by any means, but more structured than much of the organised chaos I had seen up to that point. It was mostly superficial; one didn't have to dig much deeper to realise why Colombia was one of the world's most dangerous countries at least during those times. Colombia was different and hard to explain, it was dangerous and infinitely complex. The guerrillas were fighting the government, the Army fought the rebels, the drug producers were supported by some guerrillas, and at other times were fighting both the guerrillas and the government. With little state control, and too much money and power on the line, there was little opportunity for a sustainable peace. It was a gold rush for private security companies; you could make serious money with less risks and without many of the complications seen in a high intensity conflict, like in Iraq or Afghanistan. The kidnap and ransom business was at a peak level, much to the enjoyment of narcotics traffickers looking to diversify their portfolio so to say, opportunistic criminals and also problem-solvers and insurance companies.

We were heavily armed, and well trained, but now I know that we were operating under a false sense of security as no weapons in the world could save you if Colombia decided to eat you alive, you would just be another statistic in a long line of missing people. I had been met by a local driver, just someone from the taxi company. Our minivan was heading to an apartment hotel close to the beautiful Parque 93, where I would meet Dirk in the lobby the following morning.

When I thought about it, I had gotten very little input on the mission and the players involved so far. The setup with Dirk had been handled from Sweden so all I could do was to trust that they had a plan.

My initial reason, at least my cover story and mission in Panama was done and dusted. I had learned Spanish, a reasonable ask in the world of intelligence, and I had become working proficient. The second objective was to learn the ropes and get a feel for Latin America. Which I had already done. I had good exposure to the local life and made a few unexpected excursions. But for the third objective collecting information about the conflict, drug trade and the Darien region, which might have been the more important objective, I had pretty much failed. The reasons of course were that I had been spending too much time chasing girls and looking for bad men in Venezuela. I had to wing it if I got questions, act confident and rely on my ability to talk much about things on which I knew little. The trick was confidence, building in details borrowing from my wider variety of experiences.

I slowly took a sip from my water bottle, I wasn't completely sure what they expected from me, and neither were they as this was a first for everyone. I guess it was mostly to grease the wheels to ensure a smooth arrival of the team.

The receptionist was cute. I was only booked for a night so when she asked when I would be checking out, I told her that I would make arrangements after breakfast. 'Okay,' she said and smiled, 'Don't wander too far at night as it might be unsafe.' For a second, it felt like a threat, but I am sure that she was just looking out for her guests. And her cheeky smile almost made me ask her out, but I had to focus on the mission at hand this time.

I had a short nap, as it was a humid day. I looked out over the park from my balcony and got hit with a strange feeling. I started to think about where life had taken me. It felt like I got to where I wanted to be, but it felt like a vacuum. The teenager on that static bike during selection could never even have dreamt about doing what I was doing right now. The operators dream, uncharted and structured chaos. It felt like I was an actor, like it was almost made up. On the other hand, this was the nature of the job, I guess. I was still a bit too "army-fied", as I sometimes missed the officialdom of things. I think Panama had messed with my head a little, I felt very distant from the IRP at that moment, even if I was thriving in the hot zone.

I didn't wander off too far that night. Bogota was interesting as with many cities that exist between the first and third worlds, where one could have a middle-class, hipster night out, and also possibly be shot or kidnapped. I decided to have dinner at the nearby Bogota Beer company, my first of many visits. The insurgency felt far away in the humid, funky Bogota night – good food, craft beer and a cosmopolitan vibe with a Latino twist. It seduced me, in fact so much so that for a moment, Bogota had projected a feeling that made me want to settle down there. The tranquil vibes lured me in.

Dirk was early, I was sitting in the lobby, and hadn't finished my coffee. He was short with ropey muscles, a well-maintained beard and moustache accompanied by his long grey hair tied up in a ponytail. His jeans and baseball cap were bleached by the sun. He looked exactly how one would expect a retired American operator to look. He transmitted a "Delta Force vibe", although at that point I had had limited experience with Delta Force guys, perhaps just intuition, or movies.

I was about to get up to greet him.

'Sit, sit. Relax, I'll have a coffee too.' He waved at the reception girl. *'Cafe con leche, por favor.* So did you have good trip, slept okay?'

He was like the cosy, but probably lethal, grandfather you never had. His moustache was characteristically discoloured from smoking. It reminded me of my own grandfather. He took out a case of cigarillos from his pocket. 'Do you mind? Want one?'

'Go ahead, no thank you,' I replied.

He complained about the traffic and how hard it had become to find decent parking. 'Did you find a good place to eat yesterday?' he asked.

'Yeah, I went to the Bogota Beer company, it was really good.'

'Good choice,' he said. 'A bit overpriced though. Will you be ready to go in 10 minutes? You can bring your gear with you, as you are moving to a new place.'

He navigated the streets like a local, but his driving style was Western, a bit on the safe side. We arrived at the gates of Military Police Battalion No.13 just outside of Bogota. It was a rundown regiment looking like something from the Belize jungles with a colonial flair. We were just waved through. That had been a common theme the last year. I was astonished at how much they trusted you when you were in the loop. It was a decent-sized regiment with a myriad of one-storey barracks, storage units and exercise areas all intertwined with each other. It didn't have the organisation of a Western regiment, but it seemed to work.

We drove up to a cluster of barracks that was located on top of a hill in the most northern part of the regiment. When I got out of the car it felt like I was slapped in the face with a hot wet cloth. The humidity was excruciating. Up until then I had mostly been moving between AC-equipped areas, so I was only starting to acclimatise. I hoped they at least had a fan in the room otherwise it would be a bitch to sleep in. Three operator type guys were having beers sitting in plastic chairs outside the barracks.

'Fresh meat, welcome,' one said as he raised his bottle of Club Colombia beer.

'Don't mind them, they have been here too long,' Dirk said.

We entered a small office in what looked like officer's barracks.

'This is Major Gustave, our liaison with the Colombian Army here, and this is Tony. I believe you have met before.'

We had met him previously; it was Mr T from MC Consulting. Tony smiled like a boy that had just been caught lying when I shook his hand. I now saw the true 'use' of Tony. He was the middleman, but who was he really? Just the right man in the right place? Still military? British intelligence? He was going to introduce us to the Colombian Army unit that housed us and to the multinational team assisting the Colombian Army. The time we had spent in the UK training for Mr D with MC Consulting had been to vet us, that was clear to me now. I had five days before the rest of the patrol arrived and I had been assigned a QM-like role, preparing our group's equipment, weapons, ID cards, vehicles et cetera. I also used the time to get acquainted with the surrounding areas.

We were equipped with the Colombian Army's Israeli Galil Carbine and a Sig Sauer pistol.[1] I was familiar with the Sig Sauer, as the Swedish police uses it in many versions, and the Galil is a favourite carbine of mine. I liked it better than the more popular M4, as it was robust and had a nice feel to it. Many complained about the weight and the lack of rails et cetera. But as always, it's not the tools, it's the carpenter. The Galil was regarded by many as an older generation weapon, but old school is not always worse, and newer is not always better. Weapons and kit have always been plentiful on the operator scene, and we had our pick. Sometimes it adds value, sometimes it doesn't but for a piece of gear to add value one must master the basics first. For example, a red dot sight can help a poor shot to get by, but it can make a good shot a professional. And it's always like that, aim points, NVGs, laser pointers, satnav, et cetera. If you master the basics – become proficient with iron sights, learn to navigate with a map at night, be confident in controlling a night ambush through signals then one operates and builds on a firm foundation. A key lesson was

---

1   The Galil is an Israeli designed assault rifle, and widely used throughout the world. The Sig Sauer pistol is used by military, security, intelligence, and police officials around the world.

to understand which tools were needed; the fancy stuff was not necessary for every job. One must be confident with every tool in the toolbox, a carefully selected choice of weaponry and technology, each having a specific function and a part to play in practicing the craft.

I didn't feel that arriving five days before the others was truly necessary, at least not yet, but it all depended on what was going to happen next and in how much of a hurry they were. Tony, Dirk and a few of the local officers were going to hold a week-long familiarisation training exercise and introduction before we were transferred to the active unit that was stationed up north, closer to the Panamanian border. I had been trying to get some more information about the mission, but I was given the mushroom treatment, kept in the dark and fed shit. I guessed that they wanted to hold on to it until we were all assembled. Military security is a principle of war after all – the fuckers.

The good part was that I had a lot of range time. I was good, reasonably modest too, but I was out of practice and needed to get the rust off. They had a massive shooting complex within the perimeter of the regiment. It had two long-range sniper stations, a 360 degree fire CQB village, and a large favela-style settlement designed for urban warfare, as well as regular ranges. It was well kept and more advanced than what I had expected. But on reflection, an Army that had been battling an insurgency for more than 60 years would certainly know something about shooting ranges. They had less tech, but the ranges were all well-built. I knew they used it, as the MP battalion was not exactly out of work and were doing missions almost daily in settings ranging from the jungle to the favela.

Every night I had dinner with Tony and Dirk. They both lived off base, so they picked me up and I had the privilege of enjoying a new establishment every night. Even though I spent a lot of private time with them, they managed to keep their backgrounds in the background. I knew better than to ask them straight out as this is a no-no in the business. I had a feeling that Dirk was ex SF and had probably worked with, or at least under, the CIA. At that point he was working for a US government contractor in the private security field and seemed to have been based in Colombia for some time. He was most likely a liaison between the US government agencies and the private or semi-private contractors on the ground.

Tony was a former SAS operative who had become a rock star in the private security sector and then moved on to become operations manager for different security companies in Africa and Iraq. For some time while living in Brazil he led some important private security work for Garda World. He did not seem to be connected directly to any government agency, but still used his influence to introduce many government players to each other in the private contractor world. It started to hit me how massive the government-private cooperation really was, and I probably only saw a very small part of it. Governments had always used private contractors to do their dirty work, so that was nothing new. It was a win-win for them having deniability and not having to count any casualties as their own. We saw a lot of that in Iraq in 2003–2004. Blackwater, Aegis, Triple Canopy, et cetera. I understood why they did it. The money was enormous, a team leader in Iraq could make $30,000 to $40,000 per month. If they survived for a few months, they would bring home a lot of money. For many that would go straight to their families, and for others, well I guess there were many ways to blow a few hundred k.

The part that didn't surprise me was how the military and intelligence units hid their personnel in private companies. If a country couldn't legally have their forces operating in another country, they just embedded them as a part of a private military company and voila boots on the ground. Prior to the Iraq and Afghanistan Wars, it was not unheard of, but the scale of it was larger than I could have ever imagined. I couldn't help thinking how complicated it would be when the shit hit the fan.

We had dinner at Salto de Angel the night before the rest of the patrol was due to arrive. It was an upscale club and restaurant in the heart of Bogota. The line to get in was like a mile long, but that didn't matter to us, because we just walked past it like we owned the place. Tony waved and smiled at the bouncer, letting out a cool, '*Todo bien?*'

The bouncer responded with, '*Chevere,*' and a nod while letting us through.

'Are you excited to see your colleagues tomorrow?' Tony asked while sipping on his pint.

'I am, but I have had it pretty decent on my own,' I replied.

Tony nodded. 'That's the problem; you lose contact with reality and get stuck in this fantasy world.'

Dirk laughed, 'And we have been in that loop for 25 years.'

'Did you make any arrangements for tomorrow?' Tony asked.

It was my little 'mission' to pick up the rest of the patrol from the airport the next day. 'Arrangements and arrangements. I am taking two cars: I'll be driving one and Carlos the other.'

Tony looked at me. 'Do you have a man inside the airport?'

I looked back, 'A man inside the airport? No, Tony, I don't have a man inside the airport. Why would I have that and how would I arrange that? It's just a pickup!'

Tony pressed his lips together and then said, 'I am just checking to see that you covered all your bases.'

'Are you messing with me or is there something I missed? I mean we'll take a 9mm each, but we aren't expecting any issues.'

Tony sipped on his beer and smiled, 'I am just checking.'

He always did that, put things in your head that might be valid or not, at least he made you think. I thought to myself, 'Was this was just a regular pick up, or had I become soft after being away from the Army for such a long time? It was probably alright; he would not let me go if there was a real problem.'

The next morning, we were running late. There had been a traffic accident, so it was moving slowly. But immigration always took time so we would be fine. I probably looked like an eighties cop or drug dealer with my two-day shadow and Hawaiian shirt. It was a hot day and I had sweat stains on my back, but I had stopped caring about that. Carlos and I managed to find a parking spot just outside the exit of the terminal. They had landed 20 minutes earlier. 'I'll go and show myself inside.'

'Okay,' Carlos replied and nodded before lighting a cigarette.

It felt a little Bruce Willis.

It was the usual "bring everyone you know and their friends to pick up one relative" chaos at the airport. Nonetheless, I immediately saw our guys walking out as most of them were over 6'1". It was like a group of beacons walking out of the exit. They dressed the same way we usually did but seeing it from the other side with civilian eyes made me realise what everyone else had been pointing out to us so far. I think it was hard living the military life half of the time and trying to adapt to being a civilian during these short bursts. As Alan at the FRU said, 'It's a lifestyle and an attitude.' At least we weren't in civvies and combat boots this time. Overall, I agreed it wasn't the clothing as much as the glow around them.

I gave Mr R a man-hug, one of those with a double pat on the back. 'You all look very operatory,' I said.

'And you look like a retired alcoholic', Lieutenant C said.

It gave me a very good feeling to see the patrol again. It gave me that distinct feeling of home and something familiar.

On the way back Mr A said, 'You just disappeared into thin air. We thought something was fishy when Lieutenant B came back from that SATCOM course you were supposed to be on. I asked him how you were, and he said you didn't attend the course. Ha-ha, that shit backfired on them.'

On our return Dirk, Tony and the Commander of the MP battalion held an in-depth briefing for all of us. 'Welcome, gentlemen. I know you had a long day travelling and are eager to get drunk on the town.' We were going to take them to Salto de Angel that night. It was Friday after all, and the party was about to start.

We were going to be a part of Joint Task Force Omega. The Omega project was a Colombian initiative which included about 10,000 to 15,000 men and women from different units in the army, police, and government with the objective to strike against the Revolutionary Armed Forces of Colombia[2] and the narcotics trade. It was started in the early 2000s and was in parts lead from the Larandia FOB near Caquetá in southern Colombia. The Larandia FOB already had a small group of US Army advisors and instructors to assist the Colombian forces. We were going to be attached to a unit within JTF Omega that had the Call sign White Raven. It was a unit exclusively manned by foreign soldiers. It was a strike team and had an agenda separate from the Colombian agenda. While it was still to take down bad guys, it usually contained more local interests from the serving crews' home governments.

The briefing continued. 'For all worldly concerns you are contractors, you don't wear a uniform, you don't fight under a flag. You are just good guys fighting bad guys, and whatever you report home to your respective bosses, I don't want to know, and I don't care.' As we speak, your Major is training some of these guys in Arctic Warfare, in return you will get a bit of field experience here as well as us getting knowledge transfer from you, especially on the recon side of things. You will spend a week here to get up to speed and get accustomed to some of the SOPs and how they are run here. There will be a lot of heli time, I promise you that. Okay, you have your personal guide that will help you settle in, the van for tonight's dinner leaves at 19:00 and we start tomorrow at 07:00, no excuses.'

On our way to the accommodation, Mr A said, 'What was up with the no excuses thing?'

Mr R was quick on the ball. 'It means heavy drinking and lack of sleep before operating heavy machinery.'

Mr A smiled 'Oh, the best kind then!'

It was definitely weird; drinking in the Swedish Army, especially during a duty week, is a no-no. But overseas it was always more relaxed, and our morals

---

2   This is a translation from the Spanish: *Fuerzas Armadas Revolucionarias de Colombia – Ejército del Pueblo*, FARC–EP or simply known as FARC.

never seemed to follow the Swedish way when we got other offers. It was not good, but we had a lot of fun. I can't deny that.

As I sat down and watched them unpack, I opened a beer. Mr R looked at me, 'You got beer?'

I pointed to the fridge in the small kitchen, 'It's the only thing I got.'

We were on our ear, or perhaps a more Swedish saying, "pretty round under our feet" when we headed into town. The roads were closed around the city centre, as there were festivities, and we were dropped short of our destination. The others were ahead of us as Mr A, Mr R, and I were dragging our feet. Two metres in front of us, a Land Rover turned in and blocked the sidewalk. The driver stopped in front of a pair of gates, appearing as if he was heading to his house. We walked around the back of the Land Rover and were about to continue down the sidewalk when the driver rolled down the window and shouted to Mr A, 'Do you want to see something?'

The man was British and had long grey and brown hair. He was in his fifties and looked like Donald Sutherland. Mr A walked up to him. The driver held up a green apple. Mr R moved closer while I observed from my position a little further back and to the left. As Mr A neared the window the man in the car said, 'Don't let this town…'

He suddenly pulled a knife and Mr R reacted immediately, shouting, 'Knife!' pulling Mr A backwards, grabbing his shirt.

The man in the car, not bothered by the commotion, waited until we were all a safe distance from the car before continuing, '…eat you up.'

With that, he took the small fruit knife sliced a piece of his apple and ate it. We could hear an evil laugh coming from the Land Rover as the gates opened and he drove in.

'Fuck me, that was a Kubrick moment,' Mr A said. 'What a surreal guy.'

It was surreal indeed. Colombia was full of surreal people and experiences. It had a psychedelic vibe to it from time to time. This could have been a close call, but the guy just wanted to have a piece of his apple in a dramatic way. Still, I must give Mr R credit for his razor-sharp instinct despite being in a half-drunk state. In the club the party was in full swing, we were drinking, smoking, and enjoying the big rope swings at the bar. Mr R, who was a ladies' man, had full attention on the dance floor as he wore his signature tight shirt that almost popped the buttons. He could actually pop the buttons if he flexed his chest and he had done so many times before.

It was after 04:00 before we were back at the barracks. We had fun, and it was like a reunion of old friends that hadn't seen each other in 20 years. The humidity was crushing, and I sat outside drinking a Budweiser and listening to the cicadas.

Lieutenant C joined me, 'This is how we should have it all the time.' I nodded. It's a different pace, not as stiff and boring as at home. 'I hope it lasts,' Lieutenant C said as he cracked open his beer.

My hangover hadn't kicked in yet, but Mr A always had notorious hangovers and looked like a corpse.

'I am glad you all made it; I was dubious for a while,' Dirk said. The sun was scorching; it was going to be a brutal day.

The first day was spent with weapons familiarisation and showing them how we fought. They tried to throw us into any and every situation and we handled it. We had been doing this together for a while, the cohesiveness, and battle drills kicked in – a bit of a hangover wasn't going to throw us, and we nailed the contact drills. We were also getting used to the radio equipment, and medical stuff. On day number two, our medic spent time with the local ambulance service to freshen up his skills, while we were learning radio work, call signs and code sheets, and getting familiar with the reporting SOPs. The evening was spent with parts of the MP unit drilling CQB. They did it old school, going for more risky and aggressive strategies. We call it "playing it brave" in Sweden.

Day three, we spent half a day working in the built-up favela. The risky techniques we had seen being practiced the day before were paying off. Fighting in the favela was a different game: always outnumbered, every inch was hostile, speed in, hit your target and speed out was always key as one had to minimise time in the danger zone. The enemy was nowhere and everywhere, they would always know you were coming, the perfect intelligence system for this type of urban warfare. We had to ensure surprise by doing the unexpected – keeping them on their toes and also get out before they scrambled all their soldiers in response. One of the officers that trained with us said, 'It's a nightmare and I have seen it so many times. One wrong turn or being too slow will "leave you to your faith" to meet your preferred choice of maker. The favela can eat you up never to be found. Avoid it at all costs!' It felt like another dimension of Northern Ireland, just a bit more whimsical and colourful, but not to be underestimated.

As we were having a late lunch, Mr A said, 'I am glad we don't drink every night.'

He was right, it was heavy work. Even if I was more acclimatised than the others, being a soldier in this heat took its toll. Tony approached our table.

'The MPs send their best and that they are very impressed with your planning skills.'

As we hadn't done anything out of the ordinary really, nothing spectacular by our standards, I think they were just impressed that not only the leaders, but every soldier could plan, lead, and execute a mission. That's one of the perks of coming from a small army: everyone needs to be able to do everything to a reasonable standard and leadership is taught and practiced by everyone. In my opinion, leadership through the ranks strengthens the dynamic. Most of the Americans we had met argued that it would weaken a group. I guess it's just about attitude and culture.

Perhaps a more Swedish and/or Nordic model includes leadership that is never weakened by accepting the ideas or inputs from group members and subordinates; or by the fact that every one of the members could do the same job as the team leader. No one would ever ruin a mission or challenge the team leader at a critical moment, as this would be counterproductive, but rather their responsibility would be to bring forward dynamic solutions at the right moment.[3]

When we got to the mess hall, I heard the distinct symmetrical chopping sound of a helicopter in the distance. It sounded like a Huey, but whatever it was, it was our ride. The next two and a half days and nights would be heli practice. She was beautiful, a bit of an aged lady, a Bell 212. We were all familiar with the type, even if it wasn't our standard ride. The pilot looked relaxed as he stepped out from the cockpit in shorts and a Hawaiian shirt. Yes, the Hawaiian shirt was a thing back then.

'Hello, my name is Vlad, and we are going to spend a great deal of time together.' He had a heavy Eastern European accent and continued, 'Before you ask, yes, I am Russian. That's why I have this slight, almost unnoticeable, accent.'

He got us all with his humour. I find it interesting how many Westerners do not realise the humour and sophistication of Russians. Perhaps it was part of the old Cold War story of dividing the world into good and bad only with nothing in between. Vlad had been flying helicopters for private security companies for decades, mostly in Africa and more recently in Iraq. He had worked for Eeben Barlow's South African Executive Outcomes in the late 1980s and 1990s, "when mercenaries were mercenaries", and of course one day, some may look back at my contemporaries and also reflect on "the good old days" and all that.

---

3   See forthcoming book on a Ranger's lessons on leadership and practice.

'So, let's take her out for a spin or rather, let's do that after we go through some basics and dos and don'ts.' Vlad was far less conservative than any other pilot we had flown with. We could basically do whatever we wanted, as long as, well as he put it, 'don't try to kill me.'

The helicopter struggled on the steep climb up the hillside leaving the base and the mesh seats felt a bit loose in the sharp banking turns. Vlad struggled with the controls from time to time. Maintenance and upkeep were a constant and recurring theme during my time in Latin America, and I remember thinking, 'I really hope they maintained this bird.' Although I guessed that they probably did some minimum level of maintenance as the chopper was privately registered.

'For you to trust me as a pilot, it's important for you to see what I can do,' Vlad said over the crackly intercom. Seconds after that, he pushed the nose forward and we found ourselves in a rollercoaster drop.

'Shit, this is going fast, and the helicopter feels heavy,' I thought while holding on to the seat. He pushed us in to a full nosedive. We had done this in smaller and more agile helicopters, but the 212 was bulky and sluggish.

The ground was approaching at an alarming rate. You could definitely feel a few Gs as Vlad pulled back on the stick. Keeping a high velocity, and pulling up just in the nick of time, he took us on a ride just a few metres above the surface of the river. In the hard banks, we were basically left to the integrity of our harnesses. Vlad clearly knew what he was doing, and oozed confidence, although he had a touch too much courage – or "swollen balls" – for my liking. We spent the night doing touch-and-go, embus and debus, long approaches, short approaches, roof landings, loading of injured soldiers, et cetera.

It had been a long day, but we sharpened up on our heli skills and the particular SOPs of our friend, Vlad. He was flying way too many hours in a row to be legal, but given where we were, it was the least of our concerns. As our patrol had a late-night beer outside our barracks, Mr R said, 'I wonder what our actual mission will be?'

Lieutenant C looked up, 'Assisting White Raven within the framework of JTF Omega.'

Mr A looked at Lieutenant C, 'That's such a fucking officer kind of answer! We all know that, but what is the exact nature of the mission? DA, QRF, recon?'

Lieutenant C's reply was short and to the point, 'Well, even a fucking officer can't know everything!'

'Nothing new under the sun, then' said Mr R, as he sipped his beer.

'Two short bursts, one longer burst, and observe the hits.'

I was struggling a bit with the M-60 machine gun. The sun had just popped over the horizon and we were given a door gunner crash course by two Colombians who were well versed in the role. We had all previously done the training at one point or another, but door gunner duties weren't our specialty. It's a different skill set: the movement, the speed, the distance to target and the elevation of the gun. One has to shoot by instinct rather than calculation. Similar to the lessons with rifles and pistol, it was a case of a new "natural" alignment, eyes open and across the sights but in harmony with the motion. It's a game of experience and less of precision, at its core one must be able to cover ground troops in a safe and efficient way.

The last two days were spent on an exercise field a short flight south of the base. It was supposed to be the live fire-heli interaction exercise, with the main focus on small arms and M-60 sequenced and coordinated fire from the helicopter. The door gunner instructors had many tricks up their sleeves and were talking a lot about giving accurate cover through a jungle canopy, without seeing the ground, and how to pick reference points. It was impressive and clearly not their first rodeo.

Unsurprisingly, Mr A was the best out of all of us, as he had a lifetime of experience as a machine gunner, but we were all good enough to pass the critical eyes of our instructors. On the last day, we finished off with a full-on live fire mission, extracting a kidnapping and ransom (K&R) team from a hot landing zone which also provided some CQB action. Like Lieutenant C, I was happy to see that we over performed. Even though this was familiarisation, we maintained a good standard and every instructor we had met up until then, had been more than satisfied with us. We landed at our barracks after dark, where we were met by the Battalion Commander. He wanted to see us in the briefing room after we unloaded our equipment.

'Tony and Dirk send their best regards and wish you the best of luck. They had to leave early. It has been a pleasure preparing you to join JTF Omega. You will fly out to FOB Larandia at 06:00 tomorrow morning. You will bring all your kit and weapons as you won't demob from here. You will report directly to the base commander. Expect to be operational directly on arrival as the team you are relieving left tonight. Any questions?'

It was more like a monologue than a briefing. I guess he was keen on getting home to his family. Lieutenant C stood up and took the officer's responsibility, thanked them for their time and for training us and gave him a few patches from IRP as a memento. I hated these formalities.

'Couldn't we just shake hands and thank each other like regular people?' I thought, but I knew the importance of ceremony in the military.

The heli was bobbing a bit, we could feel the lift of the aircraft, it was that moment when the helicopter wants to get off the ground, but the pilot holds it back. We had live rounds in our rifles and were kitted to go. Vlad was doing the take-off clearance with the tower; his Spanish was interesting to say the least.

'That M-60 isn't only for decoration,' he said on the intercom. We all looked at each other, and I laughed as we sat lined up like schoolgirls in the back.

'It's mine,' said Mr A. Well, he was the best and it was right up his alley, we couldn't deny him popping his door gunner cherry.

As we left the city perimeter, the jungle was thickening under us. The intercom crackled, 'You didn't ask for this by words, but your faces tell me all I need to know,' said Vlad. We looked at each other, Lieutenant C shrugged his shoulders. Seconds later, *Fortunate Son* was blasting through the intercom.

Vlad broke in, 'You can thank me later' as he smiled and pushed the stick forward. He was right, *Fortunate Son* created that Vietnam era magic we had been fed with in every war movie we had ever seen. It was magical flying low over the canopy, having Mr A locked and loaded in the door and heading out for violence. Lieutenant C tapped one of his magazines against the helmet he didn't have. It was pure movie magic; this was a moment to remember.

It's an almost four-hour flight from Bogota to Larandia which is located just outside the south border of the demilitarised zone. It had a small airstrip and was a closed Colombian Army base; hence it looked like most FOBs. The dust was intense as Vlad put us down on the side of the sun-dried landing strip. Sandbags and hescos all around: we were home again. A jeep was waiting for us. The slightly overweight driver wore a white shirt, stained with a variety of things. His name was John.

'Welcome to Farclandia,' he said. I raised my eyebrows almost without realising. He must have been like the third or fourth 'John' that I had met in a short period of time. 'I get it that it was a cover name, but a bit of creativity wouldn't hurt,' I thought.

He took us to a compound within the base along the northern perimeter. It was surrounded by a fence covered with mesh fabric and had quite a few antennas sticking up.

'One could never tell this was a secret place,' Mr R said and rolled his eyes. He was right, special units were never good at blending in.

'Leave your gear in the car for now,' John said and walked in under a small hangar like structure without walls.

'Again, welcome to Larandia FOB, gents.' He had a very generic English accent, a crisp BBC type that one couldn't exactly pinpoint. He wiped his forehead with a textile napkin before returning it to his pocket. He looked out of place, perhaps like a stereotypical accountant or somebody's dad.

'Surrounding us is the Larandia FOB.' He pointed in a sweeping motion with his hand. 'It's currently inhabited by 7th Special Forces Group, assisting the Colombians CERTE programme.' CERTE, or *Centro de Re-entrenamiento Táctico Del Ejército*, directly translates to Army Tactical Retraining Centre. The Colombian Army usually deployed their units for 90 days in combat operations, followed by 30 days of training, before another 90 days of operations. This was done to sustain a high level of skill in the units, as deployment generally provided valuable experience, but lacks the keeping and building of core skills.

The USSF, and sometimes other countries, assisted the Colombian Army in running their CERTE by adding specialist training and insight to help the soldiers do an even better job. This was obviously not a freebie from the US government. It basically gave them unrestricted access to the Colombian military landscape, allowing them opportunities to achieve their own and possibly covert objectives.

John continued, 'We are not included in the USSF training deal, mostly because we don't want to include them in ours. We don't work for the US Army, we work for a higher power, and we don't mix well together with army people. We only share this beautiful location.'

The irony in John's comment wasn't lost on me. I recognised the 'arrangement.' It sounded like a typical intelligence operation, which never went well with regular armed forces. I had often thought about the fact that we never tried to help each other. There was always a degree of competition, not for glory but essentially to keep people from stealing your job. It was not only happening in the Swedish Army, but everywhere.[4]

As John continued his briefing, it became clear to me what we were doing here. This was a boutique mission shop and a bespoke information collection point. Controlled disruption was the main game here involving typical missions like surveillance of certain organised crime organisations and smaller terrorist units that trained under the wings of FARC (primarily Middle Eastern pay-and-play customers),[5] specialised counter surveillance and probing and

---

4 Unit survival and getting funding was critical.
5 Other groups who were not affiliated with FARC, many didn't even have the same ideology. They were just paying for the training.

neutralising elements of the FARC. Most missions were airborne, photography, mapping, radio and GPS jamming, radio surveillance and of course direct action with the complementary snatch and grab raid from time to time.

Controlled disruption is a game of cause-and-effect, where one provokes reactions while monitoring logistics, radio chatter, data traffic et cetera, to map out the chain of command, key players, locations, and movements. This is usually a long game and at our level we seldom went for the strike. However, the information that we collected was usually the basis for other units' direct action. I liked this type of work. Sometimes it could be unsatisfying to never see or even remotely hear about the results, but intelligence was the core, the epicentre where everything starts, creating a butterfly effect. It's like the evil mastermind's plan for world domination, except that we were the good guys. Relatively good, anyway.

John was head of operations and station chief. A middle-aged man, balding, with a noticeable paunch, he was smart, and maintained an air of mystery. It was unclear to whom he reported. He had three operation managers and four communication specialists in his team. The comms centre and the four operators were strictly off-limits for everyone except a select few. Also, there was a 'tech and equipment' department which consisted of two gentlemen that serviced, and handed out, gear. Each crew had their own medic, but we also had a standalone paramedic on the base. If we needed a doctor, we had to use the medical bay of the main FOB. Two men made up a combined geocell/photo analyst team. They catered to all our mapping needs, taking care of visual material, assisting in operation briefings, and preparing the physical target packs. In terms of air operations, we had three birds with a pilot each and two flight mechanics that were also weapons specialists.

There were only a few vehicles attached to the White Raven unit, and they were seldom used. Ground operations were tried and tested in the early days, but it was more or less impossible to successfully conduct any kind of covert ground movements. There were four operational teams. Pink was the main photo surveillance team and was permanently assigned to Bird 1 that was rigged with video and photo equipment. The helicopter itself was fitted with a double FLIR-dome and 360 degree rotating Hasselblad triple camera under the fuselage.

Juliet was a jamming and signal tracking team that always had one of the comms specialists attached. They flew in Bird 3, as it was permanently fitted for the purpose. Black was a QRF and DA team and flew in Bird 2. It carried double M-60s and was mostly stripped for carrying personnel and medevac duties. Tropical was the off-duty team, with an assortment of base chores and standby tasks. We had a rotating schedule with one week in each team. So, three weeks "on" and one week "off". That wasn't really the case, as you were always "on" in some capacity when deployed. Missions weren't flown every day, more like twice a week, on average, and on larger operations the teams were merged and mixed.

We were going to spend the first week in briefings and familiarisation flights, while also supporting the Black team when needed, as the previous rotation had left the day before we got in. The tempo was relaxed but the attitude sharp and focused. It was the perfect combination, like they had taken out all the crap that the military likes to do but kept the ultra-professionalism. So even if most of the teams looked like beach bums, I never felt safer.

It was a feeling of being in the right company, but still very exposed if something went down. Looking at their ongoing operations the planning was immaculate. Every conceivable scenario was considered. We quickly understood that, if shit went down, we would be on our own for a substantial amount of time. Each bird was equipped with extensive demolition gear to destroy all equipment if we needed to abandon ship or make a hasty withdrawal. If something went wrong, limiting knowledge of our presence and purpose was crucial. The CSAR protocol was mostly down to us, though we had the Colombian and US military detachments as a last resort. But it was sensitive as we were not an agency, just ghosts that everyone wanted in the good times, but disposable in the bad times.

The teams at the time were mostly American and British, with a few locals, they were Central American superstars. The supervisor of the comms team had a distinct German accent. As usual, we never discussed specifics about anyone's background. But we all knew we were qualified in one way or another. The most common deployment length seemed to be around three months, but sometimes they switched earlier and very rarely all at once.

Each team that had been there had left their signature or made an improvement to the compound. The bar was a neat structure with intricate woodwork. It was signed 'Diego's Pride', which led my thoughts to San Diego. Maybe they were a unit belonging to the navy base. I started to wonder if we were allowed to build something or leave a signature of our own. Mr A was a skilled carpenter and Mr R an electrician. So, we had a few people who were good with their hands.

Mr R laughed and looked at me, 'You are already thinking about what changes you want to make aren't you?'

'How the fuck did you know that?'

Mr R smirked, 'You zoned out in that legendary way only you do.' He continued, 'Maybe a wooden ranger tab with a twist for the bar?'

I replied, 'Isn't that a bit obvious? Everyone that passes through here probably has a similar background.'

I half-zoned out again. 'But maybe something Arctic, that's us and very unique?'

Lieutenant C had been walking behind us. 'Well, before we start planning our decorations, we might actually focus on doing something useful first.'

'We will', I thought as we headed out to the helicopter pad.

It was our first familiarisation flight. We had one extra operator from 'Juliet' and one of the geocell guys too. He really knew this neck of the woods like the back of his hand, it made sense as he spent every day staring at maps. The landscape was majestic, similar to the north but somehow different. The forest was exchanged for jungle, but the vastness and remoteness were the same – breathtaking and haunting. From time to time, we would see small settlements quickly appear through holes in the canopy, and they would disappear just as quickly. The small roads and trails would dissolve into a wall of green and then appear again in the most unexpected direction.

It was clear that one needed to study the area and be familiar with the terrain to be able to deliver. We had brought some camera gear for photo practice. The jigs and bipods were fixed to the helicopter and although that helped, it was still tricky. I had difficulty getting the focus right on the quick overpasses of groups of houses or parts of trails. I had to practice.

On every flight, an appointed "navigator" that tracked and followed along on the map, gave the team a heads-ups and countdowns before action. This was especially important when the terrain was complicated, which it certainly was. It helped, but being a navigator was a task that required laser focus and constant commentary, leaving no time to relax and enjoy the sights.

Our spirits were high after returning from our first flight. Even though it was a training run, it felt like we had something to offer, and this would be a unique period in our lives. Or maybe it was the "Fortunate Son" feeling that was still lingering in us. Later that night we had a briefing for the coming week. We were to man team Black and fly daily familiarisation exercises in all roles. The only real mission that week would take place in six days, and we were going to be the ones to lead it. One kind of gets into the mode: prepping, flying, prepping, then beer, BBQ and some darts or volleyball. I struggled a bit with the humidity, but that was just a minor inconvenience. The group agreed that, throughout our military careers, this was the best we had ever had it. But I guess that we credited that feeling to the hard groundwork we had done to get to that point.

As the week progressed, I lost at darts and volleyball every night. I was most disturbed by losing at darts. Lieutenant C commented many times, 'You are a strange puppy. You don't like regular sports and don't even feel the competitive gene when doing them, but weird shit like darts and pool and cards make you tick. I don't get it!'

He was right; I had had weird athletic preferences since high school. I was bitter as a kid when it came to sports. Since I wasn't any good, I was never invited to play or participate. So, I developed a hatred instead, usually rooting for the team or individual that most people didn't like. I can clearly remember when some friends invited me to go and watch the Andre Agassi v Boris Becker match in Stockholm. Of course, nobody cheered for Becker except for me. The same thing happened in the Olympic ice hockey final; I rooted for another country and not Sweden. A bit of that weirdness still lives in me today.

We sat and chatted the night before our first mission. We were well prepared. Not in an overworked way, just ready. It was a straightforward task. We were going as Pink and were flying along an established route with the purpose of taking comparative pictures of several targets, looking to detect any increase or decrease in activity and searching for indicators and triggers of change. The belt hanging from the M-60 dropped down in a fixed box and swayed with the movements of the helicopter as it made minimal but precise turns. We were flying low, very low. I could almost touch the foliage. The pilots took different routes approaching various ground paths which allowed minimal warning to any potential hostile elements. You could hear, or rather feel, the gyro warming up on the central camera. It's the same feeling as when the landing gear is raised on a commercial aircraft. Mr A was manning the defence, Mr R was behind the camera, Lieutenant C operated the gyro video, and I was stuck with navigation. It was the task I least wanted, but I thought that I may as well take the bull by the horns.

The pilot helped me to find our entry point. As we were just above the trees, we basically had no reference points. I felt my ass crack getting sweaty as I didn't want to fuck up the first run. As soon as we hit the path, I felt more confident. I had studied the charts and all the photographs. I just needed to stop looking for changes in the landscape. My job was to prepare the spotters and photo crew in time for the checkpoints and count them in. They were basically blind back there and without a line-up they would miss the target.

'Charlie Brown... Five... Four... Three... Two... One!' I heard activity in the back, they had to move around to track the target.

'Good, or do you need more time?' I asked.

'No, no, perfect. I think it was spot on,' said Mr R on the raspy communications.

'Guns! Guns, ten o'clock!' It was Mr A calling out as we passed a clearing.

Vlad broke in over the intercom, 'Very common sight. Most people are armed in one way or another in this neighbourhood. If you see a shoulder-ready RPG, you let me know.'

There was a low risk of engagement on this path as we utilised nap-of-the-earth (NOE) flight – low and fast. It was basically just a swoosh over their heads, and we were gone. If they had a heads-up, maybe, but as the route over the checkpoints was different every time it was not easy for hostile units to efficiently position spotters. Helicopters were high value targets though, so we needed to be sharp. The army had a downed heli a few years earlier, which reminded us of the threat. White Raven had zero casualties at that point, but small arms fire was a constant risk. Vlad pushed the helicopter flying at low altitude and high velocity. It was a hectic job for everyone to keep up. Running Pink team was no walk in the park. It took roughly two hours before we got back to base. I was drenched, mostly due to the heat, humidity, and concentration.

After a photo mission, one took the flash drives out and headed straight to the geocell to conduct analyses. They had a thorough debrief where they recapped the mission and looked through the material. They were very familiar with the route, so they knew exactly which questions to ask and what to look out for and they wanted to debrief us while our memories were still fresh. They took particular interest of the sighting of the armed men. The position had been carefully noted by the spotters and we got good images as well.

It looked like a scout patrol: 11 of them, AK47s, AK74s, two PKMs. The analysts had not seen activity that close to the DMZ in a while and never that far west.

'Interesting. I think we will try to provoke these gentlemen in the future,' the analyst said.

They would analyse this type of thing for hours and no one was surprised when shortly after a target pack turned up. It was just the first of many, a perfect evening, warm, and in good company – the beer was cold and the BBQ hot – it was the life for me. Vlad, on the other hand, was pulling a late night with the mechanics. 'The right rudder was sluggish,' he said, which didn't sound good at all. I mostly tried not to think about it and hoped they didn't use too much duct tape.

A few weeks had passed, and we mostly did routine tasks. We were getting comfortable in our roles and time just seemed to float by with us unaware and in cruise control. The minute hand of the clock had just passed midnight on the last Saturday of our duty week, and we had one day left on Black before shifting to Tropical for a week. I had had a hard time sleeping lately due to the humidity. It only became bearable around 01:00 – 02:00.

Boom, boom, boom. Three loud explosions with almost no separation detonated like a rolling thunder. I bolted from my bed and 30 seconds later I was running out of the barracks with my plate carrier hanging over my shoulder and my Galil in my right hand.[6] I heard small arms fire hammering away from the southern perimeter. I observed two more explosions around 500 metres south. They hit the field below the army's barracks. It was unmistakably medium mortar rounds (possibly 84mm) that were coming at us. In case of an attack on the base, Pink and Tropical were supposed to secure our sector in the north, while Juliet held the compound and Black was to go airborne. Classic stand to drills, with an airborne reaction force. I could see Lieutenant C, Vlad and Mr A as we scrambled to the helipad our single focus was doing what was required, as Arnold put it, 'get to the chopper.' The rest were 30 seconds behind. The small arms fire had intensified as the army pushed back in the south and three more grenades splashed down 250 metres west of the airstrip.

'You need to keep this bitch alive until we are airborne,' Vlad shouted as we approached the helicopter. We were at the northern end of the base which was exposed. Until we were airborne, we were vulnerable, especially if the enemy decided to take a stab from two directions. But at that point it was all happening closer to the southern perimeter. Lieutenant C was on the radio, Mr A and I manned the two M-60s, one in each door and the rest were ready for ground action/laser tagging and spotting. It felt like forever before the helicopter started. We had eight ammo boxes in each door and more stashed in the back, we could make a dent if needed.

The Colombian Army reported to Lieutenant C, 'Tree line south southwest.' The base was surrounded by cleared fields about 250 metres wide, then from there it descended into dense jungle. The army was counting on us to get airborne and keep pushing the enemy back so they had time to regroup.

---

6   A plate carrier is a protective vest, which as the name suggests provides the operator with some protection from gunshot.

Except for the mortars it was unlikely that they had access to anything better than AKs, PKMs and RPGs. Not great firepower, but handled right, still lethal, and effective.

All my limbs were trying to find small things to grip as the helicopter banked very sharply. I was practically hanging outside in the harness, with my feet on the skids desperately trying to find a stable position. Vlad did a sharp and steep dive in the direction of the tree line to avoid early detection.

'Confirm clear field?' as Vlad completed the last turn positioning us to engage.

'Field clear, no visual.' It was Lieutenant C making sure we had no friendlies from the army that had pushed out to the field. The firing had stopped just a minute earlier, the insurgents no doubt knew the chopper was in flight. It was our turn to show our teeth. We had the tree line on the right, and we were going to do switch sweeps. In this manoeuvre, one goes alongside the last known point of contact and for each sweep you push the enemy in front of you from the point of contact or chase them on, depending on how far along they have managed to retreat. Since the heli sweeps were to-and-from, only one door is in action at a time.

'Right door, ready. Three... Two... One... Hot!' Mr A opened up and the tracers were like a light sabre in the night.

'Stand by, stand by.' Mr A ceased fire and Vlad was ready to bank. I was coming up. Mr A had worked the tree line, and we were now coming in over the canopy. I had fewer reference points, so I had to try to keep the tracers in a straight line.

'Left door, ready. Three... Two... One...' I saw three insurgent tracers breaking through the canopy and passing in front of the helicopter. In a split second I had a target. My eyes never left the spot where the enemy tracers broke the canopy, as I turned the M-60 slightly. The recoil felt rhythmic, and the position was stable. I saw my tracers piercing the spot. It was beautiful. Long bursts following the line, considering that they could have pushed more to the side or back. A lethal dance, but I was in step.

'Two more turns then the army is moving in.' The army had geared up and were ready for a ground pursuit. It was too dangerous to have a heli covering the ground attack in the jungle, as one needed great margins, coordination, communications, and rehearsal, and even then, it was close to impossible to cover troops that one couldn't see.

After two more turns, we did a few laps around the FOB to see if we could identify any approaching enemy forces, and or targets of opportunity. After landing, we started refuelling, and reloading. We were on 10 minute warning QRF standby until the morning.

John called us to a morning briefing. 'Good job last night. Quick response time: we were quicker than the perimeter watch from the army.' He looked satisfied like we had won something. I felt different. We had worked together the previous night, like a unit and not competitors. Maybe he was trying to boost morale, who knows, but we were soldiers, and by our nature we fought in groups, units, like a pack of wolves.

John continued, 'They found 11 dead bad guys. Six were in our zone. Well done on the shooting, but we must not lose track of what we are here to do. We have nothing more to do with this. We participated in the defence of the FOB, and now the follow up operations is the army's business. We need to poke around where we spotted the gunmen. During the last few weeks, we have reason to suspect that they are opening a new supply route to Central America. Money, drugs, and people that they need to hide.'

He paused and paced for a while, looking pensive he said, 'So our mission is to force them to use the new route, so that we can try to find out where it ends and where they are shipping out from.'

The plan was simple: stay away from the new route and provoke, engage, and disrupt the enemy on the known routes, trying to get them to abandon them and use the new one. And we simultaneously kept up our scheduled flights to maintain the illusion of regular groundwork. The jamming team played a key role as they could monitor their Motorolas.

Over the next two months we worked hard at provoking and stirring things up. We did five raids and kept up the pressure almost around the clock. The teams became more fixed in specific roles as the workload increased. We managed to open up the new route and we mapped it almost all the way to the end. It was bustling with activity, but they had an ace up their sleeve in the last 50km stretch, they appeared to just vanish into thin air. We suspected that they had made their way to the coast, through smaller arterial routes, and tunnels, from where they were transported to their final destination. John said that some friends in the blue business, both the Navy and private maritime security companies, hadn't picked up anything along the coast. I learned later that the Army and our intelligence colleagues used Pistris, a maritime private security company, and one of the major anti-piracy contractors, to follow up on our smuggler friends.

We were excited to follow this through to the end as we, at least in this small project, were part of uncovering and opening up a major trafficking route.

Three months had passed quickly. The teams had become really solid in their specialist roles, and we had made a few good connections that we felt would provide us with a fruitful exchange in the future. Sweden felt distant at this point. Sometimes I forgot entirely that we were a part of the Swedish Army. We were definitely in a bubble. I liked it but I had to be careful not to forget where my allegiances lie. We were "friends" now, but I didn't for a second doubt that they would use you for any purpose that they saw fit should the winds shift. The moment echoed the saying often mentioned in *realpolitik* and intelligence circles, that there are no friends, only interests.

We were about to start our thousandth BBQ when John called Lieutenant C to his office. I didn't think much of it, as Lieutenant C's role as a team leader was slightly more pronounced now than it had previously been. Not even close to army level, but just a little more formal when it came to receiving orders and briefings.

As Lieutenant C came back, he said, 'Grab a beer and join me for a couple of minutes.' We walked behind the barracks and circled around Lieutenant C.

'I just spoke to the Major. It's time, we got the call.'

We all knew what that meant, it was our 'first real deal' – what we had been preparing for. This had just been an appetiser. It was time for us to pack up and get back home. It felt a bit sad to leave, but also, we were heading towards what we had been waiting for, our first sanctioned mission. Vlad gave us a show ride back to base, doing helicopter acrobatics. We would all miss the crazy Russian, the bubble, and the cowboy times as we buckled up for our next rodeo.

This episode provides a glimpse of how weird it could be back then; how competitive it was and how much stupidity was involved. But it also shows some fun times. Of course, a lot of valuable connections and friendships were formed that perhaps couldn't happen in the same way today. The consequences could have been huge if something had happened – casualties or disappearances. Years later the command of the IRP got some heat for this unsanctioned mission. But ultimately no heads rolled when it surfaced, as we had managed to establish ourselves on a higher level by then.

As I boarded the flight home, I felt like something between an elite soldier, a chancer, and a spy – some James Bond shit indeed. I was glad to have lived it.

13

Balkan Blues

'As we were running towards the car I reported, 'QRF leaving base location,'
I wanted the boys to know we were coming.'

I landed in Sweden with mixed feelings, leaving Latin America, where I had found adventure, and finally dipped my toes in the murky waters of special operations. I would miss the autonomy, but I was happy to reunite with the rest of the platoon. I had been away for almost five months, and the others for three. We seemed to be the ones that won the golden ticket. None of the other patrols had been away on missions and adventures in the same way. But they hadn't been lazy either, they had honed their skills, and I was surprised at how technically proficient some of them had become. I almost felt jealous of them, but they had more reasons to be jealous.

We had been out and about while they had been kicking dust at the regiment. The military system is very unfair like that, especially when it comes to a small country like Sweden. Deployment time is everything and when it comes down to core business, it is the altar at which we all wish to serve. And the more deployment time one has, the more experienced one becomes, and the more gigs one gets. So even if it was the luck of the draw that we got deployed early, it was very likely we would be picked first again for the next "premium" mission. Mostly because on average we brought more to the table. I understood the logic behind it, but over time it would potentially leave good operators on the bench because of a fluke in the initial selection. It is important for everyone to get their first deployment under the belt, especially, if you want to have a diverse and flexible unit. Unfortunately, at that point, combat was what everyone was looking for. The desire fades over time and for some it is replaced by a need, and for others it becomes an evil imperative. But the result was that no one, on the outside, understood why one sought combat over anything else as a young operator.

My patrol had been out and about, but no one had officially been deployed yet, as what we did in Latin America was never something that would be recognised anywhere, or by anyone. Yet it was still experience and the ones that needed to know, well they knew. The mix was strange as military units acknowledge deployments with medals, ribbons, and badges, but in the world of covert ops, the citations are carried on the inside, and the medals locked away, never to be handed to the recipient.

The whole platoon was excited. It was finally game time. An official, secret deployment in the service of the King. Of course, he wasn't directly involved, but he is the top brass, the symbolic if not true commander, of the Swedish Armed Forces. It was what we had all been looking forward to. Naturally, there was a lot of speculation among us at that point. We had Afghanistan, a fresh and newly established deployment, which unfortunately had already resulted in the death of two operators from the SSG unit. They were the first official combat casualties since the mission in the Congo. We had Iraq, which was mostly a support and training mission at that point, although there had been quite a few missions in Iraq, by other units similar to ours, but mostly in an embedded role.

Africa was another possibility. As early as 2003, we had FJS IK (SIG) LRRP units included in the French-led Artemis operation. We also had the Balkans including Bosnia and Kosovo, but that deployment had been running for an eternity and Kosovo was on its 14th rotation. It was a new version of a classic peacekeeping mission, with NATO being big brother with the established power dynamic and relative peace, there was absolutely no action, so Kosovo was out of the question, at least in our minds.

We were assembled by the Major in the briefing room. 'Gentlemen, it's time to show our value to those who are watching, those who wanted to disband us, those who supported us to get this far. To show what their money and trust got them.'

I had never been more excited. The build up and intensity in the moment is hard to describe. 'This has to be world war level epic', I thought.

The Major shook the mouse to wake up the computer, and the projector sprung to life. It showed a list of personnel, four patrols made up of three operators and an officer, and a support element. I saw my own name. It was me, Mr A, and Mr N, led by Captain B I smiled. Tight patrols and ranking up the leadership, something big was coming. And Captain B! I don't know to this day how he ended up as commander of my patrol, but this was something I had hoped for from the beginning. I knew the beer-drinking days were over, as he was way too professional. I liked that.

The Major continued. 'You are going to Kosovo, to be a part of the ISTAR element there.'

My whole body froze. I resisted the urge to stand up and scream, 'What the fuck, Kosovo? Kosovo? KOSOVO?' The home of Swedish feel-good coffee-and-cake type of military men. Were we being punished? And if so, why?

The Major continued his presentation, and the 10 men that weren't included in the Kosovo list showed on the screen. 'And you are going to form one squad plus a small support function and go with Captain L to Afghanistan, serving as a Military Observation Team.'

As we left the presentation, my mind was spinning. We were going to fucking Kosovo and the others were going, with a former French Foreign Legion captain, to Afghanistan. 'What the fuck had happened?' I thought. It was not jealousy, it was a lack of understanding and a bit of envy, but I couldn't wrap my head around it. Captain B collected his "new" patrol outside the briefing room. He wanted us to assemble for a quick, private chat in our barracks.

I think I was the most disappointed of us all, though I tried to hold it back. It was Captain B's style, and I didn't want to be the one fucking with it. 'I can see that some of you are disappointed, and you expected something like Afghanistan. I get it. We have all trained and honed our skills for a long time. But I can tell you, this is something totally different and when this deployment is done, and in the future when you have many more under your belt, you will look back at Kosovo as one of the – if not the most – premium deployment. We are not hunting orcs this time. We are going straight for Sauron!' I trusted Captain B, but we knew his job was to motivate us, and I am not sure if the *Lord of the Rings* comparison helped or made it worse. I mean I had just had a taste of *Apocalypse Now*, but this was not the time for FOMO…mission first, always!

We were going to have a month of pre-deployment training at home and then attach to a British ISR unit that had already been established a few years before. It was a loose form of attachment – we would take over a few of their missions, but also run our own and support other units from different countries with surveillance and intelligence. The pre-deployment training was mostly focused on establishing new roles in the reshuffled team, and country-conflict familiarisation. We were to top up our combat readiness training just to be prepared should anything go down. Mr N was appointed as photo operator and primary driver, while Mr A was of course the dedicated LMG gunner. I was 2iC and signals guy. In a team this small, the appointed duties are more designed around an area of responsibility but with a wide assortment of tasks, as running operations with four guys requires all hands on deck at all times. The 2iC's focus was mostly mission and equipment preparation responsibilities. I was used to that role and was comfortable with it, although it came with a shitload of work. The comms, on the other hand, was really nothing worth mentioning as there would be no HF, just the standard small rig, SATCOM and some handhelds.

The military infrastructure in Kosovo at the time was extremely well-developed and synchronised. It was practically littered with international forces, most of them having a peacekeeping and monitoring role in addition to training the newly established departments of the police and other government agencies. That was both good and bad. The good part was that it was easy to blend in with other military forces. The hard part was not to stand out from those forces, which was sometimes easier said than done. It meant that you had to be extremely low-key when mingling, as military personnel are sensitive to new or unusual equipment, language, and general looks.

We were going to rotate in as part of the Swedish Contingent KS14B. Not as an established part of the conventional force, but rather an added specialist capability – incognito. The logistics would be owned by them, and we had to come in under the radar, as the "bad guys" monitored all nation's troop movements and rotations to detect any irregularities or irregular units. So, it was basically our cover, and it was a good one. Our real equipment had already been sent down through the military logistics system and we were rotating down in standard issue kit that we had taken out just for this part of the mission. We would look exactly like everyone else when it came to weapons, kit, and uniform. Even our nametags were fake. We would also use the standard kit if we needed to go to one of the Swedish bases or blend in for operational reasons.

We had just arrived at Västerås Airport, it was reasonably small, an hour and a half northwest of Stockholm, and frequently used for troop deployments. You could feel the testosterone oozing from the weekend warriors getting ready to board the plane. The Swedish peacekeeping mission was well populated with weekend warriors, some had good experience, but it was a game of levels. It was like they were going to participate in the War of the Worlds. Many of these guys had no standing in an equivalent Territorial Army, Reserve Force or Home Guard. They were often veterans with historical service, who were called up from civvie street for one mission, given some training and sent on their way. I mean no disrespect here, they served and made a difference, but their level of professionalism and training differed vastly from ours and for many of them it was more or less a safe way to get away from the wife and kids for a while.

Our cover was that we were a technical unit since their pre-deployment training was conducted at a different location than the regular troops' and there were no other technical units of this kind on this deployment. But the gunslingers would never know, as they were too excited to stand guard in front of the gate of the Swedish camp and get a glimpse of power that they would live off for the rest of their lives. Their friends would never hear the end of the story about the time when he or she "went to war".[1]

The only downside was that we were probably the most jacked-up "technical" unit that had ever existed. There was not even a splash of nerd in any of us, and the standard mechanic paunch was missing. I don't want to honk our own horn here, but regular units often hold a very basic physical standard, except for the occasional gym rats and runners. We were operators at the peak of our training and fitness, with a 38 year old captain that could beat us all if necessary.

Mr A sat next to me on the plane and asked me, 'So how does it feel to have gone through years of intensive, hard and highly specialised training to end up on the weekend warrior cattle transport?'

I gave him a hard look. 'And fuck you too!'

He laughed out loud. We were in the same boat but, Mr A was happy if he just had a gym, food, and his Minimi. He was more easily pleased than most of us.

He continued, 'Stop thinking about it, we are still in the army man. Your James Bond shit kind of dreams will come your way one day, just be happy. Imagine how much gym time we will have!' He didn't know how right – and wrong – he was at that moment, and neither did I.

We were based at a Portuguese base outside Pristina. The Brits had a compound within the base, and we had a compound within that compound,

---

1 This may come across a little strong but there was a specific context in Kosovo at the time, and this cannot be compared to some contemporary peacekeeping missions especially in Africa where blue helmets operate in a complex security context such as Mali, and DRC, and the now closed Darfur mission. In 2023 there were a number of peacekeepers injured in Kosovo, following a violent protest. There certainly are brave and talented peacekeepers, and they are given their due, and we salute the Swedish and soldiers from all nationalities who died in the line of duty.

so it was the regular "onion setup", as Captain B called it. It was a well-planned and structured compound. We had our own covert entry and exit for both civilian and military vehicles. This was particularly important when running covert operations with civvie cars, as one didn't want to burn them by driving into, and out of, a military base.

I was bunking with Mr N in the old barracks that had previously been used by the Gurkhas. Now the British unit in place was the Green Howards, although they were rebadged as the Yorkshire Regiment during their deployment. As with most deployments, the first week was all about getting settled and getting your bearings. Since we were living on "someone else's" base, we didn't have to worry about the lower Maslow things like guard duty, catering et cetera. We drove the main routes to get some on-the-ground familiarization and the rest was gear, gear and more gear. As the 2iC of my patrol, my schedule was hectic as we were planning to share some equipment with the British. That meant a lot of haggling between the 2iCs to work out a system that suited everyone and, most of all, setting boundaries. They had equipment we were not allowed to use, and we had "gifts" that they were not even allowed to see. We had some lengthy initial discussions, but we quickly discovered that the Brits were easy-going, and most of all practical, and over a beer or two most things were sorted.

I was surprised at how poorly equipped they were. We had all the bells and whistles when it came to kit. They, on the other hand, were a line infantry unit that had seen considerably more action than any of us, with little invest-ment in their kit. In practice, an ISTAR-role was not particularly hush-hush or special to them. But, as always, and returning to the recurring theme it's never the tools but the carpenter.

We were not only playing the ISTAR game there. We would assist them by taking over a few operations, but more than 50 percent of our deploy-ment would be separate and our own show. On one of the first days, we had a briefing with a gentleman from the Swedish Secret Service. They were running a SCOTT unit down there, mixed with police and military intelligence opera-tors, and he wanted to set up some boundaries and ways of communication, so that we didn't step into each other's operations. He also asked if we would be kind enough to report all Swedish civilian movement that we could see. What he meant by that was mostly cars, he wanted licence plate numbers. We asked if he was looking for something in particular. He told us outright that they monitored everyone and kept track of them once they got home. This was, of course, highly illegal and served as another blunt reminder that rules and laws never apply to intelligence units. So, even law-abiding citizens and civilians may be monitored by someone. Even if someone is "boring as fuck", chances are they are still on someone's spreadsheet. Maybe even in mine.

The organisation for us looked like this. Captain R led the unit. He was not formally attached to the regiment at the time. He did his basic training and first few years as an Arctic Ranger officer at the regiment but was attached to many different units afterwards. He was like a freelancer but with K4 as his home. Explosives were his bread-and-butter; he would later be a part of forming the Swedish IED investigative capability. So, he was poking around everywhere and was often attached to cloak and dagger agencies and units, as his experience and knowledge gave him a unique role. He was short and round. Not fat, but strong. He was a rugby player and had a massive scar from a blast injury on his calf.

He was probably the most experienced operator, but he wasn't typical military material. Or rather, he was not typical officer material. He was an operator down to the core and didn't care much for the fanciness usually applied by most officers. He was a practical man who enjoyed beer and bending the rules, as long as it achieved results.

Lieutenant B was in charge of the support unit and, of course, all technical stuff, including delivering reports securely back home. The support unit was manned by four soldiers, half of the original squad-sized unit. Captain T, an officer at the regiment but never attached to IRP before, was our QM. He was tall and thin and wore glasses. Not a typical ranger guy, but very humble and smart; on the level of Lieutenant B He had vast experience with logistics and was NATO-qualified for planning and leading airdrops. This made him an important addition when it came to navigating the international and cooperative logistics that we operated in, and relied on, in this multinational theatre.

Then we had the four patrols – Romeo 12 to Romeo 15. We were the second patrol, so our call sign was Romeo 13. As a half-superstitious man that spits over his left shoulder three times when a black cat crosses the street, it felt like a sign. I was passing through our private armoury on the fourth day, just as the support unit was getting it unpacked and organised. Mr B, the support unit sergeant, was racking all the weapons.

He was in his thirties and had that classic hippie look. Long hair, thin frame and the kind of person you didn't have to ask if he played *Dungeons and Dragons* or watched *Star Trek*, and if asked things like 'Is there an end to the universe?' he would give you an educated answer. But he was definitely more dangerous than he looked, and he was a genius when it came to computers, extremely humble and professional.

He looked up and said, 'Look at this, we are ready for a proper war.' He wasn't joking. We had more weapons than I had seen in a while. Barret .50s, modified PSG 90 sniper rifles, M/86 Carl Gustav Recoilless, AT4s, Benelli breach shotguns, Minimis, MMGs, HMGs, remote detonation systems for mines and explosives, decoy explosives pre-hidden in toys and plastic rocks. It looked like they were preparing for an invasion rather than some covert intelligence operations.

Captain T came up behind me and patted my shoulder, 'I'll make sure you will *never* be held back by equipment.'

He was good like that, he really cared about us never coming up short on anything. That also went for stuff like coffee and snacks. 'Nothing ruins good combat as much as shitty coffee.' He had a point.

Mr N and the drivers from the other patrols were giving the civilian cars a once over with the support guys. They needed some TLC, and we also got some new additions for our own operations. Our mechanic, a hardcore petrol head, was on the hunt for a Nitrous Oxide (NOS) kit. He wanted to do an experiment with a throttle valve that would be just right when you needed that extra push.

I was called to a briefing with Captain B, and the fun was about to start. The target was a rural mansion an hour and a half north of our position. It had been under surveillance previously, but the OP was shut down due to the risk of detection. Our first mission was to open a new, better OP a bit further away, as we had better equipment for long range photography and video recording.

We were looking for Dušan, one of the Major players in the conflict that predated the 1999 war. He was wanted for war crimes, a dodgy and morally challenged guy. Dušan had been very good at keeping a low profile and for years had moved between friendly countries, which allowed him to live with impunity. SIGINT, provided by the Americans, had picked up chatter indicating that he was coming home to meet his mother, who was ill. They didn't know how or when, but they knew that the mansion was a place of interest. It was a luxury mansion in the middle of a field, and it was heavily guarded by former Spetsnaz. They had good resources and did a lot of probing patrols in the surrounding areas, looking for the likes of us. They clearly knew what they were doing and operated on a level above the regular muscle.

Opening a new OP is always a beautiful thing as you get to set the tone according to your preferences. You leave your footprint, without leaving any actual footprint. We were going to be inserted in two nights' time, so it wouldn't be too stressful. It would be an approximately 14 day operation, potentially being relieved by Romeo 12. It was not difficult to figure out why we, specifically, got the first mission. Our team had the most collective experience and one of the best photo techs in Mr N.

I headed to the geocell, run by the British detachment, to order the maps and satellite images we needed. It was a small container in the British compound, manned by a staff sergeant and a corporal. It was crammed with the monitors, printers, and a big map table in the middle.

'Hello. I need some maps made.'

The corporal looked up. 'That is what we do. What do you need?'

I showed him the operational area. 'What kind of detail do you need?'

'One overlook and two zoomed in on these areas, like 1:25,000,' I replied, pointing at the two specific zones.

The staff sergeant looked up from his computer. 'I think we can do better.' He pulled up satellite images and low-level aircraft recon pictures. 'We have this from four days ago. The satellite pass is about two weeks old, but combined with the flybys it will give you a good picture. Do you want the maps marked?'

These guys had access to interesting resources. I was expecting a traditional geocell, but these gentlemen had access to current surveillance material. The surveillance pictures usually seeped downstream to the geocell over time, but it seemed they were working with two to three day old photos, which by geocell standards, was very good.

'We will have it ready in an hour.'

As I left, I had that feeling you get after a good round of shopping, or when the service was really good, making you feel appreciated on a level that inclines you to leave a tip.

On my way back, I stopped to see if I could manage to borrow one of the Brits' FLIR units.[2] It was way better than ours and would prove a vital asset. I felt relaxed.

This is what we had been doing for a few years, so we were confident, this was just a different location. We were going in green, meaning that we were fully kitted and in uniform, in the back of a civilian van driven by our support guys in civvies. I remember the last time we did this during an exercise, and I hoped for a smoother outcome. Every fourth day, we would do a rolling combined drop-off/pick-up, where we would hand over USB sticks and memory cards, exchange poop bags and pee bottles for fresh ones and get new water and USB sticks. We could transmit data from the OP, but that was a risk since the

2   Thermal imaging.

SATCOM left a wider footprint, so it would only be done if we had a positive ID, and UHF would be used as regular means of communication.

The night before we were due to head out, we were briefed by an "identification expert" from an unknown agency. She was talking about the ageing process and concealment methods and gave us tools to make a positive identification of our target. The target pack only contained a few blurry pictures that were about ten years old. It had no associated vehicles but did indicate a few persons of interest (POI) in his environment. So, it would definitely be a hard call, and this is if he actually showed up at all. Chatter can be anything, but apparently it was enough for them to prompt a new OP at the location. If we got a positive ID during those two weeks, we would act as an anchor OP and lead a direct action from there. I silently hoped that would happen, as I wanted to do this full circle and see it through to the end.

We were walking out with heavy Bergens to the enclosed yard where the van had been parked. The van had been given a shabby foil job[3] by us that made it look used and dull. It made it easier to change the colour of the vehicle more often to keep it flying under the radar. The licence plates had been removed as they hadn't decided which plates they were going with.

When it came to our civilian cars in Kosovo and the Balkans, we considered a few things: in the central region one used a certain type of licence plate, but in the Northern, Kosovo Serb dominated region, we used another type, in the Kosovo Albanian South it was yet again another type. There were pre-designated zones on the map where it was necessary to switch plates, to not stick out or be in danger from local "patriots".[4] So, each vehicle carried different sets of plates that were changed regularly and also switched intra unit, as the local police had a lot of informers on their payroll that were not pulling in the same direction as us. Maybe they weren't pulling against us, some didn't pull in any direction, except the general direction of money.

The van had reinforced springs, but it still felt heavy. A lot of equipment goes into opening an OP. It was 21:00 and we had to get rolling as we still had to do an infiltration, scout an OP location, build it, and have eyes on the target before first light.

Captain R stepped out of the operations centre that was located next to the yard. He had his hands in his pockets and looked at us. 'Ready?'

We nodded.

---

3   To change the paint colour or look of the vehicle.
4   The licence plate issue came to a head at the time of writing this book 2022-2023.

'Let's take a Bravo Two Zero picture so we get that over and done with.'

It was a standing joke as it was considered bad luck to take a pre-mission picture, but we knew it was inevitable, so we did. I hate that picture to this day. We look like trolls. In a certain light, one just doesn't look the part. I would say that most teams going in like that, all painted up and ready, really don't resemble the picture that Hollywood likes to paint.

The drivers came out after they had decided on which licence plates to use. They wore plain clothing and came armed with the AK5D (short), Glock and a shotgun between the seats. Illegal checkpoints were common in the rural and border regions, but not so much where we were going. It was too central. But there had been reports of the mansion's security team stopping cars at "random" on adjacent roads. So, our drop off had been carefully calculated to avoid the neighbouring roads. The only downside was that we needed to pass through a field, but the terrain was like a roller coaster which assisted in finding a decent low line that would provide us with cover.

Mr A had his hand on the door handle as the vehicle commander started the countdown.

'Approaching. Mirrors clear. Standby, standby.' You start tensing your muscles at this point, to be ready for explosive work.

'Three...' Mr A popped open the door.

'Two... One... Go!'

We had done exits like this many, many times before. It was fluid and calm as it should be. Like a string of pearls, we exited the rolling van and headed towards the bushes just next to the road. As we pushed into them, I could feel thorns penetrating my uniform sleeves. I closed my eyes and looked down as I pushed through, so that I didn't poke my eyes out. We took up defensive positions in a small clearing. Except for the wind rustling through the leaves, everything was quiet. All senses were heightened. The first few minutes of a new operation would give one a clear hint on whether you were in trouble or not. The only difference to an exercise was that the rounds in my magazine were meant to kill. I felt calm.

After two minutes, Mr N headed out from the side to check and, if necessary, cover our tracks from the drop off.

He returned quickly and whispered, 'Clean drop, absolutely nothing.'

I heard dogs barking in the distance and my thoughts were on the ASP baton[5] in my kit. I knew we had to kill them, if necessary, but I hoped it

---

5 ASP is the company name, and these are often expanding batons.

wouldn't come to that. Killing bad guys is one thing, but dogs… I would do it, but it would leave scars.

We had three map reconnoitred goose eggs – these were areas identified to build an OP through a map appreciation, that at least on paper, filled the requirements. We were heading towards location number two, as that was the one for which we had the highest hopes.

The vegetation was light, broken forest, fields and dense bush at the cross-over between the forest and field. The bushes were our target as there was limited opportunity to build a "normal" forest OP. And that was the reason we brought short poles, panels, and short nets instead of the larger ones.

Navigation through the well-defined landscape was easy. We had a short break in a small group of trees, stopping short of goose egg two. 'Now it was time to see if the maps held up to the real world,' I thought, I couldn't really blame the geocell if they didn't, but I secretly would anyway. We could see the mansion, all lit up about three kilometres away in a small valley. It was quiet and there was no movement on the roads. The plan was to cross a field, move into the forested patch above the mansion and then carefully move through the forest. About one kilometre from the mansion, we would set up an OP at the bushy edge of the forest. It might seem like an obvious spot, but the forest pushed another 500 metres towards the mansion and our planned OP was still around a kilometre away. There were many spots closer and perhaps more well suited – including the one that had been used before – on the other side of the valley, around 200-300 metres from the mansion. However, those places were probably where they would look first.

We spotted some 4x4 vehicles driving in the fields across the valley. 'Most likely, it was nothing,' I thought to myself, 'Just a part of the weird Balkan night habits that includes driving in fields and shooting into the air to cele-brate or let off some steam.' As we reached goose egg two, we immediately saw a problem. The forest was thick with dense bush, which restricted our move-ment, so moving through the forest as we planned proved impossible. Our only option was to move carefully between the forest and the field – it was brinksmanship, and, in this case, we were literally on the edge. The surface was hard which meant we wouldn't leave any tracks. 'Not all bad,' I thought, as we didn't have to stop and cover our tracks as much.

Captain B and I sat outside the spot we had found on the outskirts of goose egg two. As we couldn't use the interior of the forest, we were somewhat limited in our approach. Mr A and Mr N kept a tight perimeter watch, as we wanted the area in front of our OP to be untouched. We looked through our binoculars,

'Free view over the gate, the balcony, the front and west yard inside of the walls,' said Captain B.

'946 metres to the main gate,' I added.

'Pretty decent,' Captain B said and then looked behind him. 'It's a fucking dense bush.'

It was like a majestic aggressive wall of bush daring you to try and get through, just waiting to hurt you.

We decided to stay in that spot – the goose egg was good. First light was in five hours, so we had to get going. Mr A kept perimeter-watch with the Minimi, while Captain B and I would strip down to our uniforms and goggles. That way, our eyes would be protected, and without our extra kit, we would be able to push ourselves through the bush. Captain B then crawled underneath the bush searching for a better spot a bit deeper in. It was like we were animals adapting to an ecosystem we didn't know – we knew the principles were the same, but just different terrain – but we learned fast. I took the poles and panels and pushed in after him. I positioned myself next to Captain B I was surprised at how we got in there. It was like we were surrounded by an avalanche of dense leafy and thorned bush with tiny branches, and exactly zero room to move.

'Get on your back next to me,' Captain B said. 'I will try to push up the bush with my knees, so you get some room, then you slide a panel on top of your knees. I'll let go and insert a pole, and we'll make ourselves some room like that.'

It felt like we would have hours of work ahead of us, but we were dedicated and to be frank we had no other option available. After about half an hour, we managed to get up four roof panels, which gave us a small square house. Not exactly spacious but at least it was big enough for us to stand on all fours next to each other. We started working on the sides to get a bit more space. We added two more roof panels towards the front, where the eye of the OP would be, and managed to clear up some space in the back, were the entry tunnel was. Here, at least, was room to sit on a Bergen. I felt like we had just battle tested a military IKEA OP assembly. It was 03:45 when we put up the last drapes, mesh and net covering over the sides and the eye. I looked around. This was a small fucking OP, tiny really. I brought Mr N in to start setting up the photo equipment. As he was close to 200 centimetres tall, he looked at me and whispered, 'This will be pure pain.'

I found a small area in the back where all our Bergens would fit, and I pulled in Mr A, who was outside on guard duty. At 04:45, Captain B went outside for first-light checks. He was out a good 10 minutes. He got back and smiled saying, 'Fucking perfect! I mean it, I couldn't find us myself!' That was a good rating coming from him, as he left nothing to chance.

'First-light checks complete, eyes-on,' I reported in.

So, in this three metre long by two and a half metre wide by one-metre-high box, we managed to cram in four big soldiers, kit, and Bergens. We were no OP amateurs, but I was a little impressed myself, to be honest.

In the eye[6] we had a video on a mount which we had made ourselves and was attached to a Swarovski tube bino. The camera had a 1000mm mirror lens and was manned by a seated camera and video operator. The assistant was positioned to the right and captures in writing what the photo operator recounts. Behind the photo operator was the sleeping position, with one's legs half-across the OP. In the back sat the guard on a backpack. This was also the spot for peeing in a bottle and pooping in a bag, assisted by the guard. As if the space wasn't small enough already, there were two poles in the middle that we had to try not to knock down. We could, at least, take comfort from knowing that we set up a good OP and we had eyes-on the target in good time.

Manning an OP like this becomes really boring mostly because we had to follow a very strict schedule. Four hours in the eye (switching between photo and notes after two hours to keep sharp), sleeping for four hours, guard duty for four hours. And it goes on and on like that. In no time one's body starts hurting, as you never really get to stretch it out. Over the following days we started to map out the compound, drawing sketches, scheduling their routines, and mapping out the players, both permanent and visitors. It's more work than you can imagine when it's a permanent home to more than twelve people. At peak times we had to wake the sleeper to help take notes. You can imagine how thrilled they were about that.

'Look at C3. He kicks that ball day-in and day-out but never scores,' said Mr N as he watched through the camera while I took notes. C3 was the second oldest boy. I had started to structure all the POI in field files and indexed them with their respective picture number. Our memory cards started to fill up quickly. It's usually like that at the start as one begins to profile everyone. Once the board is set, it's a never-ending stream of notes, photos, and growing files.

I asked Captain B, 'Should we ask for an exchange tonight?' I was acting slightly in my own interest, since I knew that, as 2iC, I would be going with Mr A

6   The outlook point of the OP.

'Good idea. Run it by Zero and let's see what they can manage.' "Zero" was the ops room call sign. A few hours later our request was approved. It was going to happen at 22:00. The duffel bag had a shitty smell to it when I closed it. It was filled with poop bags, piss bottles, empty water bottles, flash drives, logs, and files, all put together like a beautiful potpourri. The trash bag came with an inventory list as I had checked off what we sent away to make sure we had left nothing behind. They would double-check it at the receiving end to see that I didn't miss anything.

It was time to go, and at 20:45 I pushed the bag positioned in front of me through the tunnel. Mr A grabbed it and pulled it out the other end when I was close to the exit. I savoured the feeling of standing up. It was beautiful. I had never looked forward to a supply run as much as this one. It took us 45 minutes to walk to the drop-off and it was mostly quiet except for a few shots we heard in the distance. It was not in our direction or the OP's, so it didn't bother us much.

The radio crackled coming alive. 'Five minutes.' And we moved from our layup to the side of the road.

'Confirm lights.'

'Lights.'

'Passenger back.'

They rolled up slowly in one of their sedans. Mr B opened the passenger door in the back and threw out a duffel bag. Mr A built up some momentum and threw ours in.

They were off and it was silent again. Back in the OP I took inventory of what we had received. Some kind person in the support squad had put four Snickers in there as a surprise. That's the kind of thing that will buy you infinite credibility in those situations. Over the first week manning the OP, we had two exchanges, and the rest was mostly routine. We built up extensive logs and profiles and got more specific target requests from HQ as the information started to get analysed at their end.

I was on guard duty one night at around 23:00. It had been dry and hot, so being on guard duty at this time was a luxury. It had been quiet at the mansion that day and I saw the notary and the photo operator switch places to keep awake. Suddenly the sound of shots fired broke the silence. Eight in quick succession, 7.62 AK. I slid down from the Bergen, pressing down on the ground, hugging it, and trying to get as much cover as possible. I heard the bullets crackling in the bushes around and over us. Within a few seconds we had to decide if we were fired upon or if they were firing in our direction.

Another round of shots rang out, and the bullets whizzed by. I crawled up to the eye to check. It was too dark to make out all the detail, but we saw the firing point outside the west wall. It was a group of people and it seemed like they were handing the weapon around.

We discovered that we were downrange of their target practice. Not optimal. But we were suitably convinced that we were not having some form of long-distance contact situation and decided to keep our heads down and hope for the best. They continued for about 45 minutes before they returned to the compound. In the morning, we spotted the "target" – an old tractor tire about 250 metres uphill from the compound, right in our direction. We hoped that they would pick another target the next time. It was obviously a fluke, but a reasonably common practice in the area was to fire in the direction of suspicious spots to flush out hidden elements – speculative fire or others may call it recon by fire. In Kosovo, many did this under the guise of legally shooting at targets on their own property.

Our second week was coming to an end. Nothing spectacular had gone down at that point and the possibility for a DA was slim. It had been good to get a feeling for intense target traffic and it had been a learning curve for all of us. We were ordered to hand over to Romeo 12 on the 15th day. They had decided to run the OP for a few more rotations to confirm the intelligence.

The day and night before handover were incredibly busy. I had to list all the gear that we were leaving, what we had shipped out, and the detail of it all. At 23:12 the new patrol arrived. They were excited to get going, maybe even overzealous but either way their willingness did not negate established rules, and principles and they had to wait patiently while their 2iC and I did the equipment handover. It required me to show him all the gear, him cross-checking it with the list and then both of us signing a copy through the ever-so-crisp NVG – quite an administrative ordeal, but certainly a necessary one. We were all happy to be on our way back, especially the ones that hadn't been out of the OP for two weeks with their only relief being the occasional first-light checks. I looked around in the van and there were many tired faces, but all still professionally alert – as expected.

The vehicle commander leaned back, 'You all smell like shit, just to let you know.'

It was good to know, and he was not wrong.

Back at the base we provided an info dump at the analysts' station followed by a short debrief by the brass and then the painful, but necessary, gear and kit check before the maintenance could start during the early morning hours.

We were soon ready to go again. It was good to be back at base, doing routine duties, manning the QRF, working out, swinging a few beers, recharging our batteries. The platoon had not been sitting on their asses twiddling their thumbs either. They had transformed and kitted out three new vans and two sedans. These were newly acquired through the channels of our quartermaster, Captain T. The vehicles had been repainted, rear suspension reinforced and fitted with a black box that could hold two photo operators at a time. An improvised cooling system was in place to extend the endurance of the guys manning it.

A new small "FOB" for civilian operations had been opened in a safe house just outside town for more covert entry and exit as it is crucial not to have the cars exposed. Poor discipline and not following protocol can get you caught or killed. While walking into the yard I saw Mr S and Mr P doing some trial photo shoots through the thinned-out mesh that was the cover behind the tinted back windows.

'Look at this! You couldn't believe it was taken from in here, could you?'

I looked at the picture and the craftsmanship of the construction. It was flawless, like it was factory-fitted.

'Mr B and Mr H from support did the welding and carpentry.'

'Stunning, they did a damned fine job!'

'Hey!' It was Captain R shouting at me while peeking out from the ops room. 'Where is the rest of your patrol?'

I shrugged my shoulders, 'Gym? Sleeping? Mess hall? I don't know.'

'Gather your herd and see me back here in ops in 15 minutes!'

Just my luck! Gathering the herd on a day off is always a mission. Although the base was small, there were many places that they could be, and 15 minutes is not a lot of time. The fact that you are the bearer of bad news doesn't help, either. Mr A was sitting shirtless outside the barracks, and as we say in Sweden, "licking up some sun". He had his signature protein shaker on the side. That could mean two things I thought, 'he had either just come back from the gym, or he had started drinking," (on his day off) as he loved to mix rum and Coke in that shaker.

'Have you already started drinking?'

He looked at me with his hand out to cover the sun which shone directly into his eyes. Squinting, he said, 'I was just about to take a sip.'

'Well, that's good then. No more sips, and do you know where the rest are?'

'Mr N is sleeping, and Captain B just went for a run.'

'Okay, you get Mr N, I'll intercept Captain B and we'll meet back in the ops centre in 10 minutes.' I could see him smiling behind his hand. 'What is going on?'

'I don't know. Captain R called for us.'

He took his hand down. 'Sweet, sweet action, Brother!' he replied as he got up from his chair and walked towards the barracks. Mr A was always up for action. He wanted to put lead down-range.

We got to the ops room a few minutes late as it took me longer than expected to catch up with the ultra-fast Captain B.

'Good! All assembled,' said Captain R as he started his briefing. 'Situation, Romeo 12 is manning the OP, Romeo 14 is on forward QRF duty and Romeo 15 is down at the German Prizren Airbase in the south.' They were participating as an ARF in a planned operation, that we soon would be a part of. An operation run by the Italian *Carabinieri* special ops unit *Gruppo di Intervento Speciale* or *GIS*. They were going for a high-value target, but they have had problems getting close to him. To make matters worse he and his family had good connections with the government and local population which made it hard to get near him. They would likely play the humanitarian card as he had the status of a local saint. A bit like Escobar, a man that divided public opinion, but for better or worse had the local inhabitants ready to die for him.

They needed him extradited before they could take action. 'This would be my second state-sponsored kidnapping in a year', I thought to myself and smiled. Armed with three vehicle-borne units, the *GIS* would lead the raid. Our own Romeo 15 was providing helicopter cover, standing by to support from the air or the ground. That was the initial plan, at least. The village of the HVT was a nasty place, we had no friends there. As soon as the raid commenced, we would only have a brief window of opportunity while they were sizing us up and assembling their own forces. So, it had to be a quick in-and-out. The regional KFOR QRF (about a company size) would be on standby, unknowingly, and would move in when we were finished, because there almost certainly would be unrest. They wouldn't know what had happened unless something went badly wrong. We needed to be gone before KFOR arrived. The official version would be that it was a search and seizure mission for weapons, and they would find plenty. We desperately wanted to avoid a "Black Hawk Down" situation, although it was doubtful that our HVT would be able to respond as General Mohamed Farrah Aideed had.

Our role was to provide more muscle, as one of the GIS teams had to lend a few guys to another operation.

'The raid starts at 03:00 tonight. A mutual friend is here and would like to say a few words.'

Jacque from DGSE appeared from the other room. '*Bonjour*, nice to see you again.' He almost looked happy. 'I heard you boys are going on a small excursion tonight. As you might know, we hit a snag with our *Carabinieri* friends.' He paced a few steps. 'I get it that they have first dibs and will clean out that house.' He tightened his lips and licked them. 'But it would be of great interest to me to know the ID of the HVT, and any casualties.' He paced a few more steps. 'Pictures would be greatly appreciated, and the favour would not be forgotten.' He smiled. 'I'll be back tomorrow to see if you caught anything tonight.' He waved weirdly as he left the ops room.

Captain R stepped up into the middle of the room. 'So do what you can. Try to negotiate the photos before the raid. I will set the stage and say that we have Swedish interests in this, non-conflicting just confirming.' Our orders were to be at the Italian base 45 minutes north at 19:00 for the final mission briefing and, hopefully, dinner. Just after 18:00 we loaded our car and made the final preparations. It wasn't much, just the regular kit and some added gear for handling prisoners. Captain B shouted to Mr N, 'Bring your trainers, you and I are runners.' To be a runner means that one carries less kit and wears running shoes. The purpose is to be lighter and quicker so you could intercept people trying to flee. One usually picked avid runners as they were the quickest in the group.

The Italian base was picturesque, to say the least. One could easily have been in a small Italian mountain village with the small, round café tables with chequered tablecloths outside of the mess hall and the doves flying out of the open kitchen window. The flutter of wings and smell of coffee added to the surreal visit. The base housed an infantry company, a few engineer platoons and one MP platoon. They had the setup of most bases with a smaller compound, for more shadowy units, inside the main compound. We were waved straight through and parked at the back of five cars that were already lined up in a column. As we stepped out of the car, a man whistled at us from the door of one of the barracks and waved with his arm for us to come over. I looked at my watch, we were 10 minutes early.

'Are we late?' I looked at Captain B

'No, but then I don't know how the Italian time system works.'

Usually, when you interact with foreign units that you are not familiar with, you abide by the rank system a bit more. To state the obvious, many countries seemed to appreciate that. In practice that meant that Captain B had to take the role of the spokesperson. This is, of course, how it works in any army but after a few years being on the operator side of things, the lines become blurred, and interaction is based more upon what you know and what your role is. No one is afraid to speak up, as it should be.

The barracks looked like a high-school gymnasium. Plastic chairs in different colours spread out in front of a stretched-out sheet that became a makeshift projector screen. There was loud chatter and at least half of them were smoking.

'Welcome, welcome, *ciao*,' the officer that met us in the door said in broken English. His name was Lorenzo, and he was some kind of liaison officer.

'Sit down here, it will start in a few minutes,' he said as he pointed to a group of plastic chairs in the back. We got a few looks from the crowd but, other than that, our presence was barely noticed.

An Italian officer stood up in front of the crowd and quietened them in Italian. After him, a short and slightly overweight man with thin hair stood up. He was wearing a white shirt with the sleeves sloppily rolled up. He didn't inspire confidence, and the fact that he was sweating visibly while fiddling with his folder, it was just business as usual for the official – he was going to give the task and leave the motivational stuff to our individual teams and units.

'Okay, everyone here?' His gaze swept over the crowd like a substitute schoolteacher.

The liaison officer that greeted us stood up. 'All here, all here.'

The man in the white shirt continued. 'If you have a problem with understanding English, just let me know and we will get someone up here to translate.' He didn't even introduce himself. He looked like a regular American office worker, a bulging briefcase type. He had what could have been a midwestern, but fairly generic, accent. CIA, FBI, DEA? We would never know. Once again, the Americans were orchestrating an "extradition". I looked at Captain B He was ready as always to take notes. Mr A was clueless; he just wanted to let rip with his Minimi. Mr N was eyeing up the girl in the corner, who with her tight top, and medic armband looked like a nurse.

The white-shirted man presented the target packs on the projector. "Vigilant" was the main target. His brother, "Bismarck", was suspected to be there as well as a few cousins, wives, and children.

'The surveillance situation has been really hard on this one. The neighbourhood is so hostile that we have not been able to have any ground sensors deliver anything of significant value. We detected his arrival through Airscan, but we have been very careful not to overuse it since they will be gone in an instant if they get a whiff of us.'

Airscan is a private contractor, run by the CIA for covert intelligence gathering. It was a small private plane with an extremely potent camera underneath that was capable of taking still shots and providing a live feed to an operations centre. For additional flexibility, the camera could be controlled by the operator in the plane or remotely.

'Remember that the local police and government are in on protecting these guys, so in this case, they are to be seen as the enemy.'

He lifted up his glasses as he looked up, exhaled and continued with his matter-of-fact explanation, 'They will defend themselves, they are heavily armed, and they don't fear death. We will be outnumbered; this is the risk we face. We would never achieve our mission goals if we processed the targets through the regular system. This operation would never have been approved by KFOR anyway. But fighting terrorism has never been a democratic process.'

He continued with the operational aspects of the mission. We would wait at a staging area just outside of the village. The heli would be out of hearing range. We would charge through the village at high speed in a convoy. The first three vehicles would be GIS, then us and finally a GIS van. The first vehicle would ram the gates and Vehicles One, Two and Three would drive into the compound. The compound was at a dead-end, the village was outside the main gates, the back of the compound was towards the forest. The plan was for us to stop outside and provide cover at the gates facing towards the village. GIS would conduct a rolling entry. It would be loud as they expected violence. They would do a sweep and collect the targets in the van and then get out.

It was a situation where we needed to act loud and big enough to create an illusion of a larger force to deter a counterattack. As the white shirt guy went through the mission line up, he presented Captain B, who stood up in his best officer manner and nodded.

'Okay Gentlemen, you leave here at 02:00. No mission creep, that will get you killed one by one.' All the squad commanders were called forward at the end to review the mission details.

Captain B whispered, 'Come with me, we need to make sure we make the Frenchman happy.' At the table with a map overlooking the compound, the squad leaders shook hands and introduced themselves.

The white shirt guy looked around. 'Everyone happy?'

Captain B started. 'My commander said he called you earlier today about the special Swedish request?'

The white shirt nodded. 'Yes, yes. Captain R called earlier. So, what do you need?'

Captain B looked tense. 'We have a common interest in these individuals. We are looking for someone.'

The white shirt looked irritated. 'Looking for someone?'

Captain B used his calmest voice. 'We need to confirm if a few POI are among these, that's all.'

The white shirt said, 'Go on.'

'So preferably we want to photograph all of those captured and casualties, if any. As I said, it's not a conflict of interests here. Just confirming. It will be handled discretely regardless of the outcome.'

The white shirt looked at the GIS commander, Matteo. 'If you have no trouble at the gate, you can send a man to the door, help take out the prisoners and then, when we have cleared the house, you can have a quick walkthrough if time permits. Time is crucial here, if we are short, it's a no-go.'

The white shirt guy looked at Captain B, 'Okay one man and be quick. No gear or documents, and you don't touch anything inside. Clear?'

'Crystal. This is our man,' he said, pointing at me.

When we got out of the briefing, we saw Mr A and Mr N were sitting outside the mess hall at one of the small round tables, having coffee. Mr A saw us and said, 'Dinner was awesome but look at this shit. Midget coffee cups! I had to order four of them.'

'You are culturally flawed' said Captain B. I, as a self-proclaimed coffee connoisseur, didn't mind at all. I also had four cups, but for very different reasons. We were the operator version of coffee and cake Swedish military men, much more kick ass, and definitely the A side.

Waiting at the staging area we started to run through checklists. We had all the windows rolled down, firstly because it was a hot night and secondly for operational reasons, as when we got to the gate, we had to be able to shout through the car if necessary. We heard the chatter on the radio. Units were checking in. Our colleagues from Romeo 15 were in a holding pattern. The hot nurse that Mr N had checked out reported ready. She and a doctor were 10 minutes away from the staging area. External medical support is a must, but most soldiers and operators are well trained for medical emergencies since we all want to make it home. It was 5 minutes before go time, and most of the GIS were still outside their cars smoking. A very Italian style of operating.

Mr N drove with Captain B riding shotgun. Mr A and I were in the back. He was eating his second protein bar.

'You want some?' he asked while chewing and held a half-eaten bar in front of me.

I didn't want any. My stomach was rumbling from the Italian dinner. 'Maybe it was the birds in the kitchen or the four espressos that would take me out after all', I thought. I heard the final radio check 'GIS Alpha march ready, Bravo march ready… Move out' and that was it, 'No turning back, but who would want to anyway,' I thought. The convoy started rolling. I could see absolutely nothing in front of me as the convoy bolted down the winding road leading to the compound and the dry clay created a massive dust cloud. Mr N was a solid driver and had studied the route extensively and practiced it on the airstrip with cones. You could see the occasional glare of a brake light in front of us which was understandable as we were travelling at speeds approaching 100 km/h. I heard the metal squeaking as the first car rammed the gate. We slid on the gravel a bit, as Mr N braked sharply to avoid hitting the wall. I was out before the car had stopped. I scanned the points of likely contact: windows, windows, windows, roofs, roofs, windows. The heli was all blacked out. It banked hard and low over the village and the mansion, where it sounded like a company sized assault was in progress. Only 15 seconds had elapsed since they rammed the gates. I heard the first flashbang go off with its distinct double thump. Another, and then shots fired, short bursts and double taps. I looked over my shoulder. I could see a flash going off on the second floor. I heard screaming and another double tap. You could see that people had started to wake up and peaked out behind the curtains.

Captain B shouted, 'We got this. Go!'

I jogged towards the door and helped the GIS guy outside cover the northern sector. I could see movement and lights being turned on in the nearby houses. There was a ruckus on the second floor, but it sounded like the GIS had cleared it.

The GIS operator shouted, 'They are coming out, Bismarck first!' I received Bismarck at the door. He was hooded and zipped. I lined him up on the side of the entrance as it was a blind spot for the village. He was shaking profusely, and I needed to tap him twice with my boot, so he didn't fall over. In the next 90 seconds, nine people were dragged out of the house, four of them kids. They were screaming and crying. The kids weren't hooded and a girl, who must have been about 8 years old, had burn marks on her cheek, probably from the flashbang.

Vigilant was squirming, so I pressed the muzzle of my rifle hard into his shoulder and he got the message, and immediately stopped. Except for the sobbing kids, it was quiet.

'All out,' said the third GIS operator, joining us outside. The three of us quickly patted down the nine and secured their ties. The kids had no idea what was happening. They had stopped crying and were looking with big eyes at the masked, armed men handling them. I took out my pocket camera. I knew I could only do three minutes of video recording, so I had to be fast.

'You got this?' I looked at the door man to see if he was covering me.

'*Si, si.*' When you have shell-shocked bad guys that one wants to document, they are usually hanging their heads in surrender and acceptance. As I took off their hoods one by one, I grabbed their hair and tilted their heads back.[7] Most of them had cuts and bruises on their faces. The woman was bleeding from her ear. I had to pinch Vigilant's eyelid as he initially refused to open them. The only ones looking straight into the camera were the kids. The whole thing took less than a minute and we quickly bagged their heads again.

I looked back at the door. Duffel bags were being brought out and one could see the shape of the occasional computer poke through the canvas bags.

The third man said, 'It's good, go in and do your thing. They are on the second floor.'

I did a quick sweep of the ground floor. I could see the blackened wall from the flashbang in the kids' room. They were putting a tourniquet on a man at the bottom of the staircase. It looked like he had been shot in the groin and chest. He was twisting his neck in pain.

'Hold his head,' I said. The medic grabbed his head by his blood-soaked hair, and I got my ID shot.

'Good?'

'All good. I am going up,' I replied. The ugly nature of our business.

In the bedroom, Bismarck's wife lay on the bed. She had been shot. There was a Makarov hanging in a shoulder holster on the wardrobe knob a small distance away from her but, in my opinion she could hardly have reached it. In the room next to her, one of the cousins – clearly dead – was lying face down in a pool of blood halfway out the door. A Kalashnikov had been kicked away from his hands and left a trail of blood. I wasn't squeamish, but if I could avoid handling dead people I would. I put my boot under his shoulder to lift his upper body a bit and turned his head so I could see his face, which looked empty.

On my way out, I grabbed two bags with gear.

'You done?' It was the commander of the GIS.

'All done.'

---

7   The main reason for the hoods is to restrict visual input and increase sensory depri-
    vation. It strengthens the feeling of isolation, fear and stress, which is part of the
    preparation for the later interrogation. It is commonly referred to as 'locking in the
    battlefield emotions.' Ear defenders are also used to add to this effect.

At the bottom of the stairs, I saw the wounded man again, but now he was dead. They had cut his tourniquet and removed the bandages to get rid of any loose ends. Out in the yard, the van was backed up towards the gate, and they had loaded up all the targets and the others. The commander and I came with the last four bags adding them to the loaded cargo, and then the van left, followed by the third car.

'Let's go!' shouted Captain B. Almost all of the windows had their lights turned on and people were looking out. This was the dangerous part as at this stage the locals knew that we were not a massive crew. Mr N had backed up so we could be the tail car behind Two and One.

'Go, go, go! We don't want to be here alone!'

The drive back was a bit slower, but not much. The helicopter lingered while we made our way back through the village.

'How many shots did you fire?' asked an excited Mr A.

'Not even one.'

'Well, at least you got blood on your boot. That's always something!'

I looked down at my right Meindl Desert Fox. It had blood over the front and down the inner side. 'They were just broken in and this stain would be hard to remove', I thought. I checked one more time that I had turned off the pocket camera. I didn't want to fuck up the pictures. As we passed the staging area and came up on the main road, we could see the KFOR convoy. They must have been put in motion early on or possibly been moved closer to the area beforehand since they managed to get here so quickly. Unfortunately, they would have a long night of grunt work ahead of them, cordoning off that village.

It had been a very quick raid, less than 10 minutes from start to finish. In total, we got nine people and 17 duffel bags full of gear and equipment. We rolled into the Italian compound about 10 minutes after the main convoy. An American Black Hawk was about to leave the ground. I wondered where they were taking them. An Italian NATO base wasn't a farfetched guess. There must have been many interested parties but if it was only the Americans, they would have done it themselves. I knew Bismarck and his wife were wanted by the Italians, and I thought, perhaps they would split up the targets. I wondered what would happen to the children. They would probably never see their parents again. Maybe they would be cared for by Italian Child Protective Services. I could only hope that they would learn to live with this one day.

The white shirt entered the briefing room. 'That went better than expected. I thought we were going to have problems with the villagers, but maybe they decided not to choose sides after all.'

I felt my camera in my chest pocket. 'If they only knew', I thought. Here I am, one insignificant Swedish operator, just a cog in the big machine, betraying whatever intelligence agency the white shirt guy was working for and the Italians for the French. It was a dangerous game, a game of loyalties, and the French had cashed in on a debt that we had owed. I also realised at this point why Captain B had chosen me. One, he could trust me. Two, if this backfired, it would be traced back to me and only me. Luckily, deals with intelligence agencies never backfire. Do they?

When we got back to our own base it was the morning rush hour. We had just missed the breakfast cut-off. Mr A proclaimed, 'After this briefing, we have to be able to get something to eat. Right? It's still a kitchen. Right?'

Everyone in the car laughed as it was not unexpected, but always funny, how different our priorities were. Captain R met us in the yard as we rolled in. 'The good news precedes you. The *Carabinieri* send their compliments.' He looked at me and my boots and asked, 'Are you okay?'

'Yes, of course', I said and gave a brief explanation.

We then had a short debriefing. 'Good work! And now we forget about this, okay?'

Of course, nothing ever exists in this line of work. When you think about it, you never really get credit for your work as it is always forgotten, hidden, or stashed away. Most of the time, it isn't even documented. But on the other hand, I asked myself, 'Would I like to get credit for this type of work?' Should someone call my mother and tell her that we assisted in killing a few bad guys and ruined four children's lives forever, for unclear reasons but mostly for the greater good? No, not getting credit was probably better.

'You two!' Captain R pointed at me and Captain B, 'You have a date with the French at MAIN tomorrow. Write a short report on the standalone computer and print it. Don't give it to them digitally and refer to us as a support unit. I trust the French, but only when the stars are aligned, and we have a downhill bike ride with a tail wind.' It was a game of interests; national, political, economic and we provided the mechanism.

He was right. The French often switched sides. We had been working with them for quite some time, had trained with them and been trained by them. But that meant nothing at the end of the day, and what just happened was of course their reason to bring us aboard in the first place. We knew that they would come and ask for a favour at some point. And this was just one of many.

Captain B and I went to the officers' bar that had just opened to get some lunch before we cracked on with our report to the French. I had never been inside the *Black Bear* before, as the British have a strong position on frater-nising between the ranks, at least on the surface that is. Just as we sat down a British captain approached our table. He was not very tall, rather thin, and weakly built, with bright red hair and a moustache that looked like some-thing out of *Downton Abbey*. He struck me as the type that had never gotten dirt under his fingernails, and I wouldn't have been surprised if he was there to keep the military lineage alive in some so-called prominent family – just another hangover from an overly classist society.

'I must insist, captain. I know this man is a sergeant.'

We both looked at him. 'He is with me. Is that a problem?'

The British captain looked bothered. 'Yes, this is an officers' bar. The men have their own bar.' Captain B looked at him and then looked at me. He started to dig around in his chest pocket, fished out a fistful of slip-on ranks and flipped through them. He carried many different ranks, as a lot of coun-tries were very particular about working with other ranks. In some cases, to participate in an HQ liaison meeting you had to be at least a major.

'Ah, here it is!' he said. He removed my sergeant's rank from my chest and replaced it with a major's rank.

'So, the sergeant has just received a field promotion. It looks like he is outranking all of us now. So, a "Sir" would be appropriate, Captain.'

The Brit looked at Captain B, 'This is not right! You will hear about this!' As he walked back to his table, we heard some muted laughing from the bar. We had our lunch, but I never returned to the *Black Bear*, mostly because the toast wasn't that good.

After a good night's sleep, the rest of the patrol had a day of getting the gear back in shape and helping the support unit finish prepping the civilian cars. Captain B and I went to MAIN, or KFOR MAIN as it was called. It was a large multinational base, like a small city that housed most HQ functions of all the participating countries. It was bustling with activity, and it had a lot of shops and a wide selection of restaurants. It carried the vibe that it had been there for too long, like most of the US bases do after a while.

Mr A had sent an order with us. 'I know they have a Burger King there. You buy me the largest meal on the menu and a few extra cheeseburgers, okay? I don't care if it's cold when you get back!' I once again wondered how he could stay on 8 per cent body fat. He was a food/fitness enigma, and the jealousy was real but never mentioned of course.

We were to meet Jacque at one of the many sandwich restaurants. I didn't mind as I was looking forward to something other than the Portuguese food that was not bad for being army food just very repetitive. It was a hot day and Jacque wasn't wearing his signature leather jacket. He sat on a bench outside, in the cooling shadow of a couple of trees. He wore linen trousers and a linen shirt, casually buttoned down with rolled-up sleeves. He looked like he came straight out of the French Riviera. So much for being subtle and blending in. I was sure that he had a civvie beret and scarf in his car, but probably thought that it would tip the scale in terms of stereotypical Frenchness.

He greeted us in his usual, overly friendly way. 'Nice to see you gents again. Let's have lunch here and then we can go to my office. It's just next to the main building.'

That was him making sure that we didn't try to hand over anything at lunch. I felt disappointed that he didn't think more highly of us. As we sat down, he went on about his vacation plans and that he couldn't wait to get back to France. Of course, he had a house by the sea.

In a silent moment, I thought I was being funny when I said, 'I can see by the way you are dressed that you are already at the Riviera mentally.'

He looked at me sharply. 'This is how cultivated people dress for summer.'

My remark didn't go down well. Every culture had their hang-ups and some amount of pretentiousness. 'Cultivated my ass,' I thought, 'I mean we are here under the murkiest of conditions.' Captain B shot me a "stop talking" look. He never liked it when I was too relaxed in distinguished company.

Luckily, Jacque lightened up the situation. 'Give me your sandwich and I will show you some French culture.' I pushed my plate towards him. He stood up, asked for something at the counter and came back with a jar.

'Trust me, once you start with Dijon mustard, you never go back,' he said as he spread a thick layer of grey goop on my sandwich. I had tried Dijon before, of course, but not like this. The intensity, the nose burn, the lingering taste was unlike anything I'd had before. He got me hooked and, thanks to Jacque, I am still a Dijon addict to this day, with no plans of getting off the stuff. I also came to appreciate the linen look myself not that many years later.

We walked into his office, it was just an empty room with a few chairs and a desk he had borrowed from the French HQ.

He leaned back in his office chair. 'So, I heard you got something for me.'

Captain B slid an envelope across the table. 'The flash drive has video and stills, cut out and indexed. The report is short and compressed, just a brief timeline of the events.'

Jacque opened the folded papers and read through them. 'Good, good! This is better than I had ever expected.'

'You trained us. Why would you expect less?' I asked.

Captain B gave me the "shut up" look again, but I knew Jacques was onboard this time.

Jacques laughed. 'I just fine-tuned you.' He folded the paper back into the envelope. 'I spoke to the Major and asked for your assistance in a future project. I hope you are good with that.'

We nodded making eye contact for a moment. He always brought the most interesting work, so how could we say no?

Mr A was waiting for us in the yard when we came back. He was almost dancing in anticipation. 'Did you get the Burger King?'

I showed him the bag from the back. He dug through it as soon as I gave it to him, 'Oh man, was this the biggest meal? You should have gone to the American base instead as they know how to properly size portions.' But he still ate it and looked happy. The next two to three weeks was mostly routine for the IRP. We worked on route reconnaissance and strengthening the safe house, working mostly in plain clothing. We had a few days in the mountains where we manned an HF radio relay station and doubled as a QRF for a British operation in the north. The never-ending QRF duties.

We spent the third week on a French base near the Serbian border serving as a forward QRF for a British OP. It was one of their long-standing Ops in the northwest. It was their show, but they were running a bit short on personnel, and we were more than happy to help out. Being a forward QRF means that one sets up at a location closer to the OP allowing faster reaction times. Sometimes it meant setting up a temporary position at a rural location, but the preference is friendly bases nearby. Our reaction time from start to out of the gates should be less than 3 minutes. During sensitive phases of the operation like infiltrations, extraction, drop-offs, or on OP requests, one should reduce the reaction time even more. This is often done by relocating even further forward. The combat readiness preparation may include being locked and loaded with the car running, sometimes just minutes away from the OP. For example, the QRF may be parked on a small side road just waiting for the order. But most of the time these duties were routine, and that was good because it meant that nothing bad had happened. But one always had the "fireman dilemma": you didn't want it to be a fire, but you still wanted to play ball.

We were eating well though; the French food at the base was mostly okay – although French cuisine is questionable at times. Besides that, we were in a rhythm of working out, chasing the sun, and waiting, waiting, and waiting some more. On the evening of the fifth day of our week with the French, we were having dinner and Mr A was five days into a debate with the team about whether asking for seconds was acceptable. The portions were too small for his liking. I had just taken my first bite as I heard a PTT push on the radio. It was not uncommon, but I removed the radio from my chest pocket and put it on the table in front of me. I turned down the volume as I assumed they were going to report something.

'Contact, contact, contact!' I heard that the RTO was out of breath, I could tell he was running, and this dinner had just become a "leave your trays and bolt" scene.

As we were running towards the car I reported, 'QRF leaving base location,' I wanted the boys to know that we were coming. We were armed to the teeth and ready to fuck things up. Mr N was driving, and he was pushing it. More than once we had extremely close calls in the many narrow tunnels. Captain B politely reminded Mr N that we would be of no use if we didn't get there. I was managing the radio. I kept it open and was waiting for positive reporting[8] from the OP crew.

'Broke contact, ERV 1. ERV 1 out.'

I knew they were hauling a heavy load if they had their kit with them. We were just minutes out of ERV 1,[9] a small back road below a ridge that was almost in a valley, so not optimal from a tactical perspective – good for speed but with the possibility for ambush. We took up positions on top of the ridge.

'Friends on the ridge.'

'Wilco.'

It was still all silent. No shots or people were heard or seen. Mr A saw the group coming in from the side, 150 metres to the west.

He alerted me. 'Visual, continue on your path.'

Captain B told Mr A, 'Hold their trail while we load up.'

They were out of breath. That's what running with Bergens does to you.

Captain B grabbed the squad leader. 'Did you break contact or are they still tracking? Any wounded?'

'No, no, we are good,' he said as he almost tumbled down the steep ridge side towards the car. Mr N had already prepped the car. He would have to be well versed in Tetris to fit four more people and gear in one car. For some

8   Push rather than pull reporting. Awaiting an update.
9   Emergency rendezvous.

reason that I can't remember, we were short of cars. It was really stupid, but we managed. We squeezed everyone in and got all the gear inside.

'Pick up complete,' I reported to HQ as we started to roll down the road.

'We are going to stay in the air until you are back to base.' It was the airborne unit that had been activated on the "contact" call. It was Romeo 14 in a German helicopter from our base. They still had some flying time, but it was always good with air support, since one never knew what complications could arise. Captain B took out his notebook and started with some field notes on the contact report. The crew was still jacked up on adrenaline and they were a bit rowdy.

So, it didn't take long for Captain B to change his approach and he soon simplified his questions. 'Listen! Equipment, do you have it all or did you leave it?'

Their 2iC replied, 'No, no, we got everything. We broke down the OP, everything is accounted for.' This was important, as if they hadn't, we would need to send in a larger uniformed unit to recover the equipment before it fell into the wrong hands.

We watered and sugared them up a bit, as their adrenaline was coming down. We were out on the main road.

Captain B continued, 'Squad leader, tell me in short what happened, how many and which types of weapons they had and what your actions were.' The squad leader explained and after a few minutes it became clearer. They hadn't fired back, they hadn't seen them, they hadn't been followed. So basically, it was more likely that they had been in the line of fire of some people's target practice, like we had been in our first OP. It was their experience and it's easy with hindsight to tell them they should have kept their cool. But I still felt a bit of disappointment. Nonetheless, I respected their call. Better safe than sorry, and we all know it's a very different story to take the decision on the ground than analysing it in the safety of a car on the way home. One thing was absolutely certain though: this OP was now closed forever. I didn't really know what they were observing there, so I couldn't assess how damaging it would be. That was up to the analysts to decide.

In the daily brief the next morning, we were told that Romeo 12 was being pulled from their third rotation in the OP that we had opened. Intelligence had come through that it was highly unlikely that the target would show up, so there was no use utilising more resources and risking exposure. It was mentioned that there was a potential opportunity for one patrol to go on two days' R&R in Greece and Macedonia, which would be a nice treat.

Otherwise, it would be a lazy day. The ones off duty were to represent us in the base's annual 5 kilometre running competition that afternoon and James Blunt was performing. He came for the British boys, of course, but we had nothing better to do so we figured that we'd tag along. But before all of that, Captain B had booked the kill house outside the Swedish base, Camp Victoria, on the outskirts of Pristina. The adjacent old open mine allowed for 360 degree fire drills and the use of explosives too. We needed it; the range on the camp was small and so were most of the ranges on the bases we had visited up to that point.

We had to kit-down and wore our standard issue gear keeping the rest in our cars while we headed up to the Swedish camp to collect the range keys. We didn't want too many prying eyes or nosey questions. The Swedes had a few smaller detachments on other bases, including MOT teams, so it was not unreasonable that we showed up.

Captain B came back to the car after collecting the range keys. 'We are staying for lunch.'

We looked at him. 'I asked the guard and it's meatballs, potatoes and home-made lingonberry jam.'

He didn't need to say more, as this was one of the Swedish national dishes and a much-needed break from the grub we were getting elsewhere. The mess hall experience was like being the new kids having lunch in the high school cafeteria for the first time: you know people are looking, even though they try not to. We didn't care and enjoyed two servings and proper Swedish coffee. Mr A's debate about two helpings could be put to bed but maybe it was because we had home court advantage on this occasion. It shortened our range time, but it was all worth it.

We were back late and "unfortunately" missed the 5-kilometre running competition. Captain R popped his head out from the ops room and said, 'So you fuckers decided you were just leaving us alone with the running competition?'

Captain B was quick with a reply. 'Erm, we needed to do some extra range work as the Minimi had some problems.'

Captain R squinted. 'Is that so? I heard that you assholes had a delicious meatball lunch and took your time with that.'

We all looked guilty.

'Next time, you take me along. Oh, and by the way, you can forget about James Blunt tonight. You are QRF for Romeo 12's extraction. The other patrol needed a break,' Captain R said as he walked back into the ops room.

Instant karma, I guess, so I never got to see James Blunt in action. But it was okay since I was not a massive fan of his anyway, and we needed to give those guns a good scrub. I suppose it was fitting that Blunt returned to Kosovo to boost the morale of the British boys. He was a fan favourite, and although his music wasn't exactly hard rock, he had the credentials. Having served in Kosovo during the turbulent 1999 campaign, he did forward reconnaissance with a cavalry unit identifying targets for the NATO bombing campaign. Years later I read that he had drawn inspiration for his song *No Bravery* from his operational experience.

It was an uneventful and calm night. They pulled Romeo 12 before midnight, and they didn't smell too bad when they arrived. We stood down at 01:30 and were ready for some well-earned sleep.

My barracks door was pulled open and Mr N, whose bunk was above mine, was sitting straight up.

'What the fuck is happening?'

I looked at my watch, it was 04:32. We had only had a few hours of sleep.

It was Mr A. 'Sorry, fellows. Don't kill the messenger but it's all hands on deck. Briefing room in 5 minutes.'

Mr N was groaning from the top bunk. 'Motherfucking army! Never lets you sleep properly… assholes!'

I silently nodded in agreement. Everyone was on base; the whole of Kosovo was filled with military. So why did they need us, of all people? Captain R met all the newly woken patrols. I did the smart thing and passed the ops room, next to the briefing room, as they always had coffee on the brew.

Mr A saw my coffee cup as I sat down next to him. 'You get fucking coffee and do it secretly without hooking up anyone else?'

'We can go halfsies on my cup.'

'Fuck you! I don't want your cooties.'

Actually, it was the other way around. I should have been worried about his cooties. I think he even managed to sleep with a Norwegian intelligence captain that been staying at our base from time to time. Later, he came around and took a few sips.

'Sorry for waking you all up early this morning. We have a situation.' He struggled a bit; you knew it was going to be something different.

'Upon the return of Romeo 12, it was discovered that Mr R had lost his weapon mounted NVG.'

Shit! This was no joke. I tried not to look at Mr R, but my head turned towards him, without thinking. It looked like he was breaking into molecules on the inside and just wanted to disappear. This was a major incident on many levels. Firstly, we were to leave no trace behind. Secondly, it was the latest generation NVG, a gift from the US. So, the incident could potentially compromise another foreign state. Thirdly, it was sensitive technology that we didn't want falling into the wrong hands. It would have been better to lose a rifle.

How could this have happened? You would notice if you lost your weapon mounted NVG, but when tired it would be easy to think that you stashed it. The NVG unit is attached to the picatinny rail with a mount and secured with a strap. Sure, it could have been broken under unfortunate circumstances. But there was also the 2iC's role. NVGs were included in his checks before leaving the OP. This was often done by physically confirming that it was in its pocket or making sure it was secure on the weapon. This check was repeated at every stop, before the pickup and again in the pickup vehicle for exactly this reason, so that he could easily identify on what stretch an item was lost. So, there must have been a string of failures. These were top-level operators; all of them, especially Mr R. And this was the kind of shit that could have you on guard duty for the rest of your life.

'We will figure out what happened at a later stage. Right now, we need to do damage control before it turns into an international incident. I need five people to go to the Swedish camp after this meeting and pick up four regular Swedish KFOR jeeps and three metal detectors that I have borrowed. You will all wear standard equipment and patches. We will be a regular Swedish unit, out looking for something. The locals will see it as business as usual.'

We were leaving at 06:00. Romeo 12 and Romeo 14 would start at the OP. Our team and Romeo 15 would start at the pickup point. I gave Mr R a pat on the pack as we left the briefing. He needed it as this would leave deep scars within him. But don't be fooled that top-tier units never fuck up. We do. The difference is usually in how we handle the mistakes and how we implement the lessons we learn from them. You would, most likely, never hear about them, because when you did it was usually in the form of an operation that went all FUBAR[10] and caused an international scandal. This time, it wouldn't be an international scandal, though. Romeo 12 found the NVG themselves after just 45 minutes of looking along the extraction path close to the OP. It was snagged in a small bush.

10 Fucked Up Beyond All Recognition.

It was concluded that he hadn't tied it according to regulations and just wrapped the security lanyard around the rail. When the NVG snapped out of its mount, which sometimes happens, nothing kept it attached to the weapon. We didn't end up changing our SOPs over this, but it was still a wake-up call for all of us and a reminder that there were reasons for the things we did. Picking up the slack if we made mistakes. I guess they got quite a few stern talks after this incident, but nothing formally ever happened, and no one really talked about it much after that. Mr R still works in a top tier unit today and when we see each other from time to time, I can see that it still haunts him.

14

Boots on the Ground, Contact!

'Stand by for contact. I flicked off the safety of the AK between my legs and grasped the pistol grip.'

We had a decent warm-up since our deployment started. Most patrols had engaged in many different types of work and were getting more and more comfortable in their roles. We had done a lot of green and semi-green (uniformed and covert) work up until then, but I could feel that the winds of change were blowing us into more of a civilian covert operations role. We were getting ready. Safe houses and vehicles were being prepared, and mission requests were pouring into the HQ. Nobody said anything, but I could see it: they were gearing up. We had to be selective with the missions we took on, so we didn't branch out too far from Special Operations and kept our path narrow.

Over the next couple of weeks, we did contract work for the Germans. They had been running helicopters up and down the central and northern region for a while to establish a normal presence. Once that was established, they required assistance with heli surveillance on those routes, mostly photography. We were definitely up to the task, and it was good practice for all of us to level-up our photo skills so that we did not have to rely solely on Mr N. Since we didn't have any Swedish heli resources, we were happy to trade services with the Germans. They had already shown great hospitality in providing us with air transport.

In fact, we technically had a Swedish aviation unit, a few HKP 9A (MBB Bo 105) anti-tank helicopters, based in the US Camp Bondsteel in the South. They arrived there just after us. They were the first modern Swedish overseas helicopter unit ever deployed. The problem was that they didn't want to fly. To be fair the pilots probably did, but they had restrictions from Stockholm, so they were of no use to us. We would go on to have the same problem in Afghanistan once the Swedish helicopters were deployed there. They had restrictions on flying time, no flying in bad weather, no hot LZs. Only high altitude, pre-planned strategic flights.[1] The government was so careful with the use of helicopters that they basically served no purpose, as a result, we have always had to rely on other nations' airborne capabilities as they would fly rain or shine.

We had a clear direction for the coming period, it was North. The Serbian border encircled Kosovo to the north and east. Serbia had always disputed Kosovo's independence. Claims that Kosovo was a part of the Serbian Republic had created a domestic and international conflict. To put it broadly, the Serbian-friendly part of the population, the Kosovo Serbs, were therefore living in the north, with the town of Mitrovica as their stronghold.

The Serbian and Kosovo Serbian feelings towards NATO forces were far from friendly after the NATO-led bombing campaign of Serbia – the Yugoslavian Campaign – in 1999. The NATO led air campaign was hailed by many as some sort of justification of how air power alone can win a war. But as we know it was aided by a strong land-based operation and tremendous amounts of international diplomatic pressure. The result of the successful campaign was a shaky peace, and the birth of KFOR, the UN sanctioned, and NATO led peacekeeping mission in Kosovo.[2] The north was, without a doubt, the most complicated area to operate in for the NATO-led KFOR troops.

Riots and disturbances were common occurrences in the North and running civilian operations wasn't easy as the climate amongst the population almost resembled the one in Northern Ireland. The north was filled with collaborators, traitors, mercenaries, and paramilitary groups sponsored by the Serbian government. And, of course, Serbian Special Forces units and intelligence.

This was an area of great interest to us, and to many other units in the intelligence world. It was a tap of information that was just waiting to be turned on. However, there were a few problems with operating in the north. Most of the available KFOR bases in the region were under heavy surveillance and that burned any intelligence operations run from them immediately. But the alternative was running operations from Central Kosovo. That was safer but affected the operational window due to travel time and communications.

---

1   See forthcoming volume on my experiences in Afghanistan.
2   This campaign perhaps helped teach some of the wrong lessons, which impacted the Iraq and Afghanistan Wars in the early 2000s.

We wanted to open a safe house outside Mitrovica, to give us extended range and more long-term exposure. Foxtrot operations were possible, but we would be burned as soon as we opened our mouths. So, the main focus would be more permanent static and mobile surveillance, as we could do that effortlessly. But, more importantly, we would start to build up and run some sources and assets.

So, what is a safe house in this context?

A safe house is an operational asset run professionally by either the agency's own personnel or a source, depending on the location. The safe house is usually deeper into hostile territory, though there are exceptions. For example, the Swedish Embassy in Berlin has its own safe house, in case of terrorist attacks. It's a common practice that many countries have safe houses in foreign territories. For our purposes, in the operational area, a safe house is always located in a hostile region. The safe house is a sleeping resource that can provide active assistance. It can resupply a ground team with explosives and ammunition, hide teams that are on the run or provide communications and medical care. It can be used for surveillance or as a secret FOB (black) for operational teams. The safe house is always secret, in the old-fashioned sense. Most often, knowledge about it is kept at a unit level or lower. It's one of those classic Hollywood "need to know" things. But even people in one's unit that will never use it, will never know about it. It is usually managed by the handler of the source or, if it's manned by your own personnel, by a dedicated safe house manager. The biggest danger to a good safe house lies within your own ranks. Your government, your army or allied forces could, intentionally or unintentionally, give away the location of a safe house. So OPSEC surrounding safe houses is critical and those in the know are anal about it. As you can see, running a safe house is a delicate process and opening one is even more delicate. It takes time. If you are recruiting and running your own sources, it can take many years.

In our case, we were going to use a source and asset that had been recruited and run up by German intelligence. He was a family man, with a wife and three kids. Originally from Mitrovica, he had moved to Munich and was recruited by German Intelligence, the *Bundesnachrichtendiest*. The Germans ran him as a community source for some time as he was in part politically, but foremost personally, motivated. After the war, he was convinced to return to Mitrovica to re-establish himself and his family. At that point he worked as a teacher but also functioned as a "ground sensor". His handle was "Fabian".

Why the Germans let us tap into 'Fabian' was way above my pay grade, but in my experience if you were pulling out of a region your assets and sources were handed to other agencies if they were still producing actionable intelligence. A deal usually followed, with the new agency occasionally providing intelligence or running bespoke missions on the other agency's behalf.

But it was not done quickly, as it had to be approached with caution. It was important not to be over-eager. Even more importantly, the asset needed to be vetted by the new agency – in this case us. We had to re-establish his loyalties, motives, and goals.[3] It could be tricky with ideologically driven people. Money-driven cases are always easier but, of course, less reliable since you need to be the highest bidder. In cases like this, you had to assume that the source will still "leak" to the agency that recruited him, in our case the Germans. It was a part of the game that could be managed as long as one was aware of it. Here again the interests of the two states had to align. The true reliability of Fabian would only be known when we had a major operational success or two.

Although we were trained for this, it was a step into uncharted terrain for the IRP. As a unit, we had never run a full-scale hybrid operation like that before. It would prove our flexibility and professionalism, as this was usually something reserved for very different units. It would also give us all a clear indication of the direction in which the unit was heading. Other circuit professionals were going to realise that we were here to stay. I think a lot of our popularity came from us being easier to talk to than many of our colleagues. We also had a broad-spectrum operational capability over the whole range of civilian and military intelligence operations. Fabian was to be taken over and handled by us. He was handled within our unit, but the handler will remain anonymous. Not even a made-up name or an initial can be accredited to this person, as I value my freedom and the safety of the persons involved. We only knew him by the mission identifier 'Joshua.'

So, behind the scenes there was an asset takeover and planning for a safe house, which meant that the patrols were about to start the groundwork. Captain Rhad called us to a late-night briefing. To state the obvious, late-night info usually meant that something was in the pipeline.

'Gentlemen, we have really hit the ground running on this deployment and we are not going to stop now. I know you are all eager to get up north where the action is and you will, shortly.'

---

3   In the world of intelligence, the general motivators are described in the acronym MICE: Money, Ideology, Compromise, Ego. Sometimes there would be a combination and interplay between the motivators.

Romeo 14 and Romeo 15 were designated with civilian and military route reconnoitring up north. It's not that the NATO supplied maps were inaccurate in any way, but one always has to double check. For us, route reconnaissance was done to establish our own waypoint system, ERVs, possible holding areas, et cetera. Since NATO was leaking like a sieve, their system could be thrown in the trash from day one.

Route reconnaissance was intensive and precise work, with a lot of supporting photography, checking signals, et cetera. So, these two patrols had to buckle up.

Captain R continued, 'As for Romeo 12 and Romeo 13, do you remember the first OP you manned? There are new leads on some POI close to an HVT.'

It was the mansion gig 2.0. But it was different this time. The first time around, the target pack was slim, and the background information was limited. The HVT was just referred to with a short designation like N21, but he had now become "Tailor". He probably always was, but we weren't trusted enough the first time around. Captain R didn't have much more info for us, other than that we were manning an urban OP for a week each, while the other patrol acted as QRF. Operations were going to be run from the German base in the town of Prizren located in the southwest, closer to the Albanian border. Romeo 15 had already been there when they acted as ARF for the GIS raid. They said that it was very organised and pleasant. We were excited to go, and we were expected at 22:00 the following evening.

As we were leaving the briefing, I looked at Captain B. 'Wasn't it odd how he gave us the codename for the HVT and also mentioned that there would be a beefier target pack?'

Captain B looked at me. 'Well, maybe that was what he had!'

I wasn't satisfied. 'But why not leave it to the briefing we would get down in Prizren anyway?'

Captain B shrugged his shoulders. To me it felt like Captain R slipped up and then covered it. Or it could just have been me overthinking it again. 'Will you start with the gear tonight?'

'Yeah, I'll get on it right away. We need building material and paint. I guess we can get what we need from the Germans, but just in case.'

Captain B nodded, 'Sounds good. I'll go and put the prima donnas to work.'

Captain R had said earlier, 'Give me a call if you need anything down there or if it gets shitty.'

'We would if needed, but we probably wouldn't need to,' I thought. The Germans were always solid, like clockwork.

It was around 18:00 when we left our base. We were going to the US base, Camp Bondsteel, which was located not too far east from Prizren. Our QM had managed to wring out some AP 5.56 and IR tracer[4] from them. We needed to restock, and the delivery from Sweden was dragging. I think the factory was having delivery problems and, at the same time, the Yanks and the Brits swallowed enormous amounts of ammo in Afghanistan and Iraq. It had been a strained situation on that front since 2003. We had decided we were having dinner at Camp Bondsteel, as they had the typical American all-in menu. If you could imagine it, they had it including an ice cream bar. Mr A was shouting for Burger King, of course, but the rumours were that the steak was good that day so we thought we might have to split up. When we arrived at Bondsteel, I went to the armoury with Mr N while the others were visiting the PX.[5] We were to meet up at the cars two hours later if we didn't see each other at dinner.

The armoury guards waved us through after checking our credentials and orders. A very jacked sergeant met us. 'Sir, what can I do for you?'

I looked at him and pointed at my rank. 'No need to "Sir" me or him. We are all sergeants.' I smiled and tried to look friendly he looked at me like I was an idiot and said nothing. I knew the Americans were very 'Sir-y' but come on, it was late in the evening and no was one around to see.

'Do you have your order?'

I fiddled around in my chest pocket. 'Here. Our QM, Captain T, called it in.'

He looked at the wrinkled paper. 'Ah, you're picking up the special. I didn't know you Swedes had this much fun. I was thinking you were just assembling IKEA furniture and shit.'

I looked at Mr N, who shrugged his shoulders. 'No idea. It's just AP and IR.'

A few minutes later he was rolling out a cart from the vault. I didn't look right to me. 'I think we were only supposed to have AP and IR. That looks like 40mm frags on top. And… .50 incendiary?'

The sergeant showed me the order. 'It's all here. He called in a bit later and topped up.'

In total, it was 20 boxes of 5.56, 10 boxes of mixed .50, four crates of 40mm frag and two crates of flashbangs. I signed off on the order and the sergeant helped us to the car. We would need to split this up later, it was heavy in an already-full car. We were ready for battle.

---

4   Armour piercing and infrared illumination tracer rounds.
5   Post Exchange or PX is a store authorised to sell merchandise to military personnel and certain civilians.

'You gentlemen have a nice evening and have fun,' the sergeant said.

'Well, you too, Sir.' I tried to be funny but got nothing but that crickets feeling.

Then the sergeant turned his head before he went inside and shouted, 'That was kind of funny.'

We had our steak and got back to the vehicles. We were running late, so we had to skip the ice cream. Mr N grunted, 'All the way here, and no ice cream.'

I looked at him, 'Why didn't you take a cone to go?'

Mr N grimaced, 'Why did you have to wait until now to suggest that?'

We hadn't seen the others yet, but in the distance, we saw something that looked like a group of housewives coming back from champagne and shopping. 'What the fuck is going on?' asked Mr N, 'I see like 15 bags. We don't have room for that shit.'

Mr N rolled down the window as they approached the car. 'Did you all go Sex in The City over dinner? This is not an NYC cab!'

Captain B looked a bit embarrassed and tried to get off the hook replying with an even cheesier, 'While in Rome.'

Mr A opened the boot. 'Holy shit! You two have also been shopping!' He was using his excited voice.

'Well, Mr A, we have balls and don't waste space on candy and protein bars.'

'Fuck that. Now we have both,' said an upbeat Mr A. Nothing could ever break his stride or spirit.

We left Bondsteel very heavily loaded. We were glad that we didn't have to drive far like that. When we arrived at the gates of Prizren AB, I glanced at my watch – 21:50. Captain B went to the guard hut to show our credentials.

Halfway to the hut, a German officer showed up on the other side of the iron gates like a shadow. 'Captain B?'

Captain B looked at him. 'Yes...'

'We have been expecting you. Follow me.' It's no joke, those were his actual words. He waved at the guards to open the gates. The German was a *Hauptfeldwebel*, the equivalent of master sergeant or something similar. He was around 200 centimetres tall and really athletic. His uniform couldn't hide the fact that he was kind of jacked. As the gates had almost opened, he started to run in front of our cars at a steady pace. He didn't max out, but he was quick.

He ran towards a part at the southern end of the base close to the outer perimeter. It was a compound surrounded by high fences, at least four metres high. The fence was carefully meshed all the way to the top, not a gap as far as the eye could see. It had been done with the utmost care and craftsmanship. As he approached the gates to the fenced compound they opened at the perfect distance. He didn't even need to stop running. It was a cinematic experience. 'Unbelievable', I thought, it was either that or the perfect athlete would have pole vaulted over the fence. The gates were closed behind us by two guards, posted on the inside. The compound was big – very big for a hush-hush one. It had six neat rows of permanent rubber tents. Across the road from the tents was a large hangar. Further down I could see a gas station, a medical centre and ammunition lockers. There was also a small gate on the other side of the compound that led straight out to a back road. In the middle of all this, close to the gates, was a guard hut. Everything was in tiptop shape. Not even the large, and probably old, hangar had any rust or flaking paint.

The German pointed with sharp movements and directed us to park on two spots next to the second tent in the row. As we exited the cars he said once again, 'Follow me.' So, we did.

We entered the tent and there were 20 beds, all were made up with fresh, white linen and a towel set neatly folded on the pillow. At the foot of each bed there was a numbered locker with a complimentary lock and key hanging outside, ready to go. At the side of each bed stood a full-sized cabinet and professionally mounted rows of electrical outlets.

At the far end, each tent had a TV lounge, a small kitchen with a fully stocked fridge and a toilet with a shower unit. It was just short of a hotel. No, it was a hotel. After giving us a quick tour, the *Hauptfeldwebel* stopped in the middle of the tent, handed Captain B the keys to an ammo locker and said, 'Breakfast will be available in the first tent from 05:00. If you need medical attention, there is a nurse in the medical container 24/7.

Mr N's ears piqued. 'The briefing will start at 08:15 tomorrow in the hangar. If you need anything, or have any questions, I am available through the guard hut at any hour, day, or night.'

'Yisses, the Germans weren't kidding around', I thought. I had seen organised before, but the Germans left everyone else in the dust. The reception, the facility, the attention to detail. It was magnificent! I would not mind spending two weeks there, or at least the one week that we were QRF.

Mr N pointed out, 'It seems like we are the only ones here, right?'

Indeed, we were. If this was how they treated their guests, we had a lot to learn from them.

After getting the best sleep we'd had in months and being fed a robust German breakfast, we all headed over to the hangar with a coffee in hand.

The doors were open, and someone was putting out a few chairs in front of a projector screen. All the chairs were the same colour, unlike the Italians, and I won't even mention the Latin Americans. The hangar was big. I saw two helicopters sticking out from under the tarps. At least 15 civilian vehicles were neatly covered, as were several motorcycles and two German riot vehicles. The corporal who was putting the chairs out smiled and excused himself in broken English.

Shortly after we had sat down, a German major entered the hangar followed by the white-shirted man that had briefed us on the GIS raid. He had now changed to a light blue shirt. The sleeves were rolled up and it confirmed my thoughts that he had never been in a military unit, my thoughts went back to my first time in my unit when I was reprimanded about my sleeves. I thought, 'No one had given him a talking to about sleeves,' but then I got pulled back to the moment by the type of shirt, you know, the ones that should be avoided if it's hot and you sweat a lot. I had become a fashion critic; it was just a question of style.

I tapped Captain B, 'Who is that guy? He never introduced himself last time around?'

Captain B leaned towards me. 'US intelligence liaison.'

He didn't introduce himself this time, either. 'Good morning, gentlemen. Good to see you again.'

I looked around. It was only Romeo 12, my patrol and two German medics or doctors, who were listening from the side, inside the hangar.

'My colleague that is supposed to be holding the briefing is running a bit late, but I think I can start with the basics.'

He introduced the German major, predictably named Hans. His nametag confirmed it. As he was about to continue, the hangar door opened. 'Sorry I am late. I had a last-minute briefing.'

It was a woman in her forties, good looking with brown hair put up in a tight bun. I almost expected her to wear a business suit, but she wore a worn-out pair of jeans and something that could have been a 5.11 shirt. She immediately took the floor and the blue shirt sat down at the end of the front row. Major Hans stood like a stone statue next to the projector screen.

She continued. 'My name is Linn, and I am the operational liaison for Operation SAVILLE ROW. Gentlemen, we are hunting big game here. This is Tailor.' She clicked on the mouse to change pictures.

I immediately recognised him. It was Radovan Karadžić, but just to make sure I had to double check and read his name in the caption under the picture.

I looked at Captain B and whispered, 'It's the damned Butcher of Bosnia.' He was as surprised as me. At the mansion gig, we had been looking for some junior POI that was in Tailor's suspected entourage. It was not the time for us to know back then as we had not been a part of the operation yet and they kept the circle tight.

Radovan Karadžić was a well-known HVT, maybe even the premium target in the Balkan conflict. He was the Serbian President from 1992 to 1996 and during the Bosnian war, was wanted for genocide, crimes against humanity and an assortment of other war crimes. He had been on the run since 1996 and was the last big fish out there that hadn't been caught and brought to the International Criminal Court at The Hague to stand trial. He had slipped away from justice several times. It was hard for intelligence agencies to maintain any traction in pursuing him as he seemed to vaporise into thin air as soon as they had the smallest lead. He still had too many friends in high places.

We were a part of this op mainly because we came from "outside" of the circle and were guaranteed to not have any divergent tendencies, but also because we had proven ourselves as a unit. This was a big operation that included many resources. Airscan, mobile units, ground units and air units, mostly run from different places. We again, just a small cog in a big wheel. Major Hans was commanding a few of the ground units, one aerial unit and us. It was kept extremely tight, and most units didn't know about other players – as it should be.

SIGINT had indicated the possibility that Radovan Karadžić would surface, so it was all hands on deck. Our task was to open and man an urban OP in an asset-acquired apartment overlooking one of the locations where it was thought he might show up. An absolute positive ID was required before there would be an arrest attempt.

We were going to be provided with civilian cars by the Germans. The prep of the apartment was incredibly good. The "owner" was on vacation, and he would be "renting" it out. They had pictures of the whole apartment. Corridors, elevators, garage, the whole package, all very well prepared. The owner was also one of two that had rooftop access. It provided even more cover and could be a trigger point. He said that the manager, who had the other key to the roof, hadn't been there in more than a year.

The apartment complex had a regular main entrance, with both stairs and elevators. The elevators ran all the way up from the garage. It also had a small fire-escape staircase leading from the garage, through every floor, to the roof. His apartment was at the end of a corridor and by the exit to the fire-escape.

It was not uncomplicated, though. You don't just take four guys with duffel bags and waltz in there. The OP would not be the hard part, the entry and exit would be. We had 48 hours to prepare, familiarise with the cars and tweak our equipment.

'I want to be able to use that rooftop option,' said Captain B as we sat around the table in our tent. He was right. The pictures of the roof showed that it would be easy enough to set up a really good observation post there. Captain B continued, 'I am thinking a Swarovski on the roof.'

Mr N shook his head. 'We have two lenses, a 1000mm and a 700mm, two cameras and one video. I would say we go for photo on the roof as well and keep the 700mm downstairs if we need to change.'

Captain B looked like he was thinking. 'Okay, I like that. Double barrels in the right direction. If the situation permits, let's go for that.'

I was painting net-reinforced mesh outside the hangar. It was for the rooftop. We decided on concrete grey about a third of the way up, and then a bit lighter as it would reflect the sky if looking from below but also provided the illusion of concrete from the air. The roof was filled with rubble, so we also backed up with a darker shade to blend in better if we needed to look more like an object.

The two days of prep time left us with a lot of time to spare, but the feeling that this was really big was lingering over us. It was not due to its complexity or danger; it was just the target. Realistically, chances were slim that he would show. It usually is the case when you have people that have been fugitives for this long that when they get caught, its most likely because someone stumbled over them, or they were involved in an accident or something. At least, that is what the statistics say. 'But this could be it for us,' I thought. Anyway, just being selected to be a part of it felt like a weird honour.

We took the cars for a spin, made ourselves familiar with the operational surroundings and did two very careful drive-bys. When inserting oneself in an urban OP, the night is not generally your friend like it is when you are working in the green. You want to pick a low-activity time, but not so low that you are sticking out. We also preferred a bit of dark as it would be harder to spot our appearances. We had decided to go for 21:00. The street was busy enough, but fewer people were moving into, and out of, the building. We were not being dropped off but would drive ourselves in and out. Technically it was not the preferred option, but in this case, it was less of a risk than having to deal with several crews going in and out.

It was just a few hours until we were leaving. It was a 25 minute drive. Major Hans gave us a last pep talk, 'Intel is still pointing in the same direction, but the indicators have not strengthened, so the overall reliability is slightly lower than when the OP was planned. But it doesn't mean anything other than that they haven't picked up anymore triggers, so in my opinion that makes it highly likely that he is on the move as the pattern usually goes like that.'

I looked at Mr N. He confirmed that he was thinking the same thing. 'Patterns! If they had a pattern on this guy, we wouldn't be there. Good intelligence doesn't stop when people move, it usually increases.'

I wondered what their source was. Linn had mentioned that they had SIGINT. If they had that and it was so precise that they would pick out this location, it felt unnatural that they lost it. You don't just pick up precise fragments like that and then, all of a sudden, you have nothing. It could happen, of course, but my feeling was that this was asset-driven intelligence, maybe supported by chatter.

But on the other hand, I wasn't complaining. It was the right move; I would have done the same. If you had even the tiniest shred of information on a HVT like this, putting together an operation of this magnitude was a small price to pay. Romeo 12 would leave a few minutes after us and would be driving within 5 minutes' reach of the apartment during the infiltration. Contact was very unlikely at that point. The biggest danger was being burned and if we were, we would probably never know.

It was a very quiet drive with only the short breaks for reporting waypoints. We only had a few minutes left to reach the apartment complex. Mr A was finishing his second power bar and threw the wrapper on the floor.

I looked at him, 'Are you going to leave it there?'

He finished chewing and looked at me. 'You people are so into this no-traces shit that you have forgotten what a normal car looks like. Normal cars have trash on the floor.'

He was right, normal cars did. We had actually kitted the car with a bit of selected local trash to make it look normal if anyone looked into it. He had bought his power bar at the supermarket, so it could stay put.

We turned into our street and immediately saw blue lights flashing down the street, just short of the turn off into to our garage. It was the police. Was it a checkpoint, or something else? We only had seconds to decide. A police checkpoint would definitely burn us. The options were to continue along our planned route and drive past them or turn early and abort.

Captain B said, 'Wait, wait.' He was just reassuring Mr N, who was driving, that a decision would come in time and that we needed to get closer to see what it was about. 'Stay with the plan.'

We had just moments before our last chance to turn off the street in a natural way would be gone. It was two police cars. The officers were negotiating with two agitated men that had had a small fender bender. It was perfect since they caught all the attention on the street. They didn't even look our way as we passed them and made the turn down to the garage, located under the apartment complex. The entry down to the garage was built in true Balkan style: steep as fuck and in the simplest way possible. Mr N needed to press down hard on the breaks to keep the heavy car from rolling. Captain B, who rode shotgun, had the remote that we got to open the garage door. He pressed it, but nothing happened. He started the remote dance when you try to aim at different locations to find the receiver. The garage door didn't move an inch. 'Did we change batteries in this one?' he asked with a slightly irritated voice.

I replied, 'Of course. I double-checked, and I also have a spare with me.'

After what seemed like an eternity, Mr N snatched the remote out of Captain B's hand and pushed it hard. The garage door cracked open and started to roll up.

'What did you do different?'

Mr N smiled. 'Magic fingers,' he said as he drove into the garage.

I knew Captain B wasn't happy about what had happened, and he probably took it as a personal failure of sorts. But we had other things to think about. In truth it was minor thing, and part of the friction of real operations.

The parking area was half filled with cars and was planned in the tightest way possible. The floor had that shiny surface that made the tyres squeal a bit when you turned at low speeds. We had parking spot number 46. It was between a wall and a pole, so Mr N needed to back up twice to line up straight enough to be able to fit in. The tyres squealed as he turned the steering wheel.

Captain B looked unhappy. 'Fuck, this is loud.'

'Relax, this is how it sounds when anyone is parking here,' I said.

As we finally crammed ourselves into the parking spot and turned off the car, we sat and observed for a moment. Everything was silent. The elevator was about 25 metres away and the ordinary staircase was through a door to the left. We were going for the fire-escape staircase that was 10 metres to the right of the elevator. It ran outside the building but was encapsulated in concrete so you couldn't see if someone was moving in it. That was going to be our way in. We quickly grabbed two bags each. I took a quick look inside the car to check that we hadn't left anything behind.

That was the critical moment. From that point until we were inside the apartment, we were at risk. We had to move quickly but silently. We passed the elevator, which had a note on it. I couldn't understand the text but the sign – tools in a circle, taken straight from the Word clip-art library – told us everything we needed to know.

The door was painted red and needed to be jiggled a bit before it would open. It was a good sign that the door wasn't used a lot. I looked up the staircase as I took point. It was a weird circular, concrete staircase; pitch dark except for the light provided through a tiny square hole every five metres. It was super-tight, and I needed to hold one of the bags to my chest to avoid constantly scraping against the walls. I get that this was meant for escape, but it would be a challenge to climb eight floors silently.

We moved slowly to keep the sound to a minimum. Every time we reached a new floor and the area where the door was, it was a relief as you could stretch out for a few seconds. It took us 15 minutes to get to our floor and I was soaked in sweat by the time we got there. We were standing on the platform outside the door leading to the eighth floor. The stairs that continued up to the roof were blocked by a gate. Mr N and I were going to do a quick reconnaissance of the rooftop while the others waited on the platform.

The roof was even better in reality, than we had seen in our intelligence package. It would be easy to build a super OP in a pile of construction rubble. It would cater to a sitting camera operator and one person sleeping.

When we came down to the platform, we confirmed that we had a "go" on the rooftop. To minimise our movements, we had planned to split the teams on the platform. The roof team would lock themselves in and stay on the roof and never change with the apartment team. We had packed and prepped just for this so that it would be an easy split.

Captain B nodded, 'It's a go, then.'

The apartment was just on the other side of the fire door and to the right. Mr A and I were going to tag team on the roof, so we just made sure Mr N and Captain B made it into the apartment before we continued up to the roof. I was slightly disappointed that I would never see the apartment, but the gentle breeze soon changed my mind.

It took us a few hours to carefully build our OP. I was happy that we had taken more mesh net than initially planned. We were going to be two people up there for a long time so, with the help of two of the three wooden pallets already on the roof, we were able to create a chair-like construction that was comfortable enough and allowed for quickly switching focus. The resting person could lie down fully stretched-out or sit comfortably below the photo operator. We could also seat two people side by side, so one could work the camera and the other as a spotter with the Swarovski at the same time.

At 01:22, we reported eyes-on. We had done test shoots on all locations. We had even greater reach than we had expected. We knew that the apartment would take longer to get ready, so we didn't expect them to have eyes-on until a few hours later.

At 04:55, the radio crackled. 'Romeo 13A, eyes-on.'

Then the waiting game began. Both locations had a map of the target location, with pre-designated points of interest. The target was a small, walled-in townhouse located in between two residential high-rises.

Mr A looked at me as I was busy with observation. 'They can only see 25 per cent of what they are supposed to. We cover roughly 150 per cent.' I looked at the map. They could only see three spots on the side of the target. The apartment coverage hadn't panned out as we expected, so it was a good thing that we had better luck on the roof. The neighbourhood was very busy during daytime so to take a bit of the load from me and Mr A, we totally let go of the side that the apartment could cover and let them handle it. From about 05:00 to 19:00, both of us needed to be observing most of the time, since the traffic was intense. The interaction around the townhouse was not that much, but we started to create files on the few persons who were moving in and out and around it. Then we divided the calmer nights for longer and more uninterrupted opportunities to sleep.

More than half of the operation was over and day four had passed without triggers. Except for the regular reports, it had been quiet. We didn't complain, as we were comfortable up there. The weather had been absolutely perfect, we had a good rolling system and I have to say that I appreciated Mr A's insistence on bringing chocolate. It elevated the morning coffee experience.

The sun was setting, and it was that moment when the sky turns pinkish. I was looking out over the horizon as I was having my cold MRE. Is this really what my life had boiled down to? If you had asked me two years earlier, I wouldn't have thought that I was going to sit and enjoy dinner in the sunset, manning an urban OP in southern Kosovo. Things had happened so quickly, and many things had changed since 2002. Basic training felt like ages ago and even Colombia felt like a distant and foggy memory. For the first time since arriving, I remembered how bitter I was that we were going to Kosovo and not Afghanistan. I had not felt that way even once since we had boots on the ground. Even if this was it, if the rest of the deployment was only QRF duties, I would be satisfied. It had already exceeded my expectations by far.

Mr A tapped me with his boot. 'Hey, time to get up. I have news.'

I looked at my watch: 04:37. It was time to get up anyway. I took a few minutes to shake off the sleep before I sat down next to Mr A. 'What happened? New players showing up early?'

Mr A was still looking through the Swarovski. 'Even better. A mobile unit started trailing a vehicle that had previously been linked to the townhouse and an older man has been observed in the back. They picked them up as they crossed the Macedonian border 30 minutes ago. Airscan just reported wheels-up and will join in 20 minutes or so. Their ETA if they are coming here is approximately two hours.'

The chatter on the radio was more intense, but still short and effective. We had taken around 100 test photos, so we would be able to switch seamlessly around the target.

'Is it a bit over-exposed?'

Mr A leaned in behind the camera. 'Technically, yes, but see how much crisper the detail is. So, it's a minor sacrifice.'

We were adjusting the settings as the light changed quickly in the morning.

'Target 75 per cent likely heading towards Mike 41; 15 minutes out.'

Mike 41 was the designation of the townhouse. The moment of truth was approaching and knowing that the apartment would not be able to see them if they were going into the townhouse upped the ante for us.

'Mobile lost them at Whisky 31.'

There was a moment of static and then the humming transmission of the Airscan crew broke the silence. 'Passing Whisky 15.'

The mobile team lost them at an intersection, it was a bit complicated due to heavy traffic, traffic light timing, and roadwork. Airscan narrated their movements, similar to an FAC low level talk-down. They were just minutes out. I saw the black Mercedes turning onto the long street. We had them 100 per cent at our 12 o'clock, then it was just one right turn before they were at the townhouse. I started snapping away. Mr A had the radio. 'Romeo 13B, visual.'

The Airscan team stopped reporting and the frequency was kept open. It was more or less up to us now. As they were turning right, they had about 50 metres to go to the townhouse. I felt the tension and the slight adrenaline rush that manifests in a rushing feeling down your neck. I had good pictures of the car and the plates, so now it was all about the pax. The Mercedes slowed down and turned into the driveway. It stopped on the sidewalk in front of the closed wooden gates.

'Target stopped short. Gates Mike 41.'

I looked at the shots of the car standing still. The focus was good and the detail crisp. I expected someone to come out of the house or get out of the car to open the gates so that they could drive in, but it didn't happen. The car was turned off as it stood across the sidewalk with the nose towards the gates. A man in his late thirties exited on the driver's side. "Snap, snap, snap." I could hear Mr A's pen carving into the paper, making quick notes. The man yawned and stretched his arms over his head. A woman, around the same age, exited from the passenger's side. They were exchanging some words.

The radio crackled, 'Confirm ID.'

The younger couple was moving to the back of their respective sides of the car. The rear doors were already open, but no one had gotten out yet.

Mr A pushed the PTT, 'Standby, standby.'

The driver helped an older lady get out of the back left. I snapped 10 more frames. I got good shots of all three of them. Now we just needed to wait for the guest of honour. The driver and the old lady walked around the back and started talking to the last passenger that still hadn't gotten out of the car.

With the help of the driver, an elderly man exited the car. He leaned on the car for support while he half-stretched his legs. I fired off 20 to 30 shots in a rapid succession.

'All out of the vehicle,' Mr A reported.

I had only seen his profile. I needed him to turn around so I could see his face.

The radio crackled again. 'Confirm ID.'

As the old man let go of the car, he turned around to talk to the older lady who was still standing at the back of the car. I saw his face. The shutter made a sound like something full auto. I had probably taken 50 frames.

'Confirm ID.'

Mr A saw that I had full-frontal pics now. 'Standby, standby.'

I zoomed in on the camera display and picked up the printed reference picture we had. I looked at the camera and the picture, trying to follow the facial lines and looking for similarities.

'Look!'

Mr A leaned in and studied the new photo and the reference for a few seconds. We looked at each other and almost simultaneously shook our heads. It wasn't him. He had a somewhat similar appearance at a brief glance, but it was not him. It felt good to be sure. We had concurred in just a few seconds, but I felt the weight on my shoulders as I pressed the PTT. Everyone was waiting for me to make the call. I literally decided the short-term outcome of all resources that were on their toes right then.

'ID negative. ID negative. Romeo 13B.' I was sure. 'Airscan, stand down. All mobile, stand down.'

We kept monitoring them as they unloaded the vehicle. It looked like they had been on a vacation or something. Maybe that is why the house had only been visited a few times by people staying for short periods of time, probably watering the flowers or something. The people made no effort to conceal themselves and took their time to get into the house. The car was never driven through the gates and was parked weirdly across the sidewalk, but that's how they roll in the Balkans. It felt like I had been standing on the starting line of a race but that the countdown had stopped at one, but no gun fire. I felt dissatisfied with the result but was satisfied with the quality of the pictures and how we had handled it. We only had one day left in the OP. Time had flown by. In 24 hours, the next night, we would be relieved by Romeo 12. We had made the decision with Captain B that the apartment-OP was going to be closed and that Romeo 12 would only man the roof. They would just expand it a bit so that they could work two cameras from there.

Romeo 13A started dismantling their OP during the day. One hour before the handover, I met Captain B and Mr N down at the gate, let them in and led them up to the roof.

'Damn! You have been living like kings up here. The apartment was horrible.' They enjoyed the fresh breeze as Captain B continued, 'We should have moved up earlier.'

I pointed at the OP, 'We don't have enough material to cover all four of us. You had no choice.'

'Romeo 12 is bringing in more material, so they can expand the OP,' I said. I had to update my inventory list as we were waiting. Captain B was eager to get home, but I could have stayed.

When I met Romeo 12 at the gate, they looked as sweaty as we probably did, even if they carried a lighter load. The handover was quick, and the way down was much more enjoyable than coming up, even if we were weighed down by piss bottles and poop bags. As we left the garage, I watched Mr A opening a Snickers bar.

He looked at me. 'What? One on the way in, and one on the way out. It's a classic.'

I shook my head, but secretly wished I could do the same. Major Hans debriefed us on our return. He had an analyst with him that wanted to "confirm" our decision on the target. He concurred quickly. Now we just had to kick back and enjoy another week of German hospitality.

On the last day of our QRF-week, both Romeo 14 and Romeo 15 joined us. They were going to run the OP for another two weeks. The intelligence had dried up, but it was decided to track the townhouse for a bit longer. We left Prizren airbase at dusk two days later. I felt happy that I had had the opportunity to participate in opening one rural and one urban OP. Captain B was a little unhappy. He didn't say anything, but you could tell as he became short and snappy, because he missed the 'action'. But he had to settle and accept that the action was a false lead and that this was a unit effort and not an individual game. Those were his own words when I first got him as platoon commander back during basic. Sometimes even the teacher needs to be reminded.

During the days after we arrived back, we had to get up to speed with the work that Romeo 14 and Romeo 15 had done over the two weeks since we had been gone. They had conducted a massive mapping effort in the north and created a completely new waypoint system. They had also done the planning for setting up a relay station, as communications were spotty at best up there.

Captain R met us at the morning briefing. 'Welcome back. I hope you had a good time and enjoyed the Sauerkraut!' He looked at me. 'When I hear your voice on the radio, you sound like one of those olden-times news announcers with a stick up their butt, not like a 20 something operator.'

The safe house was in motion. The handler had met with Fabian a few times and we were going to start developing it. We were to finish a few loose ends that Romeo 14 and Romeo 15 hadn't had time to wrap up. We were also to find a suitable location for an equipment handover to Fabian. It had to be outside the northern zone as it would be dangerous for both us and him to do it in his neck of the woods. Fabian did weekly trips to Pristina in his role as a teacher, so him moving was nothing new. We had to find a location that could be used during the daytime as he seldom travelled at night. It would be done on his call when he had a bit of a break, so we needed to get this ready as soon as possible.

But first we were going to do two days of familiarisation runs along the mapped routes that Romeo 14 had made. That meant that we would be travelling in two civilian cars. We would loosely be working together, in the same vicinity rather than in a convoy. Mr A and I teamed up, as usual. We would make our way up to the Mitrovica region and drive through the waypoint system[6] from the west. Captain B and Mr N would drive through the system from the east. We would eventually pass each other halfway, do a full circle and return home. Familiarisation was important when you were breaking

6   Way points on a map. This was a part of the process before formal routes were set.

into a new region. It might seem like a waste to do empty runs, but it would become very valuable when you become operational there.

It was a different vibe the further north you pushed. Less and less NATO presence and a stronger local identity. From time to time, one could see Serbian or Russian flags and murals of the Serbian War heroes or war criminals, depending on which side you were on.

Mr A was driving. 'Next left,' I said.

We stopped at a pre-reconnoitred spot in the northern license plate change zone. It was a small side road where one could get off and on the main road in exactly a minute. It didn't seem to be used much as the grass had no tracks from being driven on. It was a good and a bad thing: it would provide privacy, but it would leave traces.

'It's set number two today.' We had eight numbered licence plate sets in the reserve tire compartment. We stepped out of the car to listen for a few seconds. All was quiet – one could hear traffic from far away. We had electric screwdrivers to make a quick change. Just 30 seconds later we rolled out with confidence. It was our version of a Formula 1 pit stop. We were on the main road again, still with no other cars in sight.

We met the other part of the team more than halfway in. Mr A had adopted the Balkan driving style with a heavy foot to boot. It wasn't really a meeting as we barely looked at each other when passing. It had been a full day of driving. We finished the waypoint work that was left, and I had also taken the liberty of reconnoitring some good handover spots. I presented them at the briefing. Captain B looked at me as if I had been too excited on the handover reconnaissance, but he didn't say anything.[7]

Captain R remarked, 'This spot you found was not bad.' I had marked it as "Bree" on my map. It was just off the main road, probably 30 minutes north of Pristina. A small back road that led to a picnic spot, it had several entries and exits. It was quiet and you could easily overlook oncoming traffic, as it was up a small hill with a kind of viewpoint attached to it. It didn't seem to be a popular weekday spot. We had taken a few pictures just in case it could be used.

'Fabian is doing a run back from Pristina tomorrow. I will pass on information about "Bree" and see what he thinks about it. The QM and Lieutenant B should have prepared a package. Go and see them tonight, so you know it's all in order for tomorrow. This might be a fastball.'

---

7 Captain B thought that I should have done that specific recce at another time or consulted with him first.

As we walked out, Captain B asked, 'Why did you name it Bree? Sounds like the cheese?'

I looked at him. 'No, it's simpler than that. You know the village where Gandalf is supposed to meet Frodo in the first *Lord of the Rings* book? That's Bree, since the *Prancing Pony* was too long.'

He looked at me like I was stupid and laughed.

They had indeed prepared a package for Fabian. Secure emergency communication, medical kit, chargers and refills of our most common batteries and a lot of small goodies that could be needed. But the primary thing was a small relay station. It was built from scratch by the support squad, and programmed by Mr B It was intended to be used if we were doing operations close to the Serbian border, where coverage was non-existent. It was a variable effect short burst frequency hopping unit that would leave a minimal footprint for Serbian or other SIGINT units to follow. Of course, it still presented a risk so it would have to be used with caution.

Everything that they had, fitted in a bag that was stock and locally sourced, nothing could lead back to us. A folder was also included. It was an emergency plan, how and when he could activate extraction for himself and his family. We were to allow him to read it once and then burn it. I flipped through the folder.

'How did you manage to prearrange asylum for him?'

Captain T looked at me. 'We didn't. I am not even sure we will be picking them up if the shit hits the fan. The fragments that he knows are not worth rocking the boat for.' The life of the asset, filled with empty promises.

Captain B and I were to do the handover. Mr A and Mr N would be SAP. They would do a drive-by and then linger in the area in case a QRF response was needed. This was the kind of meeting that was not registered by the operations room. Only Captain R would know if something happened. The SAP had rolled out 15 minutes before we set off. I was driving for a change. We had about 20 minutes to go. We would be there on time, neither late nor early.

As we took the on-ramp to the highway, I said to Captain B, 'It feels like we are out in deep waters.'

He snapped his head around and looked at me. 'What, doing this handover?'

He probably thought that I meant that I had a bad feeling about the current mission. 'No, no, no. About the IRP. With everything we have been doing lately: sources, assets. It feels like we are winging a lot of things. Not the military parts and surveillance, but when we are setting up our own show like this.'

He took an extended pause. 'You know, I have spent half my life around intelligence people. Big agencies, small agencies. It doesn't matter, they are all winging it all the time. They fail horribly more times than they win, and their view of the greater good is definitely different to yours and mine.' He reflected for almost a minute. 'So, I think it's better to keep it in-house. With this setup, we are at least serving our own needs and we have to stand by our own decisions as it directly affects our people on the ground. We can't hide behind an anonymous agency when things go up shit creek.'

He was right. I needed to mentally leave the point of no return and accept what we were and what we were trying to become. We were good at this, probably better than many veterans in the business. Was this due to our technical skills? Experience? No, it was about our ability to keep a professional and humble attitude at all times. When I thought about it, I laughed out loud as I visualised Mr A as the poster boy for our professional attitude.

'What now?' asked Captain B.

'I was just thinking about us having a professional attitude, and then about Mr A eating a Snickers bar in the car.'

Captain B looked at me. 'He is a damned fine soldier. He lightens things up. Imagine if all of us were like you and me. Life would be like a funeral.'

I looked at him. Why did he include me in the stiff and boring section? That did not resonate with me. Or did it? I hoped to God that was not how I appeared to others.

'750 metres, right turn.'

Maybe he forgot that I had done the reconnaissance on this spot, but I kept my mouth shut this time. The SAP had reported "all clear" as we were a few minutes out. We were going to be a few minutes early. I felt calm as a biscuit,[8] almost on a level where you risk relaxing too much and become sloppy. I needed to snap out of it and feel a bit of tension. We arrived at the viewpoint parking. You could hear the birds chirping as we closed the car doors. Other than the birds, it was silent. I did a quick sweep. It would be extremely hard to get eyes on this spot. Where would I put the OP if the tables were turned? Probably on the other side of the lake, but it would only give you a narrow tunnel that you could observe through the big pine trees. I concluded that it would be a challenge if someone were to attempt it.

I could see a small cloud of dust down the road. It gave us an early warning that a vehicle was approaching. An older, dark blue BMW was fighting its way

---

8   When a cucumber just will not do.

up the hill. I could identify Fabian as he turned in and parked in the direction of the exit. He exited the car and left the engine running.

'Kill the engine!'

He turned his ear towards me as he couldn't hear me.

I stepped closer to his car. 'Kill the engine. I need to be able to hear.'

'Sorry I am late,' Fabian said as he stretched out his hand to greet us. He looked older than he was. His eyes were tired, and his hair was thinning. His English was perfect, except for a weird thing he did with the R's. I wanted him to ask for it, and he did.

'You have something for me from Joshua?'

He loaded the bag in his trunk and covered it loosely with a dirty blanket.

'You know what to do with it?'

He looked at me. 'Yes, it has all been covered.' He headed back to the driver's side; he was eager to roll.

'One more thing.' Captain B handed me the folder and I held it up in front of him. 'Read.'

He flipped down the glasses he had resting on his forehead. Half a minute later, he put them back on his forehead.

'Questions?'

He looked at me. 'No.' He shook our hands. 'I'd better be going now. Nice meeting you both.'

'Drive safe,' I said as he closed his door. He waved as he started driving down one of the exit paths. I looked at my watch; it had taken less than 3 minutes in total. It felt longer.

I looked at Captain B. 'You didn't say a single word. Isn't that weird?'

'What would you have me say? You had it.'

I looked at him. 'I did, but it was just a bit weird that you didn't utter a single word.'

'Whatever. I'll get the thermos.'

The thermos was a mug with an integrated gas burner in it, similar to a Jetboil mug. We used it for coffee and to burn documents. We burned the messages intended for Fabian and put the lid back, since we needed to dispose of the ashes at home. We waited for 10 minutes before we left through one of the other exits.

'Who comes up with all of these cover names and identifiers?' I asked as we were waiting for the gates to open back at base.

'What is it with all of these weird questions today?' Captain B replied.

'I mean, I wouldn't choose Joshua. Who gets named Joshua these days?'

Captain B sighed. 'I don't know. You'll have to ask someone else and stop analysing everything.'

He sounded like a father being tired of answering his kid's ridiculous questions all day. It was true though. I did think a lot about the small things that probably didn't matter in the end. But I wanted answers. Of course, these were hard to come by.

We had a late-morning briefing. As we were only two patrols on base, it made no sense to have it in our absence.

'All went well this morning?' was Captain R's opening question.

'It did,' answered Captain B.

'I just want to remind you that everything we do regarding Fabian, stays within the involved patrols.' He looked at us. 'So that means that it's off limits even to Romeo 14 and Romeo 15.'

I motioned for him to stop. 'We understood you when you said it the first time. Not our first rodeo.' I sounded unusually cocky. I did not know where that had come from.

He did not laugh or even smile. With a serious tone, that I hadn't heard in a long time, he said, 'This is a far more dangerous game than most things we have done. Make one wrong move, and people start dying. Don't forget that!'

Maybe we needed a reminder of the seriousness. One started getting sloppy when things became routine. Routine could never be a thing when you were working in the deep end. It reminded me of the feeling I had when we drove to meet up with Fabian. I had to get myself into gear as I was too relaxed.

Romeo 14 and Romeo 15 had not seen any action at the OP up until then. The expansion of the OP had been very successful. They were switching the next day and were doing their last week before the OP would be closed. The location was good, so the building equipment would be left at Prizren. Romeo 14 or Romeo 15 would write instructions for the OP, so it could easily be reactivated. It felt good that we had been an early part of that.

Captain R continued, 'Tomorrow, we have a joint gig with our French friends. Not joint in the sense that they will actively participate, but they will provide a base and chip in with the QRF.'

We were going to do mobile reconnaissance in a village very close to the Serbian border, northeast of Mitrovica. This was in the rural "Wild West" of the north. We were tasked with confirming the route and looking for signs of paramilitary activity. It was not going to be static, just a drive-through looking for triggers. They had a few places of interest and vehicles that would indicate increased activity.

If they called the Fabian handover a fastball, this was an ultra-fastball. The tasks were routine, but the area was hairy as fuck. We already knew that there was a shitload of paramilitary activity up there, and now we were looking for Serbian and Russian influence. The window was short. I think they had picked this up late in the intelligence tombola. If we could prove the presence of known players, it would be a game changer as they would probably be able to get their piggy bank refilled and continue running operations in the north. So, we were not looking for persons this time, just evidence of pro Serbian activity. Associated vehicles and general triggers would be enough to confirm their presence.

We were chosen because now we had the infrastructure to run ops in the north. We had the resources, and we were in a submissive form of relationship with the French. Captain R justified it by saying that we also had interests in this. Maybe we did, maybe we didn't. I didn't know enough about what was happening in the background to make that call, but it gave me a bad feeling just going out for a drive-by like this. The indicators were weak, and it felt like this was done on a whim, just because they could. This was a highly dangerous region, and I expected any operation there to have a more dedicated purpose and more detail. I had the distinct feeling that we were being used to provoke something, to rattle the cage. I didn't mind those kinds of missions, but I preferred to know when I was a part of one.

I was going to take the lead on the ground – kind of, at least. Mr N was driving, I was going as commander and Mr A would provide muscle and do photography. Captain B would lead Romeo 12, since his rank was needed for liaison duties. They would leave that night and install themselves as uniformed QRF with two vehicles at the northern French base. They would also add a French element as a QRF. It felt like they were almost expecting shit to go down.

We had the last briefing at 15:00, just before the QRF was bound to leave. We reviewed the surveillance photos from the previous spring. It was a small village, with a main road going through it. So, they were not foreign to traffic, but the roads were more like dirt tracks. At some points they were very narrow and there was no margin of error. The lighting seemed to be poor, as usual, so the photo part would be a challenge. A small video box in the back would be the best solution, with a handheld back-up camera fitted with a 150mm standard zoom lens. This, combined with manual observation, was probably the best we could accomplish.

We were looking for activity in nine locations and we had seven cars that were associated with Serbian paramilitary organisers, aka Serbian intelligence, on our list. We needed to bring fresh licence plates for this, never used with strong local ties. They couldn't just be from the north. We were going to have to switch plates later than usual and deeper into the northern zone, as we were taking the eastern route up.

Mr A looked up from the maps. 'We need to get ready for some pew-pew.'

We did. We needed to bring more lead than usual as we couldn't really go heavier on the weapons. But we still needed to be able to hold out for a while. Extra frags and smoke were a given.

The rules of engagement were also reviewed. Up until then we had been operating under ROE "Black", which meant that one could engage suspected threats without any triggers and fire at suspected enemy positions without a present threat. It was a very inclusive ROE and pretty much allowed you to do anything. This only applied to "green" units that openly wore uniform, though. For covert units, it was more complicated, and the legal framework was a bit murky, especially as we weren't working with the "full support" of the Swedish government. So, if something happened, one had to see how it would pan out. For the sake of simplicity, we can say that ROE "Black" also applied to us when we did grey and black work. Most regular units in the Balkans would work under ROE "Blue", which was more of a policing style of ROE. You could use appropriate force when being openly threatened, to save your life or the lives of others. It was more like a self-defence thing. And it required you to use the least amount of force to reach your objective; it necessitated one to be flexible relying on different methods of engagement as a situation developed.

The difference boiled down to how to handle the aftermath of a contact. If you worked green, or in plain clothing but in an official role, it was straight-forward as you followed protocol and established SOPs that had no problems being investigated by officials afterwards. But when you were doing grey or black work – in places you probably shouldn't have been and that were only approved by a small circle of middle-ranking commanders – the top brass would of course never acknowledge it if something went down. The international and political pressure and consequences would be significant.

Depending on the particular and exact dynamics of what we were doing, the main thing was to survive, and to make what had happened look like something else entirely – and that couldn't be remotely connected to one's unit, allies, or country, at least not officially. It might end up looking shady but would be hard to pin on anyone. This was commonly done by having your own people be the first to respond to the scene, cleaning it up and setting the tone for when the regular units arrived on the scene.

Usually when it involved paramilitary groups and criminal organizations that had been fired at by government units, one removed casings if 5.56 had been used, and was replaced with different casings. The Russian 7.62 × 39 was more commonly used by the enemy. One cleaned up remains of grenades, dropped magazines and leftover medical equipment. The cleaning effort stood in proportion to what was required – this was largely based on the context. We considered two main questions: was the scene left to be discovered by local authorities, or was one of our own going to take the lead in the investigation?

This was something we always took into account when we were QRF to our own operations. The level of prep usually consisted of preparing the chain of command in case of an incident and always carrying an ammo box of empty 7.62 × 39 casings and a "spare" AK47 if needed.

The rest had left, and the base was quiet. Only the three of us and the support squad were still at the base. We had finished our preparations at around 18:00 but weren't due to leave until 17:00 the next day.

As we walked to the mess hall, Mr A said, 'I would have liked to bring the Minimi with.'

'I know you would. If we weren't going into this "black", you could have taken it. Maybe next time.'

The infamous chicken was served that night. There was nothing wrong with it, but they always spiced it weirdly. Luckily, they had a sandwich bar where one could make your own sandwich. Since I got hooked on the Dijon-train, they always have a jar there. I had also recently managed to get Mr N hooked on it, so we often resorted to making sandwiches when the canteen food was crappy. Sometimes it almost looked like we were competing to see who could add the most Dijon.

'You are missing out on protein, boys. You are going to turn all thin and French if you keep eating that shit,' Mr A said as he inhaled his second serving of chicken.

Later that evening we watched a movie with the support squad in the briefing room, with chips and a few beers. We slept in the next morning, as we had a long day and night ahead of us. Even if you had a lot of time on your hands, and everything was ready to go, you still just hung around and waited. It was like checking out of a hotel and leaving for the airport. It was just a form of active waiting as your mind had already left. The military had us well trained in "hurry up and wait".

We decided last night that we would go to the gym at 11:00 and then have a late brunch. As Mr N and I bunked together, we waited in the corridor of the barracks for Mr A to show up. He was never late for activities like gym. I knocked on his door, but there was no reply.

'He probably left for some pre-gym,' said Mr N.

I turned the doorknob, it was open. Mr A was lying in bed, looking pale. He was half-asleep and woke up as we approached, 'I am so sorry, guys. I have been up all night, puking and shitting. I think I am running a fever.'

It reeked a bit from the bucket next to his bed. 'I'll tell the nurse to drop by. It sounds like you got food poisoning or something.'

Mr A looked sharply into my eyes as he grabbed my arm. 'You do *not* send the nurse here. I am this close to banging her,' he said, holding his finger and thumb close together. 'I will clean up and go to see her instead.'

He might have been sick, but he hadn't lost his game. That was clear.

'I am so sorry to leave you guys in this situation. I don't think I can go tonight.' No shit. He was not going anywhere.

'Don't worry about it. We have lots of people ready to go. I'll come and check on you in a bit.'

Mr N looked at me and clapped my shoulder as we were heading to the ops room. 'Sometimes it has its perks to be French.'

He was not wrong. It was probably the chicken that had wrecked him.

Captain R was having coffee in the ops room. 'Morning, boys. Ready for tonight?'

'Mostly. We had a minor complication.' We gave him the rundown of the situation. It was not a big deal. We just needed to add one person to handle the camera and be the muscle. My suggestion was to take any of the guys from support. They were very capable and would just need a short briefing.

Captain R leaned back in his chair and wiggled it from side to side. He looked past us and was clearly thinking.

I asked, 'Should I go and get Lieutenant B and see what we can arrange?'

After an additional 30 seconds of silence he said, 'I will go with you.'

I probably looked a bit surprised. 'Aren't you leading from here?'

'I am, but I'll brief Captain T. He can do it. It's just monitoring, and all the heavy lifting has already been done. Plus, I need to get out and roll a bit. Get some air.'

It was an unexpected turn of events, but a good one. I was very happy to have Captain R on board. He was funny and one of the most experienced people on the mission.

He didn't need a briefing, of course, and just said 'I'll be ready in the yard at 16:50.'

Mr N and I skipped the gym and went straight to brunch instead.

'Damn! Mr A will not be happy when he hears that he is missing out riding with Captain R.'

I took a second to think about what he said and replied, 'But if he wasn't sick, Captain R wouldn't be riding at all.'

Mr N looked like he had had a stroke and he stopped chewing. 'You know what that is 100 per cent correct.' Then he continued eating.

I took the grab-bag as we were about to leave for the yard. 'Ready?'

Mr N slung his weapon over his shoulder. 'Ready as can be.' He had an old, worn hoodie with jeans and trainers. I wore jeans, trainers, and the Velcro-modified shirt I had bought at H&M years earlier. We looked like we belonged on the other side of the fence.

The time was 16:52. Mr N and I were sitting in the vehicle with the doors open, just waiting for Captain R. The communications check was done, QRF was on high readiness, and we were good to go. I only noticed Captain R as he sat down in the middle of the backseat.

'Sorry I am late. I am good to go.'

I looked back and saw that he was sitting with an LMG between his legs. 'Appropriately armed, I see.'

Captain R smiled, 'My weapon of choice. If needed, I don't want to be stuck with you two having only those short BB guns.'

It was good to have him on board.

Mr N looked at me as we pulled out of the gates. 'Never mention this to Mr A, he will leave the army.'

Mr A would go ballistic. I had denied him his dream, but I was in no position to deny Captain R.

'You are running the show. I am just muscle,' said Captain R as he fiddled with his seatbelt. He was good like that, never any pride or jealousy or backseat driving. The situation would not have been like this with Captain B, for example, as he would have assumed command by rank. Different schools, but both were top-notch officers. As we were rolling north, Captain R kept us entertained with stories about Iraq and Afghanistan. He had had a lot of doors open to him with his explosive skills, usually weird and unexpected ones, but definitely premium.

As dusk turned into darkness, the car got more silent. We became more focused as we moved deeper and deeper into the badlands. Only the occasional radio report and short navigational command broke the silence. We hadn't seen another car in a long time and the feeling of travelling through a deserted wasteland was mounting. We had turned off the main road to make our way to the point where we would change licence plates. It was just five kilometres away, up a steep road and then to the right. We would change the plates and start heading towards the target area.

As we started to drive up the steep and narrow road that led uphill, I was looking down the sides. There was nothing to the left but a 15 metre drop. To the right was a 5 metre drop, but littered with trees so you would probably stop quickly if you drove over the edge.

Mr N said, 'I am not sure I would like to drive here on icy winter roads.'

Neither would I, that was certain. The steep drops on either side of the road faded out and transitioned into deep ditches as we got further up the hill. The road changed its course through the terrain. The incline flattened out a bit as we came around a corner. When we had completed the turn, I saw a small fire at the side of the road. Two oil drums and a plank lying between them. Men with weapons could be seen in our headlights.

By muscle memory, I pushed the PTT on the radio lying in my lap. 'Stand by for contact.'

I flicked off the safety of the AK between my legs and grasped the pistol grip. I knew at that point that we had no chance of any quick and easy backing manoeuvres out of the situation.

'I count six… seven… no, eight weapons at the ready,' Mr N called out.

Following standard SOPs, we were wearing transparent safety glasses and ear plugs when we were riding in those areas. I had taken out my left earplug. It was a habit of mine when I was working the radio. The distance was 15 metres and less than 10 seconds had elapsed since we saw the fire.

'Ready in the back? Fire!'

My voice was calm and low. I could feel the barrel of the Minimi moving up between my, and Mr N's, seats. Out of the corner of my left eye, I could see the tension in Mr N's arms. With my right eye, I could see one of the men at the roadblock start to move the stock of his AK towards his shoulder. The world moved in slow motion. I didn't get to finish that observation, as the Minimi started pounding on my left. The throbbing in my left ear was instant and excruciating.

The first burst from the Minimi rang out leaving the windshield penetrated but still in place. I got my AK waist high and continued the movement by violently stabbing my barrel through the windshield; it fell out onto the hood on my second stab. Mr N had already started backing up. I had the stock on my shoulder, and I could see the tracers from the Minimi pounding out to the left.

The shadow of the man at the right side of the road lined up with the red dot in my aim point. Even though the car was moving, my aim was steady. I fired five rapid shots and saw the tracers[9] penetrating the middle of the shadow. He fell to the ground. I switched to the man running for cover in the direction of the right-hand ditch. I fired six times until he fell down and the upper part of his body was hanging in the ditch with his legs left on the road.

I screamed to Mr N after the burst from the Minimi, 'Tree line!'

I wasn't sure if he had heard me, but it was the one logical place to stop as the ditch would provide cover and it was just before the most complicated part. The distance was 30 to 45 metres to the checkpoint. I kept laying down fire, together with Captain R on the LMG. I saw muzzle flashes lightning up from the enemy side.

As Mr N came to a stop at the tree line, I yelled, '*Avsittning*!' (debus) I didn't need to say the command to get us out of the vehicle. Everyone knew exactly what was happening. The commands were just flowing, they came instinctively. I got out on the right, and I assumed a kneeling position, when I saw a man running in the ditch towards my side. He was running away. I clenched my teeth to control the adrenaline and fired twice. He stopped in his tracks and fell to the ground.

Captain R had gotten out on the left side, as there was more room. He was in prone position next to the car and Mr N had taken up a position in the ditch. They laid down a barrage of fire. I scanned the checkpoint and saw nothing.

I picked up the radio. 'Contact, contact, contact! 500 metres south CP21 on black.'

'Wilco. QRF already en route.'

I changed my magazine for the second time before moving back to a kneeling position. It was quiet. I heard the muted commands as Mr N covered Captain R while he changed the Minimi's barrel. The adrenaline was spiking, and I slid on the gravel as I sprinted around the back of the car with the grab-bag.

'Coming around!'

My left ear had a loud and constant ringing – it sounded like a beep and felt more like a vacuum.

I pulled out the NVGs and swept the surrounding area. Nothing. 'Let's take the ground past them. I'll go right and you two go left.'

We quickly mounted the NVGs.

---

9   With an IR magazine I often had every other round as a tracer, or every third with four tracers in the bottom and the LMG was often four regular rounds to one tracer.

The radio crackled. 'Inbound, eight minutes.'

'Roger.'

We advanced 45 metres up to the checkpoint; I counted eight bodies and half of them hadn't survived the LMG's first burst.

'R, cover!' I threw the pocket camera to Mr N, for him to take pictures of the bad guys. I pulled up a waterproof olive drab bag from the grab-bag.

'Broke contact. Location secured.' Mr N and I started going through their pockets, dumping notebooks and maps into the bag, the whole ordeal took only took a few minutes. We jogged back towards our car. Mr N was covering while we were cleaning it out, packing the camera and making it ready. We would not travel far in this baby.

'We got visual on lights.'

I picked up the radio. 'We are standing behind our car. You'll see us in 45 seconds.' I could see six military jeeps coming up the road. The adrenaline had dropped significantly at that point, and I felt that calm, but mixed with a half-high feeling. Like after a great gym session, just multiplied by 100. The first four vehicles were French. They quickly drove past the checkpoint and made a cordon. The commander of the French was a guy dressed in 5.11 clothing,[10] while the rest of his crew was uniformed.

'Everyone good?' he asked in broken English.

'Yeah, we are good.'

I looked around at Captain R and Mr N. They were in good shape. Captain B was jogging up the road as the other Romeo members were holding the tail of the convoy.

'Captain R, what the fuck? Are you guys okay?' He had had no clue about the switch.

'We are all good. I just witnessed the baptism of your two boys. Fantastic results,' he said as he gave me and Mr N a pat on the shoulder.

'Okay,' said Captain B 'The drill now is that we will secure all the equipment from our car, remove the plates, clean the car of 5.56 and then leave. The main, and unaware, QRF will be called in 15 minutes. The local police will probably arrive after them. These are Jacque's guys, led by Simon.' He pointed at the man in the 5.11 clothing. They will clean up the rest and make the case work.' I could see Simon's guys were raking up 5.56 casings from the ground.

---

10 The brand 5.11 provides clothing for security professionals and is often used in the field.

We swiftly moved our gear to our vehicles in the convoy and it only took a few minutes to clean the car.

Simon whistled at Captain B, 'You guys need to move. The QRF is rolling, and I don't want you to meet them on your way down. Take the eastern route, they will come from the western one. We will clean this up.'

Romeo 12 was driving the cars down. I was looking out the window.

'Are you good?' asked Captain B again.

I nodded. 'It was pretty intense.'

He smiled. 'You three are now the first fire-baptised operators in the platoon. And I missed it!' he said and laughed. It was a bit out of character for Captain B, but he sounded genuinely happy with it. Technically, we got our fire-baptism in Colombia. But that was way different than this. This had an intensity that was out of this world.

I put on a pair of ComTacs ear defenders as we started our homebound journey. I was worried about fucked-up hearing affecting my future career.

As we rolled into our base hours later, a long night started with debriefings about what had happened and our actions, et cetera. It almost felt like an interrogation at times, but I knew the protocol. This was how things were run. Inside, I had the distinct feeling of wanting to party, drink, dance, and do things like that. But this was not the time – not yet anyway. Captain T and Lieutenant B were leading the debriefing and information download. Captain R sat on two chairs as he was unit commander and also a participant.

Captain R looked at Captain B, Captain T and Lieutenant B, 'And the loot? The French will know we cleaned them out, but I want to hand it up our own channels. Not so much because they need it but to show them that we can produce results, it will be beneficial in coming years.'

Lieutenant B suggested, 'Give the French access to it directly, but tell them we want it back. And we document the loot before we hand it over.'

Captain R looked around the table. 'If no one has any objections, I think we go with Lieutenant B's idea. We need to keep in good standing with the French.'

Late that night, once the equipment was taken care of and we had showered, we could get some shuteye. We had already decided not to brief Mr A until the morning. I felt like it was going to be impossible to sleep but as soon as my head hit the pillow, I drifted off.

The alarm started to torment me at 06:30. My left ear was buzzing, the earplug I had put in had fallen out while I was asleep. The plan was that I was to be at the base doctor at 07:00 to check my ear. Then Jacques was coming down from KFOR MAIN, at 09:00.

I sat on the stretcher at the base doctor, as he asked me what happened.

I was still watching the hot nurse taking notes. 'We were performing a vehicle drill, and I lost my ear defender at the most intense moment.'

He looked into my ear. 'The eardrum is intact. Only time will tell how it will heal. Trauma like this will very likely affect your hearing with age. It can also leave permanent hearing loss or cause tinnitus. But you need sound-rest and always wear an earplug in your left ear. And I would recommend double ear defenders if you have to participate in something noisy.'

The beep or ringing was lower and more in the background than the previous day. It felt like I was going to be okay in time.

We met Captain B at breakfast. 'I want you all in the briefing room at 08:00. Bring Mr A, and don't tell him about yesterday.'

I knocked on Mr A's door and opened it. He woke up as I entered his room and looked at me with sleepy eyes. 'Are you guys back already?'

I smiled. 'We are. How are you feeling?

He turned around in his bed. 'It feels like someone ran me over with a freight train, but much better, thanks.'

'Captain B wants us all in the briefing room at 08:00. That's in 20 minutes, do you want me to bring breakfast?'

'Nah, I'll eat after the briefing. Did it go well?'

'It was different,' I replied, leaving the excitement out of it.

Captain B had assembled all of Romeo 12 and Romeo 13. He gave a short summary of the previous night's events.

When it hit Mr A what had happened, he rolled his eyes. 'Sick once in 10 years and this happens! But I am genuinely happy for you guys.' He took it better than I thought he would.

'So now we are all on the same information level, and here is where it stays. Romeo 14 and Romeo 15 will be told that we did a mission, had a contact, and that's it.'

This is the type of contact one keeps in a small circle.

'Also, you can join the briefing with Jacque at 10:00 instead of 09:00. He wanted an hour with the officers first.'

Mr A tapped my shoulder as we were leaving the briefing. 'You know what? That was my Minimi that Captain R used. So, technically, she has seen combat.'

I tilted my head. 'Well, technically, you are right.' I had to give him that one.

Mr A continued. 'Good luck with the admin. I am going to sleep this shit off now.'

We were sitting with Romeo 12 outside of the briefing room, 10 minutes early.

Captain R popped his head out. 'Are you all here?'

Mr R did a quick sweep. 'Yes, all present.'

Captain R opened the door. 'You can come in.'

Jacque started off. 'Good to see you again.' He stood up and shook our hands. 'The op took a different course than we expected, but I have reviewed what came out of this and its better than what the original plan would have brought us. This took both our camps one or two steps in the right direction.' He continued to brief us on Simon's actions and what was happening next. He threw a brown dossier on the table and flipped it open. 'This is the official report, so from KFOR's side, this is a closed case. They will probably increase patrols and do some analytical work in the coming weeks, but to all intents and purposes it's done.'

I quickly read the first page. The conclusion was a clash between a paramilitary group and organised crime. It was consistent with evidence on the ground, including a car previously connected to a local crime group. The narrative was that the "victorious" group was suspected to have managed to flee the scene before KFOR forces arrived. There was possibly some truth in the last part, as we managed to get away before KFOR arrived.

I laughed on the inside. Imagine that the car had ties to organised crime! It's funny how lies so easily became the truth when the right people signed off on it.

'I will finally go on vacation, but I am sure we will meet again in the future. Thank you.' He shook our hands and waved to the officers as he left.

Captain R took the floor. 'Well done yesterday. The loot was very fruitful. Serbian maps and frequencies, positions, call signs, inventory lists. As far as mapping out the paramilitaries and Serbian involvement goes, it was pure gold.'

Mr N asked, 'Did he take the intel?'

Captain R paced two steps. 'No. He got copies of everything and was very satisfied with that. You might not have seen it in his expression, but he was really impressed with the results. The same goes for Simon.' He paused for half a minute. 'And so am I. From what I saw yesterday from all involved, but especially from the parts of Romeo 13 that I rode with, I can say with confidence that you are world-class operators. That's why I have prepared these.' He laid out two papers on the table. 'I have written one letter of commendation for Mr N for resolute and professional action under fire. And one for Max for resolute and professional leadership under fire.' People looked around the table and gave us approving nods. Captain R continued, 'This is not something I can hand in anywhere since we barely exist and the mission was not sanctioned by anyone, so it would be unwise. After all, we still have no medals or other honours for efforts in peacetime. But that might change sometime in the future. So, I will save these in case it becomes relevant, and if the situation permits in the future.'

I could see the pride in Captain B's eyes. My journey from basic to here flashed before my eyes and it felt unreal, me here, and now this. It was a humbling experience.

'Alright, that is all. I want Romeo 13 to stay behind. The rest are dismissed.'

Captain R told us to get a coffee in the ops room. He was waiting for a friend he wanted us to meet.

'Take your cups and get in here.' We had waited for just 10 minutes, when we were called in. At the other end of the table sat Colonel X. He got up from his chair and walked towards us to greet us.

'I am so glad I got the chance to say, "Hi" again. I was in the neighbourhood on another errand, and I have a few minutes before leaving for Sweden again.' He was one of the early enablers that had helped to set up the platoon, fund it under the radar and he had introduced the Major to the right people. He had helped us, although from the shadows but at the highest level.

'I have always believed in you but seeing you here, delivering outstanding results, warms my heart.' I could see that he meant it. He was one of those genuine people, even though he was deep into the cloak and dagger game. 'I can tell you that the chatter about your unit is more than flattering. Don't be surprised if you get more very high-quality work shortly.'

He got up and shook Captain R's hand. 'Sit, sit. I need to rush; I have a flight to catch. I will keep things level at home. I will see to it that the right people know who to credit for this. Good to see you all. Keep up the good work!' He carried the loot, now placed in a sealed security bag, with him.

As he left, Captain R said, 'It's all coming together nicely. Soon we will be Sweden's most wanted military resource that no one knows about.' His phrase reminded me of the A-Team's 'I love it when a plan comes together.'

As we walked down the corridor, he shouted, 'After-action beers tonight. It's mandatory. My treat. In the yard, 19:00. Don't be late!'

15

Surveillance: finding the Jackal

'I sometimes wondered if I should have chosen differently, been a door-kicker? But I knew what I was. I was a thinker and a player. And I played.'

All Romeo call signs were back on base again after being separated for almost a month. The pace was slower and the previous month's contact was fading in my memory. We had been assisting the Swedish SCOTT unit with some foxtrot and mobile surveillance in central downtown Pristina. They were looking for people involved in human trafficking and weapons smuggling. It was not great action since the gangs had adjusted their modus operandi. My personal two cents' worth was that they probably had someone on the inside. Not in the SCOTT unit, but halfway up in the Swedish police. They were not very good with secrets and the joint operation in Kosovo was an open book.

We had two men out of action. The 2iC of Romeo 14 had sprained his ankle while running. The second guy was unexpected. It was Mr Q, Romeo 12's LMG gunner. I didn't know him well, but Mr A was tight with him. Romeo 12 had been out on a two-day operation, doing QRF work or something similar for the Brits. Maybe they were doing pickups and drop-offs. I don't remember. Shortly after the operation Mr Q had disappeared. In this environment it was not really something you noticed straight away as people came and went all the time, doing weird stuff.

Captain B found us at lunch. 'Big assembly in the movie room after lunch.' We had got a movie room by then; earlier, we had used the briefing room, but the carpenters of the support unit had been busy in their spare time. They constructed a movie room with 30 seats in a movie theatre style. It was equipped with a projector, DVD player and some kind of game console. I am not a gamer so I couldn't tell you what kind it was. A small bar was also installed outside the movie theatre. We appreciated it very much, as we didn't have to use the briefing room anymore, and also, operational information could now be left out in the briefing room.

Captain R said, 'I have some sad news.' It felt like someone had died. 'We had to let Mr Q go.'

They had to let Mr Q go? What did that even mean? Did he quit? Was he injured? Did he have to go home for personal reasons?

Captain R kept it short and effective, like pulling off a band-aid. 'Mr Q had been involved in a bar fight while visiting his parents before we deployed. He had been arrested by the police, interrogated, and then let go. He hadn't informed anyone of this, in fear that he would lose his position in the IRP and had gone on with his deployment. Since he had been a no-show in Sweden when his trial started, he was wanted by the police.'

'Of course, they didn't know he had deployed or even that he was serving in an active military unit. The Major had been informed by a friend at HQ, who was the military/police liaison in Sweden. He had recognised Mr Q's name as he had helped with organising off the record background checks when we had been recruited. The officers had known this for a few weeks and had been trying to figure out what to do with him. They confronted Mr Q after a few weeks, and he was straight up about it.

The commanders said that Mr Q should have come to them before the deployment, as a bar fight was not sufficient grounds to get him disqualified from the operation. The unit could have helped him get off the hook with probation or something light. Now he was a wanted man and the risks of having him in the unit were too great. Of course, we could have protected him here, but there was also life after deployment. And this would surface at one point or another in the future and it could have a very bad impact on the IRP's reputation.

The decision had been made; he was cut lose. He was discharged from the IRP, and officially that meant he was dishonourably discharged from the cover unit we were serving in. Together with Mr Q, it was decided that he would be assigned to a regular Swedish KFOR unit. On paper, we had deployed as the cover unit, but it needed to be tweaked a bit as our cover was a non-existent unit. Colonel X assisted the Major to accomplish this. He had to sign a bunch of NDA papers and he was taken to the Finnish camp in the south. We had arranged, through some friends from Finnish intelligence, that he would be apprehended by the Finnish MP and then transported by them to Sweden. All of this to avoid any questions and unnecessary attention. He asked if he couldn't fly home and report himself to the police. We could have arranged that, of course, but having a wanted man using service identities and such was just too big of a risk. We were not going to take risks for someone who had been dishonest.

Captain R's final words were, 'So the lesson here is: if you have problems like this, not coming to us straight away will not count in your favour down the line.' He looked over the silent movie room. 'Anyone else carrying secrets, now is a good time to speak up.'

We all sat in silence. It could have happened to any one of us. Getting a bit too drunk and punching someone in the face in a bar is easily done. We all felt for him. The repercussions of this, in our eyes, minor infraction was severe. But we also knew the price for compromising the unit's integrity. I actually think he would still have been here if he had told the Major when it had happened. The Major was sneaky and well-connected and could easily have made this disappear. He could probably still have done it, but no one wanted to stick their neck out that far for a man who couldn't be honest with something like that.

I saw that Mr R, my friend, and the long-time commander of Mr Q, didn't take this well. It hurt him on a personal level – I get that. Losing one of your guys was hard, especially if this was news to Mr R as well. Then it would have felt like he had been lied to by one of his own. Mr R always claimed that he never knew anything about it. I don't know if it was true or not, but if he had known about it, he would have been at risk as well if they had found out. So, it felt weird to know that Mr Q was sitting in the brig at the Swedish camp for a punch, while we were looking for people who were wanted for Genocide. Life is not fair at times, and this was one of those times.

Mr Q needed to be replaced, otherwise we were stuck with an incomplete patrol. At home they had been busy for a while, looking for new candidates who would be suitable to recruit to the IRP, or at least be offered a spot on the selections. For as long as I had been here, there had never been talks about recruiting more people. I guess they needed to see how this all panned out first before they even started to look for people. A guy that had been working at the regiment for a while had bleeped on their radar, as he had shown extraordinary capabilities. He had been working in the regiment as an NCO, basically since we had started our selection training.

I couldn't imagine who it could be but since I had joined the IRP, I had been out of the regimental loop and did not really keep track of people working there anymore. He had been through a mini-selection and a background check. The offer he got was that, if he took this "vacancy", he was in the loop.

He would have to go through selection and do the full operator training at the next possible opportunity. He had accepted and was being rotated down the following week. This is how it was starting up something new, we had limited reserves. The rest of the IRP was in Afghanistan. I wondered why they didn't man Romeo 12 with a guy from the support unit. That would have been so much smoother, in my opinion. But it was clear that they needed to think about the future. It was not sustainable for the IRP to be just us forever. And if they thought he was capable, then worth a shot. He was working for one of the Swedish elite units, so he wasn't an inexperienced soldier. But he still wasn't an operator.

'How does it feel to have a replacement that you never met just put in like this?' I asked Mr R as we pulled a gym session.

'I don't know. He will never replace Mr Q, of course, but I trust the Major and Captain K If they say he is good, he's good enough for me.'

It was always a process bringing a guy from the outside into a tight group like this. It would shift the group dynamics, and the group's social process would be dialled back close to zero. They had to start over again. But it would be easy enough to bring him up to speed, as he was probably eager to prove himself. It was not all bad, as we needed to get used to people coming and going. These patrol constellations wouldn't last forever, and we needed to pop the bubble sooner rather than later.

Exactly a week after Mr Q had "disappeared", we had just come back after a day's training in the "mine", doing vehicle drills all day long.

'I can tell she's been in combat. She feels more aggressive now.' It was Mr A commenting on his Minimi. The only thing missing was him giving her a name. Actually, he probably already had, and I just missed it. Either way I wasn't going to ask.

Captain R came out into the yard. 'Hey, the new guy has arrived. Go and introduce yourselves. They are in the bar. And be nice! He is one of us now.'

We were quite excited, as we all wanted to know who Mr Secret was.

'If I knew you could just slide in on a shrimp sandwich instead of doing years of highly specialised and demanding training, I might have opted for that route instead,' Mr A said. He was not completely happy with this. He didn't yet know that he would become one of his better, and long-term, friends down the line.

'Bro, he's still from the regiment. It's not like they put an infantry guy here at random. And remember, the Major selected us all. So, if you trust him in selecting you, it shouldn't be a problem,' Mr N said.

Mr A walked away with his LMG and grunted, 'Well, he selected quite a few assholes as well, so I don't know about that!'

I immediately recognised the man shaking hands in the middle of the room. I had done KBS School with him. It was the 42nd man, the man that missed *baskerprovet* because he had injured his foot on a parachute jump. He looked different now, more mature. I hadn't seen him in years, and I didn't even know that he was working at the regiment.

'Wasn't it yesterday that I saw you,' I said as I approached him to give him a man hug with a pat on the back.

He looked surprised and genuinely happy to see me. 'I had no idea you were working here, but I am not surprised.'

He had an interesting story. After basic, he left the regiment and started at the Coastal Ranger regiment – or rather started and restarted. When you transferred from one elite unit to another, it went like this. First you needed to go through selection again. If accepted, you would do a "patrol course". It was a course run by all elite regiments once a year, to be able to take on transfers from similar regiments. The paratroops ran one, we did, and the Coastal Rangers did too.

The course was often around 16 to 18 weeks and was like a compressed version of basic training at the regiment. But the "basic" was taken out of it, as all candidates had already completed ranger or paratroop training. So, the requirements were high, and it was usually a brutal course that included all the requisites to earn the unit's insignia. If one successfully passed the Coastal Ranger patrol course, you would be allowed to wear their trident insignia. So, he had both the trident and the ranger tab. As he had cleared the patrol course, he was working as an NCO at their newly formed Boarding Unit.[1] He was a part of the sniper detail. Then he had recently transferred back to the regiment to work as an assistant to Captain J, who had taken over the sniper platoon at the Regiment from Captain L, who was engaged in working with the IRP in Afghanistan.

He definitely brought a lot to the table. I was happy to see him and that he had had the ability to make interesting choices after basic. Romeo 12 would spend the coming weeks drilling SOPs with him and getting him ready so

---

1   It was an amphibious unit, for boarding, searching, hostage rescue and DA on vessels. This was experimental at first and was organised under the Coastal Rangers, until it was transferred to the Amphibious Corps. Swedish SF now has their own unit called Sea transport unit.

that they could become operational again. It felt like a fresh breeze getting some new blood in the unit. It seemed that the whole unit's spirits were lifted again, after the ordeal with Mr Q had left us despondent. It had been a good few weeks for us, and we had ample time to work on proficiency on a personal and patrol level. Even though we all loved our work, you felt quite quickly that your proficiency started dropping slightly when you took away regular training. Our skills needed to be maintained. In fairness, when I say that the proficiency dropped, I am nitpicking. It could be a split-second of lost speed here and there, so it was nothing major. But the feeling of reclaiming that peak level of skill again, and pushing beyond your limits, was wonderful.

Romeo 12 and Romeo 14 were busy with training and work. We hadn't spotted anything in our pipeline yet, so we were hoping that we would be put back into work up north soon. Captain R and Lieutenant B called us in to an afternoon briefing with Romeo 15. You seldom saw Lieutenant B at the regular briefings, he was always busy with something technical.

'I hope you haven't become too soft from holding your dicks for a few weeks.'

Mr D from Romeo 15 was quick in his comeback. 'Well, we still have lead in our pencils. So, think about that, Old Man!' That was the privilege of being short of 30, in a world where 40 was considered old.

'I have a very special gift for you guys. Do you remember Linn?' Linn was the US ops liaison on the Radovan Karadžić operation that we had all been a part of. We hadn't seen her again after she had briefed us. Romeo 15 had never met her. She had invited two "selected" teams. I don't know what the selection criteria was, but I guess that we had met her before, and we hadn't made fools of ourselves. And Romeo 12 was temporarily out of service, so I guess Romeo 15 was just in the right place at the right time.

We had been invited to get Airscan training. That meant we would spend two weeks up in KFOR Main were they had one of their operations centres. The other one was located at Camp Bondsteel, but that was usually off limits for us. The training was meant to give us more understanding of the capability and limitations. It was also meant to give us proficiency in analysing imagery and operating it remotely so we could have our own personnel manning their ops centre when we used it for our operations. Lieutenant B was going because he was a technical officer and was the right guy to have when it came to this. He was also going to be the Airscan liaison, responsible for the teams that would man it in future.

The training was to start in two days. It would be an all-day thing, with a 07:00 start up at MAIN every morning. A few night sessions were also planned during the training. We were all strangely excited about this. Usually, technical training wasn't our favourite, but this was different. It felt interesting and also opened a door to a new world. This was in the early years of UAVs. Sweden had just started training the first batch of heavy UAV pilots a few years prior. We had had one person from the regiment participating. It was a two-year training course that essentially made them real pilots in the process. They flew school fighter jets during their training. That had always been an inaccessible world for most of us. We had to remember that this was far from flying UAVs, but it was still good development for us as a unit.

We were back in the school benches again. We all looked the part, kitted up with pen and paper, eyes wide open and ears dialled in for learning. A guy name Mike, 35-ish years old, not too nerdy looking, with an American southern accent, received us. He worked for the Airscan company and had a "government" background. That could have meant anything, but usually when they were unspecific like that, they belonged to some hush-hush unit. He didn't seem like a military guy, maybe former Agency, or NSA. He was going to head the training. You immediately felt that he did this a lot, teaching operators. But, as always, before we could start with the introduction, we had more papers to sign. NDAs, secrecy statements, the usual. I didn't even read them anymore. I just looked for the dates, so I knew how long I needed to be silent.

Airscan had started in 1989 and was basically a US government contractor that supplied manned and unmanned ISR aerial solutions. They had developed their own sensors and built their own hardware and software to be able to provide encrypted true real-time data downlinks and uplinks. Two of their main selling points were time over target and altitude. Which sounds like a cakewalk today, but I can assure you that it wasn't back in 2006.

The company was divided into several divisions. The mother company was a private concern with a regular ownership structure. It served a variety of government agencies, from environmental to police. Mike came from their special division that only provided services to selected government agencies. It was entirely owned by an undisclosed organisation, which was a joint CIA and NSA front company. Of course, Mike didn't tell us all of that during the introduction, but I learned about it over the coming years as we did a lot of work with them.

The first few days were mostly filled with theory, showing different capabilities and technical details, range, and endurance. A lot of example images and videos were shown. It was impressive even if we weren't unfamiliar with high-quality, long-range images. After the first couple of days, we started with the practical part of the training, watching their ongoing operations, and having the finer details explained to us: how to efficiently command a manned asset, for example, and how to combine that with remote controlled action. Some parts were similar to the FAC game. You needed to think ahead and at the same time follow along. Since they were working at altitude and flying considerably slower than fighter jets, one had – thanks to the sensors – a fair degree of wiggle room.

A lot of the work in the beginning was getting used to looking at this type of footage. It took a while to be able to accurately spot what you were looking for. Mr A had a weirdly intuitive talent for this. We didn't expect it, as he had never shown these kinds of skills before.

He claimed, 'It's just like a video game', so all his hours in front of *Call of Duty* finally paid off.

In the beginning of the second week, it was time for a written exam. To receive clearance to work independently in the ops room, you had to pass two theoretical tests and a "flight exam", where you independently planned and executed a training mission. We all passed the theoretical exam. Some of us had a narrower margin than others, but a pass is a pass and anything above the pass mark means that you are neglecting your friends.

In the middle of the second week, we were off after 12:00 on Wednesday since we were doing night ops the following three nights. We knew that Romeo 12 was in the kill house running SOPs. It was just a 15 minute drive from us, so we decided to join in. They were doing president drills when we got there.

'Looking good,' I greeted the 42nd man (from now on called 'Mr 42'). 'How is it going?'

'I hope I am doing well. It's a lot to take in but, man, I wish I had been on board with you guys from the beginning. The number of resources you have, and the perfect mix of guys. It's a dream!'

'Well, you are already knee-deep into it, so you will be stuck with us for a while.'

Mr R had set up a competition as the last shooting exercise before lunch. 'Let's see if we can beat the shit out of Romeo 13, which is not that much of a challenge,' he said laughing.

It was simple: two 9mm rounds in the magazine, draw from the drop leg holster, and shoot two trap clay targets. It was all timed and the team that hit the targets with the best collective time would win.

Mr R and I were the last pair out and were doing a head-to-head. I knew we were at a similar level in terms of marksmanship and the score was almost a tie, with a tiny advantage to Romeo 12. I took my magazine out of my Glock and removed one bullet.

'If I take out both of the clays with one shot, you will add one second to your total time. If I don't, you win, obviously.'

Mr R looked at me, 'Is this just so you can have something to blame when you lose?'

I looked at him. 'We will see. Do you accept?'

Mr R laughed. 'Of course I accept. You just handed me a walkover since you are afraid of my lightning quick draw. Let's go!'

I was putting my whole team at risk. I gambled with the results, just to be cocky. Since the clays were too far apart, I needed to shoot off the one-legged stand on the right and hope it fell to the left and took the second clay with it in the fall. I managed to pull something similar back home once, but it mostly came down to pure luck as it was impossible to control the way in which the stand falls.

'Hands on your head. Ready? Three... Two... One...', beep. I got a perfect draw and fired instinctively as the gun reached the muscle memory position. Fuck! I should have aimed more, as the accuracy when looking over the barrel could be a centimetre either way, and the leg of the stand was just one and a half centimetres wide. And even if I managed to get both clays on the ground, they had to break. Those were the rules. The wooden leg of the first stand snapped and splinters flew as the bullet penetrated the middle of the leg. The stand, light as a feather, spun into the air for a split second as the broken leg swung sideways and hit the second stand. It wobbled, and the second clay fell to the ground.

'Fuck!' Mr R shouted as we holstered our weapons. 'They have to break. They look intact from here,' he muttered as we approached the targets. As I picked up the clays, I saw that they were almost intact except for very small pieces that had chipped off both of them.

'Look.' I held them up for all to see. Breakage is breakage.

Mr R kicked the dust with his boot. 'This is not acceptable. You have unbelievable luck. It's not even skill, it's just a fucking fluke!'

It was just extreme luck at exactly the right moment. I could probably not have replicated that even if I tried all day. But what pissed him off even more was that I was quicker to draw and fire. That bugged him more than the loss itself, I think.

As we cleared the targets off the range and were about to leave home for lunch, Mr R tapped my shoulder. 'Hey, I need to talk to you when we get home. Something has happened. Can we talk in my room before lunch?' He looked serious.

I had no clue what it was about. 'Of course. I'll come over straight away when we get back.' On the way back, I wondered what it could be. Had something happened to him personally? Was he leaving the IRP? I knew his father was not well, maybe something had happened to him.

Mr A was upbeat in the car home, probably because it was lunchtime. 'Good for you that you shoot like Lucky Luke. If you had lost, I would have kicked your ass. I broke my personal best with my efforts and wouldn't have wanted it to go to waste.'

I knocked on Mr R's door. 'It's open.'

He was still stashing his gear from the shooting.

'So, what's happening?'

Mr R stopped fiddling with his stuff and sat down. 'Mr DD was killed last week.' I felt a lump in my throat, pulled out a chair and sat down. I was shocked, as this was not even on my radar.

Mr DD was a mutual friend. He was not from the regiment but had been in a specialised CSAR unit from the Air Force. He had quit the armed forces about six months before we deployed to Kosovo. He had jumped on the PMC train, like many others at the time. He had first been contracted by a Kuwaiti trucking company to set up SOPs and build a security organisation for them. It was deep waters for him, and probably for most of us at the time. He wanted me and Mr R to join him; he had taken three of our other mutual friends with him. We had had a lot of contact with him over email, as he sent bunches of documents to me and Mr R, for us to check and give our input. You could see from his work that it was not his bread and butter, and Mr R and I were both worried that they were just winging it down there. He was a good soldier but setting up a security detail was not for him, not then. But he was determined to make it work. They had managed to do a few route reconnaissance missions in Iraq, particularly around Basra.

The company they were working for was not very serious and also stopped paying them, so they parted ways after a while. One of them went back to Sweden, the other found work as a PMC operator at Castle Gate Security in Iraq, doing convoy security. Mr DD found work at Genric, a UK based security contractor. He emailed and said he was happy to finally be working at a proper company. He liked it there and said that he could get us in, if we just let him know. This was not the first PMC offer that had crossed our paths and the contractor life had always appealed to us. With the state of affairs of the Swedish army at the time, we strongly considered going down the PMC route – for the money, the stability and of course the adventure. You never knew if the army would pull the plug on the IRP and then we would be left with nothing. We had discussed taking the PMC path quite recently, but the arguments got weaker and weaker by the day as at that moment we had it all, except perhaps the money.

I looked at Mr R across the table. 'Do you know what happened?'

The answer was in line with what Iraq and Afghanistan had become in those days. 'IED attack on his convoy outside Baghdad.'

He didn't even get to see his 30th birthday. Mr DD was 26 or 27 at the time. One of the friends that had been in Kuwait with him was helping his parents and brother with the funeral.

'The funeral is going to be in two weeks. I asked Captain B, and it's okay for us to go. We need to pay for the flights ourselves.' I thought about the "we" in that sentence. Mr R was obviously going, but he had asked for me as well. I was not sure about that, but I didn't mention anything at that moment as it would have been tactless.

I left it at, 'Okay.' Soldiers in their twenties are immortal, or at least we think we are. We know that we are not, but I can only compare it to the arrogance of teenagers who thinks they will never get old.

I went to find Captain B after my meeting with Mr R, 'You got a minute? I need to talk to you about that funeral business.'

He stopped walking. 'I heard what happened. I am so sorry that you lost your friend.'

I replied, 'What did Mr R say about the funeral?'

Captain B looked a bit confused. 'Erm, he asked if you and him could go to the funeral. I spoke with Captain R and it's approved, at your own expense.'

I looked at Captain B, 'Would you go?'

He looked at me, even more confused. 'If it was important, yes. But I would consider the impact on the operations before I left.'

It was a typical Captain B answer, mission first. I guess he had a point. I was sad that Mr DD was gone, but did I know him well enough to go to his funeral? I knew that we had an operation coming up after the Airscan training ended. In all honesty, I didn't want to miss that. Call it fear of missing out, ego or operational discipline, but I had made up my mind.

'I am not going.'

Captain B looked at me. 'What?'

I repeated myself and added, 'Mr R didn't clear asking for leave with me first. It's all good, I would have done the same and he didn't know. But I am staying.'

Captain B looked at me. 'Okay, I respect that.' Then he added, 'Good choice.'

Now I had the unenviable task of telling Mr R. I went for a run and avoided him until after dinner, when I bumped into him at the gym. 'Shit, it had to happen sometime, why not now?' I thought. 'Hey, I am not going to the funeral. I spoke to Captain B.'

He stopped doing dips, jumped down from the rack and wiped his forehead with a towel. 'You are not coming to the funeral?'

I squirmed a bit, feeling massively uncomfortable. 'I am sorry. I don't feel it and I don't want to miss the upcoming operation.'

He stopped wiping. 'Okay, okay.' The "okays" had the same feeling as "suit yourself", but they were deeper.

I continued, 'I know it sounds wonky and I care deeply for Mr DD But I am just not a funeral guy. Are you sure you are okay with this? Otherwise, I will go with you.'

He looked up. 'No, no, it's good. You should do what is best for you.'

It was a bit of an uncomfortable moment, as we were on two different sides of the playing field on this. I knew he would accept it eventually, but for now it was a bit tense. He left the gym without looking back. I felt like an asshole, but I had to do what I felt was right here. Maybe I was wrong. What was missing the operation compared to having one last chance to say your final goodbyes to a friend? The "approval" from Captain B made me feel even more confused. He was not known for his social sensitivity.

The funeral situation left me with an uncomfortable feeling for the rest of the week. I was happy that we were still doing the course at MAIN and allowed for the dust to settle a bit. After doing our night runs with Airscan, we started with the final exams. It was a great learning experience as we were going to evaluate each other's performances. Strangely enough, it was not in the usual competitive spirit, so it provided us with several good lessons.

My exam went great, except for the fact that I managed to mix up the cars that I was following during a sensor switch. The image jumped a bit when you switched sensors. One needed to really lock in on your position on the map and find reference points, especially when zooming out and during times of heavy traffic. It was a classic 'noob-operator' mistake. I should have waited until after the intersection.

'This will happen to all of you at one point or another, but you were the first ever to manage it on the exam run,' Mike said. It was good laughs all around, but I had to shake the feeling of failure that I loved to hold on to from situations like this.

We were all approved as Airscan operators. Did we get a diploma? Not even a plastic card. The only thing that happened was that you were put on a list of approved operators that could be scheduled to work in the ops room. Lieutenant B held an information briefing with the other officers when we had finished the course, as this would expand our operational capability significantly. We could now plan and schedule our own missions – more or less, at least. They still had to be preapproved by the Americans and they obviously had first dibs if they needed to use the asset.

It struck me how few ground assets the Americans had in the Balkans. Of course, I didn't have any deeper insight into their intelligence organisation. But over time one observed which players were in the circle and which weren't. The Americans had a lot of analysts, liaisons, and technical units like SIGINT providers. It seemed like they ran most missions with foreign operators, to whom they provided the background muscle and baseline intelligence. It was a good way to work, as ground resources were valuable, and they probably had more need for them in Iraq and Afghanistan during those challenging years. The hunt for 9/11 terrorists was pushing on hard and swallowing enormous resources.

I didn't complain, but it would have been nice to be able to act on Swedish baseline intelligence occasionally. But I guess we were lacking that, or we just had a different focus at the time. Mr R had left earlier that morning to fly home and prepare for the funeral. He was going to be away for two weeks, as he would combine it with some R&R. Lieutenant B and the support unit would run range tests of Fabian's safe house relay with Romeo 14. They needed to find out how far and wide it could reach. They had managed to get Fabian to mount a directional antenna, which was hidden in his chimney. They wanted more reach up north.

'What were they trying to reach? The Serbian border? Or beyond?' I thought. The relay tests were going to be run as open green units, with standard kit and borrowed Swedish patrol cars. It was easier, as we didn't need so many resources when going green. The stakes were higher for civilian ops further north.

They had also started with Fabian and us running DLB drops. A DLB is a dead letterbox. It was usually a hidden location where you could leave messages, memory cards, et cetera. for the other party to pick up at a later time. It was safe, provided that you could change them regularly. The reason was that Fabian's intelligence reporting had increased. Something was brewing up north and there were allegations of gun running. The only reason I knew this, was because we were initially tasked to assist in the relay tests and running DLB operations. However, it was changed at the last minute, as an opportunity to open up an old OP had emerged, and we were deemed more suitable for the task.

Captain T held the briefing together with a British sergeant. The British had used the OP earlier this year, but nothing ever came from that operation. The sergeant showed us how they had used it. It was a perfect spot, very unlikely and not very "OP-like". It was not suitable for any construction; it was in a bushy streak at the edge of a cliff. It had a road running close to it, so people were moving around there during daytime. The idea was to find a covert base to act as an LUP, in the forest 20 minutes away from the cliff. After dark, the patrol would move to the cliff from the LUP and maintain a standing/sitting OP there. They would just use a net or two to cover them and move back to the LUP before first light to sleep there.

Sometimes one didn't need fancy or complicated solutions. The key lay in simplicity. The suspected gunrunning would take place after dark, as the factory was a regular factory during the day. The operation would boil down to the ability to observe and document events over a decent distance in the dark. We had the gear and the know-how, but it was an art as much as a science, it required both knowledge of, and a feeling for the setting. I was decent enough at this, but Mr N and Mr A excelled at it. They were really good at using a fast shutter in low light conditions. In the dark one usually used a slow shutter, to let in as much light as possible. This didn't work when you were taking pictures of moving objects and adding an NVG unit to the camera. It complicated matters, but they had mastered the perfect compromise between shutter speed and light.

This was going to be a weekend warrior type of gig. The operation was only going to be five days long, including more than a day for infiltration. The intelligence had been clear, so the timeframe was very specific. This was also going to be our first OP doing our own Airscan. If we had a positive target, we would use Airscan to see where it ended up. This would mitigate the risk of burning the receiver by using ground units, in remote areas at night.

As it was time for yet another OP gig, I was thinking about the roles, what I expected and what others expected. People had become accustomed to door-kicking soldiers fighting their way forward, street by street. The same thing had happened in Vietnam, but just that it was a jungle setting rather than urban warfare. During World War II, brave men were parachuting over Arnhem or storming the beaches of Normandy. That was what people had come to expect from soldiering. Maybe that is even what I had come to expect from soldiering. The picture that most people had about military operations was quite far from reality. They only saw the action and never the heavy lifting that led up to the action. Intelligence was just something that floated around in the air, picked up by old men in dark cellars.

Just think about it. In the Bin Laden operation, for example, Navy Seals flew in with two birds, landed, fired a few shots, and left. The whole shebang was over in under 40 minutes including flying in, and the shooting probably in around 10 to 15 minutes, and they had forever written themselves into the history books as the brave and resolute men that killed Bin Laden. But think about how they got there. They didn't just Google Bin Laden's address and set off on the raid. Imagine the countless years of groundwork leading up to that. SIGINT, OSINT, HUMINT.

People balanced on the edge of a razor blade for years, quietly poking around, collecting information, and following up on endless leads. The initial discussions and investigations about a "courier" linked to Bin Laden started as early as 2002, and the analysts and investigators just worked the leads from there. Of course there was a lot of "dirty" work involved, like the activities at Guantanamo and other black sites. When Bin Laden's courier was traced, and his compound identified, the US intelligence agencies spent 10s of millions of dollars to fund the work, and eventually set up an OP not far from his compound and gathered info over months. They then handed it all over to the strike team and disappeared into the shadows again, maybe receiving a few pats on the back or "attaboys". Then the grind continued. This was supported by geospatial, and SIGINT – although on a smaller scale, we worked to similar principles in our mission in the north of Kosovo.

We all played our part, but some didn't have the luxury of simply playing a part. They had to live it. They had to; it was the only way. It was a delicate way of life. I sometimes wondered if I should have chosen differently, been a door-kicker? But I knew what I was; I was a thinker and a player. And I played. This was our calling; this was our way of life.

Mr A was preparing small bags of protein powder to take with him. 'My body is weakening. This hard routine is killing me. Just look at this.' I looked at him as he ran his hand over his 8 per cent body fat eight-pack.

'Yeah, your body is going down the drain alright.' He didn't catch the irony in my reply. 'Don't forget to mark the bags. They need to go on the inventory list.'

Lieutenant B came into the prep room. 'I need you to take the big SATCOM. There is something wonky with the small unit. It doesn't want to play ball with the hardware encryption. Mr B will look into it, but for now take the big one so there are no hiccups.'

The big unit was not really that much bigger. The fold-up dish had a larger circumference, but the main drawback was that we needed to take a car battery to power it, while the small unit ran on a motorcycle battery. I remembered the car battery on the island exercise. So, it was going to be a heavy haul again. The support unit had come a long way with experimenting with UV panels and inverters, but it wasn't solid enough and had not been tested for standalone operations just yet.

In practice, monitoring gun runners was very similar to that of armed groups. There was a fine line between organised crime and ideologically motivated, paramilitary terrorist groups. The two usually went hand-in-hand: the crime financed the paramilitary activity. So, drugs, human trafficking, extortion, and kidnapping were not uncommon. Bad guys going down was always good, right? In the field it was only an academic difference – it was more about who took the lead. When it came to organised crime, some form of law enforcement usually took the lead and when it came to paramilitary activity, the military took the lead. It didn't mean that we didn't cooperate and help each other, but it was all about command and control, and what happened afterwards. For example, the military was not particularly keen on splashing out resources on organised crime, even when they were connected to our objectives.

We did what we had to do and nothing more. We knew that law enforcement agencies had interest in this operation, but they had been kept at arm's length, as this was just a small part of larger military operations up north. The eagerness of law enforcement to make arrests wouldn't serve our purposes. In reality, it meant that we would let drug trafficking and human trafficking slide. We might document it if we stumbled across it and, if the stars aligned, we might hand it down to them eventually. But most likely not, ironically for the greater good.

It was not a Bravo Two Zero departure this time. It was more like a school bus departure. For some reason, we all took this operation very lightly. It was going to be a two-day infiltration, so we would only have eyes-on target the following night. I had promised Lieutenant B to send a few test files on the Satcom halfway through the infiltration, to make sure the encryption handshake protocol was working properly.

The van rocked side to side, as we left the yard, like a boat in the waves. Mr H from support was driving, with Mr B as commander, and I was at the back. The superstructure was moving like a motherfucker, and if it annoyed us as operators, I could only imagine how it bothered our lead technician. 'Remind me to weld the suspension on this one when we get back,' Mr H told Mr B.

Mr H was a hardcore mechanic from the north. He had been attached to the regiment on and off for a long time, while also running a commercial diving firm with his father. Before we deployed, they had just finished a project with an underwater railway, running weighed-down tugs to help ships moor in a narrow harbour. He was born with grease on his hands, like an artist had paint, and as an intelligence guy could see through the bull shit.

I remember when he told me about his project, I said, 'Wow! That sounds like a massive project.'

He just looked at me like he didn't get it and replied, 'What do you mean? It was just welding track, mostly.' He was that kind of guy. Out of all of us that bought tax free Rolexes he was the only one that actually wore his Rolex Sea Dweller all the time. 'A watch is a fucking tool. If you are a pussy, you don't deserve one,' this was his input to the rest of the Rolex mafia.

Mr A was happy to be out rolling with the LMG again. He had expressed his disappointment that it was highly unlikely that we would have an enemy contact on this mission. Having contact in Kosovo, all together, was unlikely, no matter what kind of unit you were in.

'You guys ready in the back?' the commander asked, but it was not a question.

We were approaching the drop-off. I felt a bit sluggish, and I thought of the coming hours more as a chore than an exciting adventure. These things became routine, strangely enough. I have already given my position on the dangers of routine.

'Mirrors clear. Ready at the door.' Mr A was always the doorman, and he popped the door open with a firm hand.

'Three... Two... Headlights! Maintain speed! Abort drop!'

Mr A quickly closed the door. 'Ready in the back.'

'Zero, Sierra 34 aborted drop. Bravo 6 crowded. No go-around. Proceeding to Bravo 9.'[2]

We had met a vehicle on the road. It had come at speed. The timing was fortunate, as a few seconds later we would have been in the middle of unloading. The SOPs on an aborted drop were either to go around or use one of the reserve drops. In this case, a go-around would have taken too much time, so we proceeded to the pre-designated reserve drop-off point, Bravo 9. It

---

2   Sierra 34 was the vehicle's mission call sign.

didn't impose any massive changes on us other than a slightly longer infiltration. Charts were being pulled out to quickly refresh our minds on the reserve infiltration route.

We had good drop at Bravo 9 and as we sat and listened, I felt the weight of the car battery pushing on my knee. 'This is going to kill me one of these days!' I thought. It was all quiet. The breeze was almost chilly, perfect for a long infiltration. We quickly vanished, like a band of shadow warriors, into the lightly broken forest. It was not too bushy, and the trees were close enough to each other to provide cover, but far enough apart to make it easy to move through them.

We were making good speed through the night as we approached one of the fields that we had to cross. It was a farming field, with a few dirt roads running through it. We had been hearing a mechanical humming sound for the last 25 minutes. Not like UAV humming, but rather like machinery – a tractor or woodworking machine or something similar. As we carefully approached the edge of the field, we could see the source. Two tractors were farming in the moonlight, ploughing the field. It would be impossible to cross while they were active. They were working in a criss-cross manner, as one of them drove south, the other one headed north. We pulled back in the forest and looked at the map in the green light of the NVG.

'We can push north, go along the valley and pop back up here,' said Mr N as he pointed to the map.

Captain B looked at the time. 'We could, but most likely we would need to lay up here.' He pointed at the border of a recreational area that was located in the valley. 'And that would not be optimal. Too many people moving. Let's wait out these moonlight farmers. They have to go home at some point.'

It looked like they were determined to finish ploughing the field that night, and it would take a few hours, so we just had to sit tight. Farmers and their damned determination, there can be no more patient profession in the world, I mean waiting a whole season for your crops, one night's work for them was nothing.

After about two hours, the one tractor left, and it looked like the second one only had a few laps to go.

'Vehicle!' hissed Mr A. We all laid flat on the ground. If there was a way to push ourselves further down in the ground – we certainly tried. I saw headlights flickering down the dirt road that ran just 10 metres from our position at the edge of the field.

'It looks almost like a military jeep,' whispered Mr N. The jeep jumped around on the uneven dirt road. It struggled and appeared an uncomfortable ride. As it passed us, we saw that it was a British KFOR jeep.

I looked at Captain B, 'What the fuck is this? A joke?'

'I don't have a fucking clue. Any other country, okay. But the Brits?'

It was a surreal feeling to observe the combination of Balkan night-farming and a very misplaced military jeep.

The jeep passed quickly and seemed to be heading towards the main road. We had a moment of "what the fuck" feelings.

'Zero, Romeo 13. Friendlies around Bravo 31?'

'Romeo 13, Zero. You are the only ones. Trouble?'

'No, just out of interest. Out.'

This was not the time to ponder the matter. The tractor was finishing up and heading back south. We needed to push forward. We noted the time, number plate and location for a later discussion. It was not optimal to have unknown military jeeps running around in the middle of an infiltration. We only had three hours left before first light, so we needed to push on for two hours and then find an LUP for the day.

We kept a good pace, but first light started to break. 'Damn,' I thought. We needed to find an LUP in the very light forest where we found ourselves at that point. It was far away from the pre-reconnoitred, thicker, and bushier spot. The best we could find was a pit that would fit us all. We had to drape it with a small net and throw some leaves and branches over it. The guard post had to be outside, about 10 metres to the south. I had the first watch. It was going to be a four-hour stint before I could get some shuteye.

As night turned into day, I realised how little cover the forest provided. The pit covered the patrol well enough, but it was a hairy spot to be in. Anyone walking in the area could just stumble over us. After three hours, around 07:00, I heard chainsaws starting to work. The sound came from the valley just south of our location. I woke up the patrol. We had to identify what was happening and where.

I pointed at Mr N, while I whispered to Captain B, 'I am taking Mr N. We will make our way down the side of the valley and try to see what's going on.'

'Go. We've got this,' whispered Captain B

We kitted down so that we were travelling light and carefully made the 50 metre approach to the hillside that led down to the small valley. The chainsaw sounds got louder as we approached, but we couldn't see anything yet. As we made our way down the hillside, Mr N tapped my shoulder, and I froze. I looked to the left and, through a clearing in the trees I could see an army of lumberjacks in a line, cutting their way in our direction. They hadn't seen us. Like cats we backed out of our position and pulled back to the top.

'They are working on the hillside and moving in our direction. They are going to pass us if they continue like this.' It was way too risky to move the patrol in daylight. We had to dig in for the day and hope they kept to the hillside, and away from our position. We removed our face paint to stand a chance at being able to pose as regular troops out on an excursion or something if it came down to that. The threat was not lethal, but it could compromise the entire operation. I had to get some sleep, but it was hard with the lumberjacks approaching.

Three hours later, I woke up and I could see trees falling just 75 metres from us. They were still working on the hillside, and no one had been seen yet. They eventually passed our location without noticing us, but they were never more than 150 metres away. Of course, I hadn't been able to take out the SATCOM, so that was to be done that night. The lumberjacks stopped working at 17:00 and it fell silent. We were lucky, it was a close call.

We were supposed to have eyes-on at dark, but that would not happen as we still had a few hours to get to the location of the OP. Captain B decided that we would start moving at dusk. It was a risk, but we needed all the time we could get.

'Zero, Romeo 13. Eyes on target.' My watch was showing 23:14. According to the plan, we should have had eyes-on closer to 21:00, but at least we were there. We walked straight into the OP location with gear and all. We would have to find the LUP in the morning. The location was not bad. It was on the edge of a cliff. We had one man posted, 50 metres behind us and closer to the road. He covered the only realistic point of entry to this area. Mr N had set up a double mount, with camera and video, just sitting on his Bergen. So, it was basically just us sitting close to the edge of the cliff and keeping our signature down.[3]

It was so simple that I asked myself, 'Is this it?' It was, and it worked for those short missions. Lieutenant B was leading the Airscan from home and they had had eyes-on since before dusk, so we didn't miss anything. Having more than one source of information, and using different methods, was important in the processing of information, which would eventually become actionable intelligence.

It was easy to get an uplink with the SATCOM, as the satellite that I was going for was basically over the target compound. Something was not in sync,

---

3 In this context, signature refers to your body's profile, especially in moonlight conditions.

with the handshake protocol[4] dropping all the time, but it worked, and I decided that it was good enough for now. I knew that Lieutenant B and Mr B were already working on a solution back home for the small terminal which had the same issue, so they were already engaged in solving this problem. Lieutenant B indicated that they would have a solution by the next day and that I would be able to download and update myself. I was not a big fan of field updates, because things could go wrong quickly.

Except for a few test shots, it was mostly about observation as the factory had been well-documented over the years. It was fenced-in and had locked gates, so it was not a place where people loitered for no reason. Mr A pulled an all-night guard duty. As long as we refilled him with power bars every few hours, he was as happy as a cat with catnip.

The night passed without any activity whatsoever. It was calm. Airscan had returned, after some stand down, to cover between first light and when the factory opened. The British sergeant's info on earlier used LUPs held up well. A short, 20 minute walk got us to a perfect spot, far from lumberjacks and outdoor-people.

It was an area with that thick, thorn-filled, aggressive bush that we liked and that gave us peace of mind. We spent a quiet day in the LUP, mostly resting. I wanted to try to flash the SATCOM before dark. Mr B had prepared a new version of the firmware and sent it as a zip-file, with a txt-file with instructions for idiots, like me. I had done this in a classroom environment before. It was easy enough if it went as planned. I carefully copied the instructions to my notebook, just in case. The instructions included making a backup of the current version, again just in case.

I had flashed the SATCOM with the new version and was booting it up for the first time. I had a feeling that it would work and be a plug-and-play moment. Five minutes later, the "loading circle" was still spinning.

'Fuck! This is not good.' Dusk was approaching, and I remembered my "antenna incident" back during the operators' course. This could not be another of those moments.

After an endless number of restarts, resets and trying to reflash it, I understood that I had to get it back to the old version. Unfortunately, this was something that the instructions didn't cover. Trying hard to remember what I could from class, I knew I needed to wipe the hard drive clean, but I couldn't

---

4   Referring to standard encryption handshake protocol.

remember if that would also wipe the bootloader, which was required to install the backup. I hesitated for a while, contemplating the depth of the water that I was in. I decided that the firmware itself, including my backed-up version, should have a bootloader in it.

I pushed the 'delete all', and I held my breath as the back-up was trying to install. About 45 seconds later, I got an 'Installation Complete' message. It booted up correctly, but I had to set up the hardware encryption keys again. It took some time, but I managed to get an uplink with a slow transfer rate, just as before.

As soon as I got connected, a message dropped in from Lieutenant B and Mr B, 'Are you running on the new version now?'

'No. I had to flash the backup, as the new version wouldn't boot.'

'Strange. We have to look at it when you get back.'

Standard answer from computer people, always a shoulder shrug. They didn't know about the emotional damage this caused – a "computer-handicapped" operator, it would scare me for years.

'I am happy that you remembered to back up the bootloader as well. I forgot to put that in the instructions. You were trained well,' Mr B typed.

'I didn't back up the bootloader. I wiped it all.'

A few seconds passed. 'How are you online? Which version are you running?' asked Mr B.

I looked at the 'info' button. '3.21.'

'Ah. You were extremely lucky, then. You have an older version than you should have. None of the newer versions come with a bootloader. It's a security flaw.'

This was computer people in a nutshell. 'Thank you for telling me, at this point, about this – possibly MISSION CRITICAL – knowledge,' I wrote back.

I actually used capital letters, but I could feel how they shrugged their shoulders in their reply. 'Well, it worked out this time, so no harm done.'

Captain B tapped me with his foot. 'Ready to go? We are leaving in 10.'

We had eyes-on at 21:03. Mr A had volunteered for guard duty again. No one was going to stop him. I tried to get a live-feed uplink back to base, but with the handshake protocol issues it was choppy and rather useless. If we had something, we would just send it as stills and leave the recordings until we got back.

Airscan had retired and were on 20 minutes standby at a forward base, which included flying time to target. We did more test shots, and I was slightly disappointed with the results. I suppose it was what could be expected, but it would be borderline ID quality, if it came to that. I was observing through the FLIR around 01:45 in the morning.

Mr N was having an MRE as two trucks were approaching the gate. 'Man the cameras. We've got work incoming. Two military-looking trucks are approaching the gate. They look like Urals.'

Captain B took up position next to me to write down my narration of the events. He quickly reported, 'Activity on target. Airscan is a go.'

'Roger. Wheels up in five. Will confirm target location approach.'

A man got out of one of the trucks and opened the lock on the chain holding the gates. The trucks rolled in, leaving the gates open towards the back of the factory, just below us.

'The situational photo and video were good, but we won't be able to read the plates,' Mr N commented.

It was Kosovo Police force trucks. You could see the emblem on the doors. At the back of the factory there was a loading bay, and on the side of loading bay they had crammed in a 20 foot shipping container. Support legs had been welded on and were sticking out on the side. The container was for trash and leftover metal shavings from the factory production. The metal scrap had some value, so the container was locked. The trucks didn't back up to the loading bay, but they turned around, so that they were parked with their noses facing the way out and the back end alongside the loading bay.

Four men exited the trucks. They talked for a while and you a could see cigarettes being lit. They took their time and didn't seem to be in a hurry. It was good, as we needed them to hang around long enough for the Airscan to arrive, as it would be harder to find them once they reach the main road.

'We've got borderline ID. Very borderline,' complained Mr N.

One of the men jumped onto the loading bay and switched on the outdoor lights.

'Fuck! Help me strip the NVG.'

'We now had enough light to take photos without the NVG unit, but would we be quick enough to get them?' I thought. A minute later, both video and camera were refitted with new lenses.

'Got Bad Guy One.' You could hear the sound of the shutter flick open and closed.

'Number Two... and Three,' Mr N narrated his progress with the photography. Bad Guy Four was harder to get as he had his back towards the camera.

Eight green wooden crates were unloaded from the container and loaded in the back of the trucks, three in one truck and five in another. The man who had opened the gates got a small backpack from the truck and carried it into the container. They locked up and switched off the lights. It looked like they were having another cigarette in the dark.

The radio crackled. 'Approaching target area. ETA 6 minutes.'

The smoke break was already over, and the trucks started rolling towards the gates. They stopped just outside the gates and locked up. Airscan still had a few minutes to go.

'Trucks leaving target. Heading south on Serpent.' There was just silence and waiting.

Five and a half minutes later, the radio burst into life. 'Target acquired. Following north on Cobra.'

They got them, and we did too.

I quickly cleaned up Captain B's report. We had three ID pictures and half a profile on the fourth man. We hadn't managed to get the plate numbers. I had to split up the transmission into three parts and compress the files – this was double the normal amount to get them sent, as the uplink was wobbly. We decided that we would risk manning the OP during the next day as well, in the hope of possibly getting an ID on the person picking up the backpack. Captain B and Mr A did a run back to the LUP to leave a bit of equipment that we didn't need during the day and to get more food and water. As first light broke, we just moved into the bush and hoped no one would come to enjoy the view.

During the day, the factory was bustling with activity, as factories usually are. People went into, and out of, the container several times. They left trash, but nobody had yet taken the bag. At 16:45, the factory was closing for the day, and we could see employees leaving the parking lot. At that point we thought that we would not have any takers that day. At 17:05, the back door popped open and a man in his fifties, wearing a smart shirt and dress trousers, stepped out onto the loading bay. He looked around and then opened the container.

'You got this?' asked Captain B as I was manning the camera.

'I got him crisp.'

He returned with the backpack slung over his right shoulder, looked around, locked up and went back into the factory.

'We got this guy red-handed, in broad daylight,' chuckled Mr N.

Just 30 minutes after our report to HQ, we were waiting for confirmation that they wanted us to send the pictures.

'Romeo 13, Zero. You can take eyes off target. Can you make it to a pickup at ERV 3 at 04:00?'

Captain B got out the map. 'Standby.' He did a quick calculation and nodded. It was tight as fuck, but we could make it. 'Zero, Romeo 13. Affirmative on the pickup. ERV 3, 04:00. Out.'

Instead of the planned two-day extraction, they had opted to get us out from ERV 3 that night. It was at least six hours from our LUP. It was not a complicated hike but had lots of ups and downs. The ERV wasn't the best pick-up location, but I guessed it would be quiet at 04:00. We just needed to wait for dusk to move back to the LUP and start the extraction.

At 03:15, we could see the ERV. We had been pushing hard to be on time. The area was quiet, and we had time for some rest and to get something to eat. We waited for the pickup.

As Mr A closed the door, Mr H, who was driving again, looked back. 'Do you feel the suspension? Even, stable, and smooth as a dance floor!'

I hadn't even noticed, but it was a much smoother ride.

As Mr B finished the regular radio reports, he leaned back. 'I don't want to be the bearer of bad news, but just to give you a heads up: I think today's debriefing will be pretty long. They have a lot of players waiting for your material.'

Debriefings were a part of the job, but the long ones just sucked especially when tired. Except for our people, Jacque's 2iC was there, together with White Shirt, a German guy, and a representative from the GIS. White Shirt was the only one we had seen before. The rest were new faces. There were a lot of takers. It was only when you brought something to the table that you saw which parties were really involved in the operation, as they flocked like vultures circling a dying man in the desert.

Since our reports were thorough, we didn't have much to add, other than the material on the man picking up the backpack. Airscan had tailed the trucks to a remote farm at the Serbian border, where they had unloaded and left. It was suspected that the Kosovo Police were acting as a taxi service in this case. They could move around risk-free. But it was possible that they were directly involved. Romeo 14 had managed to pick up their plates. They had already been up north and managed to meet them head-on, on the highway.

'Do we have any information on that British jeep that passed us in the middle of the night?'

Captain R looked down at the table. 'Well, that was your QRF relocating. They made a… erm… navigational error.'

The QRF had had to move locations during the infiltration, as their original location had become unsuitable. They might have raised suspicion amongst a bunch of locals, so they chose to move to an alternate location during the infiltration. Nothing wrong with that, nothing at all. But what were the odds that they would fuck up the navigation, make several wrong turns and pass us? The odds were astronomical for that to happen.

Captain R continued, 'No harm done. They have been, let's say, "re-schooled" on the navigational front.'

I could just feel how much the brass in the room wanted eyes-on on the farm location. But it was easier said than done, as the location was almost on the Serbian border. 'A surveillance team might actually need to operate a possible OP on the Serbian side,' I thought. But I was too tired to think about the practicalities at that point. It had also been decided that the factory OP would be reopened and manned by the British, for the time being. So, as we had suspected for a long time, things were pointing north for all of us.

We headed to our barracks for some sleep after breakfast and Captain B commented, 'This whole thing gave me a crisp feeling.'

It really did. It was in and out, with results, in just a few days. Everything, except for the lumberjacks, was text book.

A week had gone since the factory OP, and I was surprised that we had heard nothing more about it. I thought it would be an immediate reaction, trying to figure out how to place assets in the north. Maybe they were already doing that. Maybe they already had teams up there. But what did I know? I was just a simple operator that sometimes forgot my place. The need to know more washed over me, not always the best trait for an intelligence operator. I knew that Romeo 14 and Romeo 15 had finished the relay station test successfully.

We had been briefed that it was operational, but I didn't know any details. Romeo 15 had opened a few DLBs and done a handful of handovers. I couldn't dig deeper into that, though, as I had to respect the hard limit. Trying to cross that could have endangered my career and would have made me look extremely unprofessional. I held back on the urge. It would clear up down the line. All I knew for now was that all patrols were home for the moment.

Mr R had returned from the funeral. Our relationship was back to a normal state, and he showed me pictures and brought back greetings from our mutual friends. I felt that I had made the correct decision in not going, as I would have missed the action at the factory. I didn't expand on that in front of Mr R, though.

Captain R finally broke the silence, and we had a briefing. This time, it involved the full platoon. We were going south, to the outskirts of Pristina. Once again, I had anticipated going north and we ended up going south. Who would have guessed? No foreign agencies were at the briefing, so the thought that this would be a completely in-house operation crossed my mind.

We were going to launch a large-scale mobile surveillance operation, running from Pristina all the way down to Prizren. We had a list of five vehicles, plate numbers, models, and makes. One or more of these vehicles was potentially associated with "Cossack" and possibly "Benchwarmer". Cossack was a Saudi national and Benchwarmer was Iraqi by birth. Despite the Russian-sounding codename, both of these gentlemen were Middle Eastern. Their ages weren't known, but they were both around 40 to 50. Finally, if Benchwarmer or Cossack were connected to any of these vehicles, we had to get their picture. The only file pictures that existed of the two of them were more than seven years old. These were HVTs, but I didn't recognise them from anywhere.

We would have Airscan available during the whole operation. I think they were working with their own direct intelligence triggers, as well as ours. We were running four black box vans and four lookout trigger cars, one for every van. The strategy was to create a net with these resources, covering points though which it was most likely that they would pass. This was like looking for a needle in a haystack, as we only had loose areas of interest. I didn't know what kind of intelligence had triggered this operation, but one thing was for sure: it wasn't meaty, mostly bones.

Captain T had acquired a new van for this operation as we previously only had three, and the conversion of the van would be a quick affair as we had started to perfect the art of building black boxes, finding, and using the perfect thread count on the mesh covering the lens. All the patrols could now deliver premium quality, vehicle-borne pictures at this point. Now we just needed to find the target. In the first couple of days, we realised that this would not be a 24/7 operation. We worked with Airscan and tried to cover most of the daylight hours. We needed to switch the person in the black box every four hours, due to the heat, and rotate car positions every few hours. So, we weren't static for too long.

For this operation I was paired up with Mr N – instead of my usual wingman, Mr A. I didn't mind the change though, since Mr A and I had almost run out of subjects to discuss at that point. Being the spotter-car became old quickly. It was all about looking at plates and cars, trying to spot one of the UKVs we had on the list. They weren't really full-on UKVs, but in the context they were, as the information about them was very loose and ghost-like.

'This is real police coffee and doughnut work,' said Mr N during one of our lookout-car runs.

One week in, it had become almost like going to a nine-to-five job. Wake up, roll out, work, dinner, work out, sleep, repeat. We had briefings every night and every morning, trying to improve our tactics.

Captain R held the evening briefing. 'We are a week in now. I know we are looking for a needle in a haystack here, but now it's time to show how professional we really are. Every day, we roll out as sharp as the next, right?'

He was right, of course, but we needed the reminder. We were used to this kind of work, but the looking for cars business was as monotonous as fuck. Nothing would change that.

Part of the support squad was going to man the Airscan ops centre during the rest of the operation, under the lead of Lieutenant B.

Mr A looked at me. 'Man, they got it all cushy working up at MAIN and having Burger King every day.'

Of course, he didn't mind the task, only the food. He always cracked me up.

Captain R said, 'Romeo 13, you can stay for a minute as I need to talk to you.'

'I need you to go and empty the DLB up in Mitrovica.' We were going to be pulled from the ongoing mobile op for a few days.

So, the time had come for us to serve Fabian, I thought to myself. It felt good to take a break from the mobile grind, but also to be more involved in the north. After our contact up there, it had mostly been Romeo 14 and Romeo 15 that had done the heavy lifting there.

The DLB was to be emptied the next day. It was a daytime run, so we needed to leave early. We were driving two civilian sedans, but we had to borrow one from the British as ours were needed at home. Mr A and Captain B were going to drive as an SAP team 10 minutes ahead. Mr N and I would handle the DLB. It was located at one of those "unofficial" pee break spots just south of Mitrovica, on one of those lay-bys that went like an arch from the main road and then back again. This one was about 150 metres long and was most frequently used by truckers resting for a few hours at night. About 100 metres along the lay-by, and five metres up into the forest, there was a decent-sized stone. The DLB was a half-litre PET bottle, hidden under the stone from the back. We were going to make the exchange, continue through Mitrovica and circle back on the eastern route called "Mordor 1". I think we had all watched too much *Lord of the Rings* for it to be healthy, and it showed.

This was not like our first mission up there. We were going to move in the more civilised parts of the north, so enemy contact was not the main worry. We still went prepared, of course. Mr A had asked to bring the Minimi, just for the sake of it, but was denied by Captain B.

'Well, it was worth a try,' said Mr A.

Both cars had made a successful plate change to northern plates. It was always a bit hairy in daylight, but it was very quick, and one just had to keep your cool. We had about 35 minutes left before we reached DLB. The time between the cars was roughly 15 minutes and we needed to be tighter before the DLB. Otherwise, the SAP car's info would be outdated by the time that we arrived. We had about 7 minutes to go when the first car passed the DLB.

'Let your foot off the gas for a bit. A family with kids stopped for a pee,' I said.

Mr N reduced our speed as much as possible, without driving suspiciously slowly.

'We will not be able to see if they are still there when we turn off the road. If they are, we'll make it look like a pee stop. Just keep your distance so they don't feel the need to talk.'

Mr N nodded. We were approaching the turn and 30 seconds before we were going to turn, we saw a car driving out from the rest area, 200 metres in front of us.

'I hope that was them,' I thought. After the initial turn, we saw that the lay-by was clear.

'Sometimes, Lady Luck smiles at us,' said Mr N. We rolled past the middle of the lay-by, and I could see the stone from the car. The car came to a stop. The place looked like shit.

There was trash everywhere and you needed to watch your step going up to the stone as this seemed to be a popular place to use as a bathroom. On the bright side, no one would look there. I dug up the bottle from beneath the stone and looked over my shoulder before I shook out the small plastic tube and replaced it with the one that we had brought. I could see flash cards and a rolled-up note. I wanted to read it, but I knew it was not for my eyes. I put the plastic tube in my chest pocket and closed it with its button.

As I approached the car, Mr N leaned out of the open passenger door. 'Don't forget the stone!'

I hadn't forgotten the stone, but it was good that he was focused. A smooth stone was moved from the left to the right of a slab of concrete with rebar sticking up from it. This indicated that we had emptied the DLB up and left something. Left in the middle of the slab, the stone would signal that we had emptied it, but didn't leave anything. This allowed both sides to check the status of the DLB without needing to manually check it and risk unnecessary exposure.

'Got it?' asked Mr N as I got into to the car.

'Yeah,' I replied. The routine was to not report the collection, but to report when we got on "Mordor 1".

'Zero, Romeo 13 on Mordor 1. Returning to base location.' The reporting was kept to a minimum and very few waypoints were reported. We had heard the lead car report in about 20 minutes earlier. It was a perfect gap. We stopped to switch plates once on our way back. It was a smooth ride, and we discussed how to approach the DLB reconnaissance that we were expecting to do the next day.

Back at base, we did an after-action report to Captain R and handed over the contents of the DLB.

I asked Captain R, 'Are we up for the recce tomorrow?'

'I don't know yet. I need to relieve a few of the guys from support at Airscan, as they need to crack down on the SATCOM encryption issue. So, I wouldn't count on tomorrow, but we will see. I'll let you know during the morning briefing.'

We didn't need much time to prep for a DLB reconnaissance, as there were already a few suggestions on the table.

I was reading in bed and Mr N was playing PSP in our room when someone knocked at the door.

I looked at the time, 22:15. 'Come in, it's open.'

Captain B opened the door. 'Ops room, five minutes.'

Captain R met us in the ops room. We were the only patrol there and to my knowledge, all units were back at base except for the Airscan crew. Something was afoot. 'Can you step out for a minute?' he asked the duty corporal.

As he closed the door behind him, Captain R continued, 'We have a delicate situation that involves Fabian's handler. He will be here shortly. I know you are professionals, but I still want to remind you that this never leaves the room.' The handler was a very familiar face and, for me, an unexpected choice, but it made sense.

'In the DLB, Fabian asked for an emergency meeting tomorrow. I don't know why, and I don't know if I trust him. He could be under duress or tailed. I just don't know.'

He needed muscle if something went down, and counter surveillance to assess if he was tailed or not. 'If you spot the slightest indication of an early tail, you send me an empty text on the only phone number programmed on this phone and I will walk away.'

He took out a map of central Pristina and put it on the table. 'This is the location. The meeting is at 13:15, but Fabian will get the location 15 minutes before.' I knew it well, it was a café across from the 'International Hotel', where all the expats, NGOs and journalists hung out.

'Mr A and I have the right appearance and could easily blend in at the hotel's outdoor serving area across the street. English is more common there than any other language and we could easily cover the street from there. We would be close if something happened,' I said.

Captain B nodded while pointing on the map. 'We could drop you off a few blocks south and you can walk to the hotel. We can position the car here and we would cover your blind spots. It would also be my preferred spot if I worked surveillance here.'

We looked at the handler, who nodded in agreement. 'Sounds like a plan. I don't really know what to expect, so be ready for anything.'

When the handler left, Captain R asked, 'You got this? Or do you need any support?'

Captain B looked at us. 'No, we've got this.' We withdrew to the briefing room to work out the details.

'This will primarily be counter-surveillance, in my opinion. I get that the handler is nervy, but the likelihood of a shootout in central Pristina at lunchtime is reasonably low. I'm not saying it can't happen, but I would say that it is more likely that he is tailed by Serbian intelligence or local police, if anything,' I said.

Their meeting location was good as they had to get close to be able to see what was happening. We would spot them, especially as Fabian didn't know about the location yet. Otherwise, they could have set up an observation post from the hotel, but now they wouldn't have time and would have to walk or drive in.

My Glock sat snug in my pancake holster. I had two magazines of 9mm FMJ, and two with a type of frangible. Not super weak, but the CPO/Confined spaces type. Mr A and I had loaded our AKs in the trunk of the car. We'd also taken two Benelli Tactical shotguns.

Captain B had a short huddle before rolling. 'I know you are amped, but this is a very crowded location. If shit goes down, we pull out the handler. Absolute minimal engagement, none if possible and only to save lives. We don't shoot to take down fleeing perps. The shit storm would never end. I actually don't even want to think about the consequences if it happened. Bring your ID badges, since neither the local police, nor KFOR, is informed. You need to have solid identification if we start shooting.'

Captain B hadn't anticipated how much we were going to enjoy going on this operation. It was a premium mission. The secrecy, the muscle, the risk

– what's not to love? We lived for this shit. Mr A and I were dropped two blocks from the meeting. We had spotted one of our mobile vans, but from the back, they didn't see us. Still, it was good to know we had reasonably close back-up if needed. The street was crowded. We would be 30 minutes early, which meant we had 15 minutes of advance warning when the meeting was announced. We found a very good spot on the hotel terrace. When I came out with two cups of espresso, I got the evil eye from Mr A. He knew as well as I did that this was one of the few places that had decent, large-sized filter coffee, but he kept quiet. 'Fucking miniature Italian coffees,' I whispered with a smile.

Counter surveillance on the street was about watching hands, faces, and movements. Doing foxtrot surveillance was an art form. It would be harder to spot them if they knew they were walking in on a handler meeting. A common fail was not taking white noise into consideration. For example, if you were working in a country where you didn't fit in, like Afghanistan, people would look at you even if you had a good cover. People would be vigilant, as they would be assessing if you were a threat or not. Then everyone would look like, and actually be, surveillance – in combat zones everyone becomes suspicious. You also had the factor of organised crime and regular criminality. This was particularly relevant in our mission. Criminals also ran their own surveillance looking for law enforcement. But you could often spot them. The trick was not to become a threat to them by allowing them to confuse your presence with that of law enforcement. There was also regular intelligence, which monitored groups of people, like expats and journalists assembled at a hotel.

The handler walked in; he was five minutes early. He played the part; he looked like a Regular. Captain B and Mr N were parked further down the street and were covering our blind spots and the long-range spectrum. Fabian made a sharp turn from a narrow market alley onto the street running past the hotel. He carried his leather teacher's bag that he had slung over his left shoulder. I thought to myself that "they" could have rigged a bomb in his bag and detonated it remotely. I observed his face. No signs of nervousness, a real cool customer. He smiled and waved at the handler as he approached. He had been well trained by the Germans. He was clean. To the best of our collective knowledge, he had not been followed. He leaned his bag against the table leg and took off his blazer. A kid in the corner had my eye, until she was picked up by a school transport. The mobile team was monitoring oncoming traffic, and it was calm.

We didn't know if they were doing a handover as well, or if they'd only talk. If they did a handover, I should not have been able to see it, because if

I could, so could counterintelligence. But I did see it. It happened in a split-second. With a bit of sleight of hand, it was done. If I had blinked at the wrong moment, I would have missed it. They did a table drop and I couldn't see the handler take it, I just assumed he did. So, it was well done especially from a source to a handler. Fabian had his coffee and was off 20 minutes later. I had an urge to put a long tail on him to confirm where he was going, but that was usually a no-no for sources as we put them at risk if we got burned.

The handler and the mobile unit left. Mr A and I stayed for a while to catch any slack. You could often spot surveillance when the target left as there was normally a lot happening at the same time if they were leaving to follow or breaking a static surveillance station.

We circled around to our alternate pick-up spot a few blocks away, closer to the shopping mall.

'Anything?' asked Captain B.

'Nope. It was clean. You?'

Captain B answered, 'We had a civilian policeman on foxtrot, but we also picked up on the target he was following. So, it was just coincidence.'

Back at base, we had a quick briefing with the handler. 'The emergency was not that Fabian was at risk. He picked up fairly solid evidence of Serbian SF breaching the northern border.'

We were back on the mobile surveillance circuit again, but my mind was elsewhere. All I could think about was Serbian SF on the northern border. That was not a small thing. I knew they wouldn't go into direct conflict with NATO, but that the ante had definitely been upped. We knew that. Now it was time for people with better salaries to analyse the data, keep traction and develop this into action.

All northern ops were paused for a good reason. Consideration of the broader context, and potential implications, this, more than ever, had to be played right. But for the time being, I needed to snap out of the north and focus on the Cossack and Benchwarmer game. We had been out for a few days and the other patrols had been grinding on, 'like an endless search for a grail we might never find,' I thought.

Captain R held the regular morning briefing. 'We welcome back the missing children. To get you up to speed on what has happened since you were gone…' He was silent for 15 seconds, 'Yeah, that silence got you up to speed. Romeo 13, you will find a spot along Snake Charmer South and Romeo 15 will spot for you. Fresh energy now, boys. We will not miss our chance when it comes because we are bored. You all got that?'

Snake Charmer South passed through a moderately-trafficked, urbanised area and was a common route to bypass the city, so one didn't have to get into more heavy traffic than necessary. We had found a good spot just after the "needle eye", looking out on southbound traffic coming from the north. The "needle eye" was a chokepoint, like a Z-formation. The southbound road wound down a hill just before the Z that continued through the Z and then flattened out at the bottom. The Z was a sharp right-hand turn, followed by a straight section of 50 metres and then a sharp left-hand turn. Our spot was 15 metres after the last turn. The spotter car was parked on the right-hand side of the downhill section between the turns. The heads-up would be short, but the speed would be low enough to be able to react.

We were starting a four-hour watch, and I was in the black box. As cars passed, I tried to double-check the spotters' work. So far, they hadn't missed anything. We picked up a few Swedish plates for the security police but didn't waste any frames on them. It was a warm day, and I was sitting in a mesh-style tank top. Sweat was running down my forehead and my hands were clammy. It made my fingers slip on the camera settings while I was trying to perfect my test photo. I heard the regular check-ins from Airscan. They were up in the skies searching. I saw that my test photos came out blueish. The sun was straight above us, and my white balance was probably off.

'UKV 3. VW polo, red 'VW' sign on the front, passing.' I heard the excitement in his voice. I only had about 10 seconds. I looked over the camera and saw the Polo with the red 'VW' mark on the front. I moved my head down and looked through the camera. It was aligned, as I had left it. I held the remote trigger in my hand. I held my breath. I needed to sit still and wait... wait... wait. I couldn't be too eager. If I was too eager and took the photo too early, the windshield would come out as a black hole, this would have had no value. And the shutter movement would create vibrations, I didn't want to fire too soon. Ice in the stomach now, Man! A Swedishism of nerves of steel. Although this is how I felt, these were never conscious thoughts. I couldn't afford that luxury. I gently pressed the trigger once and I heard the shutter move. I pressed the trigger again and held it down.

'Pegasus has hold on UKV 3, southbound Snake Charmer. Waiting for confirmation.' It was Airscan, saying that they had gotten a fix on the vehicle. I needed to assess who they were, and quick. I flicked the arrow-button on the camera's control pad to the left. Blurry, blurry, blurry. I reached the first picture and I had almost lost hope but then... deep breath and there it was.

All blue because the white balance was off, but perfectly crisp. The license plate, the driver, and the passenger. I could see their eyes; I could identify them and the vehicle. There was no doubt. It was Cossack riding shotgun and Benchwarmer driving. This was the first picture of any of them in seven years, and I got both. We were in business.

'Pegasus, Romeo 13A. Confirm both targets UKV3.'

'Romeo 13A, Pegasus. Say again. Both targets?'

'Romeo 13A, affirmative!'

'All ground units, Pegasus, stand down.' Mr N had to contain his desire to shout from the driver's seat. I knew this because I was strutting in my head. He looked back at me. 'You did it! You fucking did it!' I had just scored the winning goal of the World Cup.

Endorphins were rushing through my body while we drove back to base. I couldn't believe I'd got that shot. I felt happy to have found the needle in the haystack. We found it, but I got it on paper. There was a bit of back-patting in the yard. This was the intelligence version of shooting Bin Laden, but just with a camera and not a gun. The fire would come later.

Captain R met us. 'Listen up. Romeo 13 and Romeo 14 in the briefing room. The rest in the movie room. Romeo 15, did you take any pictures?'

The vehicle commander of the spotter car looked up from fiddling with his grab-bag. 'Nope, nothing.'

Captain R continued, 'Good. Romeo 13, bring the camera into the briefing room, as is. Touch nothing.'

Lieutenant B had assembled all the target packs from the patrols. They were numbered. He handed them in at the briefing room and Captain R closed the door. The camera was standing in the corner, tripod, and all.

'Now we wait,' said Captain R. No debriefing, no nothing. It felt weird. We were all excited and wanted to talk it through. We heard a knock on the door 45 minutes later. Captain R opened it and three men stepped in.

'Sorry we kept you waiting. We had some business to attend to.' He walked to the camera. 'Is this the one?'

Captain R nodded.

'Can I take a look?'

'Of course,' Captain R said.

They were Americans. I had never seen them before. The three men leaned in over the small screen as they looked at the pictures.

'Can we take the camera? We will send it back tomorrow.'

'No problem,' said Captain R.

One of the men clipped the camera off the tripod and put it in his Swiss backpack.

Mr N said, 'The lens cover.' The man with the backpack looked at him with a quizzical expression. Mr N continued, 'The lens cover fell off when you put it in your bag. That's a $5,000 lens.'

The man looked at Mr N. 'Oh, sorry. My bad!'

The man who had asked all the questions took the floor. 'You will hear this once and then forget about it.'

The man that had taken the camera walked around the table. 'Sign here, and here.' The document read "Top Secret NDA". National security, et cetera, et cetera. It meant 'Shut up forever.' Well, not quite forever.

Man Number One continued, 'On behalf of the United States of America and the US intelligence community, I want to thank you. I want to do that, as this is the only recognition you will ever get. I don't need to explain this to you, but I want you to know what you have done. Cossack is Mohammed al Tikrit and Benchwarmer is his brother, Omar al Tikrit. Both are main players involved in the logistics and funding of the 9/11 World Trade Centre terrorist attack. You see the bigger picture now, right? American ground units will handle this from now on.'

All three of them went around the table and shook our hands. 'By the way, who took the picture?'

I put my hand up like I was back in school. 'Good work! What's your name?'

As they walked out, we needed a minute to digest what we had just learned. We were actually playing a key part in capturing two of the most wanted men in the world at the time. A silent round of fist bumps said everything we needed to say. We all knew what we had done.

The pride probably radiated from our souls. For the patrols, the mission was over. I didn't like the "baby handling" part, though. It happened from time to time when you were doing sensitive stuff for other agencies, when you were not allowed to compile your intelligence and present it in a professional fashion. Rather, you were handled like a noob unit that had stumbled across gold by mistake. I guessed it had to do with the fact that we were still fresh and new players on the circuit. We would be the "noob" unit from time to time, but it would change. To be fair they knew the skill it took to take that picture.

The next day, Captain R called on me at lunch. 'I got the camera back. Come and pick it up after lunch. I also have something else for you.'

I looked at him as the Dijon mustard slightly teared up my eyes. 'What do you have for me?'

Captain R looked at me, 'I don't know.'

I stopped chewing. 'You don't know? What kind of answer is that?'

He replied, 'Just come and see me, alright?'

I was confused as I walked to the ops room. Captain R shut the door behind me. 'Here is the camera. They wiped the internal memory and kept the flash card. Don't write anything about it, just pick up a new one from Lieutenant B. We'll write it up as a technical malfunction.'

He grabbed an A2-sized brown envelope. It was sealed with security tape at the top. It said, "Top Secret, only for…" and had my name handwritten with a black felt pen.

'Who is it from?' I asked the captain.

'It came with the camera. I got specific instructions that it was for your eyes only.'

I looked at Captain R, 'Should I open it now?'

He was halfway out of the ops room when Captain R said, 'No, you open that when I have left. I don't want to know, and I shouldn't know. And neither should anyone else. Leave the door open when you leave.'

I tore off the security tape. It was strong and I almost ripped the top off the envelope. I pulled out an A2-print on photopaper. I flipped it over. It was the picture I took. It had a post-it note on the front.

'Thank you. B.'

I looked at it for a minute. I put it back in the envelope, borrowed a more discrete one from one of the drawers in the ops room and left the door open as I left. Again, words weren't necessary. But I smiled to myself as I walked down the corridor.

16

Victory At All Costs

'The heli shook violently as it followed the tiny river's contours. I looked around, only serious painted faces as far as the eye could see. It felt different this time. For the first time, we were going to hunt for a real army unit. It was a test – not just regular paramilitary or terrorist-affiliated organisations. We were going to hunt for the 63rd Parachute Brigade of the Serbian Special Forces. It was more war than anyone could have hoped for.'

The months before sitting in that shaking helicopter, we had been "recovering" from our success with the Cossack operation. In this business, you were not as good as your last operation, but only as good as your next one. It had been a few slow months watching the grass grow. Not dead-slow, but slow enough for things to become routine. We had had some close protection work, light surveillance, and manning some city OPs, and of course QRF. It was the well-known military business of waiting and waiting more than anything else. This especially applied to intelligence, as surveillance is by its nature a waiting game and it took time.

It could take years, even decades, of waiting for the moment when everything aligned. So, when I considered it "slow", it referred to the quality of the jobs we were taking on. We had recently done something called "Monitoring for signs of unrest in the community". It didn't sound bad and, of course, it was an important task, especially when it was considered in a broader, nationwide context. But this specific task was to see if there were any signs of rioting during a small religious celebration. It was like watching paint dry, especially as none of the parties involved cared about it. It sometimes felt like we had been left to our own devices, that the days of high-powered fastballs were done. We had even had time to train with other specialist units.

The north was quiet. Romeo 15 and Romeo 14 were rolling on DLB duty. Our time here was limited. Were we just in a holding pattern until our time was up? Or did they really not have anything else to offer? I couldn't stop thinking about the information from Fabian. Serbian recon troops moving over the border!

It tickled my nerves just thinking about it, but maybe they had concluded that it was nothing. And the police gun runners, what had ever happened with them? The tiredness had started to wear off and we had too much energy now. That was the problem with professional soldiers. They have to be kept fed and active, otherwise they grow restless and start coming up with stupid shit.

Mr A and I were having arm-day at the gym.

'Look at this!' said Mr A as he flexed his arms. 'Your arms are massive. Why can I never get thickness like that?'

I looked at him. 'You have been blessed enough with being able to shove anything in your mouth and still keep 7 to 8 per cent body fat, year-round with limited effort. Isn't that good enough for you?'

Mr A gave me a disappointing look. 'Arms are girl-catchers. That's what gets you laid, not abs,' he said as he started his set of z-bar curls, with 55kg on the bar, like it was breakfast.

Captain B entered the gym. 'Stop admiring your arms, ladies. We've got work. Briefing room in 10 minutes, and please shower off that testosterone before then.' It was almost a race to get out of the gym first, that's how eager we were.

'Do you think it's time to put lead downrange?' asked Mr A, trying to make himself heard over the roaring sound of the water pump in the shower room.

'Don't count on it. It's probably just playing taxi or something like that.'

Captain T was holding the briefing with Lieutenant B, as Captain R was home on official business. There was a big map of the north-eastern border on the wall, with areas of interest marked out by the geocell.

'Okay, Gentlemen, it's time for some heli work.'

The area was too sensitive and too close to the border zone to risk extensive ground recce at the time. They had got us on the "regular" border-control flights that were conducted several times a day, to show a KFOR presence at the border. They were run by an assortment of countries, but we were going to fly with the Germans, French and Italians, as they had command in the northern sector.

We would be looking for suitable vehicle pick-ups/drop-offs, helicopter landing sites, ERVs, paths, and judging road quality.

'We are back in the game we've never been out of,' continued Lieutenant B. 'This is the last stage of an intensive period of planning behind the scenes. Captain R is back in Sweden discussing this matter with the Major and Colonel X. That's the level we are on now.'

Over the following weeks, Romeo 12 and Romeo 13 were going to be a part of the border flights. These would be tweaked slightly, so that we could assess the locations. Special rigs had already been made by the support squad to fit the various helicopter types that were involved, as the flights could not stand out or show any signs of containing more than the usual surveillance equipment. We were relocating to the French base the next evening, from where we would run with the Italian and French helicopters. Romeo 12 was going to relocate to Prizren and run with the German crew.

Looking at the map, I asked Captain B, 'This feels like prep for… border ops?'

He nodded slowly. 'They didn't disclose the main objective yet, but you are right. There is nothing else there, that I know about, that would match this.'

We didn't get the full background but, as Captain R was in Sweden to meet with the higher-ups, something was definitely going down. Based on my experience so far, this was "personal preparations", when you recce'd your own insertion, ERVs, routes et cetera. I didn't feel like this was done for a third party. The terrain was very canalising and full of chokepoints. It didn't leave too many options.

Mr A pointed at the map. 'I would also look at this ridge. Everything comes down to the IRL[1] situation but, based on the satellite images and the map, I would definitely want to see if we could put a bird down there. It's tight, but it's far less obvious and it will allow for a much more remote, and covered infiltration, in whatever direction we are moving later.'

It looked tight, like a ridge-ledge that would require a hot drop-off, possibly by fast rope or rappelling. The area was far more remote and provided many more options and flexibility than the other ones, at least as far as the ground infiltration was concerned.

'Put it down as "Hotel 4". I'll run it by Captain T,' said Captain B and continued, 'Let the games begin.'

He was referring to the equipment race that would commence shortly. I had to sync with the 2iC of Romeo 14, as we needed some of their photo gear.

At 22:00 the same evening, we had a show-and-tell on how to use the attachments that the support squad had made. Mr H said, 'This attaches to the airframe here. You use this torque key, so you don't ruin the anchor point in the heli, otherwise we will have an expensive problem.'

1 In real life.

They had really outperformed themselves with the custom mounts that they had built for the French Gazelle and the Italian military UH-1 variant.

Mr H continued, 'We tried this with the photo equipment on the ground only. It should work during flight as well, at least in theory. So, when you do your respective first flights, you need to take note of what is not working. We will be on standby to fix any issues and it will be resolved before the second flight. Alright?'

It was a long night as we tweaked and packed equipment into the early hours of the morning. But the energy was high in the patrol as we had been waiting for something like this for some time. We were ready. We could afford to sleep in a bit the following morning as we were kitted and ready to go. We were going to be picked up at 18:00 by a French patrol returning from the south. We would catch a ride with them to their base and Romeo 12 would drive down to Prizren at 16:00.

Lieutenant B and Mr B from support would drive up a little ahead of us at 17:00 in their own car to make sure that we got settled in and also to adjust the mounts if needed. Mr H would follow Romeo 12 to Prizren for the same purpose. It was a quiet ride as the French weren't really talkative.

'Do you think we can have them make real size coffee, unlike the Italians?' Asked Mr A, always concerned with the food and drink options.

'I think they can, if you ask nicely in the canteen,' I replied. 'They understand English, even if they don't speak that much.'

By the look on his face, he had not considered that. 'I mean, it's no secret that they can't make coffee.'

We arrived at the French base late in the evening. The French were hospitable and friendly, but it was far from the organised German world. But we would survive, and then some. We were put in a corner of their hangar, which worked just fine. It actually provided a good amount of privacy and sleeping on a tent-bed in the breezy hangar was not bad. The only complaint I could think of was the lack of bed linen with an alpine rose scent, like the Germans had.

We were going to make our first run with the French in the morning, so the helicopter crew held a late night briefing. It was going to be a part of a familiarisation run. They would fly the regular route so we would have the opportunity to test our equipment. The helicopter could take two of us.

So, the set-up would be one camera operator and one spotter. The spotter's role was going to be important, as the camera operator had a very narrow focus during flight. The spotter's job was to find things and to see the whole picture, not just selected parts. The photography was really only supporting material.

The helicopter crew outlined the flight path before every mission, and we had a tailor-made waypoint system that was meant to give us enough heads-up for photography.

I was spotting for Mr N on the first run. This was when we would see if the equipment held up, and if we held up. At 06:30, Lieutenant B helped us to mount the equipment in the waiting Gazelle. It was a tight fit, but we managed. 'This should do it. I have put a very light locknut on the bolts but keep an eye on them so that they don't start to unscrew.'

It looked like Mr N had been mounted in the camera equipment. That's how little space there was.

'You ready?' asked the pilot. We gave him the thumbs up, and he closed the doors. I realised immediately how narrow the field of view became when the doors were closed. It was like driving through a tunnel.

The helicopter hovered for a minute while doing final checks before heading north and then following the border to the southeast. The vibrations were more intense than in the heavier helicopters we had flown in before. The Gazelle was really light, compared to the heavier Bell 412, UH-1, et cetera. The pilot was flying low and fast. It was a mission just to try to get our bearings.

'Could we gain some altitude?'

The radio hummed as the pilot replied, 'I can give you about 25 metres. Any higher and we will start to stick out.'

I would take that, it was better than nothing.

Mr B was waiting for us on the helipad as we landed, an hour and a half later. 'Did it hold up?' he half-screamed while the engine was revving down.

It did. The mounts had done their work, we as a crew barely had. We spent a few hours with the helicopter crew, analysing the material that we had produced during the flight.

'This is not good enough,' said Mr N.

It was, obvious that the photos were not up to scratch. We were going too fast and too low.

'Why can't we increase the altitude?' Captain B asked the pilot.

'It will look too different. The border-flights are quick and low. Anyone observing us would easily spot the difference in behaviour.'

'The photo quality is good, but the timing is off,' said Lieutenant B. 'The only option we have is to shift the timing.'

We decided to put fewer targets on each flight, have a straighter approach, and tighter waypoints. That was the way forward to try to overcome this unexpected problem. We also fixed the crews on each helicopter, to get more consistency with the pilots and have the same spotter and photo operator for each run.

Mr A and Captain B would be in the Italian UH-1, while Mr N and I would crew the Gazelle. It took us three days, and multiple flights, to get the feeling for this kind of race-car photography. But we got there in the end, having only one objective per flight helped. We also became more familiar with the route giving us a better flow in providing the heads-up. This in turn allowed us to get an early start with the running photography.

A week in, we had covered most of the static points. The second week was dedicated to route and path work.

Captain T came up that evening and wanted a progress report. 'Gents, I spoke to Captain R and the Major yesterday. We need to know if you are happy with this.'

Captain B looked at Captain T, 'Well, we need a bit more time. We are just a week in, but it looks promising so far.'

Captain T stood up and paced around the table. 'That's not what I am asking. I need to know – tonight – if you can use any of these points for insertion or if we need to scrap it and rethink.'

Captain B looked around the table. 'Hotel 4 is definitely solid for heli insertion. The pilot confirmed that he could do a blacked-out touch-and-go there,' said Mr N.

Captain B appeared to be thinking, as he brought his hand up over his mouth for a moment. He then said, 'It depends on the mission objective. But just analysing these as separate things, I would say we have enough to say that it's good.'

Captain T looked around. 'You will be briefed by Captain R when he gets back tomorrow. I will report this as a "go". You will do your last flights tomorrow morning and report back to base no later than 15:00. Understood?'

There was something in his voice that put a cloak of seriousness I had never seen before over the whole situation. Maybe it was the more command-like language.

'Something big is going down,' said Mr A when we left the meeting.

Captain B quickly revised the plan. We would skip the routes. 'A route is a route. It can be changed on the ground while running. I want to make sure that these places are as secure as we think they are. I have a distinct feeling that we are going to step out of a helicopter at one of them soon enough.'

We decided to skip the photography. Instead, we had two spotters running over the "Hotel" insertion points and the ERVs to get a better overview. When we flew over Hotel 4, I got an ominous feeling that we would do a night insertion there soon. I could visualise it. It wasn't a bad feeling, but I wondered who was expecting us in the forests and where were we going.

'It's been a pleasure working with you. We might see each other soon,' said the helicopter pilot as we were about to leave the base and head home.

'It's funny that they use Special Aviation Units for border patrols,' said Captain B in the car.

'Why? They are assisting in the recce and doing the insertion later.'

Captain B looked at me. 'These are not just the regular SF taxi drivers. These pilots came from the aviation unit serving the DSGS and other cloak and dagger units.'

Maybe he was right. Maybe it was strange to have a highly specialised unit doing a drop-off. They weren't even stationed here; they had come up north just for this.

We entered our base at 14:15. Just enough time to sort out the equipment before the big briefing at 15:00. All patrols were back on base, everyone was included in the briefing. This was an all-hands-on-deck situation.

Mr A offered to get coffee for all of us. 'Because this feels like it's going to be a long one.'

We sat sipping our coffees waiting for Captain R. He was late, but it gave us some time to get up to speed with what the other patrols had been up to. Romeo 14 and Romeo 15 had apparently been doing more than running DLBs the previous week. They had been hauling material to the safe house and had also stashed vehicles in the north. It seemed that it had been an intensive week. Stashing vehicles and gear in and around the safe house were not a light operation.

'Sorry I am late,' said Captain R as he closed the door. This was the first time I had seen the whole platoon assembled since I got down there, with no externals. It was only us.

Captain R continued. 'As you know, I have been in Stockholm the last week, in discussion with the Major, Colonel X and the General. After a lot of consideration, we got the go-ahead. We are probably seeing the most wartime-like mission so far, or at least as close as we'll get.'

The mission was clear, although unexpected. I had a gut feeling about this for a long time, but nothing of this magnitude. I thought we were going to do border surveillance, and maybe border patrols, to detect if any Serbian forces were moving across the border.

The reality proved more interesting. We were going to be inserted with Romeo 12 close to the border with orders to cross into Serbia to get evidence of Serbian SF movements and build-ups in the border region.

I whispered to Captain B, 'Did you know about this? This is pure Laos and Cambodia stuff.' Referring to the illegal US operations in Laos and Cambodia during the Vietnam War. Our mission was highly illegal and could have easily been considered an act of war if we were discovered.

He shook his head. 'Couldn't even have imagined it.'

'Romeo 14 and Romeo 15 will be inserting Romeo 12 on the north-eastern border stretch, via vehicle drop-off close to Victor 3. They will then man the safe house relay and standby as mission support and QRF from the safe house. Romeo 13 will do a heli insertion due north at hotel 4.' Captain R clenched his fists and looked over the room. 'This has been cleared by a small group of people. It's not cleared at a national or KFOR-level. So, if this thing goes south, we are knee-deep in the shit.'

This was, by far, the most sensitive operation of our careers.[2] It was a large-scale operation with every man in the platoon involved. And the adversary was different. Fabian's intelligence, combined with SIGINT and sources on the Serbian side, all pointed towards Serbian SF, in particular the 63rd Parachute Brigade, setting up small FOBs on their side, followed by reconnaissance missions across the Kosovo border. They were also suspected of helping to train and supply local "resistance fighters". They were not to be taken lightly. One of two Serbian Armed Forces' Special Forces brigades, and with a distinguished military history. They participated in the Battle of Košare, during the 1999 Kosovo War, but were most likely involved in many other operations during and after the conflict.

There were points of interests, already believed to be FOBs or training grounds, and a handful of border-crossing areas that they supposedly used. We were to insert and then layup on the Kosovo side of the border during the day and then probe into Serbia at night. Depending on what we found, we could layup in Serbia, but it was to be avoided if possible. The risks involved if we were compromised were too great. We would use the encrypted relay station, set up at Fabian's safe house, to maintain communication. Contact would be considered a failure and was to be avoided at all costs. The only exception was if we could engage the Serbian SF on the Kosovo side as it would be politically risk free. Either way this was dangerous, and it would be a true test.

We had three days to prep. The insertion would be at 02:30, three nights away. The base was bustling. Everyone had something to do, but it was quiet

---

2   At least up to this point. Iraq and Afghanistan is a different story.

and focused. Nothing was left to chance. Since we had time, the operational planning was more traditional, with delegation of tasks and a lot of brief backs ensuring that instructions were clearly understood. Either Captain R or Captain T were present almost everywhere, as they wanted full insight and involvement in how we were going to solve this.

The reconnaissance work in the helicopters had paid off, in that we could map out a lot of suitable routes. It was a remote area and by using Hotel 4, we would basically start in the middle of nowhere. Very few people had business there, so the main threat was the Serbs. No one could really make an accurate judgment on their activity in the region. That was why confirming their FOBs and personnel strength was the primary task.

Romeo 12 would do the less intensive south-eastern stretch. There were a few gaps in the intelligence, and we were not sure if that was also a region of interest or not.

'We will try to find a good, solid LUP there,' Captain B said, while pointing at an area 30 minutes from the border on our side. 'We will go light; daypacks and just enough equipment to stay over if necessary.'

I really needed to minimise the equipment for this mission keeping it super tight. The hard part was the camera gear. Our main focus was target acquisition, but we all know the saying: "Pictures, or it didn't happen". Mr A and Mr N had picked out a wish list of gear that they wanted to bring.

'One lens has to go,' I said like the parent forcing the kids to choose between chips or candy on a Saturday.

'We will keep the 1000mm, then,' said Mr N. He made a good case, as it was more realistic to expect that we would be a decent distance away. If we weren't, they could tweak it a bit to get more of a fisheye view. Water wouldn't be a problem, as there were plenty of freshwater sources in the mountain. Although it had been a dry summer, at least two had been confirmed by recent satellite images. We needed to take a small reserve for the infiltration, as it would be 24 hours before we could reach water, and it would entail a lot of walking uphill. The weather looked good: no rain expected, overcast conditions and moderate temperatures. The nights would be below 10 degrees Celsius, which was perfect for this kind of activity.

Mr A came back from the geocell. 'These are the E&E maps. One each.'

The E&E maps were crude and held just enough information for each team to get out. It contained hidden messages with instructions, covered by an exchange alphabet. The word to remember was 'Ponytrashi.' It was almost childish, but it didn't need to be harder. The Bergens were packed and kitted, then checked and rechecked. This shouldn't have been any different to any mission we had done up to that point, or the countless exercises throughout our military careers – we had simulated this exact mission, but it *was* different. The stakes were higher.

Most of us went with the chest rig option for this one, except for Mr A, he had always been a vest-guy.

'Don't you do tracers in the middle?' Mr A asked as we were loading magazines.

'Nah, my counting is automatic. I just need to have the final warning this time,' I replied.

I kitted day and night magazines as usual for green operations. The IR tracers were for the invisible, but deadly, night game.

We would be transported to the French base at 16:00 the next afternoon. We decided this night would be a good time for pizza and a few beers. We sat around the fire in the yard, sipping our Budweisers.

'This is the kind of shit you always train for, but never think you will do,' said Mr A.

'After this, we will have completed a full circle of recon duties,' Mr N said.

'In just the first deployment,' added Captain B.

'Here's to many more,' I said as I raised my bottle in a toast.

We had slept in, and we were going to need it. I walked quickly to not miss lunch.

'All good?' Captain B asked the table at lunch.

'I will recheck the kit and the batteries I charged overnight, just to make sure.'

He looked at me and then around the table. 'Good, good. Anything else?' It was like he searched for any signs of insecurity or doubt. A caring but piercing look. There was nothing, we were ready to go.

I knocked on the support squad's door. 'Come in,' shouted Mr B.

'Hey. I checked the charge of my batteries, and this one is full but topped out at 8.1 volts.'

Mr B grabbed the battery. 'You are well trained, measuring for yourself,' he said and smiled. Mr B was always happy when we took tech seriously and employed all the tips and tricks they had given us. 'I will just check them. Yeah, here you go. Take this one in reserve just in case they do not hold their charge well over time. It's a pretty badass operation we are starting, huh?' He was excited, like genuinely happy and he managed to transfer a bit of positivity and his kick ass attitude to me. I needed it, and I started to get amped.

'Stay frosty and see you soon.' Those were Captain R's final words to us before we left. Captain T was down at Prizren for liaison and Lieutenant B came up with us to lead from the French base.

It was sunset as we arrived. 'Look at that beautiful sunset,' Mr N commented.

'More importantly, I hope they don't serve that weird cock of wine tonight,' said Mr A.

'It's coq au vin, you grunt,' said Lieutenant B.

'Potato, potahto,' Mr A replied shrugging his shoulders.

They didn't serve coq au vin, it was lasagne. Which no one complained about, except for Lieutenant B who had slightly more refined taste buds than the rest of us. The helicopter crew held their briefing, showing us around the Bell AB 212, that we would be using. The crew was the same French crew that we flew with during the helicopter reconnaissance but, according to the markings, the helicopter was from the Italian Navy. I hadn't known that they operated any Bell AB212's, but it was not the time for more questions that didn't have any relevance.

Mr A had carefully oiled up his Minimi for the last time. 'She will perform now. She will sing the song of her people.'

It was time to go. Lieutenant B watched us load the helicopter. 'This is why it sucks to be an officer sometimes. You miss out on all the epic shit. See you soon!' Captain B was the exception in this case, but overall Lieutenant B had a point.

The Gazelle started at the same time, to give a slimmer profile to our exit. I watched the base grow smaller under us. As I looked around, I thought that we were not just operators, we were soldiers.

We flew with the Gazelle until we blacked out and broke off onto our designated path. We were flying low and tight, following the deserted valleys leading up to the mountain region.

The headset crackled. '10 minutes.' The fist was put up.[3] We recognised the flight path in the turns. We had studied it well and we had flown this near-exact path once already.

'One minute. No activity on the FLIR.' The pilots had a good visual on the approach and we had a FLIR dome underneath that would tell us if there was trouble ahead.

'Ready at the door. Three... Two... One... Go!' Jumping out of a hovering helicopter is not as hard as it looks, but it requires speed and teamwork to get

3   It's the 10 minute signal in a helicopter.

the gear out. Two on the ground and two lifting out the Bergens. After 10 seconds, we lay on our Bergens, weapons at the ready, while the rotor-wash pushed us to the ground as the heli took off.

Another 30 seconds later, with no visual, we only heard the muffled chopping of the rotors far in the distance, as the pilot dropped down into a steep valley. On the ground, we were laying still, providing 360 degree cover, listening, and observing. It was quiet. After a few minutes, we geared up and got ready to move. We had about three hours of uphill trekking to get to our LUP, where we would spend the day.

My uniform was left open wherever it could be opened. I could feel the sweat oozing out of my pores. It was a strong and heavy uphill hike. We needed to zigzag our way through the steepest parts. The navigation was easy, and the terrain was manageable. It was a bit rocky in parts and you had to step carefully, as a sprained ankle was no good for anyone.

The first break was five minutes early. We needed to stretch a bit and the extra water was like pure gold at that point. We had hauled enough heavy loads in our careers, so fortunately 10 minutes was enough to be back on track. We were as silent as we could be. That meant we rolled on our feet, even going uphill.

You could almost see the dawn break; it had taken longer than we had expected. We'd encountered some technical parts that involved light climbing, where we should have been roped up if we went by the book. We just needed to be careful – and we were. We were 15 minutes out from our LUP, and we realised that we would make it in time. The forest was almost untouched and blanketed with thick, old trees. It was not hard to find a spot for a good patrol base. A massive pine tree with low branches and a very roomy interior would be our base. It required almost no modification, except for some netting. We could watch over our incoming trail and the ridge ahead from underneath the pine canopy.

Mr A was sent out to fit a claymore on our trail. Captain B and I took a look around the vicinity while Mr N was fitting the nets. As Captain B and I got up on the ridge, we could almost see the border. It was probably 30 minutes away.

'Look, that's where we are headed tomorrow night,' Captain B whispered.

We got back to the pine tree as first light was starting to break. I sent our reports back. Communications were clear and the relay worked perfectly. Now we had to wait, eat, sleep and guard until nightfall.

Mr N was guarding and tapped my side. It was 09:05 in the morning. I immediately grabbed my rifle. That was always one's instinct when woken up. He pointed to the east, but I didn't see or hear anything. Then I heard branches breaking, loudly. It didn't sound man-made. These forests had a lot of wildlife, including 20-odd bears. The crackling came closer, and I could see something moving, straight from the east. My safety was off, and I was watching over my barrel.

A majestic moose appeared in my view. He walked around and scratched his head and antlers on the trees, breaking branches and made a ruckus. Even if he wasn't the enemy, he was still one of the guys you wanted to pass quickly. And he did, 30 minutes later we could just hear the faint sounds of him walking to the west and then turning north down the ridge. Maybe he was also heading across the border, like a not-so-secret agent.

I relieved Mr N early as it was my turn in 45 minutes, and I was already up and running. Mr N tapped my leg and offered a trade on his cinnamon oatmeal breakfast MRE that he didn't like. He wanted my chicken curry. It was an easy trade from my perspective, as the chicken curry had a chemical aftertaste, and the oatmeal was a beautiful symphony in my mouth. We could hear a pair of MiG-29s roaring in the distance. It was the Serbian Air Force patrolling the border; they did so at least twice a day.

It was yet another reminder that our opponent was a state this time, not some loosely organised Boy Scouts. Spending the day in an LUP, especially when you hadn't really started your mission, was mostly a tense wait. Everyone was eager to crack on. Our mission did include observation from the LUP, but I would have been surprised if we had seen any Serbian patrols hiking around there during the daytime – or anyone else, for that matter.

We were all awake after lunch, having had different amounts of sleep. Captain B and I looked at the map.

'If we follow the ridge to the north, we should be able to observe the border and then we can backtrack and do the same to the south. We will have seen as much as we can.'

We were going to sneak out and look for activity or the presence of sensors at the border. We stripped down, getting rid of as much equipment as we could, but saving the essential – we would travel light. You could hear the sound of our own border-patrol helicopters, but they were keeping to the southern path to not disturb us.

Two men, quietly floating through the forest, becoming one with it, without any fancy gear, was a very pure and basic form of recon. It was deeply satisfying. After just 10 minutes, travelling northwest along the ridge, we could see the border. It looked so innocent, just standing there. Wooden posts, every 25 to 50 metres, were the only things that marked the passing into another country. It was quiet on the other side and there were no real roads for at least 100 kilometres. There were no signs that people had moved around there recently.

'Ground sensors?' asked Captain B as we looked through our binoculars.

'Maybe, I don't think the Serbs have wireless stuff. Even if they do, this is not where they would use them. But they could have that Russian-built sector indicator,' I replied. A sector indicator was old technology. It was basically a hardwired unit that had a combination of ground sensors and tripwires. We also had it – and it was being phased out, because of its limited use and reliability problems. The ground sensors were shit, as they reacted to anything and everything, or nothing.

The tripwires were a bit more accurate, but with the wildlife moving around in the forest they would have time for nothing other than checking these things going off. We could observe several wildlife trails over the border, and it would be a safe bet to say that they didn't monitor any of them.

The southern part of the ridge gave us the same basic conclusions. As we came back to the patrol base, Captain B held a briefing and went over the battle plan.

'We will cross here, using an animal trail 25 minutes up the north-western ridge. Then we will push to Sierra 3, about 10 kilometres in. Depending on the time and findings on Sierra 3, we might have time to sweep by Sierra 2 on the way back.' Sierra 1 to Sierra 3 were the designations of areas that might have been used by the Serbs as FOBs. It was not likely that all of them would be active at the same time, but we would check to see if there had been traces of activity.

'Mines?' asked Mr A.

'It's probably a lower risk than in other areas as it is very remote and no fighting really took place here, but there is always a risk of mines and UXOs. So we need to tread carefully,' Captain B answered before continuing, 'We will leave at dusk so we can observe the crossing with a bit of light as well.'

We sat outside the patrol base, we were ready. A chilly breeze caressed us. Captain B gave the hand signal to move out. Mr N had point, I went second, then Captain B and Mr A last. This was the core of recon work. It was probably the work we had practiced most throughout our careers, but that we had done the least of.

It was all quiet as we observed from the ridge. Dusk had become darkness, our long-awaited friend that would give us protection and warmth as we moved through it. The signal to move on came from Captain B. In a minute or two we would be behind enemy lines, in the real sense. I was watching my sector, and I could see the border posts. One more step and I would be in Serbia. I rolled on the outside of my foot as I set it down. It felt the same, but better. I liked the distinct feeling of the stakes immediately becoming 100 times higher. I looked back and the whole patrol was now in enemy territory. I felt the focus, you could almost touch it.

The forest was easily navigated and, unsurprisingly, it was more or less the same terrain as we had had on the other side. We used a small stream as our eastern navigational boundary. I could hear it in the distance, it sounded larger than it looked on our maps. As we approached the clearing that was Sierra 3, we sat down and did a FLIR check. Nothing, just like every other result. We were going to make a sun feather probing approach[4] around the clearing, starting on the west side and moving to the east. It was about 100 metres across and could take a helicopter landing. It had a small tractor road leading into it from the north.

Everything was overgrown. Not just on the ground, even the trees had started taking over the clearing. This place hadn't been visited by anyone in years. As we slowly moved around the clearing, we couldn't find a trace of anything. The tractor road was found to be unusable as it had a massive gap about 150 metres from Sierra 3, most likely rain, and flood damage from previous years. If anyone wanted to make this an FOB, they had some serious work to do.

We had spent hours around Sierra 3, and we could confidently say that nothing had happened there. We would now be too short on time to take a look at Sierra 2 on our way home. We took the south-eastern route home, to cover some more ground. As we passed the freshwater stream on our way east, we filled up our water reserves. The clock was ticking, and we had to make our way back towards the border to get across before first light.

Back in the patrol base, we marked the ground that we had covered on the map. It had been a good night and we had managed to break a lot of new ground and fill in a few gaps. Romeo 12 was further to the southeast and had a forest ranger station in their vicinity, so they had to make do with just observing. They had two-night OPs and three-day ones, but they were not able to cross the border, at least not right then. They would probably try to see if they could push further north to clear the ranger station.

---

4   The probing pattern is as follows. Probe in, back track straight out, move to either side
    for x amount of distance and repeat.

I looked at Captain B, 'Look at the location of Sierra 2 and Sierra 1, and the ground we need to cover to get back. Why don't we just move on and stay over for the day?'

Captain B looked up and said, 'I had the same idea. There is risk involved in moving back all the time. And it gives us valuable time to see what's happening during the daytime.' It was decided. We would pack extremely light, just enough to sustain us for a couple of days while on the other side of the border.

We all got as much sleep as possible. It was too short, but we were all eager to get back into Serbia after the previous night's disappointing results. We would push in east of the stream and make our way along the seven kilometres to Sierra 2. If we had the same results there, we could probably push along half of the 16 kilometres left for Sierra 1 and find a position to lay up for the day. I handed out new batteries for the NVGs. We had plenty and I'd rather start fresh every night.

Zero[5] had confirmed that we were going to stay over. They didn't say anything for, or against, it. I guessed that they were just holding fast at this point. You could feel that the night was going to be crisp as we set off for Sierra 2. It was definitely colder up here, but it was perfect recon-weather. We knew that we might lose communications that night or the next day, as we were working on the edge of the relay coverage. We had a SATCOM if we needed it, but we needed to keep it low and slow for the time being. Crossing the border, the second time around didn't have the same magic. We were hungrier for results, we needed to get some Serbian SF in our sights.

The closer we got to Sierra 2, the more signs of human activity we saw, like quad trails. That didn't tell us that much, as it could have been forest rangers or Serbian border patrols. It was still a border, so they could definitely have a lot of legal activity on their side. Sierra 2 was 75 metres ahead of us.

I swept over it with my NVG and saw what looked like a hunter's cabin. The clearing was smaller than Sierra 3, definitely no room for a helicopter there. There had been recent activity. All-terrain vehicles had been driving and a fire had been lit. It felt more like a civilian or military training activity than military operations. There were no signs of tracked or heavy equipment. The dirt roads were better here, but still only suitable for quads, or maybe a Hägglunds 206. I covered Mr N as he made a sketch of the area.

'Did you see those hooks in the trees?'

5   Operations room at French base.

Without looking up, Mr N replied, 'What about them?'

That is exactly how I would mount a dipole antenna if I had to mount one here. And the nearest army base is 170 kilometres in that direction.' I pointed out the imaginary antenna direction.

'I'll put it on the sketch. You will have to explain it if it comes to that.'

It was a stretch, but sometimes it was all in the details. We discovered some AK casings and what looked like the tear-off part of a MRE and mesh on the ground. This could very well have been an area where resistance had been trained by Serbian forces. All the bits and pieces gave it a training camp vibe.

'Are we all good here?' asked Captain B as we reassembled at the outskirts of Sierra 2.

It felt like we were getting closer to something, at least some activity. As we were pushing deeper into Serbia, we could hear machinery working in the distance. It sounded like a generator and quads. Where there was sound, there was life. Like ghosts in the night, we floated through the forest. It felt like the stealthiest we had ever been, but it could just have been the context that gave it that feeling. When the wind blew in our direction, we clearly heard a generator in the distance. As we approached it became clearer and clearer that the sound was coming from Sierra 1.

We stopped to find ourselves a patrol base for the day. We still had a decent amount of darkness to work with, but we couldn't rush into that LUP. It needed to be solid, and we wanted to be able to do a few loops in our surroundings, to make sure we didn't have any surprises waiting for us. The forest was thick, and we had plenty of good spots available to spend the day. We found a dense bush on the side of a small ridge, which gave us a good view of the only trail in the vicinity, about 75 metres below us. The area was clear and quiet. Our spot was not as roomy as our previous one, but at least it allowed for a sitting spotter. Captain B did first-light checks. Everything had to be spotless, and nothing could be left to chance.

The sun had just let out its first rays and we were already huddled up in our bush. No one was sleeping. We were waiting for something, anything. We needed blood. Not in the literal sense, but we wanted the adrenaline. Night turned into day, the birds came alive, and it was just one of those beautiful moments in being a silent visitor, just watching – we were one with our surroundings.

I started to nod off. Mr N had first watch with Captain B. At 09:30 I was woken up. It was time to eat and sort out the toilet business before Mr A and I took over at 10:00. We were quick and let them go to sleep at 09:45. They had had a long night and needed to sleep. The generator had turned silent. I tried to establish which sounds were normal and what was new. If you really started analysing the sounds in a presumably uninhabited forest, you started wondering about many of them. You couldn't place some of them in any category you had ever heard before, but you had to either dismiss them or keep your ear on them. For practicality one ended up dismissing most of them.

Just after 12:00, we had been up for just over two hours. I thought that I heard voices, but it could just have been my mind playing tricks on me. I nudged Mr A. He also thought he might have heard something, but just as quickly it had disappeared. We listened intently; there they were again. Definitely voices, I could even discern the Serbian language that time. It could have been Croatian or Bosnian as well, but close enough. There was also a thumping sound that went along with the voices.

I carefully woke up Mr N and Captain B. You couldn't have sleepers at this critical point. The voices came closer. They sounded like what we assumed to be men, at least two of them, talking. I watched the trail. Something else was moving on the trail from east to west. I couldn't see them yet, but I could hear them clearly. After three minutes, two men on horseback appeared at the far end of our view of the trail. They wore military uniforms and backpacks, AKMs slung on their sides. They were definitely not looking for anything specific, they were relaxed and appeared to be patrolling.

The sound of the camera shutter almost made me freeze. It felt like the sound broke through the silence like an axe. It was Mr A, taking three shots. I gave him the eye, and with the slightest of nods, he indicated "I am done", or at least that is what I took from it.

The riders moved slowly down the trail. I watched them through the binoculars. I saw their patches; they were Serbian police. I recognised the sergeant ranks on one – they were most likely a border patrol unit. They certainly were not border-crossers. It took 15 minutes for them to pass us completely. They were following the trail passing north of Sierra 2 and then down in the valley on the Serbian side. It was reassuring to see them going about their business, not knowing that they were observed. Now we knew we were not alone and where there was smoke, there was always fire.

The day continued quietly. There was no more action on the trail. The generator started up again just after 17:00. As dusk approached, I changed the magazine in my carbine to a taped one; I had put tape on my night magazines to distinguish them from the daytime ones. I checked my NVG's weapon mount, it was all perfect. I didn't expect it to be anything else, but preparing for battle was a ritual. The way one did it, the sequence gave you confidence and comfort that the gear would support you in whatever you might have to do later. It was a moment of peace, but it was practical too.

I did the equipment checks just before complete darkness. We spent some time cautiously restoring the bush, to appear like no one had ever been there. As we had around seven kilometres to Sierra 1, we could afford to move slowly and with caution. We expected it to be manned and, depending on who manned it, we would potentially face a range of scenarios. We had to assume that it was an SF FOB and approach it as such. Night capabilities, roving guards in the far outer perimeter, alarm mines et cetera. So, we had to, and planned to, probe and approach carefully.

Around two kilometres out from Sierra 1 we established that it was manned. It was not manned by amateurs, but not by full-on pros either. Relaxed professionals, was my assessment. The light discipline was pretty much on point, the sound discipline was decent except for the generator. There were two blacked-out barracks in the middle. You could see some light leaking out when people moved in and out. About 15 metres away from the barracks was a container. It looked like one of those kitted mobile HQ/signal containers.

They had a few dishes on the roof and a dipole antenna set up. The tracks leading into the camp were among the best we had seen so far. We could see a few Ural trucks and quads. This was not a forest service camp, this was military. They had an entry post with sandbags at the entrance, and one in the far corner across. At least two guards were roving around the short inner perimeter. The camp seemed to be several clearings divided by forest, but we could only see a small part of it.

Including the guards, we had seen at least 10 people. Judging by the size of the barracks and the number of vehicles, we guessed that their strength was probably close to platoon sized. The probing was dead slow. We needed to keep our distance and remember that they probably had people patrolling the outer perimeter.

The patrolling guards weren't wearing NVGs, but you could see that the static guards had some kind of handheld NVG which they picked up from time to time. Smoking was a constant thing. The guards smoked more or less non-stop, and people were moving in and out of the barracks to smoke without fail. 'Bunch of chain smokers', I thought, but couldn't blame them. To each their own and all that.

We saw a variety of AKMs, and the static guards had PKM variants. We had covered about 180 degrees of the clearing. The other 180 degrees, on the eastern side closer to the barracks, were too much of a risk for that night. We needed to do a big loop-around to get a reasonable approach. We had found a few spots that could serve as day OPs, giving us a decent view of the middle, barracks, and container. We decided to set up in the second spot. It was a bit further away but would give us coverage. With the Swarovski and the 1000mm lens, we would have good possibilities to see what was happening.

We had done well without ghillie suits so far, but we had all brought half-ghillies just in case. These were basically ghillie suits without bottoms, great when sitting or lying in an OP. We carefully used the dark to set up the camera and the Swarovski. We used a rocky, tree-covered part of a slope as our OP's location.

The eye was just a pulled-back, meshed-up lens far into the branches. We had an extremely low profile. In cases like that, when the enemy was in your line of sight, the first-light checks were just done from the side. You couldn't risk a full walk around, and you didn't really need to as the risk of someone seeing the lenses was slight – the lenses were pulled in deep, and you knew the mesh would cover any glare. One just had to make sure it was suitably camouflaged in case we had people walking around our position.

We had room for two laying spotters/camera, one half-sitting guard in the back and one resting. Whether we liked it or not, we needed to rest. It would be a long day and a long night. I had the first shift, observing with Mr A, Captain B was guarding and Mr N was sleeping. Dawn was just turning into morning when we observed a six-man patrol coming back from the west.

'You got this?' I whispered to Mr A. He did. It was still low-light photography, so it wasn't passport photos, but it would do.

The patrol was talking to a man that came out of the container. I saw highly modified AKs, two M4s with mounted laser pointers, and NVGs on their heads. They were kitted light. The last guy had a Sako TRG with a night scope on it. This was definitely a recon patrol. Some of them wore Serbian camouflage, but it seemed to be mixed and matched throughout the patrol. I tried to find some identifying patches. The man who looked like the leader had something on his shoulder, but it was camouflaged with face paint. As the sun gave off a bit more light, I could finally make it out. It was a blue shield with a white parachute in it – it was the 63rd Parachute Brigade.

'Did you get the insignia and weapons?'

Mr A nodded. I'd done my best. I looked on the screen. The increasing light had helped, it was definitely ID quality pictures now.

The patrol disappeared into one of the barracks. The guards changed at 07:00. We started to count and photograph people as they started moving around for breakfast. This was definitely a platoon-sized operation. The container was manned by a different unit, but I didn't recognise their patches.

We took a lot of close-ups of the antennas. We got much more detail in the light of day. They also had an expandable mast on the side of the container. It was down at the time, but I had a feeling they might have had EW capabilities that was not only serving the needs of the SF platoon but also cross border surveillance – the evidence suggested that they could have been listening in on the Kosovo side of the border.

We had a blind spot, which we deduced was the toilet area. We also didn't know what it looked like on the other side of the container and barracks. We started to get a clear picture of what was happening. It was definitely an FOB of sorts. Still, as far as we knew, at that moment, it was just a military location, inside Serbia manned by Serbian soldiers. An interesting location and interesting resources – definitely good to know, but it didn't confirm any border breaches from their side. Even if the patrol had come back from the border, we had no proof, well not yet at least.

We didn't want to risk a change of spotters during daylight, so Mr A and I napped for a few hours each. It was a tense, but lovely, feeling being just a few hundred metres away from a Serbian SF FOB, inside Serbia. We were in the routine of observation, rest, eat, repeat. We had seen that a few people, who were moving outside the base perimeter, were stepping over or disarming alarm mines. They seemed to keep them close to the base. The mines were probably a last warning of an encroaching enemy, but with little option to keep it close to the base. Having them further out would carry a risk that wildlife would trigger them.

We managed to swap out Mr N for Mr A, who took position upfront. This was important so he could complete our sketches as he was the true artist amongst us. His ability to draw true to scale was amazing, but he needed good light to complete his work. We had refrained from even trying to use any forms of communication since we had found the container, and we were also way out of range for the relay. And we didn't know what kind of EW goodies they had in there; we weren't taking any risks. As dusk fell, Mr N was observing and Mr A guarding.

Captain B and I had a mini-meeting in the middle of the OP. 'Do we really need to see the back of those barracks?' I asked.

'No, we don't. Or rather, we do, but not now. It would take us all night. I'd rather see what that patrol is up to,' answered Captain B

We didn't expect the patrol to move out immediately after dark. Judging by the way they had come back, they seemed to have followed the ridgeline to the border. It made sense, as it provided the best cover. I wouldn't have been surprised if they used the same line again. We planned to leave quietly as darkness fell and loop back to find a suitable position at the ridge. From there, we would be able to see if these bad boys were just nosing at the border or if they were actually crossing it. For better or for worse, the generator was back on. It masked our sounds, but also it covered up the sounds of a potential approaching enemy.

We backed out from the OP, almost in a straight line. It took a bit of manoeuvring around the rocks, but we left the enemy line of sight almost immediately. We knew that the patrol hadn't left yet, but from that point onwards we needed to expect them at all times. We made a steep, but sharp, loop up to the ridge as we didn't want to lose too much time and risk missing them.

We had a clearly defined entry area for them if they used the ridgeline. We found a spot that would hide us well but would also provide a vantage point to observe the actual border crossing. We lay flat and ready, not a twitch. After an hour of waiting, we could see the shadows of the patrol moving along the ridgeline. My heart rate started to go up as I cautiously adjusted the ghillie over my head. I followed them in my weapon's sights. The safety was off and only my trigger discipline kept the bullet from leaving my barrel. None of us wanted to start an international incident.

They were making good speed and had decent patrol routines, but they moved like they felt safe and could afford to be more relaxed. I thought to myself, 'But you fucked up by using the convenient ridgeline, now we've got you.'

They stopped short of the border and observed from the ridge for a minute before they crossed into Kosovo. They headed down towards the cliffs. We couldn't see them as they made their way down. Captain B signalled that we would move behind the ridge line, pass their trail and loop in from the other side. It would give us the opportunity to see them from a distance as they had headed to a dead-end.

I flicked up my safety as we moved out. We had to keep up our speed, in silence and be aware that they might have friends following them. We moved behind the ridge, across their path and 50 metres beyond that. We found a tree line that would give us cover as we descended towards the edge. The forest was light enough to see, but dense enough to cover us. It was a metre by metre game, keeping track of all one's body parts while moving, weapons ready for contact.

I saw the sniper first. They had left him on guard duty, 25 metres behind the rest. He was observing the ridge through his scope. We had one move

– lie down and be still. This was as close as we got. We had a bit of cover from a few rocks. He occasionally did a 180 degree sweep with his scope. There was no sign that he had seen us. We saw more than half of the patrol as they worked on setting up a directional antenna. Maybe they were receiving something from someone on the inside. This was almost within line of sight to the nearest village.

Even if it was further away, it warranted deeper investigation. The patrol stayed for almost two hours before packing up. We saw them disappear over the ridgeline before we moved again. We carefully approached the ridgeline as we wanted to see if they were heading back.

As I slowly put my NVG over the ridge, while pressing hard to the ground, I could see the back of the sniper moving down the line that they came up – still unaware. They were on their way back to the FOB. We went back to the point where they had set up the antenna. Leaving Mr A as cover, we marked it on the map and drew lines to the places to which we had direct line of sight. It was our turn to move back. We had to make it back to our own main LUP before first light.

It wouldn't be a morning for sleeping. We had loads of material to compile into reports and send off and we were due to provide an update to Zero. Just after 10:00, Captain B was reading the report through one last time. 'Send it, it's good.'

We had only selected a few representative pictures for a quick transmission. I pushed the 'play' button and 45 seconds later it was sent and delivered. We had to give them a few hours to assess the new information, but we knew they would have inputs. We decided to start resting.

Mr A reflected, 'This is becoming a fucking goldmine. I hope they treat it like that.' He was more than right – it was a goldmine. We had a fix on the Serbian FOB, we knew they were moving across the border, and we knew that they had active accomplices in Kosovo. They could extract tons and tons of information, if they kept their cool, but sometimes their eagerness to have "practical" results quickly sacrificed long term outcomes. But I couldn't imagine that this would be one of those times. They just had to play it cool.

At 15:00, the radio crackled. 'Romeo 13, Zero. Stand by for transmission at 16:00. Out.' They had read and assessed our reports and now it was time to see how they would play it.

'You got this?' Captain B asked as he had half-woken up to see what was happening on the radio. He needed to get some more sleep.

'I've got it. I'll wake you up when we get something.'

Over the next hour I had too much time to think. It was never good when you started to analyse the upcoming actions of a military command. Most likely, one would end up disappointed. Sometimes I wished I could have been more like Mr A, who just waited for the orders and carried them out. Eat, sleep and repeat. It was an easy life and he saw this more as a job than anything else. Sure, he liked his job, but the specifics of what we did never bothered him too much.

He could easily spend six months on an army base just going to the gym and catching the sun. He had a more 'in the moment' way of thinking. Perhaps Zen was the way forward, but I would be fucked if I was going to find enlightenment on the Serbian border observing an SF enemy unit.

I was ready at 15:57. I saw that they had initiated the handshake protocol. At 16:02, two text messages had been sent.

> Romeo 13 Order: Surveillance of border from own side tonight. Romeo 12 being pulled and reinserted Hotel 4 in 31 hours at 23:00 +1. Prepare supply list for 18:00 hours.

The second message was about the specifics of us meeting Romeo 12 and leading them in.

I nudged Captain B and Mr N, 'It's time.'

The plan for the next 24 hours was uncomplicated. We quickly prepared a supply list of what we needed Romeo 12 to bring. That night, we were going to observe the known Serbian border crossing, but from a greater distance. Mostly to detect their presence and not as close as the last time. The following night, Mr A and I were tasked with meeting with Romeo 12 and bringing two empty Bergens to help them haul the load up the mountain.

'It will be a squeeze fitting all of us in here,' Mr N commented.

'Indeed. We should look for a slightly bigger home tonight, or find a double somewhere,' Captain B replied.

We had a lot to do that night, and dusk came quicker than usual. I did a full inventory and we packed up everything, since we were planning to find a new location.

'Do you remember the cluster of trees and bushes we saw on our side of the ridge on the first night, when we were scouting to the north about 25 minutes from here?' I asked.

Captain B nodded. 'Might be something. You and Mr A can go and check it out. Mr N and I will stay here.'

I tapped Mr A on his shoulder as he had been on guard duty. 'Let's go. We are going for a quick recce for a new home.'

We reached the point in just 17 minutes. We probably started to feel more at home and moved quicker. The balance was just in achieving efficiency but not becoming sloppy.

'This isn't as good as I remembered it,' I said to Mr A.

'What about that?' Mr A pointed back to a rock and tree formation we had just passed. I hadn't even noticed it on my way in. We backtracked for a minute, and it was much better than what we had now. It was a weird natural pit surrounded by rocks and trees. It would fit all of us and then some. It also had a view over the ridgeline, so we would be able to see better and further than we had before.

'So, you pay attention after all.' I could see Mr A smile in the green shimmer of the NVG.

'Sometimes, sometimes,' he replied.

We got back to the others and briefed them on our findings. We would hide our kit and pick it up on our way back from the patrol. The forest was silent as we moved closer to the crossing area. The generator couldn't be heard that night. They either didn't use it, or the wind could have hidden the sound. We decided to split up, with me and Mr A laying up a bit further south. We couldn't see the actual crossing, but had a better view over the south-eastern sector, in case they decided to take a new direction. Captain B and Mr N would watch over the border and down the ridgeline that they had used the previous night. Mr A and I crawled in under what would have been the perfect Christmas tree for a family during the holiday season.

Mr A was quick to pick up on that and whispered, 'Ho, ho, ho, bitches. Ranger Claus is in the house.' I just shook my head in the dark, but I had to acknowledge how much this guy actually lightened the mood. Captain R was right, I am not sure if I was a broadcaster, but Mr A had just put a spin on Bruce Willis in *Die Hard 2*.

The hours went by. It was a chilly night to be static. We could hear quads or trucks operating in the distance.

We pulled back to Captain B. 'I don't think they are passing here tonight. Shall we patrol south for an hour?'

Captain B looked at the time. 'We will stay here and keep tabs on the crossing. You two patrol south for a maximum of one hour. Stay on the right side of the border! No wondering off in the dark. No heroics.'

After travelling south for 45 minutes, we could see parts of the mountain-side and flickering lights moving down the mountain. It was much too far away to make out what was moving. There were no longer any motor sounds coming from the direction of the FOB. We decided to lie for a few minutes to watch the border. Mr A nudged my foot and nodded to the east. It was hard to make out in the NVG, but something was moving in the eastern tree line, about 100 metres in, on the Serbian side. It did not look like an animal. After a few minutes, the point-man of a patrol broke out of the tree line, into the open. He was leading a five-man patrol.

It was hard to determine if it was the same one that we had seen before, or new players. We couldn't see the sniper. Maybe he was an SAP for the patrol, maybe he was home sick or maybe he was providing cover for them as we speak. We made no sudden moves, as we might be the ones they wanted to flush out. It was easy to go from hunters to being hunted. We would be half-exposed if they came to our side of the ridge. The night covered our movements, but one wrong move could burn us.

We observed the patrol moving past us, turning off to the north-east – unwittingly avoiding the border area observed by Captain B and Mr N – and pushing in the direction of the FOB. We waited silently. My breathing slowed down, my pulse was stable, and my trigger finger was neither inside the trigger guard, nor fully to the side. We were prepared for more, but we knew that might also have been it. Roughly four minutes after we had lost the fifth man in the patrol into the darkness of the east, we saw a shadow moving on their trail. It was the sniper, wearing his half-ghillie.

He was moving closer to our ridge, but he followed the patrol's direction and passed us at a distance of roughly 50 metres. Either he hadn't spotted us, or he was a very cool customer. He didn't provide cover for them. He was looking for us, or the likes of us, by watching if the patrol's movements provoked any reaction. We were probably extremely lucky as we had settled in well before the patrol broke out into the clearing. The sniper couldn't spot us, as he probably observed the ridge from the tree line. We lay still, observing the sniper following the patrol's trail to the northeast. We gave it 20 minutes before slowly making our way down the ridge. We fell back further west, losing the visual on the border but had more protection from the western tree line. As we approached Captain B's location we were, of course, late. We approached them from the west and pulled them back to the tree line.

'What the fuck happened? It's been almost three hours,' whispered Captain B.

'We observed a similar patrol to yesterday's, sniper dragging, moving from the south. Most likely heading to the FOB. We spotted them from the ridge, and they moved 50 to 100 metres on their side of the border.'

Captain B was silent for a few seconds. 'Dragging sniper, so countermeasures. Do you think he could have spotted you?'

'Mostly likely not, as we established too early for them to have had line of sight and they didn't move into the clearing with caution. But yeah, countermeasures for sure.'

It looked like Captain B had his thinking-look, but I couldn't really be sure in the dark. 'Alright. We follow the tree line. We need to haul ass to make it back. Get the gear and move to the new patrol base.'

As we got back to our stash in the old patrol base, first light had already broken. It would be too much of a risk to re-establish the new location in the north. We needed to use it again, at least during the daytime and make for the new location the coming night.

After we had settled in again, Captain B rolled over to my side and pulled out a sketch.

'This is the FOB. This is the location where they transmitted. What are they doing in the south? Sure, border patrols and all that, but what is interesting there?'

I pulled out a map. 'If they pushed at least an hour to the east, maybe this.' I pointed to a spot from where, in theory, you could see at least two border crossings from above. One of them was unmanned, just a dirt track in the forest. We had seen them on our helicopter-recce. 'I mean, from an SF-perspective, the remoteness of this region makes it very interesting for them to poke around. And, technically, they are right to recce the area as we are here. There might also be additional units located east of the FOB where we haven't been yet. They could just be doing a very big loop, patrolling around them.'

Captain B looked at me. 'Why wouldn't they be more interested in the northeast?'

I shrugged my shoulders. 'They might be, but you have seen what's 30 minutes north. It's unsuitable for covert movement and it's easy to monitor for them with other assets. They might have a static OP or something. We are in an area where it's interesting. We have seen where they cross, it's one of the better spots.'

Captain B remained silent and appeared to be thinking for a minute. 'When we report this in, I know what kind of output Zero will expect. But in reality, we will be eight people tonight, and we have a lot of ground to cover. We know that they have at least a platoon-sized unit seven kilometres east. In my view, this requires a delicate touch. We need to play chess with the Serbs, and they will give us gold. But my feeling is that HQ wants more provocation, but that could close the tap.'

We exchanged a look. 'Okay, I will ask for updated objectives when I send the report tonight, so that we can get a feeling of what they are up to.'

I sent the report before getting some shuteye. It would be another long night ahead of us. I woke up just before nightfall and had an oatmeal MRE. The order from Zero had just came back.

I tapped Captain B, 'Look at this,' I said as I pointed to the screen. They want us to have eyes on the "transmitting location" during the night and report if there is any activity when we meet and lead in Romeo 12.

'Okay, we are going to be spread thin tonight. First things, first. We all go to the new patrol base as soon as it's dark. Mr A and you,' he pointed at me, 'Go and meet and lead Romeo 12 in. Mr N and I will observe the transmitting location from the west line. It will give us less of a heads-up, but better cover.'

Captain B looked at me. 'How should we solve the comms?'

'I can switch places with Mr N if you want?' I replied.

'No, I want you exactly where you are, I just want to know how we should divide them to be most effective,' Captain B answered.

'A radio each and I'll take the satellite terminal. You can take the Iridum and the satpager, just in case it gets hairy. You can send me reports on the satpager if you are in a tight spot and I can forward them as soon as I can.'

Captain B nodded. 'Okay, that is how we will do it. We need to move out now. Ready?'

Mr A and I left the new patrol base 35 minutes later, with one empty Bergen each. It was a good, downhill walk to Hotel 4. We knew the way back would have a burning sensation in store for the leg department. Almost simultaneous to our arrival at Hotel 4, the others reported eyes-on. Now we just had to wait for some action. The helicopter was inbound in 30 minutes.

'You cover us, and I'll help them unload. We'll sit and listen for a few minutes before we repack and then go on our way. You take point.' Mr A nodded, this suited him well.

Instead of an IR buzzsaw,[6] we were using a smaller IR screen for positive identification of the helicopter, as it was less visible if someone was watching from the valley. I could hear the faint sound of a helicopter in the distance. Mr A made his way up the hill to get a more solid position and get away from the rotor wash. I saw the blacked-out helicopter approaching. I exchanged friend-lies with the pilot. He was coming at speed. The wind almost knocked off my

---

6   A buzzsaw is an IR cyalume stick attached to a string, which is rotated do give a clear signature.

goggles. I could feel the vibration in my chest pocket. It was probably Captain B reporting activity, but we were well out of their way and the patrol would probably see the decoy Gazelle as it patrolled along the border in their sector. I had to relay Captain B's message, but first this. The Bergens were heavy as fuck as they came flying out of the deck. After 15 seconds, the helicopter was dropping down the cliff towards the valley. Half a minute later, one could only hear the muted sounds of the rotor. We stayed put for a minute before I fist-bumped Mr R

'Welcome to the north! I need to relay a message; you can start repacking in these.'

When I sent the activity report to Zero, they replied immediately. 'Romeo 13, Zero. Stand by for orders 06:00. Out.'

'Well, that will be a problem for later,' I thought.

I briefed Mr R on what was happening, the location of the Serbian patrol, our guys, and the base.

'They are all nuts back home. I have heard everything from snatching prisoners to assaulting the FOB,' he said with a low chuckle.

'Doesn't even surprise me a little. Many chefs involved?'

'Way too many chefs involved, if you ask me.'

Not surprising at all. As we suspected, we had had a bit of a tail wind and now everyone wanted in – they wanted their piece of the cake. I trusted Captain R to sort out most of the maniacs, and we would deal with the mechanics.

We started our long uphill walk to the patrol base. We arrived just before 03:00. We expected Captain B within the hour if everything went according to plan. The 2iC of Romeo 12 and I started the equipment dance, dividing and keeping track of inventory. It was a fairly quick affair and we got everything settled before Captain B returned. After a few more pleasantries and a more in-depth map briefing for Romeo 12, we dug into our new patrol base and awaited orders at 06:00.

Captain B's crew had seen almost a carbon copy of what had happened the last time the Serbians transmitted there. I managed to get the report in well before the 06:00 orders, so they would have time to consider it for the order. Lieutenant B had sent an interesting unit with Romeo 12.

It looked like a Russian broad spectrum frequency jammer. I asked Romeo 12's signaller about it. It was a modified Russian frequency jammer, but it didn't jam. It recorded frequency bands and effects used. And it could be emptied remotely. It was some home cooked electronics, courtesy of Mr B and Lieutenant B from the support squad. The orders came in at 06:00. Captain

B read through them and made his own notes before giving us the orders. It always became slightly more formal when there were more patrols involved.

'Okay, we have work ahead of us,' he started. We were to be there for another five days. German EW was on the ground in the village where they thought the receiver/transmitter was. They wanted to flush out the ground agent, so we needed to have eyes on the transmitting location every night and report activity on and off, to help them narrow their search. Secondly, Lieutenant B wanted us to place the modified jammer closer than 250 metres from the container, preferably in a high location. It would also help if we could get an antenna up. I rolled my eyes.

'Of course, just give us a few minutes and we will place the damned thing on top of the container itself,' I thought to myself.

Thirdly, they wanted a more extensive look at the supply track to the FOB and the eastern surroundings. So, all in all, three minor tasks in five days. Great, let's go. But it wasn't finished there. If we had time in the last day or two, we were to push and try to track down what the patrol did in the southeast. Maybe there was more to it than we could assess from where we were. Don't get me wrong, I was not work-shy, and I actually liked those kinds of things. But they wanted four delicate things in five days, which meant that we had to be pretty aggressive. And that was risking it all, in my opinion. We could have tapped the source for a long, long time and proceeded like ghosts in the night. Now they just wanted everything to happen at once. Maybe they had to pull the operation, maybe we were needed elsewhere. But if that was the case, the operation should have been left and resumed later.

Captain B laid out the game plan. 'Alright, many, many cooks in this. But we will focus on the most important tasks.'

Romeo 12 was going to take control and monitor the transmitting site. Half-fixed OP, two men doing two nights before being relieved. SATCOM at location. We were going to plant the frequency analyser and map out the supply track and the eastern perimeter. We left the patrol activity in the southeast for the moment, as it might have taken all the time we had, or even more.

As we knew the western side of the FOB pretty well, our initial plan was to approach from the east, as we didn't have time to loop all the way around the west. The last few hundred metres could take hours to complete. This was high risk and we managed to get Hotel 1 approved as a new ERV. We knew Romeo 14 and Romeo 15 were ground QRF, but I didn't think they had enough birds to have a full ARF for us. But Hotel 1 would do. If the shit hit the fan, we would be in pretty deep anyway. Our only chance would be to make it over the border, as they would probably be hesitant to follow. If not, we would be captured or killed on the Serbian side.

I took a look at the analyser unit. It was simple. There was only one button and, once pressed, it blinked red once. That was it, it was up and running. If it produced any results, they would have to be seen later. It was decided that we would do a double nighter. We would infil that night, plant the device, pull back west, and spend the day in a LUP there. Then continue northeast to cover the track and the eastern perimeter, before getting out on the western route. It was too much movement going in and out two nights in a row. Besides, we couldn't make the track and back in one night, starting from scratch.

We left the patrol base and the OP in the capable hands of Romeo 12 as we moved out at nightfall. We were entering uncharted territory as we crossed the border to the south, placing us just north of the track the Serbian patrol used. The forest was denser but softer. It meant that there were no branches or dry vegetation on the ground. It was a half-wet, almost thone, kind of moss. It allowed for very silent movement. We had to be careful as it was very easy to leave traces of our movements. Disturbed ground vegetation was a classic tell-tale sign of an amateur patrol moving through. We had the dry path, leading to the FOB, around 100 metres to the south.

An hour had elapsed since we crossed the border and we had been doing around two kilometres per hour. Mr A, who was point, froze in his step, so did the rest of us. About 80 to 100 metres at our 2 o'clock, we saw a patrol moving in the clearing, on the easier route. I grasped my pistol grip and flicked the safety to single shot. No sudden moves, no kneeling, no movement. Just standing dead still. I planned my actions in my head. I found a gap in the trees where I could accurately lay down fire. I made sure my weight was evenly distributed over both feet. I was as ready as I could be for contact. It was the same constellation[7] of six people. They were moving like they were in friendly territory. Their pace was steady. They were almost past us, almost, when the sniper in the back turned around to check his rear. The tension of a second felt like forever. He then resumed his forward march. They passed us and disappeared along the ridgeline.

We waited for a few minutes, until it was all quiet. We needed to push on, at our current tempo we would reach our target area at 03:00 and would only have a few hours tops to plant the device. They were running the generator

---

7 Grouping, set up, formation of a unit.

again which might or might not help us. At 02:45, we were at the exact opposite side of our first OP. We could see the side of the barracks and the container
300 metres directly ahead of us. A few individuals were moving around in the
FOB. We saw one of the static guards and a few more out smoking at the edge
of the container.

I whispered to Captain B, 'I can ghillie up and take the jammer maybe 150
to 200 metres straight in. That is as good as it gets. We can get closer, but then
we lose the elevation.'

Captain B tapped me and Mr N and pointed in the direction of the FOB.

We moved with caution as we didn't want our suits to get snagged on vegetation. The forest allowed us to melt in perfectly, it felt like it would be a cakewalk. After 45 minutes, we stopped short. A man had exited the container to
pee and smoke. The container was now 105 metres away. I needed 10 more
metres to get to a small grouping of trees that looked suitable. We waited
patiently for him to finish smoking.

The tree was better than I had thought as it had some kind of climbing vegetation growing up the trunk. I buried the unit in the moss and managed to get
one and a half metres of antenna wire out. It would be hard to detect, you had
to be looking for it. And the unit itself was hidden by a few roots sticking out
from under the moss. I covered the button with my hand and could see the
faint red flash against the fabric of my glove. I double-checked the moss where
I had kneeled and fluffed it a bit before moving back. The return journey took
only 20 minutes. It was usually faster on the way back.

We got our ghillies off, kitted up and were ready to leave towards the east,
after revising the old plan which was to go west and round the base to the
north to find an LUP. It was after 04:00 in the morning. We could see the
patrol getting back to the FOB. We sat and observed as they talked to someone
in the container before moving back to their barracks. I made some quick notes
about the timing. Captain B flicked his head, it was time to move. A decent
enough LUP appeared after 25 minutes. The area was borderline swampy in
parts, but it was in a bush that would keep us safe during the day. I tucked in
as Mr A had first watch and I was last on the guard duty list for once.

I woke up feeling like I had peed my pants. It was my right leg that had
rolled off the dry patch and down into the swampier part. Mr N filled me in
that the track we were going to map out that night didn't go due north as we
had thought. It curved south before going east and then continuing north.
We were pretty close at about 700 metres away; it was not on the map and not
visible from the aerial images. Quads had been running up and down all day.

'I think it's a loop leading to something else. Why would they build their supply track like this? It doesn't make any sense,' I commented to Captain B as we studied the map.

'Well, that's what we will find out tonight,' he replied. Our plan was simple, we were going to keep east of the loop that ran north to south until it ended, if it ended, then head west and pass the supply track, if they were not the same. Maybe we'd follow it a bit to the north, continue west and pass the FOB by a good margin, then work our way to the border and back.

'We'll keep at least 100 metres from the track and follow it around. The circuit seem to start at the FOB, circle to the east and then around a clearing and back. There has to be something there,' said Captain B before we settled in to wait for the clock to move in the right direction.

We had to wait for two hours after dark before we moved, as there was still activity on the circuit. It settled after 22:00. As we followed the eastern edge of the track, the forest got denser. We opted to go closer and started a sun feather movement instead. We had to get all the way, up close and personal, to assess it and what it was used for. Mr N and I sat five metres from the track. It was a dirt road two metres wide.

There was no sign of tracked vehicles moving there, we deduced that at most it was quads and 6x6s. In the curves you could see traces of some of them pulling a trailer. We could see the clearing but had too many trees on our side so we couldn't see inside of it. We needed to back out, move 50 metres to the right and then do another stab towards the road. When we got back to Captain B, Mr N quickly sketched out the circuit and noted the track's vitals like measurements, capacity, and material.

Mr N and I continued to make the incisions towards the circuit track, as Mr A and Captain B waited in the back. We hoped to see straight into the clearing that time. We stopped 10 metres short of the track and I refocused my NVG. At that point, all the time in the observation training theatre at the regiment came back to life. All the Soviet equipment I had memorised served its purpose. My heart jumped. Under a sloppily mounted net in the small clearing stood two SA-6 "Gainful".

It still is the NATO reporting name for the Russian 2K12 Kub SAM battery. It had an unmistakable profile on its tracked chassis. This was not an SF FOB, it was a Serbian air defence site, protected by SF. I tapped Mr N to keep watch, dismounted my head worn NVG as it was easier than taking off the weapon's mounted one. I fiddled in my chest pocket to get my standard digital pocket camera out. I used Mr N's shoulder as support to line up the NVG and the camera lens. This was very basic, but with the right adjustment of the NVG you would get at least usable pictures that looked like they were taken in a tube, which they were. I started the pocket camera inside my jacket and made sure the flash and screen were turned off. I got a few decent pictures. You could unmistakably see what it was. I had never thought I would see an SA-6 in the field during my time.

We got back to Captain B and Mr A and one thing was for sure, we knew that it was not a good place to linger. We could end up knee-deep in shit if we weren't careful. We knew the 2K12 was accompanied by at least one radar unit, most likely a 1S91 Straight flush radar unit. We looked at the sketch and the map. The clearing was divided in two by the supply track. The western part was a bit larger, and I wouldn't have been surprised if it held the radar unit.

We kept our distance as we followed the circuit track around the clearing. We didn't need to get as close again as we had seen the evidence and done what we needed to do. There was no point in taking unnecessary risks. We approached the supply road that led into the FOB. We were not going to follow it to the north, just assess it, sketch it, pass it, and then make a stab into the clearing to confirm if there was any radar present. Then we would push west and home. There had been some traffic on the supply road about an hour earlier, so we approached with caution. About 10 metres before we reached the road, we could see that the guard had a line of sight to our position. As a result, we couldn't stick our heads out. We backed out and needed to go at least 200 metres down the road to disappear behind a bend.

Mr N and I once again approached the road. It was six metres wide, recently re-gravelled, drained, and ditched. This was a properly constructed road, meant to bear heavily loaded vehicles. Mr N quickly sketched it up and we withdrew five metres to prepare to rapidly cross the road. We had almost lifted our asses to go when we heard a quad. We pressed close to the ground as it passed us on the supply road. It had an empty trailer jumping around behind it. It quickly disappeared northbound into the darkness. We waited for a minute more and then we made the dash, two at a time.

We pushed south southeast to make a final stab into the north-western clearing. Mr N and I left Captain B and Mr A 150 metres from the clearing as we moved in a straight line towards the position. We didn't need to get closer than 25 metres before we saw the 1S91 straight flush radar. We also discovered another guard post in this part of the field. We had to be really cool customers on our way out of there. I did a quick repeat of the photo session we had done the previous time. There was slightly too much forest in the way for the pictures to be crisp, but you could see the main parts. I kept a close eye on the guard at the post, who had his handheld NVG out as we withdrew.

We ended up doing a wide loop around the FOB as we didn't want to be entangled in any extended parts of this base. I had a slight feeling of relief as we crossed back over the border. I could see the first rays of light on the horizon as we approached the patrol base. Half of Romeo 12 was waiting for us. They had exchanged crews that morning after two days of activity on the transmission site. I had a lot of report work to do before getting some shuteye. As we filled in the positions and the location of the AA battery on the map, it was crystal clear that they were in the Border Exclusion Zone. It was a zone on both sides of the border that was not allowed to contain heavy weapon systems, like AA batteries. Captain B read through the pages before I sent it.

He nodded. 'You are a pro-level report writer, my friend.' Maybe I was. I was thorough at least. I pushed send.

Almost immediately, I got a reply. 'Stand by.' It meant we needed to stay on the link and wait for their reply.

Then the order came. 'Romeo 13, Romeo 12, Zero. Break OP at dawn. No cross-border activity. Extraction tomorrow, 23:00, Hotel 1. Confirm.'

'Zero, Romeo 12, Romeo 13. Wilco.'

'What's going on,' asked Captain B.

'Pull the OP at dawn tomorrow. LUP here and extract at Hotel 1 at 23:00 tomorrow night.'

Captain B looked at me. 'Have you already replied?'

I looked back, 'Of course. The order was crystal clear. Did you have anything else?'

He looked pensive, hesitated for a moment, and then finally conceded, 'No.'

Sometimes it hurt him that we were so effective and independent that his "officer's powers" of approving things weren't needed. It hit him from time to time, but mostly he knew he was needed, not for approval but for his tactical skills and leadership. But he forgot that when the regular armed forces officer nerve struck him.

I spent the day with inventory and indexing pictures. It was mostly getting ready and getting a decent night's sleep. The remainder of Romeo 12 pulled the OP the following morning and we spent another full day in the LUP. It was tight, but cosy. We definitely needed to leave as soon as it became dark, as Hotel 1 was down the mountain to the west. It was a pretty technical, steep decline, in the beginning. 'We might have to use ropes', I thought. So, we finished the inventory early and only the silent crunching of Mr A enjoying a power bar could be heard.

I did a kit-check one last time before we left the patrol base. It had served us well. It almost felt a tiny bit sad. I would happily have spent more time there. Both the patrols were lined up outside, heavily loaded, and ready to go. Romeo 13 led the way to Hotel 1 and the extraction. It took us two hours to complete the descent. We had to rope up for some parts. This was far more technical than we had expected or remembered from the recce.

'Glad we didn't take this way in,' said Mr R. He was not wrong; it would have been a bitch.

After another hour and a half of light downhill trekking and easy navigation, we reached Hotel 1. It was a clearing on a riverbank, the same river we followed partly when flying into Hotel 4. It was quiet. We had 15 minutes to secure it, but we didn't need even half of that since not even a mouse or a moose could be seen or heard. We pulled back to the tree line and got some well-deserved shoulder rest from the heavy Bergen straps that had been digging into our flesh for hours. The 2iC of Romeo 12 and I were busy with the final kit checks when we heard the distinctive chopping rotor sound break the silence. 'Incoming', I said, although it was not necessary, everyone saw the same thing.

It was majestic to see the blacked-out helicopter flying just metres above the river. It looked like a Formula 1 car as it precisely manoeuvred its way towards our pickup position. We had exchanged IR signals and were good to go. The rotor wash whipped up dust and river water, but with one skid on the bank it was easy to load. I checked the ground as I was last man in. Not a trace.

'All strapped in?' asked the pilot.

I looked around. 'All in and strapped.' As I put the last clip in my buckle, I had to hold on to my Bergen with my feet as the helicopter turned in a hard bank to the right after take-off, before levelling out and flying low over the forest. I looked around. It was the same men that rolled in, just now with better and with more extensive CVs. No one looked tired. The look was happy, or maybe satisfied is a better word.

The decoy Gazelle joined after 35 minutes, and we went back to light on after being blacked out. Then the Gazelle left northbound. I didn't recognise the route; they might have changed it.

As I looked around for a reference, the intercom crackled. 'Oh, you are not going back to the French base. It's home delivery today.'

Now it made sense, they had forgotten that detail in the order. Well, less loading and unloading gear for us. This was only the second time we had landed at our "home" base as most helicopter ops had been out of other bases. It was a running drop-off and the helicopter left as soon as we were all out. Our legs were a bit stiff as we walked through the doorway leading from our helipad to the yard.

Captain R met us in the yard. 'Welcome back, Gents. Listen up! You have 20 minutes for kit checks and inventory, then I want you in the briefing room for a debrief, reports and memory cards. And don't forget coffee!'

Captain R looked over the room as the platoon was assembled, 'It's been a good week and a half.'

We had proof of Serbian Forces crossing into Kosovo. Romeo 14 and Romeo 15 had, together with the support squad and German EW, pinned down two Serbian operatives working in Northern Kosovo. These were also linked to the police that were running guns up north, courtesy of the Serbian government. We had discovered a breach of the Border Exclusion Zone agreement by finding and documenting a Serbian AA unit close to the northern border.

We had placed a jammer close to that AA unit that was collecting information for the nerds to analyse, and we had established that Sierra 2 had probably been used as a training site the previous spring. Hell of a week. This came to be one of our last largest operations in Kosovo. Romeo 13 had been very fortunate as we had been part of all the major action so far. We had about a month left in country. The Afghanistan MOT team belonging to the IRP were already back at the regiment.

'Kosovo isn't that boring after all, is it?' asked Captain B 'No, it was not.'

A month later it was a regular Monday morning back at the regiment, "Welcome gents" Captain K was cheerful as we all sat with our coffee mugs. He gave us a short update about the progress of the operator training and when we would return – that was when we could expect to be a full platoon again. It was more than eight months away, but it was underway, that was something. After half an hour he reached the last point on the agenda "other business".

He fiddled with his computer and after a minute he got his PowerPoint up. He clicked once and the first slide was a map, a map of Afghanistan. 'Gentlemen, it's time to play in the sandbox.'